T4-AKQ-447

GARCILASO DE LA VEGA
AND THE
ITALIAN RENAISSANCE

*PENN STATE STUDIES IN ROMANCE
LITERATURES*
Editors
Frederick A. de Armas
Alan E. Knight

Refiguring the Hero:
From Peasant to Noble in Lope de Vega and
Calderón
by Dian Fox

Don Juan and the Point of Honor:
Seduction, Patriarchal Society, and Literary Tradition
by James Mandrell

Narratives of Desire:
Nineteenth-Century Spanish Fiction by Women
by Lou Charnon-Deutsch

Garcilaso de la Vega and the Italian Renaissance
by Daniel L. Heiple

DANIEL L. HEIPLE

GARCILASO DE LA VEGA AND THE ITALIAN RENAISSANCE

The Pennsylvania State University Press
University Park, Pennsylvania

\# 28219145

PQ
6392
·H45
1994

Publication of this book has been aided by a grant from The Program for Cultural Cooperation Between Spain's Ministry of Culture and United States' Universities.

Library of Congress Cataloging-in-Publication Data
Heiple, Daniel L.
    Garcilaso de la Vega and the Italian Renaissance /
Daniel L. Heiple.
        p.   cm.—(Penn State studies in romance literatures)
    Includes bibliographical references and index.
    ISBN 0–271–01016–9
    1. Vega, Garcilaso de la, 1501–1536—Criticism and interpretation.
    2. Italian literature—16th century—History and criticism.
    3. Petrarchism. 4. Renaissance—Italy.   I. Title.   II. Series.
    PQ6392.H45   1994
    861′.3—dc20   93–14208
                                                                 CIP

Copyright © 1994 The Pennsylvania State University
All rights reserved
Printed in the United States of America

Published by The Pennsylvania State University Press,
University Park, PA 16802–1003

It is the policy of The Pennsylvania State University Press to use acid-free paper for the first printing of all clothbound books. Publications on uncoated stock satisfy the minimum requirements of American National Standard for Information Sciences—Permanence of Paper for Printed Library Materials, ANSI Z39.48–1984.

Ad Marium meum

HOLY SPIRIT LIBRARY
95 2017
CABRINI COLLEGE, RADNOR, PA.

Contents

List of Illustrations

Preface

The study of the poetry of Garcilaso de la Vega (1501–1536) has often found a common reference point in the poet's sentimental biography (usually fabricated from the poetry itself) rather than in the ideas and artistic postures found in the poems. Much critical writing has concentrated on relating the poems to the poet's supposed amorous experiences, ignoring the aesthetic norms and ideas (as opposed to experiences) that inform his poetic production. The feelings expressed in the poems have been made to correspond to a series of love affairs that critics generally have used not only as a means of dating the poems but also as a source of value judgments for individual works. In this study I propose an approach to Garcilaso's poetry that moves away from the reliance on his undocumented sentimental biography and examines a number of poems from the perspectives of the idea content, the artistic technique, the expectations of genre, and the cultural and poetic milieu in which they were conceived. In these studies, I tend to view the poet less as a real lover expressing his unrequited passion and more as a serious thinker struggling with new material and norms of poetic expression; a stylist and wit who often takes a critical stance to examine with ironical reflection and sharp insight the paradoxical poetic problems of his day.

While the general focus of the study is unified, the specific arguments follow multiple lines of development. One of these arguments suggests a revaluation of Garcilaso's poetic principles and a detailed reinterpretation of a number of the poems within the context of Italian Renaissance literature and painting. It traces various types of Italian Renaissance influence, including the specific rules established by Pietro Bembo (1470–1547) for imitation, the reaction against Petrarchism initiated by Bernardo Tasso (1493–1569) and the subject matter and aesthetic norms of Italian painting. The richness of Garcilaso's Renaissance backgrounds in poetry, art, and philosophy have been inadequately studied. I hope I have re-created through textual references, quotations, exposition of debated issues, and references to paintings a part of the Renaissance ambience that inspired a number of Garcilaso's works. Few of the works discussed are actual sources. Rather than argue from the narrow confines of direct textual influence, I try to judge Garcilaso's works from the more global criteria of their general Renaissance cultural antecedents.

A second idea develops from the study of the relationship between the poetic voice, or voices, and the destined readers of the text. Parting from a more theoretical approach, this analysis sheds light on various aspects of the relationship between the writer (both poet and lover) and the readers (both critic and beloved) implied in each text. The examination of Garcilaso's poetry from this point of view provides further insights into the transformations from the *cancionero* style to the Petrarchan mode as well as highlighting several differences between Garcilaso and Juan Boscán Almogáver (1474?–1542).

A third course is suggested by the myth of Mars and Venus—soldier and lover—in Garcilaso's poetry. The violence of Mars and the opposing tenderness of Venus are re-created on various levels in Garcilaso's poetry. In the Ode they represent the opposition of planetary forces that invoke contrary emotions in earthly subjects. In Elegy II, Mars's steel and violence are pitted against Venus's softness and beauty. In Canción IV they become an allegory of the historical and psychological stages of human development from primitivism. In other poems they represent the soldier and the humanist, Garcilaso himself "tomando ora la espada, ora la pluma" (Eclogue III, 40). Even in poems, such as the sonnets, that do not specifically make reference to Mars and Venus, the themes of love and violence tend to dominate. The Petrarchan sonnets often evoke a masochistic suffering and self-inflicted torment ending in a welcomed violent death. The objectified conflict of the mythical Mars and Venus represents a dualism that finds full expression in the themes of love and violence that dominate Garcilaso's poetry.

This book began as a monographic study of Garcilaso's Ode ad florem Gnidi. The original study is to be found in Part VI, while the preceding chapters grew out of the critical background and revaluations of Garcilaso's art that seemed a necessary preliminary to the study of the ode. The most obvious gaps, the lack of studies of the eclogues, are not really defects, since recent critical studies have tended to supply the type of commentary that complements the studies in this book. The poems studied in this book, on the other hand, still suffer from old critical evaluations, a few dating back to the commentators of the sixteenth century. I hope that the study of several of the lesser known works will provide a wider basis for the appreciation of all of Garcilaso's poetry.

I have divided the book into six parts, each elaborating a central idea. Part I attacks the problematical question of sincerity in Garcilaso's art from several different points of view. Chapter 1 surveys the history of sincerity as a critical concept and shows why Garcilaso was in fact a poor subject on whom to foist the romantic ideas of sincerity. The textual evidence of his poetry suggests that sincerity was not always a preoccupation of the poet; more important it is relevant to the discussion of only one period of his poetry. Chapter 2 establishes a model for the love lyric based on more recent theoretical considerations of the role of the text as message from the poet and lover to the critic and beloved. The application of this model to the love poetry of Boscán and Garcilaso reveals several important aspects of the transformations from the *cancionero* style to the Petrarchan mode. A close study of several of Boscán's poems and Garcilaso's *coplas* suggests reasons for the development of a "rhetoric of sincerity," and highlights several of the differences between their works. Chapter 3 moves away from the problem of sincerity and examines the question of Renaissance ideas of imitation. The chapter outlines recent ideas on the theories of imitation in the Renaissance and analyzes in detail some aspects of Garcilaso's understanding and application of these ideas.

Part II provides one of the bases for a new study on Garcilaso: the poetic ideas of his Italian contemporaries. Past histories of Spanish literature have presented an oversimplified view of Italian Renaissance literature. This section examines the precepts of sixteenth-century Petrarchism as expounded by Pietro Bembo and the reaction against them by Garcilaso's contemporary, and perhaps friend, Bernardo Tasso. Bembo's *Prose della volgar lingua* sets forth very precise guidelines for imitation, the importance of which for Garcilaso's Petrarchan poetry is studied here for the first time. Tasso's brief prologues form a literary manifesto in which he outlines a new aesthetic for lyric poetry. This aesthetic in turn provides a new basis for the revaluation of Garcilaso's poetics and a number of his poems. These ideas make necessary the establishment of a clearly defined third period in Garcilaso's poetry, with fixed norms of poetics, form, and material.

Parts III and IV classify and analyze Garcilaso's sonnets. Part III studies Garcilaso's Petrarchism from his first imitations of Petrarch through his paradoxical subversion of the canons of Petrarchan expression.

Chapter 6 discusses his apprenticeship in the Petrarchan mode, also discussing the narrative implications of the sonnets within the broader context of the love situation. Chapter 7 analyzes his achievement of the Petrarchan mode. Special emphasis is placed on the analysis of the means of expression, the narrative posture, and implied narrative situation. Chapter 8 discusses those sonnets that subvert various aspects of canonized Petrarchism.

Part IV studies Garcilaso's reaction against Bembo's Petrarchism and his introduction of new approaches to and experiments with poetic material. The later sonnets, written under the influence of Bernardo Tasso's mandate for an expansion of poetic material, often imitate aspects of the classical epigram and present new thematic material, new methods, and new attitudes. Chapter 9 discusses the reaction against Petrarchism in the later love sonnets. In Chapter 10 special attention is given to the new Neoplatonic material, which had previously been noted in only two of the sonnets. This Renaissance philosophical system provides the basis for the reinterpretation of several sonnets that have been imperfectly understood because of the biographical approach to Garcilaso's poetry. Chapter 11 studies those sonnets that do not deal with love, but generally are sonnets of praise, introducing into Spanish new poetic themes that would come to dominate baroque poetry. These sonnets are arguably the most biographical and personal of all his poems, even though the love message tends to disappear.

Part V examines Garcilaso as a thinker and a wit. Chapter 12 studies in Canción IV Garcilaso's investigation and ironical resolution of the paradox of courtly love, conceived of on the one hand as an ennobling and civilizing element, and on the other as a loss of reason resulting in madness and savagery. This theme shows Garcilaso as a thinking poet interested in broader paradoxes than the simple wordplay typical of courtly love poetry. Chapter 13 studies in Elegy II the Renaissance theme of jealousy and how it undercuts the Aristotelian ideal of the Golden Mean and Horace's ideal of moderation. Not even revered classical ideas were free from Garcilaso's penetrating and probing wit.

Part VI is a study of various aspects of Garcilaso's Ode ad florem Gnidi. Chapter 14 discusses Tasso's conception of the ode and its Horatian roots, as well as Garcilaso's enthusiasm for Horace and the Horatian ambience in Naples in the 1520s and 1530s. The question of genre is reviewed in light of Herrera's relabeling of the Ode as a *canción*. The last part of the chapter analyzes various methods in which the Ode is unified, such as repetition of key words and phrases throughout, association of the various elements with civilization and barbarity, and the use of puns. Chapter 15 examines the Renaissance context of the various myths, such as the armed Venus and the opposition between Mars and Venus. This leads to a discussion of the relationship of Garcilaso and Renaissance painting, above all the group of late fifteenth- and early sixteenth-century paintings treating the theme of Mars and Venus. This chapter brings together in the same discussion one of the most exquisite poems in the Spanish language and some of the most beautiful canvases of Renaissance painting, finding common philosophical and aesthetic bases for each. The methodology of the iconological mystery is examined, and the astrological and occult aspects of Mars and Venus are analyzed in light of Renaissance occult sciences. This leads to the final analysis of Garcilaso's Ode as an iconological mystery.

All quotations from the works of Garcilaso come from Rivers's edition with commentaries (1981). The high quality of the text requires few emendations, so that they are noted here and in the notes to the text. I have changed the punctuation in the first stanza of Copla IV; capitalized the personified "Amor" (Sonnets VII, XXII, XXVII, XXXIII, and XXXV); placed an accent over "y" in Sonnet XXI (line 5) because I believe it is not the copulative, but a shortened form of "allí"; and emended an error in Sonnet XIV (line 11).

I have used Gallego Morell's edition of the commentaries by the early editors of Garcilaso's poems (*Garcilaso de la Vega y sus comentaristas*). The references are indicated by B- (plus number) for the commentaries of El Brocence, H- for those of Herrera, T- for those of Tamayo de Vargas, and A- for those by Azara.

Parts of Chapter 12 appeared in *The Hermetic Journal* (1991). I would like to thank the editor for permission to reprint them here.

I would like to thank Frederick A. de Armas for help in understanding the Venus–Mars theme in Garcilaso's poetry; Sharon Voros for her close critique of the first two chapters; Dan Eisenberg and David Darst for sending me hard-to-find materials; Daryl Bergeron for help with printing; my colleagues at Tulane; Tom Montgomery, for listening to various oral versions of these ideas and reading most carefully Chapter 4; Richard Tuttle, for information on Italian painting; Linda Carroll, for help with various Renaissance themes, especially astrology; and my research assistants at Tulane who helped with various parts of this project, Matthew Bailey, Fuencisla Zomeño, and Carlota Caulfield.

I
Garcilaso and the Rhetoric of Sincerity

1

Garcilaso's Critics and the
Question of Sincerity

In addition to the role he played in the introduction of Italianate meters
and poetic forms into Spanish, Garcilaso has always been regarded in his
own right as a major poet. Spanish Golden Age writers bestowed on him
the highly appropriate title of "el príncipe de los poetas." More than
any Spanish author, his works recall the glories of the Renaissance. The
balanced and sculptured beauty of his verses and his open criticism of
medieval Spanish literature recall classical elements of Renaissance art
and thought. Even though the beauty, perfection, and grace of his poetry
are easily appreciated, they are not easily analyzed or explained. Some
critics have tried to understand his success through stylistic studies, but
the reason most often advanced in modern times to explain Garcilaso's
superiority as an artist is his supposed sincerity.[1] In spite of critical con-
demnations of sincerity as a tool for literary analysis, many critical studies in the twentieth century have found the value of Garcilaso's poetry
to lie in the expression of his unrequited love for Isabel Freire and his
subsequent grief after her death. The poems have been analyzed as pieces
of evidence with which "to reconstruct in some manner the story of his

---

1. Even Dámaso Alonso assumes as a basis of his stylistic analysis that Garcilaso's best poetry
was written for Isabel Freire (*Poesía española* 104).

heart" (Keniston, *Garcilaso* 192). The superiority of his poetry over that of his contemporaries is often explained through reference to his alleged sincerity.

This use of sincerity as a critical tool for evaluating Garcilaso's poetry is a surprisingly late phenomenon. None of the commentators previous to the twentieth century employed the term.[2] Their praises or descriptions of the values of Garcilaso's poetry referred to the tenderness or sweetness of his poetry (Herrero García 75). Saavedra Fajardo (1584–1648) comes close to elaborating a concept of sincerity, but his real emphasis is on describing the effects of the poetry: "Fue príncipe de la líricia, i con dulzura, gravedad i maravillosa pureza de vozes descubrió los sentimientos del alma" (39). The last phrase probably refers more to the human psyche in general than to Garcilaso's own private passions. López de Sedano (1729–1801) limits his praises of Eclogue I to a listing of the stylistic effects and technical aspects: "el artificio, el decoro de las personas, la imitación de la naturaleza, la especie de la versificación, la dulzura y propiedad del estilo" (2:i). Eclogue II is praised for "la hermosura de la frase y belleza del estilo" (2:ii), and Eclogue III is praised as an imitation of ancient models: "Todo él abunda de hermosas imágines, y felices imitaciones; y respira el mismo gusto, dulzura y suavidad de los insignes originales de la antigüedad, que le sirvieron de modelo" (2:iii). Manuel José Quintana (1772–1857) ignores any idea of sincerity, finding that Garcilaso wrote poetry "con solo su particular talento auxiliado de su aplicación y buen gusto" (11). He reported that some readers had complained that Garcilaso did not put enough of himself into his poems, but let himself be swayed by his models: "Desearan algunos que se hubiese entregado más a sus propias ideas y sentimientos . . . por último quisieran que la disposición de sus églogas tuviese más unidad y hubiese más conexión entre las personas y objetos que intervienen en ellas" (12). The desire for personal feeling and greater unity would be provided by twentieth-century critics who construed the eclogues to be highly personal poems with a unity based on the poet's personal experience. Even though Quintana shows a Romantic bias, his praise of Eclogue I places even greater emphasis on the perfection of the style: "los hombres de gusto delicado han señalado la naturalidad y verdad que hay en las imágenes, la dulzura en los afectos, la belleza y armonía de los versos, la

---

2. The epithet "nuevo Sincero" used by Lope de Vega clearly refers to Sannazaro's academic name, and not to the qualities of Garcilaso's poetry. He says "El Títiro español, nuevo Sincero," which is made clear in a later verse: "Virgilio y Sanazaro" (Herrero García 80).

propiedad, elegancia y corrección del estilo. Ningún artificio, ninguna afectación, ningún exceso; todo tan conveniente y apropiado al género, todo tan natural y verdadero" (41). The main emphasis in all these commentaries clearly falls on expression and style.

The account of Garcilaso's death that Alvaro Cienfuegos included in his biography of San Francisco de Borja (1717) struck a new tone in Garcilaso studies. Cienfuegos's exceedingly sentimental and patriotically religious style and his constant exaltation of fact create for the first time a vein of sentimentality that would later be used to describe Garcilaso's love for Isabel Freire. His exaltation of Garcilaso's fame is a clear example of his exaggerated style: "La dulçura y facilidad admirable de sus numeros, la elegancia suave de su estilo en las prosas, la fertilidad prodiga de sus conceptos, y la erudicion que auia bebido en tantos forasteros arroyos, fueron en poco dias dilatando su fama, y sus corrientes por todas las naciones" (49a).

Even though he does not employ the term sincerity, nor does he mention Isabel Freire, Fernández de Navarrete's biography of Garcilaso (1850) clearly continues this direction by investing the elementary events of Garcilaso's life with sentimental and melodramatic emotional content. For example, he justifies Garcilaso's anti-*comunero*, pro-imperial stance by imagining his emotional reactions: "No permitiéndole sus cortos años comprender los justos motivos de queja que los pueblos podían tener contra un monarca, a quien amaba tiernamente, lamentaba en el alma ver a su hermano en el partido de los descontentos, y se dispuso a sacrificar las inclinaciones de la sangre a los deberes de la lealtad" (20). Such elaborations of fact are logically fictitious, and foreshadow the type of amorous sentimentality that dominates much of twentieth-century Garcilaso criticism.

Menéndez y Pelayo seems to have been the first to employ the term sincerity to describe Garcilaso's poetry. In volume 13 of his *Antología de poetas líricos castellanos* (first published 1908), he advanced the concept of sincerity by arguing that both the characters Salicio and Nemoroso in Eclogue I represented Garcilaso's love for Isabel Freire. The arguments he adduced to prove this point are based on the concept of sincerity: "Prefiero la tradición de Faría a la de Zapata; porque no es verosímil, ni posible siquiera, que la divina lamentación de Nemoroso, que es lo más tierno y apasionado que brotó de la pluma de Garcilaso, sea el eco o el reflejo de una pasión ajena. . . . Garcilaso ha puesto en aquellas estancias todo su corazón, y habla allí en nombre propio, no en el de su amigo, ni mucho menos en nombre del marido de su dama" (58). It is curious how easily his preference is elevated to the status of historical truth. The only Golden Age commentator to suggest that both Salicio and Nemoroso represented Garcilaso was the seventeenth-century Portuguese writer Manuel de Faria e Sousa, whom Menéndez y Pelayo generally distrusted. Because of this distrust he felt the need for further proof, for which he employed the argument of sincerity: "Admitida la duplicación poética del personaje de Garcilaso en la égloga primera, adquieren el prestigio de la sinceridad las inmortales quejas de Nemoroso, y se aumenta, si es posible, su extraordinaria belleza, no superada quizá por ninguna elegía castellana" (60). His argument rests on the assumption that a poem can only have real value if it represents the poet's own experience. This provides conclusive "proof" to establish the connection between Garcilaso and the two shepherds Salicio and Nemoroso. Not only was Menéndez y Pelayo the first to use the term sincerity to characterize positive values in Garcilaso's poetry, but he also elevated the concept to the level of a critical tool for establishing historical fact.

Menéndez y Pelayo's critical judgments have served as the basis for further elaborations from Navarro Tomás to Antonio Prieto. In the introduction to his ubiquitous Clásicos Castellanos edition, Navarro Tomás employed sincerity as a term of praise: "dos amores, en distintas fechas, pasaron por sus versos con singular fragancia de sinceridad" (Garcilaso, Obras 1911, ix). He further suggested that Garcilaso's "composiciones más sentidas" (xvii) were addressed to Isabel Freire.

Keniston's biography frequently employed "sincerity" as an aesthetic principle and value judgment. He not only found the chief virtue of Garcilaso's poetry to be "an accent of ardent sincerity" (Garcilaso 191), but he also attributed most of Garcilaso's poetry to his love for Isabel Freire: "That his love for her was intense and sincere is revealed in every line of his works which mentions her; indeed it is often this quality of sincerity which distinguishes his real poetry from his imitative verses" (193). The use of the verb "mentions" clearly overstates the case, for never is Isabel Freire mentioned in the poetry of Garcilaso. He summarized the argument again: "The love of Garcilaso for Isabel Freire permeates his work from beginning to end; it is she who inspired all of his verses which still have power to move and charm his readers" (202). For Keniston, the term involves not only truth in poetry, but also a quality of emotional or passionate expression. He found Garcilaso's poems addressed to Boscán that use a less formal language and some ironical distancing to lack sincerity and, hence, to be inferior: "As a whole the sonnets of this group are not of high merit,—conventional exercises in the spinning of conceits. . . . Lacking as they do, the warmth of sincerity which redeemed his first essays, and the polished elegance of his purely conventional classical reminiscences, they add little to his literary credit" (213–14). Compared with the poems that Keniston found to demonstrate sincerity, the "insincere" poems seem to be more straightforward in expression and refer to actual known events in the poet's life, whereas the "sincere" poems refer elliptically through metaphor to the poet's supposed love for Isabel Freire. Their hyperbolic use of the motifs of violence and suicide are clearly fictional. For Keniston, "sincerity" did not mean a straightforward nonmetaphorical utterance, but rather a level of emotional intensity. A poem was sincere if it conveyed the deep, anguished suffering of the unrequited lover; other types of poetic expression were insincere and false. Sincerity came to signify not only truth in poetry, but also a certain type of overwrought, emotionally charged poetry that was considered sincere because it communicated the anguish of the poet.

In 1924, Navarro Tomás revised the introduction to the Clásicos Castellanos edition to incorporate Keniston's findings. In the new version the speculation concerning Garcilaso's love for Isabel Freire was treated as truth. In the early version the speculation concerning Isabel Freire was placed after the documented facts of Garcilaso's life, but in the revised version it was integrated into the chronology of documented facts. The new introduction emphasized even more Garcilaso's sincerity: "Los rasgos esenciales de las poesías de Garcilaso son sencillez, elegancia y sinceridad" (lx). Even his will is marked by sincerity: "las notas más salientes son la ingenua y leal sinceridad de Garcilaso" (xxii).[3]

Lapesa also employed sincerity as a critical tool. His *Trayectoria de la poesía de Garcilaso* constructs a chronological trajectory simultaneously based on the stylistic innovations in Garcilaso's poetry and the poet's supposed love for Isabel Freire. His careful evaluation of Garcilaso's sources and style produced a landmark study in understanding and classifying the various influences and elements in Garcilaso's Italianate po-

---

3. I would like to thank David Darst for providing me with a photocopy of the 1924 introduction. Navarro Tomás added more "information" concerning Isabel Freire in the definitive 1936 edition. One phrase comments on her beauty: "cualidades clásicas del ideal de belleza feminina del Renacimiento" (xix). Another commentary speculates on her attitudes to the poet: "Sin duda D.ª Isabel, después de casada, no tuvo respecto a Garcilaso las atenciones amistosas con que antes le había distinguido, mudanza que en las quejas de Salicio aparece bajo proporciones de infidelidad y perjurio (Egl. I, 93, 129)" (xx).

etry. Even though Lapesa seldom employs the word "sincero," the concept lies behind many of his judgments, and final decisions regarding chronology at times are based on the love trajectory. Lapesa's good judgment and linguistic solidness give value to his study and save him from the backward approaches of Navarro Tomás and Antonio Prieto, both willing to overlook the stylistics of single poems in order to fit them into an amorous biography. Navarro Tomás believed Garcilaso's classical sonnets to be early, before he went to Naples and learned the correct Petrarchan expression (Garcilaso, *Obras* 1963, xvi). Prieto (*Garcilaso* 127) first followed Lapesa and placed Sonnet XXVIII late because its laconic style and dry wit are close to other poems from that period. He recently retracted his earlier view and placed the sonnet, the poem in which the poet claims he has never been in love, before the time that Garcilaso met Isabel Freire. Otherwise the sonnet does not make sense in Garcilaso's spiritual biography (Prieto, *La poesía* 88). Prieto justifies his new reading of Garcilaso on the last line of Sonnet XXXVI (of disputed authenticity) where the poet finds his love, in spite of his suffering, to be "única ventura." Prieto interprets this phrase to mean that Isabel Freire was Garcilaso's only love.

Rivers's critical studies represent a transformation of these ideas, while not breaking with them. Even though he never employs the word "sincerity" to describe Garcilaso's poetry, his short biography of the poet prefacing his critical edition with commentary (Garcilaso, *Obras* 1981, 11–17), adapted as the introduction of the critical guide (*Garcilaso* 11–21), lay great emphasis on the importance of Isabel Freire. In the critical edition he claimed "su gran amor, el que influye en mucha poesía líricia suya, era Isabel Freire" (13). In the study guide he appended a long footnote defending this traditional interpretation (*Garcilaso* 15). On the other hand, Rivers's critical estimations of individual poems and poetic processes avoid all dependence on the concept of a fervent sincere love. His article on the poetic epistle shows a clear understanding and appreciation of one of Garcilaso's poems that has always been a stumbling block for sentimental critics. His article "The Pastoral Paradox of Natural Art" appreciates not sincerity and passion in Garcilaso's Eclogue III, but the opposite effect of distancing and artifice to express passion. Finally, his studies on poetic language ("Some Ideas") and genres, like the study on the poetic epistles, continue to approach the poetics and conventions of literary production. While he seems to adhere to an older view of the poetry, his studies have developed a different and more sophisticated sense of Garcilaso's poetry.

I do not need to mention all uses of sincerity by modern critics, for it pervades both critical studies and histories of literature. However, the study by C. Poullain should be pointed out for the intensity of its arguments for sincerity: "La sincerité est bien, en effet, le trait essentiel de la poésie de Garcilaso, et c'est elle qui, par delá toutes les traditions littéraires, lui donne un caractère résolument moderne" ("Le Thème central" 358). The idea is repeated several times throughout the article. Poullain even claims that various episodes in Garcilaso's poetry, such as the myths of Leander, Apollo and Daphne, and Iphis and Anaxarete, represent the poet's own life and feeling: "Cette présence constante dans l'oeuvre poétique d'un épisode intensément vécu montre que la sincérité est le trait dominant de Garcilaso" (371). The conclusion returns to the question of modernity: "Le trait distinctif du poète tolédan est bien la sincérité; son oeuvre est éminemment personnelle, et pour cette raison, émouvante, et de plus, moderne: on est parfois plus près, chez lui, de la confession romantique que de la retenue classique" (372).

Garcilaso's critics were not unique in positing sincerity as the major quality of his poetry. Their work parallels the use of the concept in much poetic criticism since the eighteenth century. M. H. Abrams documents the appearance of sincerity in the Romantic period: "In this second sense, Pater's truth approximates 'sincerity' which, significantly, began in the early nineteenth century its career as the primary criterion, if not the *sine qua non,* of excellence in poetry" (318). He also notes the joining of the concepts of sincerity and spontaneity "in order to condemn neoclassic artifice" (319). And he comments on its importance in late nineteenth-century critical thought: "Sincerity, with persisting moral and characteriological implications, became a favorite Victorian test of literary virtue" (319). Patricia Ball has traced the concept of sincerity from its beginnings to our own day. Sincerity as a critical concept in poetry was introduced by the Romantics as a criterion for great poetry. It was felt that only writing that came from the inner self could be true poetic expression. This concept evolved both as a precept and aesthetic principle in reaction to the artistic distancing typical of neoclassicism. As an artistic norm sincerity demanded deep emotional involvement in the work of art. It has not disappeared from the literary scene: "The last words on sincerity and literature have not, however, been said, despite the evidence of its decline and fugitive survival" (10).

In spite of the nearly universal use of sincerity as a critical tool, it is impossible to substantiate its validity. Among the numerous authorities who could be cited on the importance of sincerity, perhaps the most instructive is I. A. Richards in his *Practical Criticism* where he attempts a definition and rational exposition of the concept. He begins viewing insincerity as a disparity between the poet's feeling and the feeling reproduced in the poem. Insincerity is a

> flaw that insinuates itself when a writer cannot himself distinguish his own genuine promptings from those he would merely like to have, or those which he hopes will make a good poem. Such failures on his part to achieve complete imaginative integrity may show themselves in exaggeration, in strained expression, in false simplicity, or perhaps in the manner of his indebtedness to other poetry. (95)

But he admits he is at a loss to define the concept or even to find a fruitful way to employ it in the analysis of poetry. Taking up a more careful scrutiny of the concept, he rejects emotional insincerity as inappropriate to literature and he dismisses the sense of sincerity that suggests spontaneity and unelaborated response. Even though he cannot provide a clear definition of the concept, he refuses to abandon it: "It will be worth while hunting a little longer for a satisfactory sense of 'sincerity'. Whatever it is, it is the quality we most insistently require in poetry" (282). From this point he shifts ground from sincerity in literature to sincerity on the part of the literary critic, and elaborates a process of formation based on Confucian mysticism. This comes to supersede any doubts he presented concerning the proper sense of the term. The pseudoreligiosity and elevated tone of this argument call into question Richards's own sincerity, although he confirms this conflated view of literary criticism in other passages. The escape to the concept of a critic who, once purified by oriental mysticism, is capable of understanding the mysteries of poetic creation does not erase the fact that he has failed (by his own admission) to define sincerity, and the Confucian gloss he substitutes hardly resolves the problem of sincerity in literature.

In fact, it is impossible to find a valid use for sincerity as a literary tool. Using clear examples, Wellek and Warren dismissed the concept as valueless: "The frequently adduced criterion of 'sincerity' is thoroughly false. . . . There is no relation between 'sincerity' and value as art. The volumes of agonizingly felt love poetry perpetrated by adolescents and the dreary (however fervently felt) religious verse which fills libraries are sufficient proof of this" (80). In 1970, Wellek returned to the question

(*Discriminations* 225–52), reacting against a proponent of sincerity who had claimed that the defining characteristic of the lyric is authentic personal experience, and that the lyric poem is a "real utterance" (226) based on "lived experience" (228). This proponent, maintaining that the "I" of every lyric poem was recounting his or her own personal experience, was only somewhat puzzled by obviously fictional poems that appear in novels. Wellek reiterated what he and Warren had proposed previously: that the "I" of lyrical poetry is a fictional mask, and the experience related is passed through artistic filters; in short, a poem is a fictional creation, even if the poet did experience a similar event or emotion. The tone of the lyric is often personal and intimate, but its metaphors and rhetoric, along with the narrative stance of the speaker, must be fictional.

Sincerity is an objectionable critical concept because it leads to notable distortions of value and even of understanding and appreciation of individual works. The most common is the invention of biographical legends, complete with emotional crises, fabricated to justify and explain so-called sincere writing from the past. These biographical fables serve to fulfill the Romantic criterion that great literature could be produced only by deep emotional experience that the work of literature re-created naturally and without artifice. Biography and fiction were conflated to prove that art was sincere, and the artist's life was rewritten to make it conform to his fiction. Mateo Alemán became a *pícaro,* not a judge, and Sá da Miranda retired to a country estate and led a celibate life because of his rejection by Isabel Freire (a commentary that conveniently overlooked his marriage). While sincerity may have worked well as a precept to free art from the rationalistic approach of eighteenth-century neoclassicism, as a critical judgment on works already created, it led to severe abuses.

Sincerity as a literary criteria creates an unsolvable problem. The authenticity of the author's feeling can be neither affirmed nor denied from the existing evidence of the poetic production. Those who believe in sincerity as a literary criteria maintain that successful poetry results from an intensity of feeling that is sincerely expressed, while lesser poetry falls short precisely because the poet's feeling was deficient, and hence the poetry is conventional and insincere. Without records of the poet's emotional involvement, those who support the concept of sincerity find proof of their convictions in the intensity of the poetry itself.

Likewise, those who deny the idea that the quality of the poetry depends on the sincerity of expression have no way to prove their arguments other than to maintain that the success of a poem depends on the craft and art of the poet. A good poet is one who has a gift for writing poetry, not one who has intense feelings. This argument likewise cannot be proved.

In its own way, New Criticism tried to deal with the question by alienating the text from extratextual points of reference. In the hands of weaker critics, such readings were liable to produce notable distortions of literary evaluation by attempting to exclude social, religious, and authorial circumstances as having any bearing on the text. In the case of some works, such as those depending on literary conventions (the *villancico,* for example) or those incorporating autobiographical references into the work (such as Lope's *La Dorotea*), one simply had to ignore the precepts of New Criticism. This critical practice, however, did serve as a way of removing in one fell swoop all of the pseudobiographical details that had come to serve as explanation of the literary text. Even though the strict application of this method failed, the intention was well perceived. One need only look at well-studied texts to see the unchecked cancerous growth that biographical, or pseudobiographical, criticism produced.

Until recently most twentieth-century critics have alleged that one of the outstanding aspects of Garcilaso's poetry was the authenticity and sincerity of his expression. Critical opinion was in agreement that his rejection by Isabel Freire and her later death in childbirth created the emotional anguish that served as the driving force behind his poetry. In 1969, M. J. Woods argued that sincerity was of no value in evaluating Garcilaso's poetry: "It soon becomes clear that the term explains nothing. . . . To say that a poem is 'sincere' means little more than that we find it persuasive or moving" (146–47). In addition, several recent critics, apparently working independently of each other, have challenged the historicity of the love for Isabel Freire, even to the point of questioning whether the poet had ever met her. In 1978, Frank Goodwyn reported the find of new documentation that placed Garcilaso in Toledo during the latter half of 1526, the time when he was supposed to have met and courted Isabel Freire. Goodwyn used this information as a springboard to launch an attack on "the Portuguese lady-in-waiting, Isabel Freire" ("New Light" 4). He discredited the only piece of evidence that links Garcilaso and Isabel Freire, the statement in the Gayango manuscript that titles Copla II as "A Doña Ysabel Freira porque se caso con un hombre fuera de su condición." He claimed the manuscript is "cluttered with errors" (5), and has other false attributions to Garcilaso. He further maintains that even if the *copla* is by Garcilaso, there is no other indication that the rest of Garcilaso's poetry was written to Isabel Freire. As further proof against Keniston's identification of Garcilaso with Nemoroso in Eclogue I, he states that the pastoral name Nemoroso corresponds better to Boscán because, as El Brocense said, "Nemus es bosque," whereas it is not, as Keniston had claimed, also a "vega" (12). His final arguments address the question of the difference between post-Romantic and Renaissance poetics and poetical expectations, concluding: "Regardless of whom Salicio and Nemoroso in the eclogues were meant to represent, they are fictitious figures in fictitious settings" (15).

In 1979, Pamela Waley and David Darst analyzed and evaluated the bases for the belief that Garcilaso wrote all of his poetry to Isabel Freire. Waley noted the slightness of the evidence connecting Garcilaso and Isabel Freire. She said of Copla II, "the tone of the poem suggests an urbane and conventional flirtation rather than a passionate and hopeless love" ("Garcilaso, Isabel" 12). She noted that Golden Age commentators were confused on the topic. El Brocense and Zapata had said Nemoroso was Boscán, and Herrera claimed it was Isabel Freire's husband Antonio de Fonseca. Only "in about 1640"[4] did Faria e Sousa associate Nemoroso with Garcilaso and his love for Isabel Freire. Waley did not advance a new theory because she did not want "to substitute conjecture for conjecture but to show how little foundation an accepted tradition can have even in twentieth-century Hispanism. Love poems provide in general an unsatisfactory basis for biography" (14).

Darst also reviewed the same pieces of "evidence," finding the sixteenth-century references to be scant indeed: "the remarks of two commentators and Luis Zapata (all three pointing to Boscán as Isabel's admirer), and the aforementioned title to a MS version of a *copla*" ("Garcilaso's Love" 264). Darst was aware of Goodwyn's article, but wanted to analyze exactly how twentieth-century critics had come to believe that Garcilaso had represented himself in Eclogue I. He found the actual evi-

---

4. This is Waley's conjecture. Faria e Sousa published his commentaries on Camões's *Lusiadas* in 1639. The commentaries on the *Rimas* were not published until 1685 and 1689, more than thirty-five years after his death in 1649. The discussion of Eclogue I that prefaces the fourth volume of *Fuente de Aganipe* (1644), identifies only Salicio as Garcilaso. The preface was reprinted as the introduction to the commentaries on Camões' eclogues in 1689. Faria e Sousa worked on his commentaries over a twenty-five-year period. The commentary identifying Salicio and Nemoroso as Garcilaso and Galatea and Elisa as Isabel Freire must postdate the 1644 preface to his own eclogues.

dence discredited, and suggested a new aesthetic reading of Garcilaso's poetry: "hopefully his poetry can now stand as it must: a monument unto itself, an artifact of intellectual inspiration rather than of personal emotion" (268).

In 1979 (from a paper read in 1977), Adrien Roig offered a revaluation of the question of identity of Salicio and Nemoroso in Eclogue I. His study is less satisfactory than those of the previous critics because he employs as evidence the fictionalizations presented in Sá da Miranda's eclogues. To replace the serious commentary of El Brocense and Herrera with suggestions taken from fictional poetry hardly seems a sound method of procedure; it results more in speculating on the identity of the characters than in focusing on the poetry itself and its aesthetic values.

In 1986, Luis Iglesias Feijoo studied Eclogue I, employing the suggestions of the above critics. He reviews the previous attitudes toward Garcilaso's poetry, and finds the older reading "plenamente convincente y no poco seductora" (62). He suggests, however, a new reading of the poems based on new criteria: "Procedamos a limpiarlos de antemano de la pátina sentimental de que nosotros, impenitentes románticos, los habíamos recubierto" (66). His new reading is based on the critical ambience of the Italian Renaissance. Of course, as he suggests early in his article, in the new reading nothing changes in the text itself, only our perception of its relation to reality.

Several critics have come to the defense of the traditional readings. Rivers in his critical guide to Garcilaso, appended a note before publication to defend the traditional stance (*Garcilaso* 15). Enrique Martínez López ("Sobre") also defended the traditional ideas, producing a detailed genealogy of Fonseca to show why Isabel Freire's husband could be called "fuera de su condición." Lapesa in the reprint of his studies on Garcilaso discusses in detail the arguments against the identification of Isabel Freire and defends his previous statements (*Garcilaso: Estudios* 199–203).

As much as one is in sympathy with readings of Garcilaso's poetry that question the importance of his love commitment, it is only fair to point out that the association of Garcilaso with the pastoral character Salicio dates to the sixteenth century, not only in the commentaries of Brocense and Herrera, but also among poets who refer to Garcilaso with the poetic name Salicio (Gallego Morell, *Antología* 65–69, 102, 153). Galatea was not, however, associated with Isabel Freire (at least in print). The association of Garcilaso with Nemoroso did not occur until the seventeenth century. In the first commentary on Eclogue I, El Brocense had dryly identified the two shephards: "Salicio es Garci-Lasso. Nemoroso, Boscán, porque *nemus* es el bosque" (B-95). Commenting on the inappropriateness of the word "degollada" in Eclogue III, El Brocense said that the dead nymph represented Isabel Freire (B-244), and he identified Nemoroso as Boscán. Herrera repeated Brocense's identification of the dead nymph with Isabel Freire, but extended the argument by placing it as a preface to his commentaries on Eclogue I. He says that Salicio was commonly held to represent Garcilaso: "éste se llama Salicio, y es ya común opinión que se entiende por G. L. mismo" (H-423). Herrera often contradicted El Brocense, probably to establish his own independence and originality. In the identification of Nemoroso, he states that since the character cannot represent Boscán in Eclogue II, then the character must represent someone else in the other eclogues. Elisa in Eclogue I is not identified (as in El Brocense), only in Eclogue III. Since this Elisa is Isabel Freire, then he concludes that Nemoroso must be her husband: "Elisa . . . La cual es doña Isabel Freire, que murió de parto; y así se deja entender, si no me engaño, que este pastor es su marido don Antonio de Fonseca" (H-423). The manner of phrasing: "así se deja entender, si no me engaño," suggests a conclusion from argument rather than from oral tradition.

Luis Zapata (1526–95) celebrated Garcilaso both as a hero in an exaggerated episode in his *Carlo Magno* and as a wit in several anecdotes in his *Miscelánea*. The anecdote in which he discusses the identification of the characters of Nemoroso and Elisa (first published in Sancha's edition of Garcilaso in 1786) must have been written after 1580 because he rejects Herrera's identification of Nemoroso as Isabel Freire's husband Antonio de Fonseca. He identifies the characters as Boscán and Isabel Freire, but confuses the numbering of the eclogues: "Estando en la corte en Toledo, Don Antonio Fonseca, caballero principal de Toro, con Doña Isabel Freile, una dama de la Emperatriz, á cuya muerte hizo Garcilaso una parte de la segunda egloga que lloró Boscán, habiendo sido su servidor antes que se casase en el nombre de Nemoroso de *nemus*, y ella en nombre de Elisa de Elisabet ó Isabel, que todo es uno" (384–85). Don Quijote also identified Boscán as Nemoroso: "como el antiguo Boscán se llamó *Nemoroso*" (Cervantes II, 533). In summary, the sixteenth-century commentators and poets identified Salicio with Garcilaso, but never suggested a real-life character for Galatea. Elisa was identified as Isabel Freire, and Nemoroso as Boscán, although Herrera suggested another identity, based on conjecture.

The identification of Galatea with Isabel Freire and Nemoroso with Garcilaso did not occur until the 1640s, and was not published until 1689. Faria e Sousa (1590–1649), the first to identify Salicio and Nemoroso with Garcilaso and Galatea and Elisa with Isabel Freire, often deduces his conclusions from shaky premises, rather than referring to known traditions. The late date of this identification and his claim to originality tend to diminish one's confidence in his arguments. He admits that the received opinion was that Boscán was Nemoroso: "aunque siempre se entendió ser Boscán el Nemoroso" (*Rimas* 211). He is sure none of the commentators had "discovered" his identification: "Pero sé, que no dizen lo que adelante he de dezir, mostrando, que Galatea, y Elisa representan a Doña Isabel Freyre" (211). The following argument is typical of the manner of his "proofs": "Y la Galatea, de que Salicio se quexa primero en la misma Egloga, tengo yo por sin duda era la propia D. Isabel Freyre: porque no tenia mucho proposito el mezclar quexas de mudanza de otra, con la muerte de otra: y le tiene mucho, quexarse della, porque sirviendola se casó con D. Antonio, y luego llorar su muerte en la segunda parte de la Egloga" (212). Whatever seems reasonable to the critic is elevated to the level of incontrovertible fact. After arguing tirelessly in the same vein to make his point, Faria e Sousa also claims that most of Garcilaso's poetry was addressed to Isabel Freire: "De sus amores fue Garcilasso muy derritido, estando ella en Palacio; y a ella son los más de sus versos" (212). None of Faria e Sousa's claims are verified; he simply argues from textual interpretation. As a further argument he claims that since Camões mentions both Salicio and Nemoroso, he must have understood that both represented Garcilaso. Faria e Sousa was certainly one of the most learned of Golden Age writers, but his arguments from conjecture concerning Garcilaso fail to convince. These arguments would not be taken up again until the twentieth century. It is impossible to deny the early date of the association of Salicio with Garcilaso and Elisa (but not Galatea) with Isabel Freire; there does exist, however, a certain confusion among the commentators that tends to diminish their credibility. In addition, the expansion of the idea from Brocense's simple identification of Elisa in Eclogue III with Isabel Freire to Faria's claim that Garcilaso was her lover and that all of his love poetry was addressed to her seems to be a case of critics elaborating on their predecessors rather than having recourse to commonly known facts. The "knowledge" of Isabel Freire was certainly not universal, as shown by Diego Serón Spinossa's 1618 *comedia* titled *Garcilaso enamorado,* which does not mention Isabel Freire, even though the author was an avid reader of Garcilaso (Gallego Morell, *El poeta* xviii).

The destruction of the myth of Isabel Freire has important consequences for the critical estimation of Garcilaso's poetry, not only for the eclogues, but for the other poems. Since most critics concurred that Garcilaso was at his best when he was most sincere, that is, when he expressed his frustrated passionate love for Isabel Freire, they then found the Ode ad florem Gnidi to be inauthentic because the poet makes an appeal on behalf of a friend. The adverse critical bias loses ground when the evidence concerning Garcilaso's love for Isabel Freire has been discredited. If the Salicio and Nemoroso of Eclogue I are in fact friends of the poet rather than personae for the author himself, then the famed and supposedly more intense eclogue actually comes to share the same situation as the ode; that is, it is a love poem written on behalf of friends.

Rather than searching for elements of sincerity in Garcilaso's poetry, it seems better to move the discussion away from the circular argument of sincerity versus poetic craft and consider why Garcilaso succeeded within the criteria of sincerity. There must be qualities in Garcilaso's poetry that suggest it is sincere, concrete reasons why legends have been elaborated to demonstrate its sincerity. Rather than allege sincerity in art, it might be wiser to analyze the strategies used for producing the impression of sincere sentiment. Not simply a critical ploy to admit the concept of sincerity in a slightly altered guise, this distinction allows us to focus on an important aspect of the Petrarchan revolution in Spain.

One reason that the criterion of sincerity has been applied to Garcilaso's poetry lies in the novelty of the Italianate style whose more sensual imagery and rhetorical posture of sincere passionate suffering have been mistaken for authenticity of feeling, and whose first-person narrative voice has been confused with the poet's own personality. The *cancionero* style, with its highly conventional and artificial conceits, relies so thoroughly on verbal play and intellectual paradox that it could never pass the Romantic criteria of sincerity and authenticity. The Italianate forms brought with them not only new syllabic and stanzaic forms, but also a new style and content with a preference for more languid expression and more concrete imagery. In addition, the emphasis of the narrative "yo" shifted from the conventionalized and intellectual expression of love to a personal and more melancholic reflective voice. These differences of style seemed to later critics to reflect a sincerity of expression. A simple comparison of the first stanza of Garcilaso's Copla IV with the opening lines of his Sonnet X makes this point.

> Acaso supo, a mi ver
> y por acierto, quereros
> quien tal yerro fue a hacer
> como partirse de veros
> donde os dejase de ver.[5]

The poem is composed of antitheses and a constant use of and play on verbal forms. The opposites, "acierto" and "yerro," paradoxically proclaim and underplay the wisdom of the rival lover. The stanza has nine verbal forms, drawn from seven very common verbs: "saber," "ver," "querer," "ir," "hacer," "partir," and "dejar." The repetition of "ver" in two different senses: as (1) "opinion" and (2) "to visit" is typical of the witty wordplay. The poetic qualities arise from the concision of expression and the constant paradoxical shifts of meaning over the taut intellectual structure.

The first quatrain of Sonnet X makes clear the difference of style and rhythm between the two:

> ¡O dulces prendas por mi mal halladas,
> dulces y alegres quando Dios quería,
> juntas estáys en la memoria mía
> y con ella en mi muerte conjuradas!

The Italianate sonnet is not free from rhetorical devices, as in the repetition of "dulces" in lines 1 and 2, but it is clearly more sensual and descriptive, depending less on intellectual artifice. The style is more languid, replacing the wordplays and paradox with clarity and simplicity of expression.

In general, critics have identified two contrasting elements that distinguish the differences between the two styles: the absence of adjectives and predominance of verbs in the early style, and the reversal of this

---

5. All quotes come from Rivers's edition with commentary (1981). Any changes I make in this edition are described in the notes. In lines 1 and 2 of this quotation I have removed the comma after "ver" and added one after "acierto."

tendency in the Italianate style. The Ode ad florem Gnidi again presents a special case because some critics have assumed that a poem written on behalf of a friend cannot have the same depth of emotional expression as one inspired by personal experience. Dámaso Alonso and Lapesa allege formal reasons to support this claim. Alonso regretted placing Garcilaso in "tan desafavorable luz" (*Poesía española* 302), and Lapesa claims the ode suffers from "adjetivación fofa" (*Garcilaso: Estudios* 221), even though the use of adjectives predominates in Garcilaso's most famous works, and oftentimes the repetition of synonymous adjectives is employed for balance and harmony, rather than meaning. Numerous examples of "adjective padding" can be found in the languid style of Garcilaso's late works, which move away from the contrastive, more nervous tautness of his earlier Italianate poems still showing the influence of the *cancionero* style. The early style tends to avoid adjectives, unless they contrast with their noun, and concentrates on verbs and verbal forms to create the rapidity of constant contrasts over an underlying tension. Sonnet IX, although not dated by Lapesa, shows the preponderance of verbal forms typical of the *cancionero* style:

> Señora mía, si yo de vos ausente
> en esta vida turo y no me muero,
> paréceme que ofendo a lo que os quiero
> y al bien de que gozaba en ser presente;

The substantive elements "yo," "vos," "vida," "a lo que os quiero," "al bien," and "ser presente" are abstract rather than concrete and visual, and they are free from modification. The four lines contain seven verbal forms and only two descriptive adjectives: "ausente" and "presente." This is a rather high number since the last ten lines also have only two adjectives, which are also conceptual: "diferente" and "tamaño." Both adjectives in the first quatrain are abstract and opposite in meaning. Their presence is not decorative; they are essential in establishing the basic paradox of the poem.

The description of Daphne's transformation into a laurel tree in Sonnet XIII is typical of the late style of the eclogues in its use of mythology and the predominance of adjectives:

> A Daphne ya los brazos le crecían
> y en luengos ramos vueltos se mostraban;

en verdes hojas vi que se tornaban
los cabellos qu'el oro escurecían;
    d'áspera corteza se cubrían
los tiernos miembros que aun bullendo 'staban;
los blandos pies en tierra se hincaban
y en torcidas raíces se volvían.

Even though the passage has an unusually high number of verbs for this period (every line ends with a verb describing the transformation), it is also replete with concrete nouns modified with descriptive adjectives, "luengos ramos," "verdes hojas," "áspera corteza," "tiernos miembros," "blandos pies," and "torcidas raíces." This type of adjectivization serves mainly to slow the pace of the poem and in essence does not add significantly to the nouns modified (further emphasized by positioning the adjective in front of the noun). This could indeed be called "adjetivación fofa," but it abounds in Garcilaso's late style; in fact, this languid sensuality is one of the outstanding achievements of his poetry. Although Alonso and Lapesa used the criteria of adjectivization to criticize the Ode, one suspects they were searching for solid reasons to explain the inferiority of the Ode ad florem Gnidi and hit on the verbal padding of the poem. This is the only poem in which they criticize the use of adjectives, but it is possible to find the same alleged fault in most of Garcilaso's pieces of his mature period.

One might wonder how the "impression or strategy of sincerity" differs from sincerity itself. At first one suspects sleight-of-hand by which the critic-magician removes sincerity from critical terminology only to reintroduce it through a fake door. We do not know that fifteenth-century *cancionero* lovers were any less sincere than sixteenth-century Petrarchan lovers. The impression we have of their poetry, however, is that they were less sincere precisely because the poetic expression is less personal and more abstract. One suspects that if they had to convert their feelings into elaborate conceptual games, then those feelings could not be deeply felt. The *cancionero* style abstracts the emotion and makes a verbal conceptual game out of the basic feeling, whereas the Petrarchans place emphasis on the suffering itself. The Petrarchans' focus on emotion and sentiment aims to create a sensation of sincerity and deeply felt emotional experiences. Since sincerity comes to form part of the artistic aim of the poet and artist, it is more logical in critical terminology to speak of a "rhetoric of sincerity" in place of sincerity and authenticity of expression, and devise critical language with which to evaluate the rhetorical strategies of sincerity.

Garcilaso's Sonnet I is still conceptual and abstract, and yet it is quite different from Spanish traditional poetry. The longer, more languid lines heighten the sense of introspection and inner musing. The playing down of the conceits allows more time to dwell on the poet's feeling, rather than his thought, and in fact the conceits are no longer intellectual, but deal with the poet's feelings.

> Quando me paro a contemplar mi 'stado
> y a ver los passos por dó m'han traýdo,
> hallo, según por do anduve perdido,
> que a mayor mal pudiera aver llegado;
>   mas quando del camino 'stó olvidado,
> a tanto mal no sé por dó é venido;
> sé que me acabo, y más é yo sentido
> ver acabar comigo mi cuydado.
>   Y acabaré, que me entregué sin arte . . .

In the first quatrain, the paradox is not based on a verbal play, but is a paradox of emotion. He finds that he could have ended up worse. Lines 7 and 8 play on the word "acabar," but the real paradox lies in his sentiment; he regrets more loosing his worry and preoccupation than he does loosing his life. The phrase "sin arte" in line 9 proclaims his innocence and lack of duplicity. The intellectual conceits of *cancionero* poetry give the impression of lacking sincere feeling, for their art lies in a constant shift of conceits and paradoxes. Petrarchan conceits, however, deal less with thought and intellectual paradoxes, and more with feelings and ironical contrasts of feelings. In addition, in this sonnet the poet proclaims his sincerity by denying his lack of duplicity. These elements together represent a strategy for producing the impression of sincerity and sentiment, aspects typical mainly of the Petrarchism of Garcilaso's middle period.

The removal of the poet's own "dolorido sentir" from the poetry makes the poetry less personal and completely destroys the argument of sincerity, demonstrating that Garcilaso's superiority must be explained by the poetry itself, not by the nobility of his suffering, as do sentimental critics in inventing supposed tears and torments to explain the poetry. We do not know if Garcilaso ever cried in his life, nor do we know if he fell in love and suffered an unrequited passion. And even if we did, could this fact suffice to explain the long-standing preference of his poetry over that of Boscán? Logically, any superiority would consist in the translation of the feeling into poetry; that is, in the act of artistic creation, not in the quality of the emotion.

If we turn to Castillejo's satires of Boscán and Garcilaso, we see that it is not only the longer line that has upset him, but it is also the concentration of feeling. He puts in the mouth of Torres Naharro the following lines:

> Pero ningún sabor tomo
> en coplas tan altaneras,
> escriptas siempre de veras,
> que corren con pies de plomo,
> muy pesadas de caderas.
>   (2:195)

The phrase "escriptas siempre de veras" seems to refer to the poetic posture and rhetorical commitment to love. Boscán states a similar idea, contrasting intellectual material with metrical sonority, in his famous letter to the Duchess of Soma. He states that the Spanish poets find the new Italianate styles to lack masculine qualities and intellectual rigor: "Otros argüían diciendo que esto principalmente había de ser para mugeres, y que ellas no curaban de cosas de sustancia, sino del son de las palabras, y de la dulzura del consonante" (166). Gracián's *Arte de agudeza* (which might be called a treatise on intellectual poetry) seems to recognize the excess of passion and lack of intellectual content. He closes with a jab at the Petrarchans, not only criticizing their lack of originality but the intensity of their feeling: "Ni todo ha de ser jocoso, ni todo amoroso, que tantos sonetos a un asunto liviano, más sentidos que entendidos, en el mismo Petrarca, en el mismo Herrera empalagan" (*Obras* 515). Gracián's short phrase "más sentidos que entendidos" criticizes the lack of intellectual and artistic distancing of the emotions from the work of art.

This intellectual distancing was summed up by Golden Age writers with the elusive concept of "artificio" as a term of praise. The nineteenth-century concept of sincerity gave the once-praised idea of "artificio" a negative connotation. Herrera often praises Garcilaso's "artificio." Covarrubias defines "artificio" as art. His definition of "artificioso" suggests duplicity: "se opone a lo natural." For *Autoridades* "artificio" is skill or even the work of art constructed by art and rules, but this and later dictionaries add to this a second or third definition by which it comes to represent duplicity. *Autoridades*'s third definition is presented as an extended meaning: "Metaphoricamente se toma por fingimiento, cautela, astucia y maña en el obrar con destreza y disimuladamente." Salvá in 1846 gives the second definition as "Disimulo, maña, cautela," leaving the sense concerning artistry as a third definition. The neoclassical collector of poetry López de Sedano still could, in 1769, praise "el artificio" of Garcilaso's poetry (2:i). Quintana, however, writing in 1807 (in a passage already cited) praised the opposite quality of the absence of artifice: "Ningún artificio, ninguna afectación" (41). "Artificio" in Renaissance art serves to distance the feelings of the artist from the artistic creation. It requires introduction of verbal plays and artificial poetical devices to avoid a confusion of authorial voice and poetic feeling. Fifteenth- and sixteenth-century poetry relied on contrived artifice; whereas, sixteenth-century poetics strove to create the illusion of true feeling and required more sensuality and sentiment; for this reason sixteenth-century poets have been preferred in modern times. The languid sensuality, called sincerity in the Petrarchan poets, passed the Romantic criterion of authenticity of feeling.

Was this judgment correct? It would seem not. We have no way of judging fifteenth-century sincerity, but we are told that Macías (fourteenth century) and Garcisánchez (sixteenth century) went insane over the intensity of their love feelings. Both wrote in the conceptual *cancionero* style. In some ways Garcilaso was a strange candidate for sincerity. In contrast to his early Petrarchan style Garcilaso's late poems show a self-awareness of style and a conscious distancing of the authorial voice, and it is his late Latinate poetry, the eclogues above all, that is most famous. These poems show a deliberate and purposeful distancing of the narrative voice from that of the poet. Much of the Petrarchan poetry relies on a poetic "yo" who suffers unrequited love, whereas in the eclogues and the ode, the poet consciously removes the poetic voice from the person who suffers to that of a disinterested narrator. This distancing is seen in several ways. The poet may place intermediary characters between the narrator and the love affair in order to distance the author's voice from the torments of love. In Eclogue I, it is the pastoral characters Salicio and Nemoroso who speak; in Eclogue II, Albanio suffers from passionate love and is cured; in Eclogue III, nymphs relate through other works of art, the sufferings of others; and in the Ode, Garcilaso pleads

on behalf of a friend. The effect of distancing the poetic voice from the
suffering creates the feeling of classical detachment in which suffering is
observed rather than felt directly (Rivers, "Pastoral Paradox"). Keniston
noted these changes, but claimed that Garcilaso's technical skills com-
pensated for the lack of sincerity in his late poetry: "More important
still as a sign of growth is the heightened plastic and pictorial power, the
atmosphere of assurance, of complete mastery of form which atones in
his later work for the lack of emotional sincerity" (*Garcilaso* 205).

The late poetry also shows a conscious distancing through the poet's
increased awareness of style. The ode, elegies, epistle, and eclogues contain discussions of style. Paradoxically it is this posture that shows an
author who is uncomfortable with the anguished personal "yo," who
distances himself and reflects outwardly on problems of style. In the Epístola a Boscán (dated 1534), Garcilaso says closeness of friendship frees
him from the task of searching for an elevated style:

> no le podrá faltar con vos materia,
> ni será menester buscar estilo
> presto, distinto d'ornamento puro
> tal cual a culta epístola conviene.
>
> (4–7)

In Elegy II (1534), also addressed to Boscán, he admits that he got carried away with an improper style:

> Mas, ¿dónde me llevó la pluma mía?,
> que a sátira me voy mi paso a paso,
> y aquesta que os escribo es elegía.
>
> (22–24)

In Eclogue III (1536) he mentions style twice in the dedicatory stanzas.
In the first instance he claims that his unaffected poetry has been appreciated: "ni desdeñes aquesta inculta parte / de mi estilo, que'n algo ya esti-
maste" (35–36). In the next stanza, he argues that the simple and
unadorned pastoral style is more expressive of the innocent soul than the
eloquence of more cultivated styles:

> Aplica, pues, un rato los sentidos
> al bajo son de mi zampoña ruda,

> indigna de llegar a tus oídos,
> pues d'ornamento y gracia va desnuda;
> mas a las veces son mejor oídos
> el puro ingenio y lengua casi muda,
> testigos limpios d'ánimo inocente,
> que la curiosidad del elocuente.
>
> (41–48)

These lines argue for the superiority of spontaneous communication (suggesting sincerity) over contrived eloquence (suggesting "artificio"), again reinforcing Garcilaso's self-proclaimed mission as a Romantic poet. The focus on style within one of Garcilaso's most eloquent poems, however, serves to distance the work by suggesting a conscious poetic effort.

The Ode ad florem Gnidi also begins with a long discussion of the subject matter and style of the poem. Even if he had a martial style, rather than a lyrical one, he would not sing of heroic deeds, but of the harshness of the flower of Gnido:

> Si de mi baxa lira
> tanto pudiesse el son que en un momento
> aplacase la ira
> del animoso viento
> y la furia del mar y el movimiento,
>
> . . . .
>
> no pienses que cantado
> sería de mí, hermosa flor de Gnido,
> el fiero Marte ayrado,
>
> . . . .
>
> mas solamente aquella
> fuerça de tu beldad seria cantada.
>
> (1–5, 11–13, 21–22)

This self-conscious attitude concerning style and material, which occurs only in the more Latinate rather than the Italianate works, suggests that in his later poems he experienced a renewed struggle with style. While at times these reflections on style seem intimate and bring the reader closer to the poet, they also make the reader more conscious of the determined labor of art, which in fact serves to distance the poem from the speaker.

The authorial distancing in Garcilaso is neither subtle nor difficult to discern. Curiously, one finds the poetic voice of the *cancionero* poems resembles more the voice of the late Latinate poetry than that of the sonnets and *canciones*. The early and late voice is witty, even jocular, while the Italianate voice is poignantly sincere and genuine. It is the latter voice that critics have identified as Garcilaso's true voice. Past criticism has invented a passionate suffering poet and supplied him with a beloved, given her a name, personality, etc. The persona of the middle period has been identified with the poet completely, reading the fictional "yo" into the life of the real "yo."

In all probability, sincerity was a misguided criterion to apply to Garcilaso's poetry. Since there exists the possibility that Garcilaso was not expressing his own emotion through the characters of Salicio and Nemoroso, we need to look at the eclogue again. We still see that the poetry is exquisitely beautiful and the emotion expressed with pathos, but there is no way we can tell from the poetry alone whether Garcilaso is expressing his own frustrated love or whether he has simply imagined it. If he is expressing his own passion, it is certain that he wishes to mask that fact from his audience. The whole poetic apparatus: the pastoral scene, the description of nature, the dedication, and the personae serve to distance the poet from the involved overwrought expression typical of late Petrarchism. In such circumstances, sincerity becomes something of a moot point. If we know that the poet is presenting his own love, does the poem become better? Or on the contrary, if he is presenting a stock pastoral competition based on the question of love between two poets who represent his friends, or even simple inventions of his poetic genius, does the poem become less beautiful? In fact, sincerity neither augments nor diminishes the poetic expression. The important point that becomes lost, when the criterion of sincerity is brought to bear upon the poem, is that Garcilaso was trying to distance the narrator from the personal pseudo-authentic "yo" that characterizes Petrarchan verse. An important aspect of Garcilaso's poetic development has been obscured by the false critical concept of sincerity.

Garcilaso's biography was rewritten to conform to the personal "yo" of the Petrarchan poems,[6] and this biography was imposed upon poems

---

6. Fernández de Navarrete does not mention Isabel Freire. Navarro Tomás's first biography (Garcilaso, *Obras* 1911) introduces the speculation on Isabel Freire after the discussion of the

that present dramatic personae and in other ways distance the narrator from the author. Whether the characters in the eclogues represent Garcilaso himself or not is highly debatable at this point. What is not debatable is that Garcilaso became explicitly self-conscious about style and expression in his later works; in them he distances the narrative voice from that of the author, by presenting dramatic characters (as in the eclogues), by assuming a philosophical stance (as in the elegies and the epistle), or by taking up the collective social voice of the classical ode. Criticism has dealt with this distancing of the authorial voices either by imposing earlier Petrarchan structures upon it, or by claiming the works to be inferior because they are not sincere. In general, sincerity has been a false criterion for judging all of Garcilaso's poetry, but especially the late poetry which aims to move away from impassioned anguish to the calmer, more reflective postures of classical art.

---

documented facts of Garcilaso's life. The later biography (Garcilaso, *Obras* 1924) conflates the two, incorporating the love story into the period in Granada.

2

Text and Message in the Love Lyric

The concentration on sincerity as an aesthetic norm in Garcilaso's poetry has obscured understanding of the complexity of the poetry as an amorous lyrical speech act consisting of text and message. The term "sincere" suggests that the sole aim of love poetry is to express the poet's love for the lady, and the greater the degree of the poet's authentic passion, the better the poetry. The love lyric, however, as a poetic message communicated from the poet and lover to the readers, both critical and amorous, creates a highly complex set of characters and relationships whose parts must be identified within the larger circumstances of the literary and amorous situations.

The lack of a definition of lyric poetry in antiquity meant that Renaissance criticism, which relied so heavily upon antiquity, either ignored a definition for the lyric, or simply missed the point (Atkinson 189–99), as did Francisco Cascales (1564–1642) whose definition ignores the reality that almost all lyric poetry treated the theme of love: "Imitación de qualquier cosa que se proponga, pero principalmente de alabanças de Dios y de los santos, y de banquetes y plazeres" (231). Formalist theories of the lyric have their roots in Romanticism and grow out of the poetic practice of that period. John Stuart Mill defined lyric as an utterance overheard. At the basis of this definition is his conception of lyric as pure emotion pouring forth from an overwrought romantic heart (Mill

348–49). Formalist criticism accepted this definition, continuing the emphasis on the author's emotional communication. Northrop Frye repeats Mill's definition, but in a context that not only isolates the text, but tends to identify the text and author: "The lyric is . . . preeminently the utterance that is overheard. The lyric poet normally pretends to be talking to himself or to someone else. . . . The poet, so to speak, turns his back on his listeners" (*Anatomy* 249–50). The Romantic conception of individualistic author survived the formalist attempts to achieve a more scientific approach to literary criticism.

Only recently have critics begun to analyze the role of the text within the complete love situation. The analysis of the characters and readers implied in the narrative moment of the text—the lyric as a poignant moment of some larger narrative situation—provides other insights into Spanish Petrarchism and especially into the revolution from the *cancionero* lyric to the Italianate style in Boscán and Garcilaso. Such an analysis looks away from the romantically passionate poet and the love situation to the text and its relationship to its readers. The shift of emphasis from the biography of the passionately sincere poet to the text, its cultural context, and its readers provides new insights into Renaissance love poetry. The Petrarchan love stance becomes at once more complex, more contrived and menacing, and much less innocent.

Each courtly love lyric refers to some circumstance or occasion of the complete love situation. Some of these become topoi, such as the praise of the eyes in Petrarchan poetry or the self-imposed silence suffered by the lover in Spanish *cancionero* poetry. From the fragments of the lyric, past critics pieced together a set of ideas, which they called a code of courtly love, to be obeyed by the lover.[1] Modern critics have felt the idea of a code, and especially the tenets of the code as worked out by past critics, to be too restrictive.[2] Parts of the courtly love code obviously came from one poet's representation of love exclusive of other broader interpretations. The code was too restrictive of the many possibilities that existed within the broad framework of courtly love.

Eugene Vance has suggested that the courtly love lyric has certain correspondences to narrative, and that these provide a more complete understanding of the role of the text and its message. He views courtly

---

1. Valency summarizes the long tradition of courtly love and its development as a literary and historical concept. The most extensive studies for Spanish literature are those of Otis Green in volume 1 of *Spain and the Western Tradition*.
2. Utley summarizes some of the criticisms of courtly love as a historical concept.

love as comprising a complete story of love shared by a society with concomitant values and known situations. The story is seldom narrated fully, but is understood by the society *in extenso,* so that it can be presented through a brief reference or through a full dramatization. The ideas of love, instead of constituting a code of conduct, were a shared social myth that could be variously understood and interpreted ("Greimas" 93–94). This conception better explains variations from author to author and certain elusive references by specific writers. In effect, individual authors were elaborating their poems in reference to a shared myth and at the same time drawing on their private understanding of the myth ("Greimas" 93–94).

Jakobson's structural diagram of linguistic communication between addresser and addressee, and involving context, message, contact, and code, has provided the basis for further theoretical elaborations of the love lyric (Jakobson 69–79). Eugene Vance ("Greimas" 97–101) and Antonio García Berrio ("Estatuto" 12–15) have suggested the use of Greimas's actantial model for the narrative to explain the courtly love lyric (Greimas 197–221). I find Greimas's model less helpful in a strict application than Vance's more general application of Jakobson's model of text as a linguistic code consisting of the speaker and implied voices, the reader (either addressed or implied), the message from speaker to reader, and the other characters either mentioned or implied by the structure. Rather than search for the characters mandated by Greimas's model, I shall search for the voices and character allusions found in Garcilaso's poems themselves. The study of these elements in the poetry (both the *cancionero* and Italianate styles) of Boscán and Garcilaso provides further insights into the transformations from one style to the other, and a deeper understanding of the nature of both styles.

In its simplest form, the love lyric is, or pretends to be, a message from the poet to the beloved through which the poet informs the beloved of his desire. One expects the lyric to correspond to the various emotional moments in a love affair, such as the feeling of longing, despair, hope, etc. Since the poem is a written message, the expression of absence is implied in the text itself. Under normal circumstances one does not write to a person in the same room. The medium of a written text suggests absence; hence, longing for presence, or complaint of absence, are perfectly logical poetic messages. A forced absence, such as rejection, is the type of block or other impediment that the text attempts to bridge. In a courtly love context, the poet may complain of the lady's cruelty or lack of attention; Petrarch is famous for the praises of his lady's beauty. Love as a message implies a desire to express love and be loved in return. The love situation involves a message whose ultimate goal is the seduction, if not physical, at least psychological, of the beloved.

This naive view of love poetry is well expressed by Mario Equicola in his *Libro de natura de amore* (1525).

> Sforzase il Poeta che de sue passione scriue con culte & dolci parole, con noue & apte sententie, con accommodate gionture mouer lo animo de l'amata uer lui & rendirse beniuolo: Il che in doi modi p̃cipuamente opera: L'uno ha in se commendatione, l'altro concintatione, doe potentissime parti di persuadere: Commendatione e quella che le laudi contiene: a tutti o uera o falsa che sia data piace & delecta per esser p̃mio & chiareza de uirtu. . . . Concitatione quella chiamano, la q̃le cõmoue li affecti: In questa bisogna essingerci esser & parer tali, quali uolemo quelli, a cui persuadere uolemo: De poeti latini uedemo l'opere piene de laude de le amate, fundamento ualidissimo di far la donna credula & obsequente: uedemo loro libri abundatissimi de lacrime, suspiri & cruciati: Via facillima ad indure donne ad misericordia, cosa humanissima & loro propria: In doi modi adunque precipuamente li poeti han tentato acquistare beniuolentia de chi amauano, laudandola da tutte parti che meritano lode, si de animo, si del corpo, & con farli intendere che per suo amore se cruciano, el desio de seruirla essere grandissimo. (187v-188)

(The poet strives to write of his passions with learned and pleasing words, with new and fitting sentences, and with well-disposed transitions in order to move the mind of the beloved towards him and to render it kindly disposed. This works in two principal ways: one is commendation, the other is excitement, two very powerful parts of persuasion. Commendation is that which contains praises. To everyone it is pleasing to receive praise, whether it be true or false, as a reward and evidence of virtue. . . . We call excitement that which moves the passions. In this it is necessary to extinguish our being and appear in the state that we want those whom we are trying to persuade. In the Latin poets we see their works full of praise of the beloved, a very valid basis for making the lady credulous and obsequious. We see their books abounding in tears, sighs, and afflictions, a very easy way to induce the ladies to pity, a very human emotion and fitting to them. In two ways then principally the poets have tried to gain the goodwill of those they love, praising them in all parts that deserve praise, whether in mind or in body, and to make them understand that they suffer for her love, the desire to serve her being very great.)

Equicola accepts love poetry at face value, but in reality the medieval and Renaissance love lyric is more complex. First of all, it is a lyric text. The speaker is not only a lover, but also a poet, and his message follows formal aesthetic rules. On one level, the aesthetic qualities of the poem are part of the message, and they represent to the beloved the wit and superiority of the lover. We know, however, that in their historical context the poems generally were circulated among readers of poetry rather than among various mistresses. William J. Kennedy has summarized the duality of voice and reader in the Petrarchan tradition: "The Petrarchan sonnet unites in a single lyric modality the chief rhetorical attributes. Its *ethos* requires a split addresser whose voice as speaker differs from that of the author. Its *pathos* demands a split addressee whose function as fictive audience—usually the speaker's beloved—differs from that of the actual reader" (20). Obviously this system also applied to courtly love poetry.

Equicola's characterization of the love situation, and what might be thought of as the archetypal love poem, seems oversimplistic and naive in the context of medieval and Renaissance love poetry. As Castillejo said in complaining of his contemporaries who wrote in the *cancionero* style, very few of them were in love:

> Antes siento
> pena de ver sin cimiento
> un tan gentil edificio,
> y unas obras tan sin vicio
> sobre ningún fundamento.
> (2:184)

He said Boscán was neither in love nor had a beloved:

> Mas trovada
> una copla muy penada,

> él mesmo confesará
> que no sabe dónde va
> ni se funda sobre nada.
>   (2:184)

Others wrote without being in love, or wrote for a friend who was in love:

> Y algunos hay, yo lo sé,
> que hacen obras fundadas
> de coplas enamoradas,
> sin tener causa por qué.
> Y esto está
> en costumbre tanto ya,
> que muchos escriben penas
> por remedar las ajenas,
> sin saber quién se las da.
>   (2:185–86)

The love lyric had become the mark of a gentleman and courtier. The beloved was secret—not to hide her identity—but because she did not exist (just as it has been claimed that Petrarch's Laura was a fiction). The absence of a beloved rather complicates the archetypal model previously described. The recipient of the message is not the beloved but other courtiers, perhaps patrons, who will be seduced by the beauty and wit of the poem to give favor to the courtier, or perhaps rivals in courtly favor who are to read the message of the poet-courtier's superiority. The role of lover and the role of poet could in these circumstances produce two different readings of the same poetic text and message. It would seem likely no text in the fifteenth and sixteenth centuries served, or was meant to serve, exclusively one purpose. Instead of author or poet, one often speaks of the hyphenated combination poet-lover, with more significance than just conceding that the medium is a poem and the message is love. In many cases, one suspects (and Castillejo confirms that suspicion) that the message and intended reader are far different from the theme of love treated in the poem and the "señora" mentioned in the text. The objection could be raised that these arguments do not apply to Garcilaso because his sincerity separated him from the general practices of the *cancionero* poets criticized by Castillejo. This is quickly answered by recalling that the first editor of Garcilaso's poetry was not Isabel Freire's, nor any mistress's, family, but the widow of his friend the poet Boscán who possessed copies of many, if not most, of his works. The duality of signaled reader (recipient of stated message) and the aesthetic reader implied in the fact of artistic composition was a conscious element in text production throughout the Golden Age. Lope de Vega treats the idea in the introductory sonnet to his *Rimas* where he characterizes his poems as wayward children who are returning home (that is, being anthologized). The amorous message is represented by their worldly existence while the aesthetic readings signaled by an anthology are represented as a retirement, if not to a religious retreat, at least from a public life (Heiple, "Lope's").

The expressions "love lyric" and "poet-lover" contain the same dualities. Not only is the message doubly encoded by the double author (poet and lover) to the dual reader (beloved and critic), but the love poem, as Vance has shown, hardly ever corresponds to the archetype of a poet-lover sending a message (with implied seduction) to the beloved. The love situation involves more than lover and beloved with an implied separation (physical or mental) that can only be bridged by a written text. The poem often displaces the object of desire, addressing the space or impediment between lover and beloved, be it separation, the lady's cruelty or the poet's resignation. Or it may include in its cast of characters the poet's helper or his rival or imply other competitors in general. Or the poem may distinguish between lover and nonlover, as does Petrarch by pointing out how he flees the crowds who mark and reject him as afflicted.

The love situation is much more complex than the archetype described by Equicola. The poet and lover-narrator are both inscribed into the message to varying degrees. In addition, the speaker who represents both poet and lover in the poem assumes a pose (aggressiveness, depression, reflection, etc.) that represents a certain moment in the love situation. The text contains a message that tries to bridge the space assumed by the need of a written message. The physical existence of the poem (text) assumes a separation or blocking element that can only be bridged by a written message. The message must address the impediment as well as suggest ways to its removal or justification of its continued existence. Among the impediments may be a rival, who of course constitutes another possible character in the plot of the love narrative assumed by the existence of the lyric text (a fragmentary moment of the larger situation).

The existence of the nonlover usually serves to define the position of the real lover, distinguishing the lover's superior sensibilities and commitments. In addition, the readers are multiple. The poem may be addressed to or imply the existence of any one of the characters, the beloved, the rival, a friend, the nonlover, or the reader of aesthetic poetry.

This suggests the model in Diagram 1.

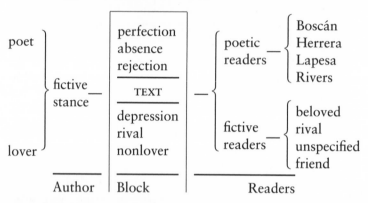

Diagram 1.

The text must be central to any model. It is produced by the author in the presence of a block or impediment that the text must bridge. The reason for the triangular scheme for the author, rather than a linear structure, such as

$$\text{or} \quad \begin{array}{l} \text{poet} \rightarrow \text{lover} \rightarrow \text{fictive stance} \rightarrow \text{TEXT} \\ \text{lover} \rightarrow \text{poet} \rightarrow \text{fictive stance} \rightarrow \text{TEXT} \end{array}$$

is that one cannot determine if the stimulus to write the poem was that of a poet or that of a lover; in fact, the model must always envision an interaction between the two impulses in the invention of the fictive posture of the textual narrator.

As discussed previously, the block may be of any of several natures that the text will imply. The block is the pretext for a written message, so it must involve a certain distance from the person addressed to make plausible a written text. The blocking force to the love relationship may not be explicitly stated in the poem, or even form part of it, but its existence is always implicit and influential in the text. Not only does it provide the pretext for the poem, but it also is influential in the fictive stance chosen by the poet-lover. The stance of the lover and the shape of the message are all part of the authorial strategy for bridging the blocking factor. The block may also be a fiction, but it exists as a pre-textual element—both pre-text and pretext—that determines the shape of the text.

The various elements I have listed as blocking devices are intended as representative rather than comprehensive. Absence is an excellent pretext for writing a love poem. The blocking space in this case is a physical space separating the lovers that the text bridges with a message. This is a common theme in Spanish *cancionero* poetry as well as Petrarchan verse. The absence or distance can be caused by rejection, in which case the poem addresses either the cruelty of the lady or the suffering of the lover as a victim seeking compassion. The claims and analysis of suffering or depression dominate Spanish fifteenth- and sixteenth-century love poetry, while the Petrarchan descriptions of the perfection of the lady found little following in Spanish poetry.

Within the area of blocking elements are the rival and the nonlover who place a stigma on the suffering lover. The nonlover again is common in Petrarch, as in "Solo e pensoso," but generally appears in Spanish poetry only in the Neoplatonic vein. Little attention has been paid to the presence of the rival in the triangle of desire (as described by Girard, *Deceit* 1–52) among the cast of characters in the love poem, and yet he is all-pervasive, especially in the Petrarchan poetry of the early sixteenth century and in Garcilaso's octosyllabic poems. I have placed the rival among the textual blocks, although the rival seldom forms the sole block in any one poem. Rather, the poet's textual strategy often addresses another blocking element and skillfully implies the presence of a rival. Although the rival is structurally different from other blocks, his presence is often implied or directly stated in the poem. The presence of the rival, either implied or stated, recalls the presence of the real rivals in the social role of poetry in a society of patronage and favor. One could envision that some poems may employ the love topic as a subtle allegory in which the beloved (at times called "dueño") is a figure for the patron and the rivals are other courtiers seeking the favor of the allegorical lady and lord.

The poet-lover can also address someone he feels will sympathize with his situation, a confidant or helper (Greimas's notion of adjuvancy; Vance 97–101). Many poems displace the object of desire and focus on the poet's suffering in order to garner sympathy for his situation. Such suffering could produce compassion for the lover from a confidant, or it could also disarm a rival by making the poet-lover so miserable a figure that one would not harm him. In this way, the poem need not distinguish between rival as block and the confidant as adjuvant because each may be moved by the same arguments.

Two readers are assumed by the author construct of poet-lover: a reader of the love message and a reader of the poem as aesthetic production. Although each is supposed by the text, and may even be indicated by the text, neither may have existed in reality. In the diagram on page 36 I called the readers inscribed in the poem the fictive readers, not because they may not have existed, but because they have entered into the fictive construct of the poem. Boscán, for example, is listed as a critical reader, and in many cases he was most likely one of the first critical readers. In Sonnets XXVIII and XXXIII, Elegy II and the Epístola, however, he is also a fictive reader because he is addressed in the text. The fictive reader may have truly been a fiction, as in the case of the poet who wrote love poems without being in love but followed the convention of presenting himself as a lover addressing a beloved. On the other hand, it is possible that some works never found an aesthetic general public and were lost before being read; or in extreme cases, they were in fact love missives that were burned by the mistress so her husband did not find them.

The use of this model permits a fuller understanding of the rhetorical stances of Boscán and Garcilaso in their love poetry. Kennedy claims that the shifts of author and reader are the chief defining characteristics of some poets:

> So narrow are its conventions, finally, that to many critics "Petrarchan" implies nothing more than a limited set of repeated themes and stylistic devices. A closer look, however, reveals that while Petrarchan diction, vocabulary, and elocutionary devices remain unchanged over whole centuries, other rhetorical strategies of voice and address distinguish individual poems, poets, and poetic movements. (20)

An analysis of the evolution of the author-reader relationship in the *coplas* and *sonetos* of Boscán and Garcilaso provides additional characteristics for understanding the transformation from the *cancionero* to the

Italianate style in Spanish poetry. The comparison of Boscán's *cancionero* poetry with his Petrarchan sonnets demonstrates these changes most dramatically. The *cancionero* poems tend to display a formula of a "yo" representing the poet-lover who directs his poem to the beloved, called "vos" and often further specified as "señora"—hereafter called the "yo → vos (señora)" formula. In the Knapp edition, twenty-one of Boscán's forty-five octosyllabic compositions are directed to the beloved (whether fictional or not does not concern this argument), with sixteen using "señora" as the form of address. Of the seventeen *coplas,* thirteen address "señora" who is in all cases but one then addressed as "vos." Boscán's seventy-six Petrarchan sonnets show a completely different pattern. Only seven of them employ the "yo → vos (señora)" formula, while some sixty-two have no specified reader. The change could not be more striking. The *coplas* established a pattern of address that could be broken, but variations from the norm were usually indicated by a title, such as "A la tristeza," "De Boscán al Almirante . . . ," and "Del mismo a un espejo." The sonnets, on the other hand, establish a completely new system. The Italianate poem is usually believed to be more sensual and sincere, while the *cancionero* poem was intellectual and contrived. The analysis of the author-reader relationship in these poems provides unexpected results. It seems contradictory that the poems could appear to become more intimate and sincere, and at the same time move from addressing the beloved to addressing an unknown and unspecified general reader. The movement could not be accidental, nor can it be without significance. But there remains the question of who is the intended reader of the Petrarchan sonnet.

The various responses to this question suggest that more investigation is needed to understand fully the roles of the readers and characters in the courtly love lyric. Eugene Vance has advanced the model of Greimas and suggests a function of the love lyric as message based on Freud's analysis of sexual humor as a device designed to disarm the rival ("Greimas" 102–5). The studies of Antonio García Berrio have analyzed this problem, also using Greimas's model ("Estatuto" 17–19). García Berrio has placed more emphasis on the actant as friend and has not identified other characters in the courtly love lyric. Mariann Sanders Regan finds the text even more personal as a creation and expression of self equivalent to the identification of one's love with one's psyche (15–82). Clearly in the face of a multitude of possible models, a study of Garcilaso's poetry employing any one of them would be premature. Instead of proposing any one theoretical solution to the questions raised by the changes from *cancionero* poetry to Petrarchism in Boscán and Garcilaso, I shall analyze the problems posed by the different readers and characters in the poems of Garcilaso, and in a way shall be suggesting a new solution based on the observations of changes within the text. To provide a background for understanding the implications of reader and characters in the sonnets of Garcilaso, I shall analyze in this chapter one *canción* and two sonnets by Boscán and the amorous octosyllabic poems by Garcilaso, reserving the discussion of Garcilaso's sonnets for Parts III and IV.

Boscán's octosyllabic Canción I treats the question of frustration and the lover's inability to adapt to rejection. Typical of most of Boscán's octosyllabic verse, it addresses the beloved with the "yo → vos (señora)" formula.

Canción I

¿Qué haré? que por quereros
mis estremos son tan claros,
que ni soy para miraros,
ni puedo dexar de veros.
  Yo no sé con vuestra ausencia
un punto de vivir ausente,
ni puedo sufrir presente,
Señora, tan gran presencia;
  de suerte que por quereros
mis estremos son tan claros,
que ni soy para miraros,
ni puedo dexar de veros.

(128)[3]

The poem addresses the question "¿Qué haré?" The lover is at an impasse, torn between two extremes of not being able to look at his beloved and not being able to stop seeing her. The *redondilla* form of the stanza cleverly contrasts "ausencia / presencia" as rhyme words in the first and fourth lines, and "ausente / presente" as rhymes in the second and third. Also noteworthy is the similarity of "-eros" and "-aros" as rhymes in the *estribillo*. The lover is unable to suffer absence and presence, leaving him

---

3. All quotations from Boscán come from the Knapp edition. I have removed the capitalization at the beginning of each line, modernized the accents, and occasionally changed the punctuation.

torn between two impossible alternatives. His actual state is defined negatively (Darst, *Juan Boscán* 35). He cannot live without her nor can he suffer being near her when she rejects him. The beloved is addressed in eight of the twelve lines. The block is not the absence of the beloved, but the poet-lover's emotional impasse.

Boscán's sonnets and Petrarchan *canciones* clearly form a cycle. The first four discuss the role of the text and the relationship between text and reader. Sonnets V and VI begin the love story proper. Not addressed to a specific reader, the sonnets encode rather surprising implications. Sonnet V announces that he has suffered from lovesickness from infancy.

Soneto V

Aun bien no fui salido de la cuna,
ni del ama de leche hube dexado,
quando el Amor me tuvo condenado
a ser de los que siguen su fortuna.

Diome luego miserias de una en una,
por hacerme costumbre en su cuidado;
después en mí de un golpe ha descargado
quanto mal hay debaxo de la luna.

En dolor fui criado y fui nacido,
dando de un triste paso en otro amargo,
tanto que si hay más paso es de la muerte.

¡O corazón que siempre has padecido!
Dime: tan fuerte mal, ¿cómo es tan largo?,
y mal tan largo, di: ¿cómo es tan fuerte?

Both poems, the octosyllabic canción and the Italianate sonnet, make manifest the poet's desire, but the sonnet does not address the beloved. The poem describes generally the lover's condition rather than any act of love. The characters found in the sonnet are the wet-nurse in line 2 (who defines his age), and the personified Amor in lines 3 and 4 who has condemned him to a lover. In line 4 he also refers to a band of lovers, of which he has formed part since childhood. This select and refined group—love was a noble passion appropriate only to the upper classes—includes the speaker whose commitment to love began in childhood. Rather than dedicate the work to a specific beloved or affair, the poet places more emphasis on his condition as lover and his suffering. He was "condenado" (3), suffered "miserias" (5), "cuidado" (6), and "quanto mal hay debaxo de la luna" (8). "Dolor" (9), "amargo" (10), "muerte" (11), and "padecido" (12) characterize his upbringing and life. The object of desire has been displaced as the poet concentrates on his commitment to and his suffering for love. From lines 3 and 4, it is clear the world consists of those who are in love and those who are not. The lover is not placed in the context of the beloved, but in that of the followers of the personified force of love. The extremities of the poet's suffering exaggerate his sacrifice. Among the lovers, the narrator of this poem has suffered extremes of love, making him the model of desire for others to follow.

Sonnet VI makes a similar point about his destiny.

Soneto VI

El alto cielo en sus movimientos,
por diversas figuras discurriendo,
en nuestro sentir flaco está influyendo
diversos y contrarios sentimientos;

y una vez mueve blandos pensamientos,
otra vez asperezas va encendiendo;
y es su uso traernos revolviendo,
agora con pesar, y ora contentos.

Fixo está en mí sin nunca hacer mudanza
de planeta ni sino en mi sentido,
clavado en mis tormentos todavía.

De ver otro hemisferio no he esperanza;
y así donde una vez me ha anochecido,
allí me estoy sin esperar el día.

The octave describes what were believed to be the normal celestial influences on earthly beings, whom Boscán identifies with "us," referring to "nuestro sentir flaco" and "es su uso traernos revolviendo." The plural "nos" in the octave contrasts with the singular "yo" in the sextet, marking the speaker off as different from all readers both present and future. The narrator refers to the usual changes and alternation of happiness and sadness caused by the celestial influences of the planets in their revolutions and movements. In lines 7 and 8 he seems to recall not only astrological influences, but also the double aspects, prosperous and adverse, of Fortune and her turning wheel. The other hemisphere in line 12 could also be a reference to the other face of Fortune. The sextet presents the narrator as an unique case for whom the heavens never change configuration and who is continuously subject to the same torments. He lost hope that a new configuration will come to him because he is buried in the darkness and despair of his present unfortunate signs and condition of unrelieved suffering.

These two sonnets single out the lover and his unique commitment to love, the first from childhood and the second from celestial determination. Like the *canción,* they stress the point that the lover is committed to love and cannot change. But the differences in style and avowed reader shift the focus. The *canción* is addressed to the beloved, and formally, at least, it limits itself to a single love affair. While the poet argues the constancy of his love, he seems to be asking, by implication, that the mistress begin a dialogue, answering the initial question "¿Qué haré?" or that she take pity on his dilemma. The poem focuses less on the lover's suffering—it does not try to re-create it—and places more emphasis on the paradox and its clever expression in the poem. The lover bases his appeal on behalf of his constancy, his dilemma, and above all his wit. The real block, unstated, is the relationship that denies the lover access to the expression of his desire. As a love message, the charm of the lover is communicated to the beloved who might be expected to take pity on him.

The two sonnets clearly address other concerns. The constancy of the lover is argued through his disposition—he was born a lover—and through celestial influences upon him. Both poems, but especially Sonnet V, dwell upon his suffering, exaggerating its duration (since childhood) and its extent (every evil on earth). The message then focuses on two elements: the longevity of the lover's commitment to love and the greatness of his suffering. Unlike the *canción,* but like most of the sonnets, these two poems are not specifically addressed to the beloved. In fact, no specific reader is identified in the poems. Are they still to be understood as addressed to the beloved? If not, who is the reader supposed to be? Who needs to be convinced of these extravagant claims of longevity of love and magnitude of suffering?

The lack of an addressed beloved does not remove the possibility that the poem is addressed to the beloved, but it certainly does not limit the implications of a reader to her alone. In fact, other readers might be an accomplice who could pity his suffering and help him, or it might be a male rival who needs to be convinced of the superiority and commitment of the narrator as a lover. The same message that could convince the beloved of the constancy and finesse of her suitor could also serve to warn rivals of the superiority and commitment of the lover. The scope of the message has broadened to bridge not only the impediment of an unresponsive mistress but also the interference of rivals. Boscán's two sonnets—the first in the series that address the problems of love as separate from the problems of how to read the textual message—are unqualified claims of territoriality directed to the beloved and to the rival. While concentrating on the lover's suffering, the sonnets imply the superiority of the lover through his lifelong celestially determined disposition. The poems serve to mark the lover as distinct and special, maintaining his superiority over rival suitors. In spite of the elegance of expression, they represent on a baser level the male's marking territory in the eyes of the desired beloved against rival males.

The poet does not claim superiority on the force and extent of his love alone, but he places additional emphasis on his suffering to invoke pity from the beloved and possibly to disarm the violence of rivals. The lover's enforced suffering gives him not only a superiority in the field of love, but it also evokes sympathy for his state. This accounts for the double thrust of territorial claims and increased emphasis on suffering. Boscán's two sonnets, in asserting his claims to superiority as a lover, are patents-of-nobility in the making. On the one hand, they mark his superiority and desirability to the beloved, and on the other, they serve to denigrate the rival both in his own estimation and in that of the beloved, both of whom are further disarmed by the protestations of suffering.

The change in the love message from the *canción* to the sonnets forms part of the move toward a rhetoric of sincerity. While wit might disarm the mistress or a patron, in effect its lack of seriousness marks it as a less than honest love poem. The Petrarchan "rhetoric of sincerity" solves the problem by making it seem that the lover has suffered greatly for the beloved. The claims of suffering and sincerity of feeling are further arguments for the lover's superiority directed to both the beloved and potential rival. The poet—the wit—who dominates the *canción* is effaced in the Petrarchan sonnets by the lover who must convince his implied readers—beloved and rivals—that he is consumed by passion and that his passion is sincere.

The *canción* has one identified reader, the beloved, but in its author construct the predominance of the poet is seen, which in turn suggests the literary reader or critic. In the sonnets, the lover's voice and message predominate, making the unnamed readers seem to be more involved in the love situation than in the critical process. This change of focus forms part of the rhetoric of sincerity, the process by which the message in the Petrarchan poem is assumed to be more sincere. The "yo → vos (señora)" formula serves to introduce a personal amorous note in the intellectual octosyllabic *coplas* to make them more personal, while the extremes of suffering and commitment in the sonnets need no personal references to the beloved to achieve intensity.

The love poems of Boscán represent only one aspect of the shifts of elements in the model proposed for the love lyric. Garcilaso's poetry offers other, and perhaps more complex, possibilities for assigning roles and understanding the effect of the message. The octosyllabic love poems attributed to Garcilaso follow the same pattern as Boscán's. Three of the eight *coplas* are not love poems. Two of them treat the subject of bad dancing and are humorous (I and VII), Copla V (also attributed with more probability to Hurtado de Mendoza) is a translation from Ovid constructed as an epigram. They are, in essence, not love poems, and they have involved titles explaining the references of address. Five of the eight *coplas* are love poems, and are addressed to the beloved, all of them addressing the lady as "vos," and two of them (VI and VIII) further referring to her as "señora." Garcilaso's Copla III fits the pattern observed in Boscán.

> Copla III
> Yo dexaré desde aquí
> de offenderos más hablando,
> porque mi morir callando
> os ha de hablar por mí.
>   Gran ofensa os tengo hecha
> hasta aquí en aver hablado,
> pues en cosa os he enojado
> que tan poco me aprovecha.
>   Derramaré desde aquí
> mis lágrimas no hablando,
> porque quien muere callando
> tiene quien hable por sí.

The authorial "yo" is a lover who addresses his beloved concerning his suffering. Although he does not call her "señora," the pattern is fulfilled in all other respects. The poem is an intimate, albeit stylized, communication addressed to the beloved. The lover will refrain from speaking and offer his suffering to speak for him. While the text bridges the gap caused by silence, it takes a rather paradoxical position that is not resolved in the poem. If the poet were really to maintain silence, he would refrain from all communication, including poetic missives. The rhyme words "hablando" and "callando" underline the central paradox of the poem. The *copla* makes clear that he has offended her in the past by speaking, and such action, in fact, did him little good. From here on his suffering (called by hyperbole, death) will speak for him. Even though Garcilaso introduces a third-person subject, "quien," it is for the effect of making a general rule rather than a reference to another third-person character. The *copla* marks the territory of the lover in the eyes of the beloved. Even when silent, this lover will be demonstrating his love, and therefore, by implication, will deserve to be loved in return for his great sacrifices and suffering, even death in the literal sense of the metaphor.[4]

Copla VIII introduces a variation on the "yo → vos (señora)" formula:

> Copla VIII
> Villancico de Garcilaso
> Nadi puede ser dichoso,
> señora, ni desdichado,
> sino que os aya mirado.
>
> Porque la gloria de veros
> en esse punto se quita
> que se piensa mereçeros;
> así que sin conoçeros,
> nadi puede ser dichoso,
> señora, ni desdichado,
> sino que os aya mirado.

Addressed to the mistress with the words "señora" and "vos," it employs the standard form of address observed in the majority of Boscán's love poetry in the *cancionero* style. For this reason, it does not need a title because its situation is familiar. There is one difference, however, for the poet does not introduce a "yo" suffering for the lady's love, but rather a general concept of "nadi" who serves as a rule for everyone. The change

---

4. The theme of silence also appears in two of the sonnets attributed to Garcilaso, XXXVIII and XXXII.

is quite significant. Of Boscán's forty-five octosyllabic poems, forty-one have a "yo" inscribed in the text. Garcilaso's *estribillo* is straightforward, playing lightly on the irony that seeing the beloved causes both happiness (because of love) and unhappiness (because she is cruel). The "señora" serves to break the phrase into two parts, typical of the popular *villancico* (Sánchez Romeralo 151). The gloss establishes a link between the glory of seeing the beloved, and how the one who sees her comes to deserve her through his suffering. It is probable that a line is missing after "quita," for it is unusual to have a single rhyme word in the gloss of a poem. Another line would probably make the gloss more intelligible, for this stanza is quite opaque, even for a genre of poetry that prides itself on complex syntax.

Through the slight variation of presenting a third-person subject in place of the regular first-person subject, Garcilaso introduces a shift in meaning. All happiness, and all unhappiness, flow from the lady, but they flow to everyone, to the lover and to his friends and his rivals. The speaker has masked his desire and his suffering by a general message. Everyone who sees her will become a rival in pursuit of the mistress, emulating the desire of others. The wordplay explained by Rivers on "conoceros" in line 7, as both "to know" and "to esteem," suggests that only those who know how to value the mistress are worthy of happiness. The unannounced speaker of the poem has subtly inserted himself into the text as one who knows that all happiness, and subsequent unhappiness from unrequited desire, come from the mistress, through the unspoken conclusion that only those who can appreciate the lady can share this happiness and be privileged to share the unhappiness. Garcilaso has focused the interest in the Girardian triangle of desire not on the rival but on the model of desire. Girard maintains that one's desire is mediated through the desires of others, and he has studied the role of the rival rather than the other through whom the rival perceives his desire. The implication seems to be in Girard that all desire is mediated and never authentic (*Deceit* 12). Like Boscán in his sonnets, Garcilaso strives to assume the role of the superior lover whom others will emulate in their desire. As the poet-lover in Copla VIII extols the mistress as the object of desire, he presents himself as the model of desire whose sensitivity and perception place him in preeminent position among the other suitors. Only those who can understand his message are worthy as lovers, and worthy to be his competitors. The text has two audiences, the mistress who is to see the poet as the best lover, and by implication the rival who must accept the poet-lover as the most worthy of the lovers, but must at the same time, if he thinks to win merit, enter into the competition. The text strives to include the male reader as rival in desire, and at the same time relegates him to a secondary position.

Copla II, the famous poem supposedly written to Isabel Freire upon her marriage to Antonio de Fonseca, makes a more obvious comparison with the rival. The title of this poem in the Gayangos manuscript is one of the few pieces of evidence linking Garcilaso to Isabel Freire: "De Garçilaso a doña Ysabel Freyra [*sic*] porque se casó con hombre fuera de su condición."

Copla II
Canción, aviéndose casado su dama
Culpa deve ser quereros,
según lo que en mí hazéys,
mas allá lo pagaréys
do no sabrán conoceros,
por mal que me conocéys.

Por quereros, ser perdido
pensava, que no culpado;
mas que todo lo aya sido,
así me lo avéys mostrado
que lo tengo bien sabido.

¡Quién pudiese no quereros
tanto como vos sabéys,
por holgarme que paguéys
lo que no an de conoceros
con lo que no conocéys¡

Even though the speaker has, according to the special circumstances outlined in the title, already lost out to the rival, he still maintains his presence in the competition and in a parting shot vows the mistress will be unhappy. He imagines, or rhetorically feigns, that a certain blame has been thrust upon him for having loved her. She does not reward him, but to the contrary abandons him. He imagines that she will pay for this treason in the rival camp. The sense of "conocer" as "appreciate" is necessary to understand the poem. They will not know how to appreciate her because she does not appreciate him. "Conoceros" in reference to the rival clearly contrasts with its rhyme word "quereros" used by the speaker. The use of the plural "sabrán" not only shows a reticence in referring directly to the rival by replacing his presence with that of many, but it also converts the struggle into a tribal affair. The rival suitor is "fuera de su condición"; hence the whole family will not be able to appreciate the beloved. If the title of the Gayangos manuscript is correct in identifying the lady as Isabel Freire, then genealogical proofs prepared by Martínez López ("El rival") demonstrating that Antonio de Fonseca was of "converso" family would provide a context that would add racist implications to the use of the plural, which is again repeated in line 14.

The *copla* distinguishes between "perdido" and "culpado," which defines more precisely the word "culpa" in the first line. Not only did he lose, but his loving somehow has become a moral fault through her treatment of him. In the repetition of the *estribillo,* the lover expresses the wish that he did not love her to the degree that she knows so well so that he could enjoy seeing her suffer the same lack of appreciation that he received from her. Not only is "conocer" employed twice, first to characterize the rival's treatment of her, and second her treatment of him, but "saber" is used of all three parties. In line 4, the rivals "no sabrán conoceros." In line 10, the lover has learned that he must suffer loss and a sense of guilt: "lo tengo bien sabido" ("lo" refers to "todo" in line 8). Finally the mistress knows how he has loved her: "tanto como vos sabéys." "Saber" as knowledge serves different purposes. The rival will not know how to appreciate the beloved; that is, his clan consists of inferior beings. The lover knows that he must suffer every indignity at the hands of the beloved, but without benefit of being reciprocated in his love. Finally, she knows how much he has loved her, but has failed to recognize him. Knowledge and knowing suffer in this poem. The rivals lack the breeding and finesse even to "know" or appreciate the beloved. The beloved refused to recognize (know) the lover even though she "knew" how much he cared. The only successful use of knowledge is that the lover is forced to realize how much he has been disdained, and that results from a twisted concept of justice.

Copla II is not a simple love missive. Inscribed in its message is the threat of unhappiness and of warring clans. The blocking element consists of an unresponsive lady and a rivalry reinforced by clan. The lover presents himself as an innocent victim to be sacrificed through the poor judgment of his beloved. He does not accept his role passively, but threatens her with future unhappiness. He takes upon himself the blame and the suffering that comes from it, but, even though he suffers as a sacrificial victim for others' faults, he casts the blame on the beloved. The first line is ironic: "Culpa deve ser quereros"; even though the poet-lover suffers for the alleged sin, he in fact casts the blame on the beloved. In this way he becomes an innocent victim who must pay through suffering and sacrifice the faults of others. Garcilaso's sonnets exploit the role of sacrificial victim; that is part of the violence and emotional intensity typical of the Petrarchan rhetoric of sincerity, but it is interesting to see it also forms part of his *cancionero* poetry.

Copla IV presents another case of rivalry between suitors:

> Copla IV
> A una partida
> Acaso supo, a mi ver
> y por acierto, quereros
> quien tal yerro fue a hazer
> como partirse de veros
> donde os dexase de ver.
>
> Imposible es que este tal,
> pensando que os conocía,
> supiese lo que hazía
> quando su bien y su mal
> junto os entregó en un día.
>
> Acertó acaso a hazer
> lo que si por conoceros
> hiziera, no podia ser:
> partirse y, con solo veros,
> dexaros siempre de ver.

Unlike Boscán's coplas, which tend to be more straightforward love missives, Garcilaso's Copla IV dwells on the competition between rival suitors. The blocking element in this poem is the rival whom the poet suggests should be forgotten, since he is not present. The speaker assumes a knowledgeable stance that allows him to pontificate on the proper way to love. To create a possible scenario into which this poem would fit, we could imagine a lady remaining faithful to an absent lover. The speaker of the poem suggests that if the lover is absent, he could not really love her. The final implication would be, that since the rival does not claim his territory as a lover, the lady should accept the love of someone who indeed knows how to love and has remained faithfully close. The "yo" has nearly disappeared, being reduced to the one reference "mi ver" in line 1, and has been replaced with another party, a rival who is the subject of all the verbs and whose presence (and absence) dominates the poem.

The beginning word of the text "acaso" places in question even the validity of the suitor's love: "Acaso . . . supo quereros."[5] The would-be lover maintains that the rival's love of the lady is correct, even if only by chance. The contrast of "acierto" and "yerro" is complete, although the impact of "acierto" has been diminished by "acaso." In spite of the correctness of his love, the rival committed the error of abandoning the beloved and never seeing her again. The *estribillo* has eight verbal forms and no adjectives, typical of *cancionero* language in general. The verbal form "ver" appears three different times, first in the sense of opinion, "a mi ver," second and third in the sense of to visit or court. The repetition of similar ideas in lines 4 and 5 suggests that a difference of meaning should be ascribed to the two phrases "partirse de ver" and "os dexase de ver." Line 4 indicates that the rival left the mistress after they fell in love and line 5 means that he continued to stay away. "Donde" in line 5 must retain its etymological sense of "de onde," that is "de donde," so the sense would be that he not only left her, but also from his absence, "de donde," he did not return to see her. Line 4 places emphasis on the suitor's having left, and line 5 reinforces that idea as a concept of abandonment. The *copla* expresses incredulity that the other lover knew what he was doing, suggesting that in reality he could not have been in love with the lady. Line 7, "pensando que os conocía," calls into doubt the validity of the relationship with the suggestion that if he had known her, or appreciated her, he could not have left her. The "bien" and "mal" of line 9 seem to be the suitor's love and his absence, abstracted to the extremes opposites of good and evil (his "acierto" and "yerro"), both of which the suitor left to his beloved in his absence.

The last stanza is the most dense and difficult because of the hyperbaton. It repeats the rhyme words and ideas of the *estribillo*. The rephrasing of "Acaso supo . . . por acierto," from the opening lines restates the paradox more concisely: "Acertó acaso." Lines 12 and 13 are nearly unintelligible: "hazer / lo que si por conoceros / hiziera, no podia ser." The intricate syntax is preparing the way for the repetition of the central

5. I changed punctuation in lines 1 and 2 to correspond to Rivers's first edition of Garcilaso, rather than the second by removing the comma after "ver" and placing it after "acierto."

paradox: how the rival could leave the mistress and never see her again. The repetition in the last two lines restates more clearly the ideas of parting and abandonment in lines 4 and 5.

My interpretation of this *copla* disagrees with that of Rivers (Garcilaso, *Obras completas* 1981, 57). Generally he ascribes a more benevolent role to the poet in this *copla*, and he sees the poem more as a compliment to the lady than a denigration of the rival: "En ella el poeta comenta la buena suerte de otro hombre, que fue capaz de dejar para siempre de ver a la dama después de haberla visto una vez. Se supone que si este hombre hubiera llegado a apreciarla de veras, no hubiera podido escaparse tan fácilmente de querer volver a contemplarla, realmente o en su imaginación." My interpretation ascribes darker motives to the poet and his attempt to cut in on the rival for the lady's favor.

Garcilaso's octosyllabic verse shows a complexity of situation and innuendo that rival the complexity of their syntax and structure. The *coplas* move from the simple "yo → vos (señora)" pattern of address to more complex messages involving the replacement of the "yo" and the introduction of rival lovers and competition. Thematically, they are closer to the first eclogue than to other *cancionero* poetry or to Garcilaso's own Petrarchan love poems. The presence of the other, that is the rival in desire, marks these poems as different from Boscán's octosyllabic poems.

The lyric poem treats a moment or occasion, which has been chosen for the poignancy of its emotional content or the irony of the situation. This moment or occasion is clearly part of a larger context that is evoked by the lyric. Inscribed within a larger framework, the poem achieves full significance when its broader implications are explored and brought to bear on the text. In this chapter, I have focused on some rather obvious elements of the poetry, the speaker and the addressed and implied readers. The consideration of these elements moves us away from the concept of author and text united in the sincerity of expression, and provides new insights into the way such poems must have functioned. The historical context of love poetry suggests a more hostile world of competition and rivalry. These themes are also found in the poetry itself, as the authors try to strike a more authentic poetic voice, one that not only pays heed to the required theme of love, whether there was a beloved or not, but adapts it to the more immediate circumstances of the other readers of poetry, the rival for courtly favors and the critic of fine poetry. The themes of rivalry and jealousy are carefully inserted into the conventionality of the love message in the poetry of Boscán and Garcilaso. A court-ier had to be a lover, and he had to write poetry to prove the elegance of his spirit and his ability to love. In the poetry of Boscán and especially of Garcilaso, the reality of the historical situation is perceived in the incorporation of the themes of territoriality and rivalry, themes that cor-respond more fully to the historical situation than the obligatory love message.

3

Garcilaso and Renaissance Modes of Imitation

In place of originality, authenticity, and sincerity, Renaissance writers developed ideas of *imitation,* a word that took on negative connotations in the nineteenth century, even coming to signify a fraud or fake. Modern critics have had to sidestep these negative meanings of the word and return to the explanations given by the classical and Renaissance rhetoricians. As recent criticism has revealed, the term had wide and varied meanings with regard to Renaissance artistic practices. Unlike Aristotle's mimesis, which usually defines art as imitation of life, the rhetorical writers were advocating the imitation of previous texts as a method of training and of mature artistic practice. Controversy among Renaissance writers concerned not the licitness of imitation, but the nature of the sources, the attitude of the artist toward the original or originals, and the closeness of the result to the sources. Some writers, such as the Ciceronians, prescribed a close faithful imitation of one master writer, and their works tend to reproduce closely the style, tone, and ideas of the original. Others, such as the Neo-Latin lyricists, advocated the competitive emulation of many authors, with results that competed with and aimed to outdo the original. These writers imitated several sources and their works show a marked distance from the original and personal application of the final poem.

In this chapter, I wish to examine some aspects of imitation in Garcilaso's Petrarchan poetry. I shall first focus on some recent views on Renaissance imitation as well as suggesting some of the ways in which these ideas are seen in Garcilaso. I shall then review the historical apologies for Garcilaso's poetry and finally analyze in some detail Garcilaso's imitation of Petrarch in his sonnets as a key to understanding his need to imitate and his reaction against it. The issues of imitation in Garcilaso are complex and essential for understanding his apprenticeship and mastery of the Italian styles. A close analysis of one aspect of his Petrarchan sonnets reveals his attitudes regarding the use of models. As Rivers has argued ("Some Ideas"), Garcilaso obviously needed to imitate the subtlety and nuance of Italian poetic expression. The fact that he needed to imitate foreign masters should not lead us to conclude he was content to re-create their successes in a new language and cultural context. As this chapter and Chapter 8 will make clear, Garcilaso not only imitated, but his rebellion against the need to imitate is also registered in his poetry. Just as Garcilaso's courtly love poetry envisions a circle of strong amorous rivals, who may represent rival courtiers competing for patronage, so too does his Petrarchan poetry suggest a strong rivalry with the master. One can only conclude that Garcilaso was a reluctant Petrarchist in light of the manner in which he corrects Petrarch's classical quotations and seeks to rework the conventions of Petrarchism into new, even unPetrarchan, ideas and postures.

The issues of imitation in Garcilaso have been clouded by apologists anxious to dismiss the implications of plagiarism. Enthralled by Garcilaso's poetry and embarrassed by the borrowings from other writers, critics have employed several strategies to guard the author against the charges of plagiarism. Curiously enough, no critic has ever dismissed Garcilaso as a plagiarist. All surviving documents have defended him against supposed attackers—who may in fact be personifications of the gnawing inner doubts of the defenders themselves. Early critics attacked the commentators for having pointed out Garcilaso's borrowings from other writers. Others have tried to ennoble imitation, looking to the Aristotelian definition of imitation as a creative act. These Aristotelian glosses overlook the rhetorical tradition where imitation signaled the copying of past masters as a method of improving style. As we have come to realize with the studies of modern theoreticians, such as Bloom and Riffaterre, poetic language is highly conventional and owes a tremendous debt to predecessors. The fact that Renaissance theoreticians and preceptists discussed and analyzed artistic creation as an imitative process is of greater help in understanding the creative process than the post-Romantic attitude of looking for originality and therefore dismissing or ridiculing the conventions necessary to poetic production.

The concepts of imitation were extremely important for the Renaissance artist. Not only was the Aristotelian concept of art as the imitation of life introduced and commented upon, but also the older rhetorical notions of imitation of models, which had survived the Middle Ages, took on renewed interest for the humanists whose aims included the restoration of the glory of classical antiquity. Recent critics have studied imitation in Garcilaso as a creative process. Anne Cruz has studied his and Boscán's growth in Petrarchism, and has demonstrated through Garcilaso's multiple sources indicated by the sixteenth-century commentators that Garcilaso favored the imitation of many models (*Imitación* 71–75). Rico has studied how a certain Petrarchan phrase constantly recurs in disguised forms throughout Garcilaso's works ("De Garcilaso"). Rivers has presented the only proper defense of Garcilaso's borrowings, arguing that imitation of the masters was a necessary step in order to learn the new Italianate style and norms of expression ("Some Ideas").

Several recent studies have revealed a variety of concepts regarding rhetorical imitation. Basing his study on classical and Renaissance rhetorical treatises on poetics, G. W. Pigman III has distinguished three separate concepts of imitation, adapted from the three categories defined by Bartolommeo Ricci in 1545: following, imitation, and emulating ("Versions" 3). Pigman's classification corresponds roughly to Ricci's three categories, but he prefers other terminology: transformative, dissimulative, and eristic (3). The first category consists of borrowing from or closely following the steps of a master with no attempt to disguise the borrowing. Even though this may consist of little more than direct copying, Pigman labels it transformative, because the original is transformed by the context of its new setting and argument. The second category, which also consists of imitation of a model, he labels dissimulative because the artists strive to disguise their sources. The source is hidden within the fabric of the new text, enhancing the new creation. Petrarch advocated this type of imitation, which explains why his references to classical myths are seldom clearly spelled out and why his quotations from classical authors are always slightly transformed and reworked into the fabric of his text.

Pigman admits that the distinction between transformative and dissimulative imitation is of little use in textual analysis. Some of Garcilaso's uses of models, however, correspond to these two categories. His direct borrowings from Ausiàs March and Petrarch, such as the beginning line of Sonnet I, "Cuando me paro a contemplar mi 'stado," seem to correspond to his Petrarchan phase in which he carefully imitated the master in order to achieve a successful standard of poetic expression. Garcilaso's borrowings from Ausiàs March are even more obviously transformative. The first quatrain of Sonnet XXVII is translated directly from March. The imitation is not hidden or disguised, but stands at the beginning of the sonnet making its source clear to those familiar with March. It is, however, used to different ends and is transformed by its new setting. Clear examples of dissimulative imitation are seen in the mythological references from the Petrarchan period, such as the Mars–Venus–Vulcan legend in Canción IV (lines 101–7) and the Orpheus myth in Sonnet XV, where the particular circumstances of the myth are recalled and worked into a new poetic idea, but the actual names of the pagan gods are never revealed.

Pigman's third category, eristic (from Greek, *eris,* 'competition'), is an important tool for understanding Garcilaso's use of models. In this type of imitation, the artist enters into competition with the master in an attempt to outdo and supersede the original. In addition to the classical sources adduced by Pigman, he discusses in depth the Renaissance treatise by Calcagnini (1532), which is of key importance in the explanation of the competitive emulation of other writers. This type of imitation is not dissimulated because the artist wishes the reader to recognize the source and appreciate the competition and victory. Garcilaso's Sonnets XVII and XVIII, as well as other works, clearly demonstrate competitive imitation in an attempt to outdo the master.

Thomas Greene distinguishes "four types of strategies of humanist imitation, each of which involves a distinct response to anachronism and each an implicit perspective on history" (38). He labels them as (1) reproductive or sacramental, (2) eclectic or exploitative, (3) heuristic, and (4) dialectical. While these categories are more subtle than those of Pigman and are particularly interesting for their perspective and attitudes regarding history, it is difficult to apply them to Garcilaso's poetry because we lack clear ideas of his historical perspective. Greene's categories work best for discussing humanists whose historical and political writings shed light on their poetic production. Other than two slighting remarks regarding previous literature in Spanish (dedicatory letter to *El cortesano* and Sonnet XXIV), Garcilaso's attitudes regarding history cannot be deduced from his works, and speculative leaps based on flimsy evidence would not be helpful in understanding his attitudes toward imitation.

Greene's first strategy of imitation, which he calls reproductive or sacramental, involves the reproduction of a canonical text whose greatness is such that one could not treat it other than as a sacred palimpsest. This may consist of simple citation or translation with an idea of fidelity to the original. Much of sixteenth-century Petrarchism relies on the enshrinement of the master and careful reproduction of his ideas, phrases, imagery and even feelings. It provides a great practice or apprenticeship, but it ignores the gap of history that separates the original from the contemporary. This type of imitation can be seen in an elementary manner in Garcilaso's translations from Fracastoro and Sannazaro in Elegy I and Eclogue II.

The second type, eclectic or exploitative, which he also refers to as *contaminatio,* consists of the quotation of many different authors in the same text: "quite simply allusions, echoes, phrases, and images from a large number of authors jostle each other indifferently" (39). This type of random quotation does not place the sources in a historical context, but simply combines them all in a fragmented mosaic. It obviously "could not mediate effectively between a past and a future if the past was fragmented, jumbled, in effect dehistoricized" (40). Again Eclogue II is a good example because Garcilaso, as he moved toward the imitation of classical writers was still apt to quote Petrarch along with Sannazaro, Virgil, and Ovid. In this poem, the numerous and heterogenous borrowings are all reduced to the timeless present of the pastoral.

In the strategy that Greene labels heuristic, the author does not try to integrate the original in the new text, but to make the quotation evident and establish a distance between the present of the author and citation, making the reader aware of the difference of sensibility and cultural values that lies between the past of the quotation and the present of the new composition. This historical distancing often consists of a modernizing touch or conclusion to the citation that makes the reader aware of the historical nature of the text being imitated and its reapplication to a modern situation.

Greene's fourth strategy for imitation is dialectical. He admits its closeness to the previous category, heuristic, but he finds in this strategy that the author attempts not only to distance historically the quotation from the present text, but also to register resistance to the imitative act itself. All writers are forced to work with and build on the conventions established by predecessors. Such necessary subservience produces a rebellion in artists wishing for independence of expression. It is this debate, the dialectic struggle between the artist and his or her model, that is registered in the text itself. Greene's first three categories correspond roughly to the three versions of imitative theory outlined by Pigman. The difference is that Greene has placed more emphasis on the historical perspective of the writer and the consciousness of anachronism. Pigman's categories are interesting because they are based on Renaissance distinctions and present the ways that some Renaissance artists and critics conceived of imitation. Greene's categories are valuable because they allow him to enter into a dialogue with and relate to modern literary theory. There is a sense, however, in which both systems are somewhat frustrating. These carefully worked out categories in Pigman and Greene are not always clear-cut in a specific passage or composition, and for that reason they are not always useful in literary analysis. Rather than discrete categories of imitation, the various modes of imitation defined by the two writers represent several broad spectrums of imitative practices. The polarities of these spectral modalities might be laid out as shown in Diagram 2.

one author ——————— many authors
closeness (Ciceronian) ——————— distance (emulation)
dissimulation/assimilation ——————— exposure of source
anachronism ——————— historical perspective

Diagram 2.

As with an equalizer, any one element can be boosted and another decreased. Establishing categories is highly risky with so many sliding scales of practice.

A further obstacle to applying these categories to literary analysis results from the attempt to discover and determine the author's intention in imitative quotations. When Garcilaso quotes Petrarch in his opening line of Sonnet I, one must, in applying these categories, try to determine his attitude toward his source, and suddenly we have entered again the slippery ground of authorial intentionality. Even so, several of the oppositions outlined above can be posited. One could hardly claim Garcilaso is hiding his quotation, since it receives maximum exposure. His attitude toward it, however, is less clear. Is he trying to incorporate and assimilate Petrarch into his own composition, is it a respectful sacramental quote, or does the author wish to compete with the original? Does he wish to reframe Petrarch's proposition, indicated by the change from "gl'anni" to "mi 'stado," in order to discuss social rank rather than time? Or are other criteria at work? How quickly we have returned (regressed) to questions of authorial intentionality, and how quickly we have lost our grip on the issues at hand. Clearly one way to resolve this impasse is to study an author's imitative practices in a large number of texts and compare it with his or her critical writings on the subject. We have no problems determining the theory and practices of Poliziano, Erasmus, or Bembo, whose theoretical expositions make clear their ideas on imitation and their imitative practices in their literary works support their theoretical views.

The case of Garcilaso is much more complex. As I shall detail in Chapters 4 and 5, it is obvious he changed imitative strategies in the middle of his Italianate period. In the remainder of this chapter, I shall review the early critics who discussed the issues of plagiarism and then analyze the quotations from Petrarch in Garcilaso's sonnets in order to delineate various imitative strategies. The study of Garcilaso's direct quotations from Petrarch, which gives a fair picture of his imitative practice, also serves as a prelude to the Petrarchan sonnets discussed in Part III. One of the approved aspects of imitation consisted of the incorporation of phrases, language, and thoughts of other poets. With the vogue of Petrarchism and Bembo's treatise on language that gave specific rules for imitating Petrarch, that is, creating new poetry using the same methods as Petrarch, one would expect Garcilaso to have a great many echoes of the master. Some critics make much of this aspect, giving the impression that Garcilaso "borrowed" heavily from Petrarch. In fact, the number of adaptations of an actual phrase from Petrarch in the poetry of Garcilaso is quite limited.

For Garcilaso, Petrarchism does not mean copious borrowing. Even though the actual quotations from Petrarch are quite reduced in number, the re-creation of Petrarchan situations and the use of Petrarchan motifs, themes, and antitheses is far greater, even though the passages cannot be directly related to specific texts of Petrarch. The body of critical opinion that defended Garcilaso against the suggestion he was a plagiarist could have looked to the poetry to see how little he actually borrowed directly from the masters. Beginning with the commentaries of El Brocense, and especially after those of Herrera, certain readers of Garcilaso began to feel that his poetry was not original, but consisted of a pastiche of many borrowings strung together as a kind of cut-and-paste collage. Even sixteenth-century writers steeped in the traditions of imitation could take offense at plagiarism. The written evidence consists less of dismissals of Garcilaso's poetry than defenses of his artistry that take offense at El Brocense for having pointed out Garcilaso's borrowings. El Brocense had already encountered this reaction before publishing his first edition of Garcilaso with commentaries (1574). In the prologue he remarked:

> A penas se divulgo este mi intento, quando luego sobre ello se leuantaron diuersas y contrarias opiniones. Pero vna de las que mas cuenta se hace, es dezir que con estas anotaciones mas afrentas se haze al Poeta, que honra, pues por ellas se descubren y manifiestan los hurtos que antes estauan encubiertos. (Keniston, *Garcilaso* 340)

El Brocense goes on to attack poets who do not imitate as inferior and stupid:

> Opinion por cierto indigna de respuesta, si hablassemos con los muy doctos, mas por satisfazer a los que tanto no lo son, digo y affirmo que no tengo por buen poeta al que no imita a los excellentes antiguos. Y si me preguntan porque entre tantos millares de Poetas como nuestra España tiene, tan pocos se pueden contar dignos deste nombre, digo que no ay otra razon, sino por que les faltan las sciencias, lenguas, y doctrina para saber imitar.

In the works of Jéronimo de Lomas Cantoral (1578) an anonymous sonnet comments on El Brocense's disclosures of sources, labeling Garcilaso a thief and accusing El Brocense of having chained the poet in commentaries (quoted in Gallego Morell, *Antología* 87):

CONTRA LAS ANOTACIONES DEL MAESTRO SANCHEZ,
CUANDO LA PRIMERA VEZ SE IMPRIMIAN. HALLOSE
ENTONCES EN CASA DE UN CAVALLERO DE SALAMANCA
    Descubierto se ha un hurto de gran fama
del ladrón Garcilaso que han cogido
con tres doseles de la Reina Dido,
y con cuatro almohadas de su cama.
    El telar de Penélope, y la trama
de las Parcas, y el arco de Cupido,
dos barriles del agua del olvido,
y un prendedero de oro de su dama.
    Probósele que havía salteado
diez años en Arcadia, y dado un tiento
en tiendas de poetas florentines.
    Es lástima de ver al desdichado
con los pies en cadena de comento
renegar de retóricos malsines.

In a sonnet using the same rhyme scheme, Jéronimo de Lomas Cantoral defended El Brocense and in the second quatrain he contradicted the main arguments of the anonymous critic as he avoided repeating the word "ladrón," which figures so prominently in the previous sonnet (Gallego Morell, *Antología* 90):

    Aquel cuya virtud tu lengua infama
si oscurecer su luz algo has podido,
mostró cruel, de madre vil nacido,
y del ajeno bien que se derrama,
    ni hurtó jamás ni es cierto lo que trama
tu condición perversa, ni él ha sido
preso, ni el bajo nombre ha merecido
que tu voz mentirosa le da y llama.
    Antes como a divino ya y dejado
de ti por hombre tal con nuevo intento
pudieras pretender diversos fines;
    sino que sólo hieren al que ha dado
el mundo justo lauro y digno asiento
¡oh fiera bestia! tus palabras ruines.

El Brocense also replied to the anonymous sonnet with another sonnet employing the same rhyme scheme. He reprinted the original sonnet with his reply in his second edition (1581; quoted Gallego Morell, *Antología* 88):

EN LAS ESPALDAS DEL MISMO PAPEL,
PONESE EL NOMBRE DEL AUTOR CONTRARIO,
CON ALGUNAS PROPIEDADES DEL MISMO

Descúbrense poetas, cuya fama
podrá tocar las ondas del olvido,
que por henchir el verso mal medido,
lo embuten de almohadas de la cama.

Y buscan consonantes de la trama
de Parcas, tela y arcos de Cupido,
sin sentir en sus versos más sentido,
que siente el prendedero de su dama.

Y quieren dar juicio, mal pecado,
que tal de Garci Lasso es el comento,
ladrando a bulto, como los mastines.

Es lástima de ver tan mal ganado,
de largos dientes, corto entendimiento,
más falsos que corcovos de rocines.

The resentment against the commentaries was widespread. Luis Zapata (1526–95), arguing against Herrera's identification of Nemoroso as Antonio de Fonseca, quipped: "algunos comentadores de Garcilaso, antes calumniadores" (385). His dissatisfaction with the commentators seems to be the same as that of the anonymous sonnet.

In the seventeenth century, Diego de Saavedra Fajardo also defended Garcilaso against the reputation of being a plagiarist. Saavedra Fajardo cleverly invents a trial with the commentators as accusers and witnesses: "a quien le hicieron cargo de muchos urtos cometidos en Toscana, de que testificaron de vista Sánchez y Herrera, . . . y hubo testigo que juró que la capa que entonces traía de luto por la muerte de Don Bernardino de Toledo era de Fracastorio para la muerte de Marco Antonio de la Torre" (125). Garcilaso speaks in his own defense, claiming that imitation is a licit practice: ". . . decía que injustamente llamaban hurtos a los que eran imitaciones" (126). He follows this defense with a list of respected classical writers who imitated their predecessors. The case he makes for his defense is ingeniously argued: "que solamente se podían llamar ladrones los que despojan y quitan al señor lo que es suio, y que así se le hacía agrabio con tal nombre, pues si se mirasen los guardarropas de Virgilio y Fracastorio, se hallarían en ellos las cosas que a él le imputaban haber hurtado" (126). This reputation has followed Garcilaso through the centuries, although critics have not attacked his poetry for plagiarism. Many have, however, served as apologists, explaining that imitation was licit practice in the Renaissance and that plagiarism as a concept is a post-Romantic notion. The previous quotations show that sixteenth- and seventeenth-century writers were quite aware of artistic integrity.

After a careful study of El Brocense's and Herrera's commentaries, one remains somewhat surprised that Garcilaso could have ever been thought a plagiarist from those commentaries or that Golden Age writers saw a need to defend him on this issue. Most editions of Garcilaso give the wrong impression by beginning with Sonnet I, whose first line, "Cuando me paro a contemplar mi 'stado," is adapted from the opening line of Petrarch's Sonnet CCXCVIII: "Quand'io mi volgo in dietro a mirar gl'anni." In spite of this beginning, the actual number of direct borrowings from Petrarch in the sonnets is quite few in number, and limited to those texts that I have classified as Petrarchan. El Brocense and Herrera between them cite seventeen actual borrowings from Petrarch in the sonnets. If we examine closely the nature of these "quotations," however, we find that their significance is much reduced; the commentators did not intend them to be regarded as sources, but only wished to point out parallel ideas, as will be demonstrated with several examples.

Only four of the seventeen are closely translated from Petrarch. They are (1) line 8 from Sonnet XVII:

y duro campo de batalla el lecho,

from Petrarch's Sonnet CCXXVI:

Et duro campo di battaglia il letto
(B-19, H-113);

(2) line 4 from Sonnet XXVI:

¡Oh cuántas esperanzas lleva el viento!,

from Petrarch's Sonnet CCCXXIX:

Quante esperanze se ne porta il vento
(B-27, H-157);

(3) line 14 from Sonnet IV:

desnudo espirtu o hombre en carne y hueso,

from Petrarch's Canzone XXXVII:

O spirto ignudo, od huom di carne, e d'ossa
(B-6, H-35);[1]

and (4) lines 6 and 7 from Sonnet VI:

busco de mi vivir consejo nuevo;
y conozco el mejor y el peor apruebo,

from lines 135–36 of Petrarch's Canzone CCLXIV:

Cerco del viver mio novo consiglio
E veggio il meglio, et al peggior m'appiglio
(B-8, H-45).

Other borrowings are obviously related to Petrarch's text, but have been changed. Even the line that Garcilaso quotes in Italian from Petrarch's Canzone XXIII as the last line of Sonnet XXII: "Non esservi passato oltra la gonna," is changed: Petrarch's line reads "essermi," not "esservi" (B-23, H-132). Many critics have, however, reported that Garcilaso copied this line literally, for example, Navarro Tomás (Garcilaso, *Obras* 1963, 224). Other passages are simply recalled through the lan-

---

1. Rivers rejects the Petrarchan source (93n.) because of a confusion resulting from Herrera's number for Petrarch. Herrera refers to Canzone IV, which is composition I, XXXVII.

guage, but are in fact changed from Petrarch's original. Such is the first line of Sonnet I:

> Cuando me paro a contemplar mi' stado,

which is modeled on the first line of Petrarch's Sonnet CCXCVIII:

> Quand'io mi volgo in dietro a mirar gl'anni
> (H-12).

Also the last tercet of Sonnet XXVI:

> Aqueste es el deseo que me lleva
> a que desee tornar a ver un día
> a quien fuera mejor nunca haber visto,

clearly comes from Petrarch's Sonnet CCCVII:

> Ch'i' chiamo il fine per lo gran desire
> Di riveder, cui non veder fu'l meglio
> (B-28, H-159),

but, as is evident, Garcilaso's tercet has been freely adapted. Line 3 of the same sonnet only recalls the Petrarchan idea:

> ¡Oh cuánto bien se acaba en solo un día!

from Petrarch's Sonnet CCLXIX:

> Com'perdi agevolmente in un mattino
> quel, che' n molt'anni a gran pena s'acquisti
> (H-156).

This could hardly be labeled a borrowing. Most remarkable in this respect is Sonnet XVIII, which relates to a Petrarchan phrase but actually contradicts its meaning. Garcilaso's final sextet argues precisely:

> Y es que yo soy de lejos inflamado
> de vuestra ardiente vista y encendido

> tanto que en vida me sostengo apenas;
> mas si de cerca soy acometido
> de vuestros ojos, luego siento elado
> cuajárseme la sangre por las venas.

Garcilaso's idea is elaborated out of Petrarch's opposite statement in Sonnet CXCIV:

> Che da lunge mi struggo e da press'ardo
> (B-20), H-119).

All commentators cite this line from Petrarch without noting that Garcilaso has cleverly reversed the terms. Herrera cites a line from Ariosto that is much closer in sense to Garcilaso's text. As I shall show in Chapter 8, this is an example of eristic competition in which Garcilaso imitates and reverses Petrarch's primary sense. Finally, El Brocense's source for Sonnet III is so transformed that one could doubt there existed a real connection. He relates Garcilaso's lines

> La mar en medio y tierras he dexado
> de cuanto bien, cuytado, yo tenía

to lines 41–43 of Petrarch's Canzone XXXVII:

> Quante montagne et acque,
> quante mar, quanti fiumi
> m'ascondon quei duo lumi
> (B-3).

To this point, I have discussed eleven of the seventeen passages cited by the commentators as borrowings from Petrarch, only four of which are direct quotations. The remaining six need no discussion as they are parallel ideas with no evidence of direct influence. Brocense gives a source in Petrarch for Garcilaso's Sonnet XIII on Daphne, and Herrera finds a source in Petrarch for the nymphs in Sonnet XI. In neither case is there a coincidence of phrasing or thought, and it is highly unlikely that Garcilaso took his information on nymphs and Daphne from oblique references in Petrarch. Since the commentators also give the correct sources in Ovid and Sannazaro, it seems they did not mean to indicate

Petrarch as a source; they were simply signaling other passages that named Daphne and the nymphs. The same is true of Sonnets VIII, XVIII, and XXV where Herrera alleges sources in Petrarch that are not at all convincing. Lapesa also discusses at length certain passages that are parallel to Petrarch, but again, none of these is a direct borrowing, and all the rest are simply imitations in the broad sense, that is, re-creations of Petrarchan topoi. Only one in Sonnet IV shows a similarity of wording (*Estudios* 79). The remaining six parallels with Petrarch noted by the commentators have so little in common that they can be rejected outright as sources.

One curious aspect of Garcilaso's borrowings from Petrarch in the sonnets is that three of the previously cited direct quotations from Petrarch are from lines in which Petrarch himself was incorporating and dissimulating a quotation from a Roman writer. It is obvious that Garcilaso took lines 6 and 7 in Sonnet VI from Petrarch because both use the words "consejo / consiglio." Garcilaso's lines

> busco de mi vivir consejo nuevo;
> y conozco el mejor y el peor apruebo

are a direct translation from lines 135–36 of Petrarch's Canzone CCLXIV:

> Cerco del viver mio novo consiglio
> E veggio il meglio, et al peggior m'appiglio
> (B-8, H-45).

This passage was also related by El Brocense and Herrera to a passage from Ovid's *Metamorphoses:*

> Video meliora, proboque, / Deteriora sequor.

This double source might pass as a coincidence or as insignificant were it not that two other passages also have double sources. Line 2 from Sonnet X:

> dulces y alegres cuando Dios quería

comes both from Petrarch's Canzone XXXVII, line 36:

> De' miei dolci pensier, mentre a Dio piacque

and from Book IV of Virgil's *Aeneid*:

> Dulces exsuviae, dum fata, Deusque sinebant
> (B-12, for Virgil; H-75–6, for
> Virgil and Petrarch).

Since "dulces exuviae" (spoils), are closer to Garcilaso's "dulces pren-das" than Petrarch's dissimulated phrase "dolci pensier," it has been more customary to attribute this borrowing to Virgil rather than Pe-trarch. Lope often related this line to Virgil. In *El divino africano*, San Agustín reads from Book IV of Virgil's *Aeneid*: "¡Ay, dulces prendas, cuando Dios quería!" (quoted in Herrero García 79). Lope also trans-lated the line from Virgil in the same way in *La gatomachia*:

> Por quien, dijo Virgilio,
> destituída de mortal auxilio,
> que llorando decía:
> ¡Ay, dulces prendas, cuando Dios quería!
> (quoted in Herrero García 80).

Contrary to the previous example, in which it cannot be affirmed that Garcilaso knew the Ovidian original, in this case it could be argued that he did not know the Petrarchan text, although the fact that both Petrarch and Garcilaso omit the fates and include God suggests Garcilaso knew both sources.

The final case of a double source is curious: it is evident that Garcilaso had both texts in mind since he borrowed from each. In Sonnet XVII, the eighth line (as previously noted) comes directly from Petrarch. The association does not end there; the following lines continue to resemble Petrarch, but in fact use the Ovidian expression to replace Petrarch's phrase:

> (Garcilaso)
> y duro campo de batalla el lecho.

Del sueño, si ay alguno, aquella parte
sola quês ser imagen de la muerte

(Petrarch)
   Et duro campo di battaglia il letto,
Il sonno è veramente, qual huom dice,
Parente de la morte: e'l cor sottrage
Aquel dolce pensier, ch'in vita il tene.
                         (CCXXVI, 8–11)

(Ovid)
Stulte, quid est somnus, gelidae nisi mortis imago?
                         (B-19, H-114)

While Petrarch says that sleep is "parente de la morte," Ovid, like Garcilaso, said it was an image of death. As I shall show in Chapter 8, this is a clear case of eristic imitation by Garcilaso. The direct quote in line 8 serves to announce the imitation, then Garcilaso proceeds to correct Petrarch's dissimulated imitation of Ovid, and finally to outdo Ovid. The double reference to Garcilaso's borrowings from Petrarch are not inconsequential since two of them show he had in mind both the Latin and Petrarchan text.

The first stanza of Canción I also simultaneously quotes Petrarch and Horace. Lapesa comments in a note: "En Garcilaso hay notas que no se dan en Petrarca, sino en el modelo de éste, es decir, en la referida oda horaciana. . . . Razón tenían Sánchez y Tamayo al citar los dos textos como fuentes del pasaje garcilasiano: el poeta ha operado por contaminación, combinando elementos de uno y otro" (*Garcilaso: Estudios* 88n) Even though contamination was a term employed by Renaissance rhetoricians, it suggests corruption and places a pejorative judgment on this process. I would prefer to view this as another example in which Garcilaso calls attention to Petrarch's dissimulated imitative style by supplying details from source. It seems when Garcilaso recognized a passage in which Petrarch had incorporated a dissimulated imitation into his text, he would imitate both texts in order to challenge the Petrarchan method of imitation. Some of the passages lead to uninteresting results, but there are also resounding successes, such as Sonnet XVII.

The purpose of this close examination of Garcilaso's direct borrowings from Petrarch has not been to discredit the commentators or to diminish the idea of influence from Petrarch. Garcilaso developed his Italian style as a Petrarchist, and his poetry clearly reflects the influence of Petrarch. What it does not show, as has often been alleged, is heavy borrowing of whole lines and passages from Petrarch. The number of passages that recall other specific passages in Petrarch is six. The number of changed passages that are translated from Petrarch is five; three of the total are from passages that Petrarch had borrowed from Latin writers. The total concerns some eleven passages in only nine of the seventeen sonnets I have classified as Petrarchan. While noteworthy, it hardly lends weight to any conclusion that finds Garcilaso's poetry to be a pastiche of borrowings from Petrarch. Garcilaso was a Petrarchist, and Petrarchan elements abound in his poetry, but not slavish copying. More often we see his independence of spirit as asserted in Sonnets IV and XXVI; or an actual reversal of the Petrarchan topos, as in Sonnet XVIII; or very subtle reworkings and elaborations of Petrarchan ideas, as in Sonnet XVII; or in the phrase that Francisco Rico finds re-created in dissimulated forms in various passages in Garcilaso's poetry ("De Garcilaso"). In the final analysis, and as the study of the Petrarchan sonnets will show, Garcilaso's Petrarchism proves to be a highly original application of the Petrarchan system.

In these three chapters I have registered my complaints with the pseudobiographical criticism that began in the sixteenth and seventeenth centuries and finally flourished among twentieth-century critics. The concepts of sincerity and authenticity have produced distorted interpretations of individual poems, such as Eclogue I, Ode ad florem Gnidi, and a number of the sonnets. As I shall show in Chapter 11, some of Garcilaso's poems are autobiographical, but autobiography functions more politically in these poems than sentimentally. In Chapter 2, I discussed the political context of courtly literature and suggested that in some cases the love story may have served as a commentary on the real courtly ambience of rivalry and intrigue. Finally, the study of the idea of imitation (and rivalry with the master or source material) provides a broader understanding of Garcilaso's poetic practices and his posture as an artist. In place of the "sincerity" that previous generations of critics believed they found in Garcilaso's poetry, I shall, in analyzing individual poems, point out Garcilaso's artistry, his engagement of philosophical ideas, and his conscious artistic manipulation of sources and existing concepts.

II
The Vernacular Renaissance

IN 1922 KENISTON IDENTIFIED Bernardo Tasso's ode, "O pastori felice" (published 1534) as the source of the metrical form of the *lira,* the stanzaic form introduced by Garcilaso and widely employed in Spanish Renaissance poetry (*Garcilaso* 334). Few critics, however, have investigated the state of ode writing in Italy at that time and the novelty—and rebelliousness—that it represented.[1] In like manner, critics have recognized that Garcilaso's late works are classical in inspiration, but most have failed to regard this aspect as an innovation, tacitly assuming that classicizing was an expected element in Renaissance literature. The imitation of classical authors in the vernacular was an innovation in Italian poetry that occurred contemporaneously with Garcilaso's own absorption and mastering of the Italian style. Among others, Navarro Tomás propagated this basic misunderstanding of the classical influences on Garcilaso's poetry in his widely disseminated Clásicos Castellanos edition of Garcilaso: "los clásicos era, no sólo un hecho corriente, sino un principio fundamental en la educación literaria de la época de Garcilaso y de todo su siglo" (*Obras* 1963, lix). A more thorough investigation of the "Vernacular Renaissance" provides a better understanding of Garcilaso's own poetical development.

Renaissance literature in Italy at the period when Garcilaso arrived in Naples fell into two major currents, depending on the language, Latin or Italian, in which it was written. In the revival of classical learning that flourished among the Italian humanists in the fifteenth and sixteenth centuries, scholars and artists had revived the study of Greek and Latin composition. They imitated the ancients in their own compositions, with the result that most Renaissance works showing classical influence were written in Latin or, more rarely, Greek. In their epigrams, odes, and elegies the humanists explored and developed classical material quite different from the topic of unrequited love that dominated vernacular poetry. The Neo-Latin ode, as formed by Filelfus and Pontanus, often addressed the pagan gods and treated themes, such as pagan myths and conjugal love, that are quite different from those of courtly love. The number of Neo-Latin poets was quite large. Even Garcilaso wrote compositions in Latin, of which four have survived.

Literature in Italian, on the other hand, was following completely different courses based on the imitation of Petrarch's *Canzoniere.* Even though the investigation and diffusion of Latin poets had begun as

---

1. Not even Dámaso Alonso in his well-known study of the *lira* (*Poesía española* 611–18).

early as the twelfth century, poetry in the vernacular continued until the beginning of the sixteenth century to employ medieval forms and subject matter. Not until the 1520s were attempts made to imitate classical poetry in the vernacular, and this movement coincided with an intense period of Petrarchan revival and influence, so that the introduction of classical elements and the classical spirit into the vernacular ran counter to the general current of Italian letters.

Sixteenth-century Petrarchism returned to a very close imitation of the medieval poet. Wilkins describes Renaissance Petrarchism as "the use of Petrarchan words, phrases, lines, metaphors, conceits, and ideas, and the adoption, for poetic purposes, of the typical Petrarchan experiences and attitudes" (281–82). Within the general imitation of Petrarch, there had come to exist two widely divergent practices. Late fifteenth-century imitators of Petrarch, such as Il Chariteo (c. 1450–1514), Il Tebaldeo (1463–1537), and Serafino dell'Aquila (1466–1500), had concentrated on the poet's rhetoric instead of his balance and harmony, and they carried Petrarchan rhetorical devices, such as conceits and antitheses, to exaggerated extremes. None of these writers has fared well in the literary histories. Wilkins says of Il Chariteo:

> [I]n the last decades of the fifteenth century there developed a new phase of Petrarchism which was destined to have great influence, both in Italy and abroad. The responsibility for the initiation of this new phase lies with the Catalan Benedicto Gareth, who came to Naples in his early youth and became, to all intents and purposes, an Italian: he was known, in Italy, as Il Chariteo. . . . [B]y no means without artistic gifts of his own—[he] devotes too much attention to . . . rhetorical devices, and exploits them energetically. His cardinal and most infectious sin is the materialization of Petrarchan metaphors, to which he gives an existential literality they were never meant to bear. His two chief companions in flamboyance were Tebaldeo and the devastatingly popular Serafino dell'Aquila. (283)

His condemnation of Serafino is even stronger:

> He was all but worshipped in his lifetime. . . . Yet he had nothing to say that was worth saying; and much of his very considerable skill in rhyme and rhythm was spent, following the leads of

Il Cariteo and Il Tebaldeo, in the effort to treat his listeners to
farfetched surprises. (176)

These historical summations give a clear idea of the state of vernacular
poetry at the end of the fifteenth century, and provide a background
for the two subsequent developments I trace in the next two chapters.
Chapter 4 analyzes in detail Bembo's calculated revival of a moderated
and balanced Petrarchism to counter the extravagances of the late
fifteenth-century Petrarchists. Chapter 5 studies Bernardo Tasso's rejection of Petrarchism and the introduction of classical themes and subject
matter into vernacular poetry. These two chapters not only show the
complexities and countercurrents of the vernacular renaissance, but
they also serve in turn as introductory material to the analysis of
Garcilaso's sonnets in Parts III and IV.

4

Pietro Bembo and Sixteenth-Century Petrarchism

Pietro Bembo (1470–1547) was an important humanist writing in both Latin and Italian. His reputation as a writer depends largely on his exposition of the theory of Neoplatonic love in *Gli asolani,* on his defense of the practice of imitating one rather than many writers, and his arguments for establishing Tuscan as the literary language of Italy. He also influenced the course of poetry by advocating a return to a balanced and moderate style through close imitation of Petrarch. In reaction to the extravagant style developed by the Petrarchists of the late fifteenth century, Bembo prescribed for Italian poetry the imitation of the best Italian poets, especially Petrarch. In his *Prose della volgar lingua* (first published 1525), Bembo outlined a future course not only for Italian poetry, but also for the Italian language. Both issues, a standard language for the Italian states and the salvation of poetry from the excesses of late fifteenth-century Petrarchists, were to be resolved in the careful and studied imitation of Petrarch, the one model that would serve to form a national idiom and poetry of good taste: "here there is one god, Petrarch, and Bembo is his prophet" (Whitfield 162).

The question of a national language for all of the Italian states had been discussed heatedly. In proposing the use of Tuscan, Bembo looked to two past masters, Boccaccio in prose and Petrarch in poetry, as models of good usage. As part of the creation of a standardized national language, Bembo argued for the return to a strict imitation of Petrarch as an ideal of moderation rather than a source of extravagant antitheses and conceits. He found in Petrarch's good taste and moderation both a standard for the unification of the language and a model for returning poetry to a more balanced tone. The close imitation of Petrarch would serve to eliminate the extravagant comparisons and questionable taste that had characterized Italian lyric poetry in the fifteenth century (Forster 26–30).

In this chapter I shall study in detail Bembo's prescriptions for structuring the sound values in poetry. Since his source was discovered fairly recently, a study of how he has adapted and transvalued his source material makes clearer the implications of his own thought. I shall then demonstrate the relevance of these ideas for Spanish literature, first attempting to reconstruct Herrera's interpretation of Bembo and Dionysius of Halicarnassus, and then approaching the more difficult task of extrapolating from Garcilaso's poetry his own interpretation and application of Bembo's ideas.

In his *Prose della vulgar lingua,* Bembo gives precise guidelines for the imitation of Petrarch, especially regarding the sound system of Italian. These generally are not stated as rules for imitating, but are presented as observations on the sound structure of Petrarch's poetry that can serve as guidelines for creating in one's own poetry the same effects of moderation that Petrarch created in his. While Bembo defended the idea of imitating one sole author, we note that his concept of imitation was quite inclusive. The writer is to imitate the manner in which the master composed and not the master's composition itself, even though it is only through a thorough analysis of the composed text that one can gain an idea of how the master worked.

In proposing a national language and a poetics based on the medieval writer Petrarch in a period of extremely sophisticated studies of Latin and Greek poetry, Bembo must have understood the necessity of placing vernacular poetry on a level with the highly revered classical literatures. Most of the participants in the dialogue of the *Prose* are major Neo-Latin poets who are opponents of composition in the vernacular. The character who defends vernacular literature and the views of the author is his deceased brother Carlo Bembo. The confrontational situation of the dialogue allowed Bembo to introduce the types of subtlety that placed vernacular poetics on a par with the complex metrics of Latin and Greek. He found this needed reinforcement in a discussion of the sound system used in vernacular poetry and a careful description of the technical aspects of the sound structure of Petrarch's poetry. In place of the complex and sophisticated metrical patterns and feet of the Latin lyric poets, Bembo offers a detailed analysis of the musicality of Petrarch's *Canzoniere.*

Bembo's observations on the sound structure of Italian, as a key to the successful imitation of Petrarch, are usually considered the heart of the book (Pettenati 69). Bembo did not identify the source of these ideas and, until recently, his editors and critics generally attributed great originality to him, often in those very passages that are directly translated out of Greek (Dionisotti 150). Far from original, as Pettenati demonstrated in 1960, Bembo's observations on the phonetic values of Italian are taken directly, even at times translated word for word, from the first-century Greek rhetorician Dionysius of Halicarnassus, whose treatise on composition had first been published by Aldus in 1508. Bembo obviously studied it and drew from it in the original Greek because a Latin translation did not appear until later in the sixteenth century. The structure of Bembo's arguments and many of the details in Book II derive directly from Dionysius's *On Literary Composition.* Bembo either translates from the Greek or, if necessary, because of the differences between the languages, adapts Dionysius's observations to the different circumstances of Italian.

A comparison of his text with that of his source proves useful for delineating Bembo's thought and limitations, and sheds light on how his ideas may have been further transvalued by Garcilaso and his chief commentator Fernando de Herrera. As a beginning step, it is useful to distinguish not only the different contexts in which Dionysius and Bembo were working, but also the different aims of the treatises. Dionysius was commenting on a literature that had flourished and left a rich legacy. Bembo was prescribing the imitation of medieval writers in an age that declared the Middle Ages to be barbaric, and he needed to defend the idea of composition in the vulgar tongue as opposed to the more prestigious Latin. Another difference comes from Dionysius's strict distinction between content and form, presented in classical rhetoric as *res* (things or subject matter) and *verba* (words or style). Dionysius carefully distinguishes between the two concepts and states explicitly he is treating style (word order) only. He makes clear he is not dealing with the choice of words, which relates to content, but to the ordering of words that have already been selected. He announces a future treatise on the correct choice of words. Since ancient Greek had a comparatively fluid word order, he posits that the arrangement of the words can create success or failure. In dealing with the more strongly patterned phrasing of Italian, Bembo would not find such a rigorous distinction to be of much use, and was forced to modify subtly the views of his source.

Bembo asserts that Petrarch's success as a poet and the balance in his style come from the fact that the sounds of his verse appropriately reinforce the stated message. His basic idea is that the successful combination of sounds in a line of poetry creates one of two effects: either *gravità* or *piacevolezza*. This distinction comes from Dionysius, who distinguishes two types of beauty in literary style: charm (*hedone*) and beauty (*to kalon*). Both words indicate beauty, but the first refers to delight, enjoyment, or pleasure; the second implies a moral sense of beauty, even signifying goodness or virtue. Roberts translates the terms as "charm and beauty" (119); Usher as "attractiveness and beauty" (91). The essence of Dionysius's distinction seems to lie between a style that creates art for art's sake and a style that has didactic qualities. The charming should be melodious and polished, while the beautiful should be noble and dignified (135). Bembo's rendering of *hedone* as *piacevolezza* hits the mark, but his rendering of *to kalon* as *gravità* (probably suggested by the traditional rhetorical distinction between *gravitas* and *suavitas*) is less accurate. To illustrate this idea, Dionysius gives examples of authors whose styles are either beautiful or charming. He names Herodotus as the master whose style encompasses equal measures of both characteristics.[1] Bembo follows Dionysius in this, substituting Dante as an example of *gravità* and Cino da Pistoia as an example of *piacevolezza,* and Petrarch as the master who excelled in both:

> Per ciò che egli può molto bene alcuna composizione essere piacevole e non grave, e allo 'ncontro alcuna altra potrà grave essere, senza piacevolezza; sì come aviene delle composizioni di messer Cino e di Dante: ché tra quelle di Dante molte son gravi, senza

1. "The styles of Thucydides and of Antiphon of Rhamnus are sure examples of beautiful composition, . . . but they are not remarkable for their charm. On the other hand, the style of the historian Ctesias of Cnidus, and that of Xenophon the disciple of Socrates, are charming in the highest possible degree, but not as beautiful as they should have been. I am speaking generally, not absolutely; I admit that in the former authors there are instances of charming, in the latter of beautiful arrangement. But the composition of Herodotus has both these qualities; it is at once charming and beautiful" (121). All quotes come from the edition by W. Rhys Roberts.

piacevolezza; e tra quelle di messer Cino molte sono piacevole, senza gravità. Non dico già tuttavolta che in quelle medesime che io gravi chiamo non vi sia qualche voce ancora piacevole, e in quelle che dico essere piacevoli alcun' altra non se ne legga scritta gravemente, ma dico per la gran parte. . . . il Petrarca l'una e l'altra di queste parte empié maravigliosamente, in maniera che scegliere non si può, in quale delle due egli fosse maggior maestro. (Pozzi 130–31)

(Therefore any composition can very well be pleasing and not grave, and on the contrary any other can be grave without a pleasant quality; such as occurs in the compositions of Cino and Dante: for among those of Dante many are grave, without pleasantness; and among those of Cino many are pleasing, without gravity. I do not claim, however, that in those I call grave there are never pleasing words, and in those that I say are pleasing one never reads some words written gravely, but I speak for the greater part. . . . Petrarch satisfies both of these aspects marvelously, in such manner that it is impossible to choose in which of the two he was the greater master.)

In addition to providing examples of each style, Dionysius characterizes charm and beauty in composition:

Under "charm" I class freshness, grace, euphony, sweetness, persuasiveness, and all similar qualities; and under "beauty" grandeur, impressiveness, solemnity, dignity, mellowness, and the like. (121)

Following Dionysius, Bembo characterizes both terms, but changes their order and subtly modifies their meaning:

sotto la gravità ripongo l'onestà, la dignità, la maestà, la magnificenza, la grandezza, e le loro somiglianti; sotto la piacevolezza ristringo la grazia, la soavità, la vaghezza, la dolcezza, gli scherzi, i giuochi, e se altro é di questa maniera. (Pozzi 130)

(under gravity I place honesty, dignity, majesty, magnificence, grandeur, and similar qualities; under the pleasant I include grace, delicacy, charm, sweetness, jokes and playfulness, and others in this manner.)

Bembo has shifted the sense of Dionysius's distinction between his stylistic possibilities to encompass two other traditional rhetorical distinctions. First is the classical rhetorical distinction between *gravitas* and *suavitas* (*utile et dulce* in Horace's terminology) which was in turn based on the rhetorical distinction between *res* and *verba,* understood as content and style. In Dionysius's distinction between the two styles, charm and beauty, both styles are assumed to reside within the category of style or *verba.* Bembo's terms constitute a basic modification of Dionysius's thought. In effect he has reintroduced the *res/verba* distinction between the didactic and entertaining elements in literature, and has changed the order of the descriptions so that the more important didactic *gravità* comes first. A second modification concerns the descriptions of the terms, which are made to correspond to another traditional rhetorical distinction, the difference between the high and low styles. Bembo is not describing a precious, amoral style, but intends *piacevolezza* to be much broader, for he has added to Dionysius's list humor and jokes. He has replaced the traditional *suavitas* with *piacevolezza;* the latter not only corresponds better to Dionysius's term, but it is a more evocative expression and includes not only the delicacy and sweetness assigned to the traditional *suavitas,* but also the humor and levity typical of the low style. Bembo's category of *gravità* consists mainly of elements indicating the thematic material of the high style, above all the idea of nobility. Dionysius's description consists of words indicating musicality and grandeur, while Bembo's list consists of words proper to nobility as a social class. Not only has Bembo modified *gravità* to incorporate other rhetorical categories, but he has also transvalued the concept to correspond to the contemporary reality of Italian court society by transforming the hero into a courtier.

Bembo's overloading of the stylistic distinction between charm and beauty with the implications of the *res/verba* distinction and the distinction between high and low styles produces several inconsistencies in his thought. For Dionysius, charm and beauty are not presented as the sole alternatives in style, as are gravity and pleasantness for Bembo. In stating that "charm" and "beauty" were two basic styles, Dionysius was not eliminating the possibilities of producing other styles, which he at times mentions. Whether he would have accepted the seventeen styles described by Hermogenes is not known, but he certainly saw more possibilities than just two effects. In addition Dionysius introduces the two terms early in his treatise and does not relate his phonetic explanations to the two concepts. Bembo, on the other hand, claims that the sounds of the letters produce either *gravità* or *piacevolezza,* and he does not allow for other possibilities, with the exception of exaggeration of the two effects. He believes that the good writer uses the sounds of words to mark the character of the subject matter. He reduces the possibilities of style to only two, which almost leaves him saying that certain words have grave sound and others have pleasing sound, a thesis so easily disproved that it would render his theories useless. Dionysius is concerned with the stylistic effects of word order. He often employs examples in which the style gives a different sense to the subject matter, such as Homer's list of cities, which becomes interesting because of the rhythm and order of the words. This presentation saves Dionysius from the implication, quite clear at times in both Bembo and Herrera, that grave words have the sound characteristics of the grave style and pleasing and jocular words have the characteristics of the pleasant style. In claiming there are only two stylistic effects, Bembo narrowly skirts the implication that words have set sound values:

> Conosciute ora queste forze tutte delle lettere, torno a dire, che secondamente che ciascuna voce le ha in sé, così ella è ora grave, ora leggiera, quando aspera, quando molle, quando d'una guisa d'altra; e quali sono poi le guise delle voci, che fanno alcuna scrittura, tale è il suono, che del mescolamento di loro esce o nella prosa o nel verso, e talora gravità genera e talora piacevolezza. (Pozzi 135)

> (Now that all the values of the letters are known, I repeat that accordingly as each word has them in it, it is now grave, now light, now harsh, now soft, now of one manner and now of another; and whatever then are the values of the words that make up any writing, so is the sound that issues from the combination of them in prose or poetry, and at times it generates gravity, other times pleasantness.)

Dionysius introduces four categories of elements that produce the two styles: "melody, rhythm, variety and appropriateness" (121) while Bembo reduced the number to three by eliminating Dionysius's fourth category. He lists the three ways in which a writer achieves the effects of *gravità* and *piacevolezza*: "e le cose poi, che empiono e compiono queste due parti, son tre, il suono, il numero, la variazione" (and the things then that create and compose these two parts are three: sound, number, and variety) (Pozzi 130). He translates and adapts Dionysius's descriptions of the sounds of the language, and then analyzes various passages from Petrarch, Dante, and Boccaccio to show how the sounds combine to produce one of the two effects.

Under the first category he discusses the sounds of the letters and the effects of rhyme and stanzaic form (Pettenati). Bembo makes varied use of his original source by (1) translating directly Dionysius's minute observations on the phonetic values of Greek, (2) adapting them to the rather different circumstances of Italian, (3) expanding on the moralized ideas implicit in Dionysius's text, and (4) providing additional observations on the sound values of those letters that do not occur in Greek. His observations on *l* and *r* are an example of direct translation from Dionysius:

> [lambda] falls pleasurably on [the ear], and is the sweetest of the semi-vowels; while [rho] has a rough quality and is the noblest of its class. (147)
>
> molle e dilicata e piacevolissima è la *l* e di tutte le sue compagne lettere dolcissima. Allo 'ncontro la *r* [è] aspera ma di generoso spirito. (Pozzi 134)
>
> (soft, delicate and most pleasing is the *l* and of all its companion letters, the sweetest. On the contrary, the *r* is harsh, but of noble spirit.)

Bembo adapted Dionysius's comments on the *s* to the context of Italian. Dionysius expressed absolute dislike for the *s*, which in Greek is a pure sibilant and occurs with far greater frequency than in Italian:

> [sigma] is an unattractive, disagreeable letter, positively offensive when used to excess. A hiss seems a sound more suited to a brute beast than to a rational being. At all events, some of the ancients used it sparingly and guardedly. There are writers who used actually to compose entire odes without a sigma. (147–49).

Bembo did not agree with Dionysius's strictures regarding the *s*, and he reformulates the original and, with the word "spesso," seems to indicate the voiced single *s* (different from the unvoiced double *ss*, which resembles more the sound in Greek):

> E questa *s*, quantunque non sia di purissimo suono, ma più tosto de spesso, non pare tuttavolta essere di così schifo e rifiutato nel nostro idioma, come ella solea essere anticamente nel greco; nel quale furono già scrittori, che per questo alcuna volta delle loro composizione fornirono senza essa. (Pozzi 134)

> (And this *s*, when it is not of purest sound, but somewhat thicker, does not always seem to be so loathsome and scorned in our language as it used to be in ancient Greek, in which there were writers who for this reason occasionally composed a work without any *s*'s.)

Bembo at times tends to moralize rather than strictly translate, although it could be argued that he is foregrounding an element implicit in Dionysius's arguments. Dionysius finds more pleasing those sounds that are aspirated, perhaps because they have more breath or *pneumatos* (spirit). In his commentary on aspirated sounds he stated: "the rough letters have the breath also added, so that they are somewhere nearer perfection than the others" (151). When ranking the vowels, he finds the alpha to be the vowel that produces the most pleasing sound: "Again, of the long vowels themselves the most euphonious is [alpha], when prolonged; for it is pronounced with the mouth open to the fullest extent, and with the breath forced upwards to the palate" (143). The sense of breath (spirit or *pneuma*) and the upward thrust provided Bembo with the suggestion for placing moral values on his phonetic observations. Bembo translates Dionysius's *pneumatos* as "spiritus," and finds the upward movement of the breath to be heavenward: "E di queste tutte miglior suono rende la *a*; con ciò sia cosa che ella più di spirito manda fuori; per ciò che con più aperte labbra ne'l manda e più al cielo ne va esso spirito" (And of all these the *a* produces the best sound; whether because it sends forth more breath [spirit]; or because it sends it out with more open lips and this breath [spirit] goes more toward heaven) (Pozzi 131).

Dionysius does not relate the two concepts of charm and beauty to the discussion of melody and rhythm, whereas for Bembo the sounds and rhythms produce either one of the two effects of gravity or pleasantness. This creates a certain confusion in Bembo's treatise, since he often simply paraphrases Dionysius's descriptions of the nature of the vowel and consonant sounds. Since Dionysius does not relate them to the previous distinction between charm and beauty, the descriptions, as paraphrased and contextualized by Bembo, fail to identify the effect they are supposed to create. One emerges from these paragraphs unsure of which of the two effects the consonant sounds create.

It is clear from his classification of the vowels (Pozzi 131–32), that the clearest concept of gravity comes from the long vowel sounds. The *a* has the best sound of all, then the *e,* then the *o*. The *i* is a weak and light sound; the *u* is the least of all sounds. The Greek letters eta and epsilon, which are transliterated into Latin alphabets as *e,* and omicron and omega, which are transliterated as *o,* allow Bembo to distinguish between close and open *e* and *o*. The vowels have better spirit when they are long or lengthened than when they are short. Bembo does not use the terms *grave* and *piacevole* to describe the vowel sounds, but does ascribe moral and ethical qualities to them, such as "better," "best," "spirit," and "dignity." Since gravity, like the high style, pertains to nobility, and the pleasing style belongs to the lower classes, the hierarchical adjectives describing the vowels imply a relation to the concepts of gravity and pleasantness.

Bembo's description of the consonants is more difficult to relate to his central thesis. He pays special attention to the double consonant sound in the *z* finding it the only surviving double sound of which Greek had three. In the discussion of these double sounds, he includes the double *s,* but does not classify it. Other consonants are related to the two principal effects only by inference. As noted, the *l* is soft, delicate, and very pleasant (Pozzi 134). The *r* is rough, but of noble sound. The *m* and *n* are intermediate between these two. The *f* is thick and full; the *g* moderately thick and full, but quicker. The thickest and fastest is the *c*. Quick and clear are the *b* and *d;* the *p* and *t* the quickest and clearest. These categories remain somewhat ambiguous since it is difficult to infer which of the two characteristics the sounds generate.

Bembo also classifies the two letters not found in Greek: the *q* and *h*. In the classification of the *q* Bembo demonstrates that his sophistication in these observations depended largely on Dionysius's superior training in grammar and phonetics. From one point of view it was not necessary for Bembo to classify the *q,* since it duplicates the sound of the *c*. In this Bembo shows that he was working more with letters (as was Dionysius) than phonemes. He does not, as he did in copying Dionysius's remarks on the other sounds, describe the production of the sound, and his observation is based on moral, rather than phonetic values: "Di povero y morto suono, spora gli altri tutti, ultimamente è la *q*; e in tanto più ancora maggiormente, che egli, senza la *u* che'l sostenga, non può aver luogo" (Of poor and dull sound quality, above all others, lastly is the *q*, and to a much greater degree, for it, without the *u* that sustains it, cannot occur) (Pozzi 134–35). His classification of the *h* is better realized, but again shows his desire to place the sounds in moral and social hierarchies: "La *h*, per ciò che non è lettera, per sè medesima niente può; ma giugne solamente pienezza e quasi polpa alla lettera, a cui ella in guisa de servente sta accanto" (The *h*, since it is not a letter, by itself can do nothing; but it only adds fullness and as it were flesh to the letter, by which it stands in the manner of a servant) (Pozzi 135).

Both Dionysius and Bembo describe the sound produced by each letter. This system works fairly well for Dionysius because each consonant sound in Greek is represented by a distinct letter of the alphabet. Bembo clearly follows Dionysius, in most cases word for word, in the description of the "sounds of the letters" in Tuscan. Like all early linguists, Bembo describes the sound of each letter, rather than the phonemic particularities of Tuscan. Pozzi demonstrates this with an example: "De altra parte è chiaro che il Bembo non distingue adeguatamente tra fonema e segno grafico, giaché parla dell'*h* ma non fa cenno della *v*, che, come è noto, no si distingueva graficamente della vocale *u*" (On the other hand it is clear that Bembo does not distinguish adequately between phoneme and graphic sign, since he speaks of the *h*, but does not mention the *v*, which, as is noted, was not distinguished graphically from the *u*) (135). Because of his attention to the letters and not the phonemes he adds a description of the *h* and *q*, but omits discussion of other sounds in Tuscan that do not occur in Greek, such as palatal *c*, *g*, *cc*, *gg*, *sc* (before *e* and *i*), and *gl* and *gn*.

Bembo includes in the category of sound the discussion of rhyme, claiming it gives "armonia e leggiadria" (135) to the vernacular, and replaces the metric feet in Latin poetry. Bembo maintains that rhymes have an effect of *gravità* when the rhyme words are furthest from each other, and of *piacevolezza* when they are close, as in couplets. The effect is even more pleasing if the lines are of seven syllables instead of eleven (Pozzi 138). He includes under sound a discussion and classification of stanzaic forms. A stanza composed of frequent rhymes is pleasing; one composed of sparse rhymes is grave. He gives examples of each from

Petrarch. He finds *piacevole* the two "sister" *canzone* "Chiare, fresche e dolci acque" and "Se'l pensier, che mi strugge." Both have exactly the same number of verses and the same rhyme scheme. They differ in that the first one ends with an hendecasyllable and the second with a heptasyllable. Any delay in coming to the rhyme produces gravity; hence the first *canzone* is slightly graver than the second. As the example of the most grave stanzaic form, he names the *canzone* "Nel dolce tempo de la prima etade." This stanza has twenty lines, only one of which is a heptasyllable, the preponderance of long lines creating gravity. These observations may have influenced Garcilaso's choice of stanzaic forms. His Canción III takes its stanza from Petrarch's "Chiare, fresche e dolci acque," one of two stanzas labeled *piacevole,* and his Canción IV takes its stanzaic form from Petrarch's "Nel dolce tempo de la prima etade." Garcilaso thus chose for two of his *canciones,* the extremes of *gravità* and *piacevolezza* as identified by Bembo.

Bembo defines number as the amount of time granted each syllable:

> il qual numero altro non è che il tempo che alle sillabe si dà, o lungo o brieve, ora per opera delle lettere che fanno le sillabe, ora per cagione degli accenti che si danno alle parole. (143)

> (number is nothing other than the time that is given to the syllables, either long or short, either by function of the letters that make up the syllables, or by reason of the accents that are given to the word.)

Bembo discusses number both in poetry and prose. He classifies the hendecasyllable *agudo* as grave, the *llano* as moderated and the *esdrújulo* as pleasing. The same is true of prose. The opening of Boccaccio's *Decamerone* is "grave e riposato" (146) because the accents fall on the penultimate syllables: "Umana cosa è l'avere compassione agli afflitti." He then rewrites the sentence, changing the main words to *esdrújulos:* "Debita cosa è l'essere compassionevole a' miseri." He finds the sound of this sentence to be "men grave" and not adjusted to the purpose that the author sought in his opening sentence.

Bembo explains that longer syllables, composed of multiple consonants and vowels (that is, diphthongs) produce a graver sound:

> Ora, venendo al tempo che le lettere danno alle voci, è da sapere che tanto maggiore gravità rendono le sillabe, cuanto elle più

lungo tempo hanno in sé per queste conto; il che aviene qualora
più vocali o più consonanti entrano in ciascuna sillaba. (150)

(Now, treating the time that the letters give to the words, one
must know that syllables create much greater gravity when they
have longer time in themselves in this count; the one that [is
greater] happens to have more vowels or more consonants in
each syllable.)

In all cases, Bembo seems to favor gravity, probably because it represents for him the dignity of the high style. He does give examples of some
words that produce a grave sound:

Per ciò che più grave suono ha in sé questa voce *destro* che
quest'altra *vestro;* e più magnifico lo rende il dire *campo* che, o
caldo o *casso* dicendosi, non di renderà. (150)

(Therefore the word *destro* has in it a graver sound than *vestro;*
and more magnificent is it rendered to say *campo* than *caldo* or
casso.)

In summary, the following rule is stipulated: "che sì come la spessezza
delle lettere accresce alle voci gravità, così la rarità porge loro piacevolezza" (so as density of the letters increases the gravity in the words, so
does thinness give them pleasantness) (Pozzi 152).

Bembo's last category, variety (Pozzi 152–56) is also adapted from Dionysius, who defined it as a change of melody and rhythm. Bembo conceives of it as a variation of gravity and pleasantness. Again the model
for variety, which is useful for avoiding monotony and *satietà,* is Petrarch, for his numerous poems on the same subject could be cloying had
he not introduced variety into the stanzaic structure of the songs. His
gravity was tempered by his pleasantness to provide relief from the same
tone and to make the two parts more impressive through their juxtaposition. Bembo believes that the poet not only must strive to vary the style of
the poem, but must also avoid mechanical evasions that become obvious
patterns in themselves: "Nel rimanente poi di questa canzone e in tutta
l'altra, e all'une rime e all'altre per ciascuna stanza dando parte, fuggì
non solamente la troppa piacevolezza o la troppa gravità, ma ancora la

troppa diligenza del fuggirle" (Then in the rest of this song and in all others, and giving part to one rhyme and the other, he avoided not only too much pleasantness or too much gravity, but also too much diligence in avoiding them) (Pozzi 155). Variety reflects his hesitation to be over-dogmatic and provides an escape from the tenuous nature and even inconsistencies inherent in his systematization of Dionysius's material. With variety, Bembo appears to say that a sound that is naturally grave in one context may achieve its opposite effect in another phonetic situation. In other words, the difference is not purely stylistic for Bembo, as it was for Dionysius; rather, it is also determined by the sense and sound of the passage. An example of Bembo's hesitancy to form hard and fast rules, or to be overdogmatic occurs in his observations on the distance between recurring rhymes (Pozzi 139). He suggests that it is better not to place four or five lines between rhyme words (moderation is his ideal), but he would trust the ear of the poet more than a fixed rule; besides, Petrarch, on occasion, broke this rule. When he finishes his discussion of the major sound effects, he will not be pinned down to a strict dogma, but claims that any sound can produce the opposite effect depending on its context and use in the poem.

After discussing the three elements that produce *gravità* and *piacevolezza,* he includes a brief discussion of decorum (Dionysius's fourth category) and persuasive style. At this point Bembo returns to the principle of moderation. He states an author must be careful with these effects because, if carried to extremes, they produce undesired results. All extremes are a vice: gravity, if overdone, can become austerity, and pleasantness can fall into degeneracy:

> quando se vede che agevolmente, procacciando la gravità, passare si può più oltra entrando nell'austerità dello stile, . . . pigliando quelle voci per oneste che sono rozze, e per grandi le ignave, e per piene di dignità le severe, e per magnifiche le pompose. E, d'altra parte, cercando la piacevolezza, puossi trascorrere e scendere al dissoluto, credendo quelle voci graziose essere, che ridicule sono, e le imbellettate vaghe, e le insiepide dolci, e le stridevoli soavi. (Pozzi 156)

> (when we see that easily, seeking gravity, one can pass beyond entering into austerity of style, . . . choosing those words as hon-

est that are coarse, as great the lazy, as full of dignity the severe and as magnificent the pompous. And, on the other hand, approaching pleasantness, one can surpass it and sink to the dissolute, believing those words to be pretty that are ridiculous, and the painted and made-up to be beautiful, and the insipid to be sweet, and the shrill to be smooth.)

These descriptive terms give a final evaluation of the grave and pleasant, by specifying the nature of their abuse.

In treating persuasion, which is not one of the items included in Dionysius's list of causes, Bembo returns to the basis of the rhetorical tradition, but not just to restate a well-known commonplace. By persuasion in this context, he indicates that the sound of the words must in themselves be persuasive: "Ma io non dico ora persuasione in generale e in universo; ma dico quella occulta virtù che, in ogni voce dimorando, commuove altrui ad assentire a cciò che egli legge" (But I do not speak of persuasion in general or universally; but I am speaking of the hidden power which, residing in every word, moves another to agree to that which he [or she] is reading) (Pozzi 157). Thus, the sound system outlined by Bembo is an integral part of the final effect and success of the composition.

As a final commentary on Bembo's exposition of the sound system that must be employed in successful composition, one must note that *piacevolezza* plays a less important role than its counterpart. Bembo nearly always speaks of creating gravity in the first place, and pleasantness is either summarized quickly or even passed over. Nearly all of the truly sonorous effects of the language are associated with gravity, and the humorous and even dissonant are associated with the effect that was defined as smooth and sweet. The distinction between the high and low style has dominated and somewhat reformed the categories from their original conception. The pleasant effect is always thought of as debasing the style, and twice he warns against such excesses, as the use of too many rhymes, "che la piacevolezza non avilsca" (so that pleasantness does not degrade) (141), or of too many heptasyllables, which "potesse avilire" (can degrade) (155). The idea of the low style constantly forces its presence into the discussion and makes the distinction between the two effects somewhat difficult.

Historians of Italian literature agree that Bembo altered significantly the course of sixteenth-century Petrarchism, not only in Italy, but in all of Europe. Bembo was a very powerful literary and ecclesiastical figure, exercising the type of authority that is difficult for us to contextualize in our own culture. Wilkins speaks of Bembo's "attainment and lordly exercise of literary dictatorship" (284), and Whitfield concludes: "His authority swelled with his age. . . . In his own day the weight of his reputation could crush a would-be rebel like Antonio Brocardo" (163). The fact that Garcilaso's friends sent his Latin poetry to Bembo for approval and that Bembo expressed high admiration for the young poet (there is no evidence he received any of the Spanish works) shows that Garcilaso was being groomed for a major literary career. Bembo's authority and influence brought about a strong reaction against the fifteenth-century Petrarchists, whom even modern critics disparage: "With Cariteo, Tebaldeo, and Serafino Aquilano, however, the [Petrarchan] style degenerated into reckless extravagance, with exaggerated conceits and hyperbole" (Weiss, 99). Bembo created a new appreciation of Petrarch and established Petrarchism as the European vogue of the sixteenth century: "The work of Serafino had been frivolous; with Pietro Bembo . . . came the return to Petrarch's form, his balanced diction and his ethos" (Forster 26). Bonora says of Bembo's influence: "Al Bembo e ai suoi seguaci il Petrarca prestava una lingua poetica perfetta, nobile e capace, come nessun'altra, di esprimere i grandi temi dell'amore e della morte" (To Bembo and his followers Petrarch provided a perfect poetic language, noble and capable as no other, of expressing the great themes of love and death) (57). Forster, who overlooks the importance of the *Prose,* sums up the effect of the influence of Bembo's poetry: "Petrarch became a classic, like Cicero or Virgil. Grace and dignity become the main stylistic criteria. Bembo quotes and elaborates Petrarchan lines and phrases, always with restraint, always with good taste, but practically never with inspiration" (28). Wilkins sums up the influence of Bembo in the early sixteenth century: "In his train hosts of Italian poets and poetesses strove to imitate Petrarch—or Bembo—or each other" (284). Both Antonio Brocardo and Bernardo Tasso (before their rebellion discussed in the next chapter) began their careers as Bemboesque Petrarchists, and each had composed an index of acceptable Petrarchan expressions. Nicolò Franco summed up best Bembo's contributions to Petrarchism in the concluding couplet to a sonnet on Bembo's death: "che se non eri tu mastron di tutti, / tutti sariemo stati Tebaldei" (for if you had not been the great master of everyone, everyone of us would have been Tebaldeos) (98).

Navagero, Boscán's instructor in Italianate forms, was a close friend of Bembo and had read the *Prose* in manuscript long before its publication in September 1525, one year before his conversation with Boscán in Granada. Bembo worked on the *Prose* over a twenty-five-year period and it was well known among his circle of Venetian friends. His first reference to beginning "alcune notazione della lingua" (Marti vi) dates from 1500. Dionysius of Halicarnassus's treatise on literary composition, which Bembo utilized so extensively in the second book of his own treatise, had first been published by Aldus in volume 1 of *Rhetores Graeci* in 1508. By 1512, Bembo had completed the first two books of his work, which he sent to various friends in that year, including Navagero (Dionisotti-Casalone 185). The third book was probably finished in 1519, when Navagero made reference in his correspondence to a work on the Italian language by Bembo (Marti viii). The conversation between Navagero and Boscán probably included a discussion of Bembo's observations. Boscán recalls that the topic of experimenting with Italian metrical forms came up while they were discussing the differences between languages: "Porque estando un día en Granada con el Navagero, . . . tratando con él en cosas de ingenio y de letras y *especialmente en las variedades de las muchas lenguas,* me dixo por qué no provara en lengua castellana sonetos y otras artes de trobas usadas por los buenos authores de Italia" (*Obras* 89; italics mine). Navagero, a humanist thoroughly competent in Greek and Latin (as was Boscán to a lesser degree), probably would have had the ideas of Dionysius and Bembo as a basis for discussing the differences between languages. Boscán seems to indicate that his first attempts to write in Italian meters were hindered by complexities that may have gone beyond the problems of scansion: "Y assí comencé a tentar este género de verso, en el qual al principio hallé alguna dificultad por ser muy artificioso y tener muchas particularidades diferentes del nuestro" (*Obras* 89). Some of these difficulties with detail may have resulted from attempting to apply the sound system expounded by Bembo. Even though Boscán on occasion recalls an image of Serafino Dell'Aquila, it seems that the Petrarchism introduced into Spain was largely that of the moderate style advocated by Bembo, and probably included careful analysis of the phonetic patterns employed in poetry.

A rereading of Garcilaso's poetry in light of Bembo's theories of sound structure is made difficult by the differences between Tuscan and Castilian and by few indications of how Garcilaso interpreted and applied Bembo's ideas. We are aided in this task by the commentaries of Fernando de Herrera, who unhesitatingly applied Bembo's terminology and

ideas to Garcilaso's poetry. While Herrera's commentaries are very helpful, we must keep in mind that Herrera took no interest in explaining or
re-creating a historical sense of Garcilaso's understanding of Bembo. To
the contrary, Herrera consistently evaluated Garcilaso's poetry according
to his own criteria and norms, which he stated as universal truths. Since
Garcilaso's understanding of Bembo can only be gleaned from his poetry
and Herrera did not formally expound his understanding of Bembo, but
only alluded to it in various commentaries, an evaluation of the influence
of Bembo on Garcilaso must depend on several speculative conclusions
based on Garcilaso's poetic practice and Herrera's seemingly random
commentaries on the subject. Even though William Ferguson has studied
Herrera's commentaries on the sound structure of the language in relationship to Herrera's own poetic production, his observations are of little
help in the elucidation of Garcilaso's poetry because he did not recognize
Herrera's source in Bembo's treatise. He therefore expounds Herrera's
thought in relation to Herrera's own poetic practice and does not take
up the question of Garcilaso's use of these ideas.

The adaptation of Bembo's ideas to the rather different circumstances
of the Spanish language confronts several obstacles. Even though Tuscan
and Castilian are very similar in many respects, a number of those elements that Bembo found to be essential in the sound system do not exist
in Spanish. Most serious is the absence of long and short vowels, the
element on which Bembo based his concepts of number and gravity. In
addition, one cannot in Spanish shorten words by apocope as freely as in
Italian, making it more difficult to alter the sound patterns. The relative
scarcity of doubled consonants in Spanish removes a good number of
possibly grave syllables. In addition, i and u occur much less frequently
in Spanish than in Italian, and almost never in final position. Garcilaso's
consonant system did, however, include two of the affricates praised by
Bembo for their gravity, the z (dz) and $ç$ (ts).

From Bembo's definition of number, one might conclude a priori that
it could not apply to Spanish at all. He defines "numero" as the time
allotted to each syllable making it either long or short (Pozzi 143). Since
Spanish generally does not have vowel lengthening, it would seem that
the concept of number could not apply. Golden Age poets and *preceptistas,* however, employ widely the terms *número* and *numeroso,* neologisms from Latin signifying "rhythm" and "rhythmical." Garcilaso himself uses the expression "verso numeroso" in Eclogue II (1105), and the
terms *número* and *numeroso* stand as praise in many poetical commen-

taries of the Golden Age. What the Spaniards meant by number is the rhythm, and even though long and short syllables do not exist in Spanish, the concept of number does exist. It cannot, without careful examination, be related to Bembo's terminology.

In spite of the lack of clear indications of how Bembo's ideas would apply to Spanish and how Garcilaso would have interpreted Bembo's rules for sound production, Herrera expressed no doubts about the veracity of Bembo's system of sound underlay or the possibility of applying it to Spanish. He uses Bembo's terminology to refer to the sound structure in Garcilaso's poetry, and in addition, found these ideas effective in the creation of his own poetry (Ferguson 11). In his introductory essay on the history of Italian forms, in reviewing Italian and Spanish authors, Herrera allotted second place to Bembo as a poet (but noted that not everyone agreed):

> Sannazaro . . . tuviera el segundo lugar en esta poesía si el Bembo no se le hubiera anticipado con la pureza y claridad de sus rimas, y con la suavidad y terneza de los números; el cual, aunque fue juzgado por duro y afectado de voces y estilo, fue sólo verdadero y primero conocedor de todas las flores, de quien se adorna la lengua italiana y latina y de él se aprendió a imitar. (H-1).

Herrera's final observation on Bembo as a master of imitation makes clear his dependence on Bembo's ideas both in his commentaries and in his own poetry.

Herrera's commentaries on Garcilaso are replete with critical concepts and vocabulary taken from Bembo's *Prose*. He summarized the effect of Garcilaso's poetry as a perfect blending of the sweet and grave: "Garcilaso es dulce y grave (la cual mezcla estima Tulio por muy difícil)" (H-1). He often uses the terms "número" and "numeroso," and occasionally "sonido." He shows little interest in variation. In Sonnet XXIV, he comments on the iambic rhythm of line 10, "con dulce son que'l curso al agua enfrena": "Lleno y numeroso verso" (H-146). He finds the rhythm to be one of the outstanding characteristics of Sonnet XIX: "este numeroso y bellísimo y afectuoso soneto" (H-120). As in Bembo, gravity is related to ideas of decorum, social class, and the concept of literary styles. Poetic elements that have "gravedad" are noble and elevated, indicated by words such as "grande," "generoso," and "noble." In Sonnet V he uses "ilustre," "noble," and "generoso" to describe the effect of the last three lines: "Todo este terceto es de espléndida y numerosa oración, con que se muestra más amoroso su enamorado intento, y más ilustres y nobles las palabras generosas" (H-40). On Sonnet XII he comments on the greatness and nobility of the sound of line 2, "loco, imposible, vano, temeroso": "Verso de grande y generoso espíritu y sonido" (H-82). However, he finds the last line of Sonnet XXIII, "por no hazer mudança en su costumbre," to lack nobility of sound: "Este es lánguido y casi muerto verso, y muy plebeyo modo de hablar. Y fue común falta en aquella edad no sólo de los nuestros, pero de los toscanos, acabar el soneto no con la fuerza y espíritu de los cuarteles, sino floja y desmayadamente" (H-137).

Herrera also accepted Bembo's distinction between *gravità* and *piacevolezza,* frequently labeling a verse as "grave" or "con gravedad." In two early commentaries, Herrera delineated the two principal methods of generating "gravedad," one depending on vowels and the other on consonants. In the first commentary, on line 1 of Sonnet I, "Cuando me paro a contemplar mi' stado," Herrera commented on the gravity created by the *a*'s and *o*'s: "Este verso por las vocales primera y cuarta, que tiene tan repetidas, es muy grave, porque son grandes y llenas y sonoras; y por eso hacen la voz numerosa con gravedad" (H-2). Goodwyn has also commented the sound patterns in this line ("Una teoría"), but he was not aware of the relationship between Bembo and Herrera's ideas. Herrera notes only the concurrence of several *a*'s and *o*'s, although the gravity of the sound clearly depends in large part on the four tonic *a*'s, while the four tonic *o*'s are less prominent. One could also refer to the sequence *a–o,* and the consonant clusters (*nd, nt, mpl, rm, st*) in this line as a source of gravity. In several places, Herrera indicates that consonants produce gravity. He recognizes that many consonants make a line grave in the commentary on line 4 of Sonnet III, "gentes, costumbres, lenguas he pasado": "El verso, que tiene muchas consonantes, es grave, tardo y lleno como éste" (H-22). He is obviously referring to the number of consonants, that is, consonant clusters, and not their individual quality of sound. Undoubtedly, he means to signal not only the internal consonant clusters in "gentes," "costumbres," and "lenguas," but also the double consonants formed by the juncture of the words, the *sc* and *sl.* In another commentary he speaks of the consonants brought together by the juncture of words. On line 2 of Sonnet VIII, "salen espirtus vivos y encendidos," he comments on the number of *s*'s: "Este verso está muy lleno de la *s,* y por esto los griegos lo llaman polysigma, cuando este elemento se dobla muchas veces. Pero aquí por no herirse una *s* con otra no es insuave sonido" (H-60). Herrera is referring to the juncture of two *s*'s between words, as occurs rarely in other lines of Garcilaso: "salidos sin" (Canción I, 41), "tetas secas" (Eclogue II, 510), and "fieras salvajes su gobierno" (Eclogue III, 340). With Dionysius's proscription of the *s* echoing in his memory, Herrera suggests that double *s*'s would produce a harsh sound, especially those brought together at the juncture of words.

Herrera added that gerunds produce gravity. Commenting on line 85 of Canción IV, "estoy cantando yo, y está sonando," he finds it a grave line whose sound reinforces both the gravity of the situation and the references to music and sound: "Estos gerundios son altas dicciones de ancho y largo espíritu, y graves en su movimiento; y la semejante cadencia del verso hace mucho afecto para el intento" (H-232). Another commentary on the *canciones* clarifies these ideas: "Escogió *ondas* por *aquas,* porque es dicción más sonora y llena y más grave" (H-215). Bembo had ranked the *o* in the third place below the *a* and *e,* while Herrera and the Spanish *preceptistas* gave priority to the *o* over the *e* (Ferguson 17). In this case, Herrera gives the *o* priority over the *a,* probably because of the effect of the double consonant and because he remembered Bembo had praised the word *onde.* Herrera concluded the previous commentary with examples of grave words. His criterion takes into account the level of diction (distinguishing between the grave and sublime) as well as the sound of the word: "más grave es *procela* que *viento, ruina* que *caída, pesadumbre* que *grandeza,* y *onda* que *agua.* Gravedad es de peso; sublimidad de dignidad; y así la voz grave significa más vehemencia, y la sublime más magnificencia y resplandor, y añade majestad a dicción grave" (H-215). In his commentaries Herrera establishes the chief ways in which the poet achieves gravity: (1) repetition of the same vowel sounds, especially the dark sonorous vowels *a* and *o,* and (2) the use of consonant clusters (especially the nasals), which occur in the verses he labels as "grave."

Bembo's opposing term, *piacevolezza,* is more difficult to render in Spanish. Herrera has less occasion to use it since he is mainly commenting on a serious poet, but the occasional use of "suave" and "dulce" seems to indicate that Herrera rendered with these Spanish terms Bembo's *piacevolezza.* Recalling that rhetorical tradition opposed *gravitas* and *suavitas,* just as Horace contrasted *utile* and *dulce,* one sees that Herrera's terms do not miss the mark, although he seems to interpret "suavidad" as more a gentleness of sound than pleasantness and lightness. He explains "suave" in his commentary on the octave of Sonnet XXVI: "Suaves son todos estos ocho primeros versos, porque la suavidad de la oración es donde no hay muchas consonantes, y se evitan los elementos ásperos" (H-155). He makes the same point about Sonnet XII, but using the word "dulce": "En este soneto se hallan muchas sinalefas. . . . Estas suenan más dulcemente que las consonantes, y por eso forman la oración blanda y delicada; pero no por eso deja de hacerse grande y llena por el concurso de ellas" (H-81). Like Dionysius and Bembo, Herrera classifies the *l* as one of the consonants producing "dulzura." He uses both "dulzura" and "suave" in reference to the sound of the *l*: "Es landacismo, donde la *l* suena muchas veces. Dionisio Alicarnáseo entre todas las semivocales da la ventaja a la *l*, por la dulzura con que las vence, y el concurso que se hace de ellas, es más suave" (H-189). In conclusion, Herrera uses "suavidad" and "dulzura" to reproduce in Spanish Bembo's concept of *piacevolezza,* but with a slight shift of meaning. While Bembo's term included the pleasant and even the jocular, encompassing the low style, Herrera's use of the term seems to indicate more a sweetness or lightness of sound, but not grandiloquence. He finds the paucity of consonants and elision to be elements, along with the *l*, that create this effect.

Herrera finds that these sounds often reinforce the meaning of the poem. The whole first quatrain of Sonnet IV has a grave sound that supports the meaning: "Todo este cuartel es artificiosísimo en composición y gravedad, y descubre su afecto con la pesadumbre de la contextura, dicciones y número" (H-31). Even the effect he labels "desmayado" and which he at times criticizes as ineffective can have an appropriate effect. Commenting on the last line of Sonnet III, "y si esto lo es, tampoco podré habello," he finds it of weak sound, but perfect for the context: "Flojo y desmayado verso, y sin ornato y composición alguna para remate de tan hermoso soneto, pero artificioso para lo que pretende; porque con aquel lasamiento y número caído y sin espíritu descubre su intención" (H-29).

Behind Herrera's profusion of descriptive terms there lies an inconsistency in thought and terminology. The grave style seems to have most of the sonorous elements: the open vowels and rich consonants. The smooth and sweet style is marked by close vowels and fewer consonants; he characterizes it as having a lack of tone and dignity that could degenerate into a "muy plebeyo modo de hablar." In his commentary on Sonnet XXV, he defends Garcilaso's ending the poem on rhyme words, "vean," etc., that lack a consonant between the rhyming vowels: "mas casi oso afirmar, que es vicio acabarse siempre en vocales, porque carecen de variación y se pierde mucha parte de la grandeza, sonoridad y número" (H-154). Fewer consonants produce a smooth sound that can, according to Herrera, degenerate to a lack of rhythm and proper sonority. The smooth and sweet is not full and sonorous, but close and rapid. While these elements could correspond in part to Bembo's *piacevolezza*, which included both humor and jokes, they do not fit Herrera's categories, which have been revised from Bembo's thought along the lines of classical rhetoric. There is a very clear sense in which the grave style, as described by Herrera, could easily be called smooth and sweet, and the other category, which treats the low classes, could be called dissonant and jarring, rather than smooth and sweet. At the base of Herrera's thought is the distinction of *res* and *verba,* the didactic and the frivolous. In this sense the didactic should be ponderous and heavy, while the frivolous would be light and attractive to the senses, rather than to the intellect. Herrera's application of these ideas to Garcilaso's poetry finds the grave style to be sonorous, and the sweet and smooth to verge on vulgarity (*plebeyo modo de hablar*) and vapidity (*desmayado*). That these effects could be labeled smooth and sweet seems to belie their essential nature.

Bembo's *Prose della vulgar lingua* provides a fundamental key not only for understanding Herrera's commentaries on Garcilaso's poetry, but also for appreciating the poetry of Garcilaso. Herrera's commentaries offer useful clarification of the adaptation of Bembo's rules to Spanish poetry. It is not unlikely that Garcilaso would have known of Bembo's rules for imitation, and that he experimented with them in a certain period, especially in the Petrarchan sonnets and *canciones* where much artful sound structuring is evident.

Garcilaso began writing sonnets in the Petrarchan manner, some of them probably within the norms of imitation established by Bembo. This sound patterning seems to occur in a limited number of poems, mainly those sonnets that one could classify as Petrarchan and the four *canciones,* while the late poetry tends to avoid Bemboesque sound structure. Eclogue III, for example, ends with alternating stanzas of sweetness and bitterness, but there is no trace of Bemboesque sound patterning, even though the ideas of pleasantness and gravity are clearly indicated by the text. The sound structure studied by Montgomery in Sonnet XXIII is based on the contrast of open and close vowels. The latter are, as the critic explains, used for the effect of heightening the sense of finality. One could also argue that they underlay the poem and its lighthearted spirit with a sense of lightness. Those sonnets that I have classified as late and as reactions against Petrarchism, however, generally do not have the sound patterning evident in the sonnets of the Petrarchan period. In addition to the lines pointed out by Herrera as grave, there are remarkable examples of sound patterning in other sonnets. Sonnet IX is a case in point: line 1 has three tonic *o*'s and four *s*'s: "Señora mía, si yo de vos ausente." Both lines 3 and 4 have three tonic *e*'s and four atonic *e*'s: "paréceme que ofendo a lo que os quiero / y al bien de que gozava en ser presente." Line 5 has four tonic *e*'s: "tras éste luego siento otro acidente." Sonnet V is probably the poem that is most carefully constructed. Lines 1 and 5 exploit the use of words employing *es,* especially *est:* "Escrito 'stá en mi alma vuestro gesto." Line 5, in addition, has four tonic *e*'s and four repetitions of *est:* "En esto estoy y estaré siempre puesto." Azara found these lines overworked, and commented: "Los versos 5 y 9 de este soneto son durísimos" (A-5). Sonnet X has a remarkably grave sound pattern in the last line, not only with four *m*'s, six *t*'s and two tonic *i*'s (fulfilling Bembo's observation that any sound, even if of one defined characteristic, can be used to the opposite effect in another sound context), but it also repeats the syllables *memor:* "verme morir entre memorias tristes."

Also important is the recurrence of rhyme. Bembo noted that fewer rhymes with more distance between them produced gravity, while closer rhymes and short lines produced pleasantness. Sonnet X, however, seems to produce a gravity in the accumulation of heavy sounds. The sextet has only two rhymes (instead of three), and each one is a variation on the other, and both consist of heavy consonant sounds: "-astes" and "-istes." Sonnet I also creates this effect with three rhymes: "-arte," "-arme," and "-ello."

The clearest idea of how Garcilaso interpreted and applied Bembo's concept of sound underlay comes from the envoi of Canción IV:

> Canción, si quien te viere se espantare
> de la instabilidad y ligereza
> y rebuelta del vago pensamiento,
> estable, grave y firme es el tormento,
> le di, . . .

> (161–65)

In these lines, Garcilaso is summarizing the effects of the poem itself, claiming that if to some people it seems to be frivolous, it does in fact treat a very serious subject. The series of three terms used to describe these effects are, as Herrera noted, opposites: "instabilidad" / "estable," "ligereza" / "grave," and "rebuelta" / "firme." Not only do the central pair of opposites "ligereza" (162) and "grave" (164) recall Bembo's stylistic terms (Bembo occasionally used *leggiadro* in place of *piacevole*), but the lines in which they are found also partake of the respective sound symbolism. Line 162 has five *i*'s, three *l*'s, three *d*'s, and a *b*, while line 164 has seven pairs of double consonants and two tonic *a*'s. The short *i* in "firme" is checked by the double consonant, making it graver than the *i*'s in line 162. Line 162 is visually much shorter and can be spoken rapidly, whereas line 164 is longer and reads much slower because of the doubled consonants and forced stops. These two lines not only serve as proof of Garcilaso's familiarity with Bembo's ideas of sound underlay, but also provide an idea of how he applied them to Spanish. To create gravity, he used double consonants and forced pauses to slow the line, while the opposite effect is created with short vowels, *l*'s, and rapid single consonants. The contrast in sense and sound is very effectively achieved.

The observations on sound structuring by Bembo open a new window to the study of Spanish Golden Age poetry. This chapter makes clear that Garcilaso employed these ideas, at least in a certain phase of his career. Ferguson has studied Herrera's use of sound patterning, Herrera being a particularly useful example because he expounds his basic ideas in his commentaries on Garcilaso's poetry and because the variants in Herrera's own poems can be dated, showing the direction in which he worked in revising his poems. The rest of Spanish Golden Age poetry is yet to be studied. A very clear example of sound patterning by Francisco de Aldana shows that Bembo's ideas had circulated beyond Garcilaso and Herrera. In the second quatrain of a sonnet, Aldana employs Bembo's sound structure to great advantage in a humorous context:

> buscan quien les absuelva esta quistión
> con viva diligencia y suma cura,
> y es tan alta, tan honda y tan oscura
> que no hay quien dalle pueda solución.
>
> (128)

Line 6 has only one double consonant and five short vowels, three *i*'s, and two tonic *u*'s. The sound of this verse underlines the jocular style, and the mock gravity of the following line, with its *a*'s and *o*'s, contrasts the two styles. The poem uses the short vowels for humor and assumes a tone of pseudogravity to talk about the profundity of the subject matter. Undoubtedly a good number of poems await analysis in future studies.

Herrera seems to have had no doubts about how sound worked in Garcilaso's poetry. In light of Bembo's theories and Garcilaso's attempts to assimilate the Italian manner, it would seem Herrera was correctly perceiving a subtle aspect of Garcilaso's poetry, and not simply inventing a sound structure based on coincidence. E. M. Wilson has commented on Herrera's dislike of certain common words, such as "alimañas" in the Ode (Wilson 174). In the case of "tamaño" used as an adjective in Sonnet IX, Herrera does not criticize the archaic or popular nature of the word, but that its sound led him to expect a conceit where none exists: "Porque no hay cosa más importuna y molesta, que el sonido y juntura de palabras cultas y numerosas, sin que resplandezca en ellas algún pensamiento grave o agudo, o alguna lumbre de erudición" (H-72). Unless Herrera is substituting one criticism to mask a deeper dislike of a popular word, he shows a much greater sensitivity to the nuances of this sound system than we understand. That he could claim such a depth of sensitivity suggests that we may be a long way from appreciating the full range and timbre of Spanish Golden Age poetry.

5

Bernardo Tasso and the Beginnings of Anti-Petrarchism

Bembo's ideas on imitation influenced Garcilaso greatly in the period of his apprenticeship in the Italianate style. The majority of his extant works, however, are not Petrarchan in inspiration, but are revivals of classical genres in vernacular verse. In these works he follows an innovation announced by the Italian poet Bernardo Tasso in the preface to his *Libro primo degli amore* in 1531 as a conscious rebellion against courtly love and Petrarchan lyric formulas. The idea of writing poetry in imitation of classical models in the vernacular was an innovation that Garcilaso and Boscán readily embraced. Their ode, elegies, epistles, eclogues, *fábula,* and *capítulo* were on the cutting edge of the new verse. Not only had they introduced Petrarchan forms of expression into Spanish, but they represent the first reaction against them. Petrarch died in 1371, and several vogues and revivals of Petrarchism had occurred. By the time Garcilaso and Boscán began writing in the Italian Petrarchan mode, the Neoplatonic ideas of love had begun to replace Petrarchism in Italian verse. Boscán wrote Neoplatonic sonnets and added a third book with a *fábula, epístolas, capítulo,* etc. Garcilaso also used Neoplatonic imagery and abandoned Petrarchan expression for the classical forms of the ode, elegy, eclogues, and epistle. This is clearly a third stage in their poetry, quite distinct from their sonnets and *canciones* in the Petrarchan mode.

Both Garcilaso and Boscán compressed into their lifetimes several centuries of developments in Italian poetry.

Boscán began experimenting with Italianate versification in 1526, one year after the appearance in print of Bembo's *Prose della volgar lingua*. Boscán's and Garcilaso's first works in Italianate verse were undoubtedly conceived within the Petrarchan tradition, and moreover probably attempted to comply with Bembo's strict canons of imitation. Their careers as Petrarchists, however, were cut short by other developments in Italian poetry. In spite of the prevailing mode of Petrarchism and the great influence of Bembo's treatise among Italian poets, other options for vernacular poetry, more in line with the Renaissance admiration for the classics, were also emerging. At the same time that many writers in Italian were following Bembo and returning to a closer imitation of Petrarch, other poets were beginning to speculate on and experiment with how to transform the lyric forms of the ancients and the humanists into the vernacular language. Trissino, Alamanni, and Tolomei were experimenting with the forms of the Pindaric ode, imitating the metrics of the strophe, antistrophe, and epode in Italian, including, in the case of Tolomei, the use of classical feet (Bonora 68). In spite of the classicizing elements in Trissino's and Alamanni's odes, their experiments tended to treat the ode as a problem of external form and they found few followers (Williamson "Form").

In 1529, Giovan Giorgio Trissino (1478–1550) published in his *Rime* ten *canzone*, three of which attempted through stanzaic irregularities and the lack of an envoi to represent the form of the Pindaric ode. Two of these (XXXI and LXV) achieved the triadic effect of the Pindaric ode by introducing a different rhyme scheme for the third and sixth stanzas. Trissino labeled these *canzone*, and it might take an attentive reader to notice that stanzas 1, 2, 4, and 5 had one rhyme scheme, while 3 and 6 had a different one. One final *canzone* (LXXVII) achieves the triadic effect through the use of longer stanzas for the third and sixth stanzas. In addition, the effect of classical versification is imitated through an unrhymed verse. These were the same methods Trissino had used in 1519 to render the choral odes in his play *Sofonisba* (Hauvette 226).

Almost contemporaneous with Tasso's development of the Horatian ode, Luigi Alamanni (1495–1556), following Trissino's lead, also experimented with the Pindaric ode. In his *Opere toscane* (1532–33), he introduced new forms in imitation of the ode. For these compositions he employed the genre name hymn in preference to ode. He indicated his attempt to imitate Pindar by labeling the stanzas *ballata, contraballata,* and *stanza,* rendering in Italian the names strophe, antistrophe, and epode (Hauvette 227). Like Trissino, he changed the length of the third and sixth stanzas and eliminated the envoi (228). Alamanni's hymns imitate Pindar in other ways, by celebrating victories, relating the victors to their family origins, and recounting historic narrations concerning their pasts.

Another option, and the one that exercised tremendous influence over Garcilaso and Boscán, was the idea of adapting classical subject matter into traditional vernacular verse forms. In the dedication to the first edition of his *Gli amore* (1531), Bernardo Tasso (1493–1569) announced this innovation. He explained that most of the poems in the volume followed the old manner of imitation of the best Provençal and Tuscan poets, but at the end he had included a few poems in a new vein that used classical subject matter in traditional Italian meters. Typical of much literary criticism on sixteenth-century poetry, critics often observe that Bernardo Tasso's poems are dedicated to Genevra Malatesta, but overlook the fact that the preface addressed to her is a literary manifesto.

Historians of Italian literature have generally given little notice to the importance of Bernardo Tasso's reaction to Bembo's prescriptions, and as a poet, he has come to hold a very minor place in the history of Italian literature. He was quite famous during his lifetime as a writer of letters, and the published collections of his letters served as models for diplomatic and personal correspondence. *Gli Amadigi,* his long *romanza,* although very popular during his lifetime, never gained the acceptance of those of his predecessors and successors, and Tasso's fame has been eclipsed by Ariosto, Boiardo, and his own son Torquato Tasso. His lyric poetry has often been compared to his letters, as the expressions of a consummate courtier. Perhaps Torquato himself, not only because of his own success, but through his expressed judgment, was partially responsible for the eclipse of his father's fame:

> mio Padre, il quale nondimeno fece professione di Cortegiano, no di Poeta, ò le sue propie lodi furono quelle, che egli meritava in corte; l'altre degli studi sono state accidentali, ò ricercate da lui dopo la sodisfattione de i Patroni che egli serviva, a i quali principalmente cercava de compiacere. (Williamson, *Bernardo* 35)

> (My father, however, was a courtier, not a poet, and his own praises were those that he earned in court; his other attainments

were incidental and were sought by him for the satisfaction of the patrons whom he served and whom he tried to please above all.)

Williamson agrees with this judgment: "This is indeed the heart of the matter, for Bernardo was not a poet but a courtier-poet. The type did not survive the renaissance" (35). In light of the changes of direction implied in Tasso's literary proclamations and as seen in his pastoral sonnets, odes, and pagan themes, these judgments dismiss his lyric unfairly. Even critics who recognize the importance of these innovations label his poetry as cold and uninspired (Toffanin, *Il cinquecento* 505). The importance of Tasso's poetic revolution has been lost among the large poetic outpouring of sixteenth-century Italy; more specifically, it has suffered in comparison with the fame of his son.

Tasso's ideas differed markedly with those implied in Alamanni's and Trissino's experiments with Pindaric verse forms. Rather than transform Italian metrical forms, he placed greater emphasis on a change in content. His proposal differs even more sharply with Bembo's idea of continuing to imitate medieval poetic material and style. His dedicatory letter clearly distinguishes between Petrarchism, most probably as proclaimed by Bembo, and a new style of imitating the best classical writers of Rome and Greece:

> De tre miei libri adunque (che tanti appunto sono) intitolati gli Amore, non potendo ora per nove occupazioni fargli tuttatre imprimere, solo in luce ne verrà il primiero, composto ad imitazione de' moderni Provenzali e di messer Francesco Petrarca. Et hovvi nella fine aggiunto alcune altre poche rime, cantate secondo la via e l'arte de gli antiqui boni poeti Greci e Latini. . . . (1)

> (Of my three books therefore (for that many are ready) entitled *The Loves,* not being able because of new duties to publish all three, only the first of them will come to light, which is written in imitation of the modern Provençals and of Francesco Petrarca. And I have at the end of the book added a few other poems, sung according to the manner and art of the ancient good Greek and Latin poets. . . .)

Tasso announced that the majority of his poems imitate the Tuscan and Provençal style—an obvious reference to courtly love poetry, especially the Italian master Petrarch. Tasso began his poetic career as a follower of Bembo. He had composed a treatise on Petrarch (now lost) that was to serve as a guide to imitation. That he called it "un tesoro della lingua" suggests it followed Bembo's principles of imitation. Even as late as 1529 he was sending poems to Bembo for correction (Cerboni Baiardi 39–40). In the prologue he states that, while most of the poems are in an older mode, he has added a few at the end that are in a new mode in imitation of the best Greek and Latin poets—not in versification and metrics, but in subject matter and style. The additional poems are contained in a section that begins on page 47. The section is not marked by a formal title, but by the fact that the previous page (46v) is blank. The poem that begins on page 47 is a long untitled poem, one of three such poems that in later editions Tasso would group together and label as "Hinni et ode."

In 1531, Bernardo Tasso did not claim to be an innovator in poetic stylistics but asserted he took his lead from others. His attitude was one of humility and almost a refusal to accept the responsibility for having broken with tradition. He states the idea of using the subject matter of the best Greek and Roman poets in Italian verse was urged on him by Antonio Brocardo:

> Ne pensate ch'io fosse stato si presuntuoso che l'avessi pubblicate giamai se prima molti letterati uomini e ben intendenti di poesia non me l'avessero persuaso; e specialmente quella ben nata e felice anima di messer Antonio Broccardo, che'n questi di, con universal danno et infinito dispiacere d'ogni spirito gentile, immaturamente passò di questa vita; il quale, se qualch'anno ancora vivuto fosse, avrebbe in questa via mandato fuori degne scritture del suo altissimo engegno. Egli non solamente me ne persuase, ma con fortissime ragioni mi dimostrò ch'io devea al tutto farlo. (3)

> (Do not think that I would have been so presumptuous to have published this if first many lettered men well versed in poetry had not persuaded me, and especially that well-born and happy soul of Antonio Broccardo, who on this day, with universal harm and infinite displeasure to every one, prematurely passed from this life, who, if he had lived another year, would have sent forth in this manner writings worthy of his very high genius. He not only persuaded me of it, but with very strong reasons he demonstrated to me that I should do it wholeheartedly.)

According to his contemporaries, Antonio Brocardo (c. 1500–1531) was a quick-witted and gifted poet whose early death cut short a brilliant career (Vitaliani 33–36). He left a very small collection of poetry, some forty-seven poems in all, which display few of the characteristics attributed to him by Tasso. Like Tasso he too began as a follower of Bembo and was a close disciple. He too had composed a vocabulary of canonized words from Petrarch and Boccaccio, listing in each case the appropriate adjective that could be used to describe the term (Vitaliani 21–22). Tasso greatly admired Brocardo who figures large in his *Libro primo*. At the end of the first section (those poems that imitate the medieval style) there are six sonnets on the death of Antonio Brocardo (44v–46). The first two sonnets are addressed to the deceased poet; the third sonnet to Brocardo's mistress Marietta Mirtilla, consoling her on the poet's death; and the last three to other friends concerning Brocardo's death. The sonnet following the sixth, the very last poem of the Petrarchan section, makes no direct reference to Brocardo, but it could be construed as the voice of the dead poet predicating his fame on his love poetry. The poem takes on a more general character in later editions where it was placed first in the *Libro primo*.

Brocardo is remembered in literary histories for the bitter controversy he sustained with Pietro Bembo. Curiously enough, that the controversy existed is well documented, but the substance of the polemic has been lost. Some critics concluded, because of Brocardo's use of the *strambotto*, a form never used by Petrarch, but much favored by his fifteenth-century imitators, that Brocardo had advocated a continuation of the fifteenth-century Petrarchan mode. Others, familiar with Tasso's praises and Sperone's dialogue, have claimed that the cause of the polemic was Brocardo's decision to imitate the classics, rather than Petrarch, in vernacular poetry. If, as Tasso claimed, Brocardo had advocated openly the imitation of the classics, then such an innovation could easily run afoul of Bembo's ideas of creating a national poetry based on medieval Italian models. The early death of Brocardo, attributed by Pietro Aretino to the sharp criticism of his poetry, obscured the particulars of this debate. Tasso, through one of his poems in the 1531 edition, also became involved in the controversy, although his smooth art of diplomacy somehow saved his friendship with Bembo. Among Tasso's additional poems in the new style are pastoral sonnets on the poetic competition between Alcippo and Titiro, which Tasso's contemporaries believed were references to Brocardo's superiority over Pietro Bembo:

> Questa sampogna al cui soave et chiaro
>> Suono, talhora a le dolc'ombre estive
>> Cantar solea ne l'antenoree rive
>> Titiro fra Pastor famoso et raro,
> Vinse Alcippo cantando . . .
>
>> (48v)

> (This reed-pipe to whose smooth and clear
>> Sound, sometimes in the sweet summer shadows,
>> Titiro famous and rare among shepherds
>> was accustomed to sing on the Paduan shores,
> was conquered by Alcippo singing . . .)

Tasso saw his friendship with Bembo threatened by this sonnet and he wrote to a mutual friend claiming the poem had been misinterpreted. He begged the friend to intercede with Bembo on his behalf, claiming the sonnet was in praise of Pan:

> Il sonetto della dedicazione della sampogna, ch'io faccio a Pan, non solo ha posto a rumore questo Studio, ma tutta Europa, perche alcuni, volendo interpretarlo non secondo la sincerità della mia intenzione, ma secondo la malizia della loro volentà, hanno detto che sotto il nome de Titiro ho voluto intendere de Monsignor Bembo. . . . Io ho sempre pensato d'onorarlo; e conosciuto ch'egli era degno d'essere onorato de ciascuno. (*Delle lettere* 1:85)

> (The sonnet on the dedication of the reed-pipe, which I wrote to Pan, has caused rumors not only in the university, but in all Europe, because some, wanting to interpret it not according to the sincerity of my intentions, but according to the viciousness of their will, have said that under the name of Titiro I meant to indicate Bembo. . . . I have always thought to honor him, and have known him to be worthy of being honored by everyone.)

While Tasso excused himself for this sonnet only, in fact, the five sonnets that follow contain further references to the same contest, and to Alcippo (a name Brocardo used for himself in his own poetry), Titiro and Brocardo's beloved Marietta Mirtilla: "Cantiam le lodi sue sotto quel faggio / dov'io vinsi a cantar Titiro anchora" (Let's sing his praises under that beech tree, where I conquered Tytiro in singing) (49); "Di latte Alcippo, et di cornuto armento, / Il piu ricco pastor di questi monti, / Che Titiro l'altr'hier vinse cantando" (With milk and horned flock, Alcippo, the richest pastor of these mountains, who the other day conquered Titiro singing) (49v); and one sonnet that praises Mirtilla ends with the phrase "Cosi cantava Alcippo" (Thus sang Alcippo) (49v), leaving little doubt as to the identity of Alcippo. The identity of Titiro, a classical name for Virgil, still remains a mystery, although it possibly refers to Bembo. The poems refer to a poetic contest for which I have found no documentation.

The final references to Brocardo in the *Libro primo* occurs in a sonnet placed penultimate among the additional poems and dedicated to Antonio Brocardo celebrating the innovations in his poetic style:

> L'orme seguendo del tuo sacro ingegno,
>   Che pellegrino in questa parte, e'n quella
>   Ha mercato d'honor salma si bella,
>   Che ricco hor poggia ove ciascun e indegno;
> Scorgo del vero stil l'antiquo segno,
>   Ch'alza la fama altrui sovr'ogni stella;
>   Non noto anchor a quest'età novella,
>   A cui salir quanto posso m'ingegno;
> Et per quel calle, ove mi fosti scorta
>   Affretto i passi al desir tardi et lenti,
>   Lasciando l'altra via fallace et torta;
> Quant'io, Brocardo, et le future genti
>   Ti debbo et poesia, c'hor si conforta
>   D'accender gli honor suoi, ch'erano spenti.
>
>   (56)

> (Following the steps of your sacred intelligence,
>   as a pilgrim in this world, and in that other,
>   your beautiful remains have a market of honor
>   which now richly rest where others are unworthy;
> I perceive the ancient sign of the true style,
>   which fame raises for others above all the stars;
>   I do not yet see innovation in this age

which I strive, as much as I can, to leave.
And along that path, where you were my guide,
   I hurry my tardy and slow steps to desire,
   leaving the other way, false and crooked.
How much do I, Brocardo, and all future people
   owe you, and poetry also, which now is gratified
   in elevating its own honors, which were spent.)

Tasso's sonnet was perhaps intended as a dedicatory poem for the post-humous collection of Brocardo's poetry, which was not published until 1538. The "salma" in line 3 would refer to the poet's literary remains, his poems now placed in a marketplace. Tasso indicates the importance of Brocardo's idea by praising the revival of the ancient style in line 5. He does not find his contemporaries to be innovative and the poet wishes to emancipate himself from such a stagnating climate (lines 7–8). In the first tercet he indicates that he is a follower in this style and condemns the old style as twisted and false. The final tercet proclaims Tasso's indebtedness to Brocardo, as well as that of future generations and of poetry itself. The final words again characterize the state of poetry, saying that its honor had been spent, the word "spenti" signaling a rebellion against sixteenth-century Petrarchism. The celebration of Brocardo's innovations using ancient styles and the condemnation of Bemboesque Petrarchism could not be clearer.

Antonio Brocardo's poetry itself suggests little of this revolution, but he was later credited with having participated in it by Speroni Sperone (1500–1588), who used a character named Antonio Brocardo to expound his views in the dialogue *Della Retorica*. The character is modeled on the real-life Brocardo, for he states his aversion to studying law, which was forced upon the real poet by his father (Vitaliani 17). In the dialogue, Brocardo outlines the study of rhetoric and oration, especially in a courtroom context. Near the end of the dialogue, he states his ideas concerning lyric poetry in the vernacular. He details the constraints placed on him in his formation as a Petrarchist:

> con speranza grandissima di ciaschedun che mi conosceva io mi diedi al far versi. Allora pieno tutto di numeri, di sentenzie, e di parole petrarchesche e boccacciane, per certi anni fei cose a' miei amici maravigliose; poscia parendomi che la mia vena s'incominciasse a seccare (periocché alcune volte mi mancava i vocaboli e,

non avendo che dire, in diversi sonetti uno istesso concetto m'era
venuto ritratto), a quello ricorsi che fa il mondo oggidì e con
grandissima diligenzia fei un rimario o vocabulario volgare: nel
quale per alfabeto ogni parola che già usarono questi due, distin-
tamente riposi; oltra di ciò in un altro libro i modi loro del des-
criver le cose, giorno, notte, ira, pace, odio, amore, paura, spe-
ranza, bellezza sì fattamente racolsi, che né parola né concetto
non usciva di me, che le novelle e i sonetti loro non me ne fossero
exempio. Vedete voi oggimai a qual bassezza discesi e in che
stretta prigione e con che lacci m'incantenai. (Pozzi 662)

(with great hope of everyone who knew me, I gave myself to writing poetry. Then all full of Petrarchan and Boccaccian rhythms,
sentences and words, for a number of years I wrote things marvel-
ing my friends. Then believing that my inspiration was beginning
to dry up [because some times words would not come and not
having anything to say, in a number of sonnets the very same conceit came depicted to me] in those recourses which everyone uses
these days; and with great diligence I made a list of rhyme words
or a vernacular vocabulary in which alphabetically every word
that those two writers had used was individually listed, and besides that in another book I listed the ways they described things:
day, night, anger, peace, hatred, love, fear, hope, beauty, so carefully collected that no word or conceit came from me that did find
an example in their novels and sonnets. Look now to what depths
I descended and in how tight a prison and with what bonds I
chained myself.)

Brocardo continues saying he saw a great discrepancy between Petrarch's
and Boccaccio's works in Tuscan, which are excellent, and their works
in Latin, which are poorly written because the period in which they lived
did not know Latin well. He then describes how he conceived of the idea
of imitating the classic poets in Tuscan. He first alludes to the attempts
of Trissino, Alamanni, and Tolomei to adapt Latin metrics to vernacular
poetry and proceeds to describe his own "more reasonable" approach:

Confirmava mia openione il vedere ogni giorno alcuni uomini,
pur toscani letterati e di grandissima fama, li quali tolti dal Petrarca, e or Tibullo, ora Ovidio, or Virgilio imitando, facevan

versi volgari; li quali, mezo tra volgari e Latini, parimente a' volgari ed a' latini spiacevano: in fra li quali chiunque con nuova
guisa di rime o senza rima niuna i latini imitava, meno errava al
mio parere, e con giudicio più ragionevole le poesie confundeva:
perciocché, togliendo a' versi la rima o del suo loco movendola,
si leva loro gran parte di quella forma volgare, che i Latini e loro
arte naturalmente aborrisce. La qual cosa sò provai io in quel
tempo, quando (quasi nuovo alchimista) lungamente mi faticai
per trovare l'eroico; il qual nome niuna guisa di rima dal Petrarca
tessuta non è degna d'appropriarsi. Moveami ancora a dover
creder così la nostra guisa di verso, il quale contra i precetti latini
senza piedi e con rime non è men dolce agli orecchi, nó men leggiadro nel caminare di qual si vuol degli antichi. (Pozzi 663–64)

(My opinion was confirmed by seeing every day some men, Tuscan writers of great fame who, rescued from Petrarch and now
imitating Tibullus, now Ovid, now Virgil, created vernacular poetry which, mixed between the vernacular and Latin, equally dis-
pleased vernacular and Latin readers. Among which whoever imitated the Latins with a new manner of rhyme, or without any
rhyme at all, erred less in my opinion, and with more reasonable
judgment blended the styles. Because removing the rhyme from
verse, or moving it from its place, one takes away a great part of
the vernacular form which the Latins and their art naturally ab-
hor. I tried this myself at that time, when [like a new alchemist]
for a long time I toiled to find the heroic mode, which name no
manner of rhyme woven from Petrarch is worthy of appropriat-
ing. It moved me to believe our manner of versification, which
goes against Latin precepts in not having feet and in having
rhyme, is no less pleasing to the ear, no less graceful in its progression than that of the ancients.)

He then states that he returned to the study of Petrarch, but from this
new and different perspective, and he found a subtlety and good taste
that he had not seen in his previous studies. Sperone's character defends
his adaptation of classical material to vernacular verse and versification,
the same manner that Tasso developed in his own lyric poetry.

In spite of numerous promises, Tasso never completely explained the
particulars of this new movement, but bits and pieces can be gleaned

from various writings. The preface to the *Libro primo* provides important, even though vague, clues for understanding how this new imitation and these transformations were to work.

> . . . gli antiqui boni poeti Greci e Latini, sciolti d'ogni obbligazione, cominciavano e fornivano i loro poemi com'a ciascun meglio parea (massimamente quelli che d'amorosi soggetti ragionano e c'hanno similitudine co' volgari, come sono epigrammi, ode et elegie); ne aveano rispetto di principiar piu con proemio che senza o, se pure il facevano, non curavano di dargli quelle parte che quel della prosa ricerca; e piu tosto secondo l'ampia licenza poetica entravano in qualunque materia, e vagando, n'uscivano in fabule, o'n qualunque altra digressione a lor voglia; et anco spesse volte senza ritornar in essa fornivano: quel che non hanno avuto ardir di far i Provenzali e Toschi e gli altri che loro stile seguirono, li quali a pena toccano pur le fabule con una parola e con un solo verso, fuor che'l Petrarca in quelle due canzoni: "Chiare, fresche et dolci acque" e "Se'l pensier che mi strugge"; le quali piene di vaghezza e di leggiadria piu per avventura poeta lo dimostrano che l'altre sue composizioni. . . .

> (. . . the good Greek and Latin poets freed from all obligations began and executed their poems as it seemed best to each one [above all those that treat amorous subjects and have a similarity with the vernacular poems, such as epigrams, odes, and elegies]; nor were they more obliged to begin with an introduction than without it, or if they did begin it so, they did not worry about giving it those parts that one seeks in prose. And more quickly according to the ample poetic license they entered into any material, and wandering, they came out of it in a fable, or in any other digression at their will, and yet many times, without returning to it, they provided that which the Provençals and Tuscans, and those others who followed their style, did not have the courage to do, and who often barely touched on a fable with only one word and with one single line, with the exception of Petrarch in those two *canzone:* "Chiare, fresche et dolci acque" [Clear, fresh, and sweet waters, CXXVI] and "Se'l pensier che mi strugge" [If the thought that destroys me, CXXV], which, full of beauty and

grace, show him by chance to be a better poet than any other of his compositions. . . .)

Even though these brief descriptions give only a vague notion of the changes implied by these new sources, it is possible to extract three major ideas concerning the transformation. First of all, running through the passage is a celebration of a new freedom from the old constraints of Petrarchism. The classical poets, "sciolti d'ogni obligatione," could construct their poems as they saw fit, or as the material demanded.[1] This newfound freedom gives an enthusiastic, celebratory tone to the passage.

Second, he advocates the use of digressions and free structuring of the material, according to the demands of content. With this he eliminates the formal structures imposed on Italian poetry, as the contrastive movements required of the "piedi" of the *canzone* strophe. Also, he states, without further explanation, that the poet is no longer confined to developing the material in any particular way, but can, following the models of the best ancient Greek and Latin poets, introduce digressions, leave lines of argument undeveloped, skip from topic to topic, and maybe back again if desired. This allows for greater freedom in development of the subject matter.

The third element mentioned by Bernardo Tasso is the use of myth and narration—fable—to replace the static lyrical lament typical of medieval courtly love poetry. Tasso claims that no medieval poet, with the exception of Petrarch in two of his songs, had the courage to introduce mythology into poetry. This discussion seems to imply a criticism of Petrarch (who only achieved the status of poet in two songs) and other courtly love poets. He advocates the imitation of the style and manner of the Greek and Latin poets, and he also encourages the modern poets to employ mythology. Fable was a popular concept among Renaissance writers, implying a formal structure and didactic ends. Especially important was the idea that fable consisted of an outer narrative cortex that covered a hidden message or mystery within.

The implications in the shift from medieval content to the use of narrative forms involves much more than a simple shift of emphasis. Even though not mentioned by Tasso, one of the most important transformations concerning the introduction of fable occurs in the change from the personal "I" of the poet-lover to the distancing typical of a third-person

---

1. Tasso may have been restating a rhetorical commonplace. Compare Godman 152.

narrator-observer. At the center of Tasso's objections is the rigidly prescribed uniformity of attitude concerning love. The code of the compromised lover of a cold disdainful beloved imposed on love poetry a uniformity of vision and expression that could only be broken by new poetic
postures and new attitudes toward love. The use of fable and a detached
narrator instead of an involved lover signaled an important revolution in
Renaissance poetry. For Tasso, the imitation of the ancients occurs in the
new subject matter treated in the poems and in the new attitudes toward
love. For example, his third ode begins (ironically paraphrasing a line
by Petrarch) by rejecting the traditional stance of the Petrarchan poet-
lover:

> Pon freno, Musa, a quel si lungo pianto,
>   Ch'Amor t'apre dal core;
> Et vestiti di ricco & lieto manto.
>   (*Libro primo* 53)

> (Hold in check, Muse, that long lament
>   which love opens from your heart,
>   and dress yourself in a rich and joyful cloak.)

Other poems break with the conventional structures of Petrarchan restraint. Among the additional poems in *Libro primo* was a sonnet to
Priapus (51v). Not only is the open sexuality startling in a Petrarchan
context, but the sexuality is not limited to female adoration: "Hore da
l'uno, hora da l'atro sesso / Offerti voti in questa, e'n quella parte" [Now
from one, now from the other sex / Votive offerings in this and that part].
Another poem to Priapus appeared in the *Libro secondo* (64), in which
a thirty-year-old virgin abandons her dedication to Diana after a dream
of her future unhappiness, in order to be seduced by the "Agreste Iddio
de gli horti" (the rustic god of the gardens). These frank expressions
of sexuality clearly go against the current of refined courtly love in
sixteenth-century Petrarchism.

In the 1534 edition of *Gli Amori*, consisting of a reprint of a much
abridged Book I and a new Book II, Tasso's move toward anti-
Petrarchism, or perhaps more precisely anti-Bemboism, is quite evident.
Sixty-three poems were dropped from Book I: all three *canzone*, the two
sestinas, the four poems in tercets, and fifty-four sonnets. The Petrarchan
imitation in the suppressed sonnets is quite clear from the first lines of

sonnets such as "Quando mi voglio in dietro a mirar l'hore" (*Libro primo* 20) and "Solo e pensoso i miei passati affani" (34). On the other hand, none of the added poems in the new classical style were eliminated, nor none of the sonnets on the death of Brocardo. The three odes that had remained unidentified as to genre in the 1531 edition were moved to a new section in the 1534 edition with nine new odes and titled "Hinni et ode." His anti-Bemboism becomes clear in two new *canzone* "Hor che con fosco uelo" (45v–48) and "Come potro giamai Notte lodarti" (72–73v). In the first Tasso uses the stanza form of Petrarch's "Chiare, fresche et dolci acque," one of the two *canzone* that Bembo had identified as "piacevole" to describe night and suffering with dark turgid imagery. In the second he uses a "graver" stanza, also of thirteen lines, but only two (instead of nine) heptasyllables, to praise the serenity and peacefulness of night, as an ideal time for lovers and writers. The two *canzone* present the two faces of night, but the peaceful vision of night is placed in a stanza Bembo would have labeled grave and the nightmarish vision is in the stanza form he singled out as "piacevole." The vision of night in the first *canzone* is hardly pleasant, as a few lines make clear:

> Tu, ch'a me sei simile,
>   Scura, com'è' l mio stato;
>   Co tuoi silentii ascolta
>   Quel, che piu d'una uolta
>   Dett'ho piagnendo con la morte a lato;
>   Et nel tuo fosco serba
>   Il tristo suon de la mia doglia acerba.
>
>   (46)

(You, who are similar to me,
  dark, as is my condition,
  with your silences you hear
  that which, more than once
  I have said crying with death at my side;
  and in your gloom guard
  the sad sound of my bitter pain.)

One notes the repeated *l*'s, and other aspects of the pleasant style in a poem whose content is grave. The poem, however, is not unsuccessful, even though it runs counter to Bembo's principles of sound patterning.

In the new preface to the *Libro secondo* (1534), Tasso speaks clearly
of his innovations in vernacular poetry. Whereas he had shown reluctance to break with the past in 1531, he begins stridently in 1534: "la
nouita de miei versi, cosa non meno inuidiosa, che diltteuole, mouera
molti a uituperarli" (the novelty of my poetry, no less enviable than delightful, will stir many to attack it) (2). He says he will be accused of not
imitating Dante and Petrarch, but he states it is impossible to repeat their
success by imitating them:

> Ma hauendo que gloriosi con un loro raro ò leggiadro stile uol-
> gare, si altamente ritratti lor diuini concetti, che impossibile sa-
> rebbe hoggimai con quelli istessi colori depinger cosa che ci pia-
> cesse, uana mi parrebbe ogni fatica, ch'io usassi non pur per
> passar auanti, ma per andarli vicino, caminando di continuo diet-
> ro l'orme loro. (2v-3)

> (But these glorious [stars] having, with their rare and graceful ver-
> nacular style, so loftily portrayed their divine conceits that it
> would be impossible today with the same colors [metaphors] to
> depict something that pleased us. Any effort I might make would
> seem useless to me, not only because one is not advancing, but
> also because one is following them closely, walking continually
> straight in their footsteps.)

Like Brocardo he complained that Petrarchism had become a confining
prison of language and thought that limited poetry to an established
vocabulary and one theme, claiming poets could no longer continue expressing "quelli istesse cose con altri parole, o con quelli istesse parole
altri pensieri" (the very same things with other words, or with the very
same words, other thoughts) (7).

Tasso's method of imitating the classical writers in vernacular poetic
forms represents a curious compromise of principle, but one that in the
long run seemed to promise better results. Rather than launch into new
and awkward metric and strophic forms, the poet had only to adapt the
new subject matter to the established familiar forms. Tasso continued to
give preference to the sonnet as the form for shorter poems, and it remained without change in its formal aspects, but treated different attitudes toward love and incorporated new material. These experiments in
new subject matter break the molds of the old medieval poetry that still

held vernacular poetry in check and had recently been renewed by Bembo as a principal plank in the formation of a national language.

In proposing the imitation of classical poetry, Tasso had as a model the imitation of the classics by the humanists writing in Latin. The imitation of the best Greek and Latin poets implied the emulation of the Renaissance Neo-Latin poets, whose poetic conventions differed significantly from those of vernacular poetry. In the "poemi aggiunti" of the 1531 *Libro primo* Tasso essayed imitation of two classical humanist genres: the epigram and the ode. For the reproduction of the epigram, he used the sonnet as the closest Italian verse form. Classical epigrams had varied greatly in their extension from two to sixteen lines of elegiac couplets (McFarlane 17), although four to ten lines were the most popular lengths. Since the sonnet is a fixed fourteen-line poem, its use for the reproduction of the epigram produced mixed results. For the classical Greek epigram, which relied much less on paradox and point, the sonnet could serve adequately. For the short pithy epigram, relying on one or two well-stated, succinct paradoxes, the sonnet was too long and roomy. The sonnet as epigram could produce a languid, repetitious style, as seen in the series of sonnets on the Armed Venus discussed in Chapter 15.

In his prologues, Tasso made several references to the best Greek and Latin poets. Among the poets of highest esteem in the early sixteenth century were the Greek epigrammatists whose poems had been collected in the *Greek Anthology*. The collection (which was first published in 1494 and saw three more editions by 1521) enjoyed great prestige throughout the Renaissance; Italian poets imitated these epigrams in Latin, and later in Italian. The epigrams regarded as most authentic, as propagated by Navagero (Rothberg 80), were the dedicatory inscriptions, which are marked by understatement rather than sharp wit. We often consider the two chief characteristics of the epigram to be brevity and point, but this conception is a seventeenth-century development based on the epigrams of Martial (Hutton, *Greek Anthology* 190). The epigrams of the *Greek Anthology,* especially the dedicatory poems, do not rely on sharply worded paradoxes and irony: "Point, in the rhetorical sense, is relatively rare in the Greek epigram of the best periods; its place is taken in the Alexandrian epigram by what we should call 'conceits'" (Hutton, *Greek Anthology* 55). As Gary J. Brown has shown, sixteenth-century commentators and critics from Lorenzo de Medici to Herrera and Lope had posited an equivalence between the classical epigram and the sonnet ("Fernando" and "Lope").

The imitation practiced by the Neo-Latin poets differed greatly from that prescribed by Bembo, which prescribes the close imitation of the style, tone, and sound, including vocabulary, imagery, and even ideas of the master Petrarch. The Neo-Latin poets not only took from numerous sources, as Tasso said, from the good Greek and Latin poets, but also viewed imitation in an eristic manner. They imitated to actualize the classical source, to make it contemporaneously relevant and even personal. As Nichols explains, the sense of loss felt by the Renaissance artists, when they looked to ancient art and literature, led them to try to revitalize the classical and to infuse it with new life. Rather than quote and re-create the authentic spirit of the past with the same words and phrases—employing only approved and canonized modifiers and verbs, as did the sixteenth-century Petrarchists—the Neo-Latin poets tried to evoke the past within a contemporary framework. Not only did the Neo-Latin poets imitate many Greek and Latin models, but their imitations were much freer, designed more as competitions than reproductions. Part of the distancing of the source allowed for a more personal expression:

> Perhaps the most surprising feature of this poetry is its intimate and personal quality, beside which the vernacular poetry of the time often seems reserved, abstract, and impersonal. Politian in his Latin epigrams sketches out for us the contours of his social world, his likes and dislikes; his shorter Latin poems in particular define a social world in a way that his equally brilliant Italian poems do not. (Nichols 1)

The Neo-Latin poets understood and adapted classical material in the terms of their own personal and cultural understanding.

A striking example of this method is Marcantonio Flaminio's poem on Hercules and Hylas (published 1529), a close imitation of Theocritus's Idyll 13. In a poem nearly the same length, Flaminio takes his reader through the opening meditation on the power of Eros, describes Hercules' love for the beautiful boy Hylas, his raising him, their sailing with Jason toward Colchos for the Golden Fleece, Hylas's capture by the nymphs in the spring, and Hercules' search and mourning for his beloved. Flaminio carefully distances his version from Theocritus's, employing different metaphors and imagery. While Theocritus ends his poem reporting that the ship's crew were angry because Hercules continued the journey on foot by land and they were short an oarsman, Flaminio adds four lines that compare the long example with Renaissance heterosexual love:

> Hos tu sollicitos Heroum doctus amores
>   Disce libens durae ferre iugum dominae,
> Nec te iam pigeat quemuis perferre laborem,
>   Omnis amor longo uincitur obsequio.

> (You, familiar with the anguished love of heroes,
> learn willingly to bear the yoke of a hard mistress,
> and don't let it annoy you now to endure any labor:
> all love is won by long obedience.)
>
> (Nichols 428–29)

The obvious discontinuity between the carefully reworked example and Flaminio's closing application or modernized understanding of the source is so great as to produce a tension between statement and implication, the sort of tension that occurs with any reapplication of classical sources to contemporary settings, what Godman has labeled "the fundamental paradoxes of literary classicism." Particularly noteworthy is "the paradox of creative subversiveness through fidelity to the classical tradition's original attribute of freedom" (151). Theocritus's idyll was also a reworking of previous texts. In addition to the Homeric epithets, it seems Theocritus is retelling, and refashioning, the episode of Hercules and Hylas in Apollonius of Rhodes's *Argonautica* (Rist 115–19). Apollonius had presented Hylas as a servant, with no allusion to a love relationship, leaving the grief of Hercules without psychological motivation. Also the last two lines of Theocritus's poem "depict Hercules' companions calling his manhood into question" (Rist 118). Theocritus is celebrating the origins of the cult of Hylas, telling a story that explains the founding of the cult with its ritualistic "threefold calling of his name," an element that is lost in Flaminio's re-creation. The treatment of homoerotic desire, which Theocritus imposed on the Apollonius story, and which serves to call into question the heroic attributes of Hercules and open him to the taunts of his crewmates, was a daring and original addition. As Godman suggests, the classical in its own contexts was often not the canonized version that we have come to view, but was in itself a startlingly original treatment of the material. We could say that Flaminio and other Neo-Latin poets chose their sources "not simply for private purposes of self-expression but because it presented them with specific opportunities to revive the freedom, the scandalousness, and the impertinence of the classical traditions of which they were the beneficiaries" (Godman 151).

Flaminio's recontextualization of the story of Hercules and Hylas revives the freedom of the original text and re-creates the sense in which the original was in the avant-garde. In Theocritus's retelling of the story, the hero, dominated by his passion, defies the canons of heroism and by implication verges on the unheroic. Flaminio again retells the story, now canonized as a classic, in a society that in the name of its religion is horrified by and severely punishes homoerotic love. The outrageous nature of this quotation and its re-creation as an example of why the Renaissance lover was bound in servitude to his mistress through the power of Eros exemplifies, as perhaps few other examples can, the ambiguity of classical imitation. The nature of the exemplum in a strict Christian Renaissance context hardly serves to ennoble the concept of courtly love portrayed at the end. In a less strict context, one might read the example as a new model of desire, which through its greater detail and extension trivializes the heterosexual gloss and exalts Hercules' desire as a superior heroic love. The tension arising out of the framework and the cultural context in which the poet has imitated and re-created his classical source serves to recall the "freedom and impertinence" of the original.

Clearly not all examples contain so much dramatic tension between the source and its new context, but this example serves to dramatize precisely the ambiguities that arise from Renaissance eristic or heuristic imitation. Flaminio has recast Theocritus's original, providing new details, metaphors, and imagery, and he has used it not, as Theocritus did, to dramatize the founding of a cult, but to make a comment on courtly love; whether to exalt it or trivialize it is not clear from the text. These then are the essential elements typical of Neo-Latin imitation of the classics. The original, be it a word, phrase, or myth, is recontextualized in the Renaissance, and perhaps even given a personal application. The authors strive to distance their works from the source, and at the same time to re-create the classical world within the framework of the Renaissance. It is this sense of personal re-creation and historical recontextualization that marks the style of Neo-Latin humanist verse. From the fragments of classical civilization, like Michelangelo's restorations of classical statues, the Neo-Latin writers reconstructed versions of classicism that were relevant for themselves personally and for their culture historically. In contrast, Bembo's idea of Petrarchism, which meant the re-creation of

Petrarch's spirit and ideas, using his very words and phrases, consisted of a close following and modeling on the work of the one master. The thoughts and feelings so poignantly expressed in Petrarch's *Canzoniere* may or may not have been relevant for poets two centuries later, but Bembo's idea of imitation, in prescribing the close re-creation of the master's language and ideas, overlooked the gaps of history and changes of style and taste. No wonder Tasso celebrates a new sense of freedom in his poetic manifesto. Sperone has his spokesman Broccardo characterize his Petrarchan formation in terms of prison, and Tasso in the prologue to his *Libro secondo* ridiculed the Petrarchan movement's adherence to the same words and ideas. Obviously a number of writers were convinced they had squeezed every possible drop of anguish from their Petrarchan sources, especially those whose interests ranged beyond the expression of frustrated desire and mental anguish.

A study of Tasso's method of imitation in two of his sonnets addressed to nymphs will make clearer his method of working, and will at the same time be relevant for the discussion of Garcilaso's Sonnet XI (a further elaboration of the same topos). The epigrams from the *Greek Anthology* that seemed the most authentic and original to the Renaissance writers were the dedicatory epigrams in Books VI, IX, and XVI. In these poems, the subject dedicates an object to a deity, oftentimes, if not fruits from the garden, an object that no longer serves: the old fisherman dedicates his nets on retiring; the old scribe dedicates his writing implements to the muses, or the aging courtesan dedicates her mirror to Venus, to cite a few common examples. The problem with imitating or re-creating this type of epigram was that the central act of a votive offering was no longer religiously or culturally relevant. Probably more bothersome than its heretical implications was its lack of sense for a Renaissance cultural context. Tasso's sonnet (discussed previously) on the dedication of Titiro's reed-pipe to Pan, now that the poet has been beaten in competition, is probably an echo of epigram VI, 82 from the *Greek Anthology* in which Pan refuses the offering of a reed-pipe because of his previously suffered passion for Syrinx. The dedication in Tasso's sonnet allows him to develop the relevant issue of the competition and Alcippo's victory over Titiro. In Tasso's sonnet the pastoral and pagan elements provide a classical setting for the central act of a current event, a poetic competition.

Tasso's nymph sonnets relate the classical elements to current love themes, more along the lines of Flaminio's poem on Hylas. In the *Greek Anthology* there are a number of epigrams dedicated to the nymphs, six of them beginning with the word *numphai*. One poem requests cures for disease from the waters (VI, 189). Others simply state that a token or carved images have been left for a drink of water, or simply left in exchange for the continued flow of water in the river (IX, 327, 328, 329; XVI, 264A). In one unusually sensual example (IX, 556), Pan asks the nymphs if Daphnis, who bathed in their waters, was as beautiful as he suspects. The problem of contextualizing these nymphs in a sophisticated courtly society must have been troubling. Pontanus, the famous Neapolitan humanist, addressed the nymphs as part of his self-recognition as a poet:

> Nymphae, quae nemorum comas virentes
> atque undas Aganippidas tenetis
> et saltus gelidos virentis Haemi,
> vos, O Thespiadum cohors dearum,
> vestris me socium choris et antris,
> vulgi avertite dentibus maligni;
> et me Castaliae liquore lymphae
> sparsum cingite laureis corollis
> cantantem modo Sapphicis labellis.

(Nymphs, who inhabit the green leaves of the woods and waters sacred to the Muses, and the cool valleys of verdant Haemus, you, o band of Thespian goddesses, save me, a member of your troop and a familiar of your caverns, from the teeth of the evil crowd; sprinkle Castalian water upon me and crown me with laurel wreaths as I sing now in sapphic mode.) (McFarlane 22–23)

An early poem by Marcantonio Flaminio (Maddison, *Marcantonio* 25) incorporates the address to the nymphs, who are asked to accept the offerings of a young man before he goes swimming in the small Rhine river in Bologna.

> Ad Nymphas Bononienses.
> Nymphae, quae parui colitis vaga flumina Rheni,
>   Et blando agrestes vtitis igne Deos,
> Liba dat haec vobis, vobis haec pulcer Iolas
>   Porricit in gelidas nigra falerna domos.

Vos puerum accipite, atque instanti arcete periclo,
  Dum vestram niueo pectore pellit aquam.
                          (Gherus II, 31–32)

(Nymphs, who inhabit the wandering flow of the tiny Rhine,
    and inspire the rustic gods with bland fire,
Beautiful Iolas makes these libations to you, offering
      them to you
  in your sparkling dwellings from dark Falernian vines.
Receive the boy, and protect him from immediate danger
  as he splashes water over your snow-white breasts.)

This poem incorporates the pagan offering into the poem as a request for protection from the nymphs, perhaps remembering their treatment of Hylas, or employing the story as a metaphor for drowning. One cannot overlook the sensuality of Flaminio's votive epigram. The nymphs with their bare breasts and the desire they provoke in the rustic gods turn nature into a sensually stimulating playground of personified deities.

Tasso imitated this situation in two different sonnets. Like the classical epigrams, each begins addressing the nymphs and each describes them briefly. Tasso relates this situation to courtly society by requesting that the nymphs recognize his love situation. In the first he asks that they listen to his love laments and hide his tears in the deep recesses of their watery abode; in the second, that they celebrate his freedom from love by marking the day and accepting his altar and offerings of flowers.

Nimphe, che'n questi chiari alti cristalli
    Vaghe scherzando al camin uostro andate;
    Et amiche d'Amore, ò de pietate,
    Guidate ogn'hor dolci amorosi balli;
Se scenda dal suo fonte, ò da le ualli
    Il uostro fiume puro, et se l'irate
    Falci, giamai le riue sue honorate
    Non spoglino di fior uermigli, o gialli;
Aprite al pianto mio l'humido seno,
    Et queste amare lagrime chiudete
    Nel piu secreto uostro herboso fondo.

Che ueder non le possa il cieco mondo.
    Poi le sprezza colei, de le cui liete
    Vaghezze'l Cielo, et di sue gratie adorno.
            (*Libro primo* 52v)

(Nymphs, who in these clear deep crystalline waters
    gracefully playing you go your way;
    and friends of Love and mercy,
    direct continually soft amorous dances;
your pure river descends from its fountain
    and from its valleys, and if the angry
    scythes never strip your honored banks
    of red and yellow flowers,
open to my weeping your humid heart
    and close these bitter tears
    in the most secret part of your grassy deep,
so the blind world cannot see them.
    For she despises them, she of whose merry
    charms and of whose graces Heaven is an ornament.)

In spite of the obvious error in the rhymes of lines 9 and 14, the poem makes good sense. In the earlier of the two poems, Tasso has eliminated the votive offering and inscribed the classical locus into the Renaissance context of courtly love, evoking the cruel mistress at the end. The main elements, the address to the nymphs and a personal application, are present, but the classical votive offering has been lost in the transference.

In the second sonnet, the speaker is no longer in love. After asking the nymphs to remember his love laments, he asks them to come forth and accept from an altar the flowers he has offered to them. This sonnet not only expresses a new idea regarding love—the speaker is free from love—but it also incorporates the pagan offering to the deities.

Nimphe, ch'al suon de la sampogna mia
    Souente alzando fuor le chiome bionde
    Di queste si correnti ò lucid'onde,
    Vdiste il duol, ch'amor dal cor mi apria.
Se sempre l'aura si tranquilla sia,
    Che non ui turbi l'acque; et se le sponde

Del uostro fiume, ogn'hor uerde et feconde
Non sentan pioggia tempestosa y ria,
Uscite fuor de liquidi christalli;
Et la mia liberta meco cantante
In queste uaghe riue et dilettose;
Che d'un altar di fior candidi et gialli
Sarete in questo di sempre honorate;
Et d'un canestro di purpuree rose.

                    (*Libro secondo* 53)

(Nymphs, who to the sound of my reed-pipe
    often raising your blonde tresses
    out of the running and so lucid waves,
    you heard the pain that love opened from my heart.
If always the breeze will be so tranquil
    that it does not disturb your waters; and if the banks
    of your river, always green and fertile,
    do not feel stormy and malicious rain,
Come forth out of your liquid crystal
    and sing with me my liberty
    on these beautiful and delightful banks,
for from an altar of white and yellow flowers
    I will always be honoring you on this day,
    and from a basket of red roses.)

These two sonnets show how Tasso has adapted the classical epigram to
the vernacular. His poems are not faithful transcriptions of a classical
model, but rather a re-creation of a classical topos that he has adapted
to his own personal situation and historical context. In both poems, the
speaker stands on the bank of the river and addresses the nymphs concerning the status of his commitments to love. Like the Neo-Latin poets
whose manner he imitates, he has brought a fragment of the past into
the present. In the first example, he eliminates the central element of the
votive offering and adapts the topos to the situation of the unrequited
courtly lover. In the second example, he assumes a new attitude unfamil-
iar to courtly love and reworks the topos to include the votive offering.
In both poems the juxtaposition of the classical and the modern is not
completely harmonious. In the first, the juxtaposition of the classical
nymphs with the posture of the medieval courtly lover seems to make

the nymphs somewhat extraneous to the central issue. In the second, the speaker seems out of place and time erecting an altar of flowers on the river bank as a votive offering. In the conflict of model and its reproduction in an emulated text, one is aware of the historical gap between the two and conscious that each suffers modification in the presence of the other.

For longer poems, Bernardo Tasso abandoned the *canzone* with its fixed structure and developed a new stanzaic form that employs shorter stanzas of five to seven lines and eliminates the formal divisions within the *canzone* stanza and the envoi at the end. This stanzaic form was called a "hymn or ode" in the second edition (1534), and it is from one of the odes published in 1534 that Garcilaso borrowed the stanzaic form of the *lira* he used in his own ode. In Book II of *Gli amore* (1534), Tasso also introduced eclogues and elegies.

The ode came to play an important role in Bernardo Tasso's poetic production. The *Libro primo degli amore* (1531), with its few poems in a new style added at the end, had three odes that we can easily imagine were experimental because of the variety of metrical forms employed. Even though one of these odes (not labeled in any way) marked the beginning of the section of new poems, it consisted of ten-line stanzas (only two of Tasso's odes, both published in 1531, exceed the five-line stanza) and seemed to resemble a *canzone* without the final envoi. Another ode had seven-line stanzas, and only one had the five-line stanzas that he would come to prefer, but not yet with the abAbB rhyme scheme to which he would give preference in the later odes.

In the 1534 reedition of the *Libro primo,* along with the new *Libro secondo,* Tasso removed the three odes from their place in the earlier edition of the first book (although the other poems follow their original order), and placed them in a special section called "Hinni et ode" to which he added nine new odes, all with five-line stanzas, and the majority with the rhyme scheme abAbB. Only one had the rhyme scheme aBabB, which Garcilaso imitated in his Ode ad florem Gnidi, and then, with the name *lira,* became so popular among Spanish poets. The *Libro terzo,* published in 1537, did not reedit the first and second books, and it had three new odes interspersed in the text in the manner of a *canzoniere*. The 1555 edition of all three books of poems with the addition of a fourth book returns to a special section of odes, called "Inni et odi," reprinting the fifteen odes from the first three books plus eighteen new odes. The 1560 edition prepared by Tasso himself reprinted all of his previously published poetry (with the exception of the Petrarchan poems that he had excluded from the *Libro primo* in 1534) and gave titles to most of the odes. It reprinted the thirty-three odes from the previous editions and added twenty-two new odes. It also included a section of thirty poems called "Salmi" which were religious poems, but which had the five-line stanzas and varied rhyme schemes of the other odes.

Finally in 1560, in his final collection of poetry, containing five books of *Gli amore,* Tasso summarized the changes contained in the odes:

> Però non le serà molesto qualhora da suoi gravi, ò importantissimi pensieri haurà la mente libera, di legger queste mie ode ò hinni fatti ad imitazione di buoni Poeti Greci e Latini, non quanto al verso, il quale in questa nostra italiana favella è imposibile d'imitare, ma ne l'inventione, ne l'ordine, e ne le figure del parlare. (Preface to Odes)

> (It will not disturb you anytime you have your mind free from your serious and very important thoughts to read these odes and hymns of mine written in imitation of good Greek and Latin poets, not in versification, which is impossible in our Italian tongue, but in invention, order, and figures of speech.)

These poems obviously were key works in Tasso's renovation of poetic material, and they represented for him an important departure from the heavy personal involvement of the courtly love tradition. Maddison describes the difference between the Renaissance ode and the *canzone:*

> Thus the humanists invented a new poetic genre, a poem celebrating contemporary experience in the ancient taste. The ode, then, became a poem of greater dignity than the *canzone* or *chanson.* At the same time it was trimmer in shape. In place of the long, sprawling strophes of the medieval poets there were the brief, agile stanzas that the ancients had used. . . . The ode . . . was learned and formal, rather than private or personal. (*Apollo* 2)

Edward Williamson argued that the ode developed not as a metrical novelty or formal experiment, but as a necessary result of a desire to transform poetic content ("Form"). Arguing that content preceded form in the innovations in poetry, he maintains that Tasso experimented with the ode to escape from the stifling conventions of Petrarchism. Ode writing is not anti-Petrarchan per se because Tasso and other poets also continued writing in the Petrarchan vein, as well as in the new form of the ode. Their experiments with the ode, as well as with the eclogue, elegy, and poetic epistle, spring not only from an appreciation of the classics, but also from a desire to find new and more ample forms of poetic expression. Tasso had no reason to criticize Petrarch and Dante, and in fact his *poetica* is full of praise for them. Personally, however, he was interested in finding a less constraining mode of expression than the imitation of the same few writers. One might say that Tasso's innovations are more anti-Bembo than anti-Petrarch. Tasso found unbearable the limitations of posture, theme, and vocabulary imposed by Bemboistic Petrarchism.

Garcilaso's friendship with Tasso, if it existed, is not documented. Tasso never once referred to Garcilaso in his poetry or his voluminous correspondence. In 1532 Tasso became secretary to Ferrante Sanseverino, prince of Salerno. Tasso was not a member of the Accademia Pontaniana, which Garcilaso attended and from which he drew his circle of friends. Garcilaso and Tasso both participated in the expedition to Tunisia, but there is no evidence of contact between them. The only concrete reference to Tasso by Garcilaso is in line 3 of his Sonnet XXIV: "a Tansillo, a Minturno, al culto Tasso," where the adjective "culto" must signal Tasso's imitation of the classics. The stanza form of the *lira*, aB-abB, which Garcilaso took from the ode "O felice pastori" (published 1534), shows a familiarity with Tasso's works. Garcilaso's use of the ode, elegy, epistle, and mythological sonnets would suggest a thorough understanding of the preface to Book I of *Gli Amore*, published 1531 and 1534. Other influences of Tasso are suggested rather than conclusive.

In spite of the inconclusive nature of the relationship of Garcilaso to Tasso, suggesting that Garcilaso may have known and admired his works, but they may not have known each other personally or been close otherwise, the works of Tasso are quite useful in the discussion of Garcilaso's work because they are so closely dated. The *Libro primo* appeared in 1531; it was reprinted in abridged form with the *Libro secondo* in 1534; the *Libro Terzo* appeared (without reprinting the other two) in 1537. Unlike the works of Tansillo (collected in the nineteenth century), Minturno (published 1559) and Telesio (published 1762 and 1808) and Caracciolo (dispersed in manuscripts or anthologies), Tasso's works have a fairly definite chronology. There is no evidence that Garcilaso knew other than the 1534 edition. Tasso eliminated a good number of Petrarchan works from the 1531 edition, but Garcilaso never echoes them in his own poetry, nor is there any suggestion that he knew parts of the 1537 edition in manuscript. One might argue that Garcilaso must have known the preface to the *Libro primo* before it was reprinted in 1534, since it would suggest that most of his surviving works were written between September 1534 and his death in October 1536, a feat that seems almost humanly impossible.

Garcilaso's imitations of Tasso do not show actual quotations of phrases as do his other imitations. Previous critics have acknowledged only two instances in which Garcilaso relied on Tasso: the use of the strophic form for his *lira* and his reworking of the *carpe diem* theme in Sonnet XXIII. I have discovered three other occasions in which Garcilaso reworked topoi treated by Tasso: the address to the nymphs in Sonnet XI, the votive offering in Sonnet VII, and the image of the faithful dog in Sonnet XXXVII. In addition, Tasso wrote a sonnet on Carthage (published 1537) and dedicated several poems to the marquis of Vasto, but there seems to be no direct relationship between these poems and Garcilaso's Sonnets XXXIII and XXI. In those four cases where Garcilaso does rework an idea of Tasso, there exists no actual relationship of phrasing or even vocabulary as occurs in Garcilaso's other imitations. In borrowing material from Tasso, Garcilaso never translated the source poem, but has completely reworked the material in his own fashion. Perhaps there is a method in this type of imitation. Garcilaso translated whole phrases from Petrarch, Horace, Ovid, Virgil, Sannazaro (1456?–1530), and Ariosto (1474–1533). Garcilaso's borrowings from the last figure occur in poems that date from 1535. One notes that Garcilaso only quotes from authors who were deceased. His borrowings from his contemporary Tasso are so freely reworked that the question of imitation cannot be resolved by pointing to phrases or lines that have been translated from the source.

If taken in the strict sense of founding a poetic school or exercising direct influence on major poets, Bernardo Tasso's poetic revolution and invention of the vernacular ode did not have great or long-lasting influence in Italy. A number of minor lyric poets of the later sixteenth century, labeled by Carducci as "suoi sparsi e brevi imitatori" (his few and limited imitators) (22), wrote odes using the meters invented by Tasso. His influence otherwise is difficult to measure. He formed part of a classicizing movement that continued unabated throughout the century, and his influence in that may be greater than previously calculated by looking for direct influence and imitators of his poetry. One might also try to gauge his influence on the mid-cinquecento Neapolitan poets, such as Angelo di Costanzo, Bernardino Rota, Luigi Tansillo, and Galeazzo di Tarsia, who departed significantly from Bembo's school of Petrarchism (Wilkins 285). Also, Tasso's son Torquato could, in this respect, be considered an important disciple. Judged from a broader point of view, the solution he provided for breaking with Petrarchism by introducing classical themes into vernacular lyric and employing vernacular metrics was successful in the long run. He was not the only innovator in this area, but his particular solution, whether attributed to him or not, was the one that came to predominate in Italian lyric.

Tasso's real success, however, is seen in foreign countries. Ronsard, who titled his collected verse *Les Amours,* introduced classical themes and odes into French poetry. Undoubtedly, Tasso's greatest success was in Spain. Garcilaso's debt to him has already been summarized and will become even clearer in the following chapters. Boscán's contact with Tasso's works did not end with Garcilaso's death. His Libro Tercero, inspired by Tasso's revolt against Petrarchism begins with a translation of Musaeus's *Fabula de Hero e Leandro,* which is quite similar to Tasso's translation of the same work in his *Libro terzo* (1537). Tasso was also quite influential for sixteenth-century poetry in Spain. The first generation of poets following Garcilaso and Boscán picked up on the Petrarchan conventions (probably because they corresponded more closely to the courtly love conventions they were already familiar with), but tended to ignore the pastoral and definitely the ode. The next generation, the poets of the Counter-Reformation, such as Fray Luis de León, Francisco de Medrano, San Juan de la Cruz, and Francisco de la Torre, found the moral stance and the philosophizing attitude of the ode a more comfortable means of expression than the intensely personal love conventions. Only Herrera, who also stamped his own interpretation for posterity on the work of Garcilaso, remained faithful to the Petrarchan forms of expression. Otherwise, Tasso's unique combination of classicism and social message, combined with a renewed interest in the vernacular, provided the right elements for his tremendous influence on sixteenth-century Spanish poetry.

The differences between Bembo and Tasso, which never came to an open polemic as in the case of Brocardo, concerned one of the basic principles of rhetorical imitation. Bembo, following Cortese, was of the school of thought that advocated the imitation of one master. In Latin prose he was a Ciceronian, claiming that one could learn Latin composition only through the study and imitation of Cicero. Opposed to this view were Poliziano, Erasmus, and Giovanfrancesco Pico della Mirandola, who proposed imitation of the best authors. They advocated the study of good writing from all periods and the judicious selection of elements from the best writers. Bembo and Giovanfrancesco Pico della Mirandola had exchanged letters on these points. The differences between Bembo and Tasso were far greater. While Bembo chose Petrarch and Boccaccio as models for imitation in the vernacular, Tasso not only advocated drawing on numerous sources (*gli antiqui boni poeti Greci e Latini*), but also proposed a radical shift in the nature of vernacular poetry through the imitation of different poetical themes and the assumption of new poetical postures. Through his great skills in diplomacy, Tasso managed to prevent an open polemic with Bembo who was very sensitive on these issues. Compared to that of his undeclared adversary, Tasso's reputation has suffered greatly, although his thought and influence on vernacular poetry may have been far greater.

III
Garcilaso's Petrarchan Sonnets

HISTORIANS OF SPANISH LITERATURE establish a clear distinction between Garcilaso's *cancionero* and Italianate styles, but often fail to recognize the variations of style and genre within the Italianate poetry. While one of the aims of Lapesa's trajectory is to distinguish between the Italianate styles, the differences are not as clear as those he establishes between *cancionero* poetry and Italianate poetry. Histories of literature often fail to perceive any differences of style in the Italianate poetry. Rivers remedies this situation by distinguishing between the two Italianate styles (*Obras* 28–31). As the previous chapters have indicated, however, the transition from Petrarchism to classicism is more complex, more systematic, and can be more fully documented than previously claimed.

Garcilaso's thirty-eight or so sonnets provide an excellent basis for studying the transformation from *cancionero* poetry through Petrarchism to the wider norms of the later anti-Petrarchan and neoclassical styles. This trajectory in Garcilaso's other poems involved a change of genre. The very names *ode*, *epístola*, *elegía* and *égloga* clearly denote classical genres, in contrast to the *canción*, a genre that belongs to the Italian medieval period and Petrarchan style. The sonnet, however, without changing name or form, spans both periods and styles and cannot be classified as uniquely medieval. Bernardo Tasso had maintained the importance of employing the metrical system of the vernacular. While he replaced the stanza of the *canzone* with the shorter one of the ode, making the transformation obvious, he continued to use the sonnet as a vehicle for new material. Thus the only way to understand the change in Garcilaso's sonnets is to study the ideas and material, for that is where the transformations occur.

Garcilaso's sonnets have often been studied as a group, and especially since the studies of Keniston, Entwistle, and Lapesa, they have been conceived of as a trajectory of love, from the sonnets treating the love, rejection, and death of Isabel Freire to those alluding to the sensual, jealous love of the mysterious lady in Naples. The classicizing sonnets, not part of the love cycle, were usually categorized as late and were considered part of the rebirth of the classical spirit in the Renaissance. A study of Garcilaso's sonnets, based not on his supposed love affairs, but on formal aspects and idea content, provides a clearer idea of his poetic development. The sonnets can be studied in many groupings and in many orders. In his *Critical Guide* Rivers proposes a structural approach. Lapesa studies them thematically. Consiglio studies their chronology. Prieto attempts to establish an amorous *canzoniere* sequence among them. My study orders them according to style (distinguishing Petrarchan sonnets from classical) and material (distinguishing Petrarchan love from Neoplatonic love and other themes).

Although several sonnets are the most studied, the selection of this canon is fairly recent. Modern critics have more or less settled on Sonnets I, V, X, XIII, and XXIII as the most important. They are the sonnets that are most often written about and the ones most frequently anthologized, although lines from other sonnets are quoted as examples of Garcilaso's attitudes toward love. The sonnets as a whole were quite popular in the sixteenth and seventeenth centuries, especially Sonnet XXIX (Alatorre, "Sobre"), Sonnet X (Herrero García 79–88), and Sonnet I (Glaser, "Cuando"). Gracián quoted a number of Garcilaso's sonnets in his *Arte de agudeza* (1648), but always as examples of *conceptismo*. His selection cannot be considered extremely instrumental in the formation of the canon of Garcilaso's sonnets, because his *conceptista* criterion leads to an erratic selection. He chose, for example, Sonnet XXI, which has never been anthologized (341). Even well-known sonnets were chosen for different reasons. He quoted Sonnet X as an example of conceits, "compuesto de conceptos" (240) and Sonnet XIV as an example of witty similes, "semejanzas conceptuosas" (283). Eighteenth- and early nineteenth-century commentators generally did not favor the sonnet as a genre, and Garcilaso's sonnets suffered from neglect or outright hostility. Azara said of the sonnets in general:

> Garcilaso en éste, y en casi todos sus sonetos, habla del amor con tantas figuras, y con ideas tan poco naturales, tan extraordinarias y confusas, que apenas se acierta con lo que quiere decir. De los italianos, a quien imitó, contrajo este mal gusto de espiritualizar, por decirlo así, las cosas más naturales y sencillas; envolviendo unos pensamientos claros en sí con mil rodeos y contraposiciones, que cansan en vez de agradar. Sus églogas son cosa muy distinta. (A-3)

Eighteenth-century critics singled out the eclogues, especially Eclogue I, as his most enduring and significant compositions. An edition consisting solely of Eclogue I appeared in 1771. Quintana called it "La mejor composición de este escritor, y acaso de la poesía castellana en el género bucólico" (41). The high praise accorded pastoral eclogues and the lukewarm reception and even hostility to the sonnets was the environment in which the first anthologies came onto the scene.

Between 1769 and 1820, there appeared five anthologies of Spanish poetry. The sonnet that appears most in these anthologies is Sonnet XXXIV (three times). Sonnets X, XIV, XXIII, and XXV were anthologized twice each, and Sonnets XI, XVI, and XXIX once each. Sonnet XXXIV appears in none of the modern anthologies and has not been the subject of any critical studies; yet it appeared in three anthologies and was the only sonnet that López de Sedano included in his anthology. Later anthologies began to settle on Sonnets X and XXIII as the most often selected, and these are the two that, along with Sonnet I, have been most often studied by modern critics. As in the selection of all canons of approved literature, some very interesting and delicately beautiful sonnets have been overlooked. Perhaps even more important, the sonnets have been selected for extraneous reasons. Certainly one of the contributing factors to the popularity of Sonnet XXIX in the sixteenth century was that it was often placed out of order at the very beginning of the collection before Boscán's poetry. In the same way, Sonnet I has attracted much critical attention, while other sonnets that share some of the same characteristics are generally overlooked. Perhaps even more damaging than the selection because of position is the selection on biographical grounds, which fixes a limited meaning for the poem, such as the standard interpretations of Sonnets X and I. Even the selection on aesthetic grounds is harmful, for there is a tendency to consecrate the poem as a masterpiece and produce a distorted interpretation by removing it from the context of the total poetic output and the aesthetic norms within which it was conceived.

Garcilaso's sonnets correspond to various tendencies. Most are amorous, but a few are sonnets of praise and employ different styles. In this part and Part IV, I study each sonnet in the context of its poetic tradition, and thus avoid the curious fragmentation produced by the canon of favorite sonnets. When Garcilaso was persuaded to adapt Italian meters to Spanish, the models he had for imitation were Petrarch and the second school of Petrarchists. For this reason, his early Italianate poetry follows Petrarch rather closely in its expression and attitudes toward love; only later do we see the results of his reaction against Petrarchism. I have divided the study of the sonnets between Parts III and IV: Part III studies Garcilaso's Petrarchism; Part IV, his reactions against the limitations of Petrarchan expression. I have classified seventeen of the thirty-eight sonnets I discuss (excluding Sonnets XXXVI and XL) as Petrarchan (Sonnets I, II, III, IV, V, VI, IX, X, XIV, XVII, XVIII, XX, XXV, XXVI, XXVII, XXXII, and XXXVIII). As I shall make clear in discussing each sonnet, the classification of Garcilaso's sonnets to narrative stance and avowed reader cannot be exact because of slight variations from poem to poem and because of changes of avowed reader within a single sonnet. Even a sonnet that addresses the beloved as "vos" and "señora" may not maintain a constant relationship of reader and speaker from line to line. For these reasons, the classification of the Petrarchan sonnets based on the relation of narrator to reader can only be a rough pigeonholing.

Every one of the Petrarchan sonnets has a first-person narrator who is identifiable as a lover. The personal note is emphasized in the anguish and suffering of the speaker. In none of the Petrarchan sonnets is the first-person narrator replaced with a third-person objectified lover as occurs in his *coplas*. Eight of the seventeen Petrarchan sonnets employ the *cancionero* formula of addressing the beloved as "vos" (Sonnets II, III, IV, V, IX, XIV, XVIII, and XXXVIII). Three of these also invoke the beloved as "señora" (II, III, and IX). The inscription of the reader / beloved into the text ranges from the maximum example in Sonnet V to the use of a single object pronoun, "os," in Sonnets IV and XIV. Sonnet IV addresses the heart in lines 7 and 8 and the beloved in line 14: "veros." Sonnet XIV contains an objectified description in the octave with a personal application in the sextet, which includes a form of address, an "os" that is somewhat confusing following, as it does, from an accepted textual emendation. Six of the seventeen sonnets are addressed to an unspecified reader (I, VI, XVII, XX, XXVI, and XXXII). The sonnets that have eliminated the avowed reader tend to involve other unidentified characters, such as vague referents to a "quien" or an unnamed passive subject ("soy tornado" in Sonnet VI). Four of the sonnets (including Sonnet IV) have other forms of address or other specified readers (IV, X, XXV, and XXVII). As mentioned above, Sonnet IV addresses the lover's heart as "tú" before addressing the beloved. Sonnet XXV has "tú" in the first quatrain and "te" in the sextet, but they do not seem to address the same subject, as the discussion of the poem will make clear. Sonnet X is addressed to the "dulces prendas" who are represented as "vos." Sonnet XXVII is addressed to "Amor"; that is, Cupid, who is addressed as "vos." Even though the beginning is clearly a dialogue between the lover and the personified figure of love, the sonnet loses the quality of dialogue and becomes more general, so that the end seems not to have a specified reader.

In summary, eight of Garcilaso's seventeen Petrarchan sonnets address the beloved as "vos" (with three of them further invoking her as "señora"); six are addressed to a general unspecified reader; and five (including Sonnet IV) have personified or other forms of address. In comparison, Boscán also has seven sonnets that employ the "yo → vos (señora)" formula, which makes them a very low percentage, only 9 percent, of his seventy-six sonnets in the Petrarchan mode. In Boscán's sonnets, the type with a general unspecified reader predominates, 82 percent, in 62 out of the 76. Assuming that Garcilaso was moving in the same direction as Boscán, we have a great number of sonnets from the transitional Petrarchan period and nearly half of the thirty-eight sonnets come from the post-Petrarchan period. Garcilaso's true Petrarchan period is seen in about a quarter of the sonnets and the four *canciones*. Within the sonnets I have classified as Petrarchan there are a number that are transitional from the *cancionero* style and others that incorporate heterogenous materials from other traditions.

In Chapter 2, I suggested that Boscán's movement from the forms of direct address in his *cancionero* poetry to no avowed reader in his Petrarchan sonnets implied a change of poetic narrative postures from that of the clever poet to a role model for desire. Garcilaso's *coplas,* however, placed emphasis not only on the wit of the poet, but also, even to a greater degree, on the problem of the rival. The change in Garcilaso's sonnets is also striking, but it does not correspond to Boscán's formulation of a role model for desire—a posture that incorporates the illusion of sincerity in order to impress both the beloved and the rival. In his Petrarchan sonnets, Garcilaso by and large abandons all references to a rival, either implied or stated. Rather, he tends to place himself as a disgraced lover in the posture of wishing for death because of his suffering. The poetic plea of Garcilaso's sonnets is that of the innocent victim who desires his own death in preference to the torments of life. Even Garcilaso's *coplas* tend to cast him in the role of innocent sufferer, such as "Culpa debe ser quereros" (Copla II). The sense of guilt and innocence becomes quite marked in the sonnets, and the elements of violence and death-wish dominate the final thoughts of most of the Petrarchan poems. René Girard's treatment of the social status of the sacrificial victim—the innocent person who has been chosen to die for the collective guilt of the social group—provides a key to understanding the imagery of several of the Petrarchan sonnets. As an amorous posture this status bestows on the victim both scorn and privilege, creating a vacillation of emotional responses (*Violence* 149–56). This posture is, as I will show, typical of a number of Garcilaso's Petrarchan sonnets.

This part consists of three chapters. Chapter 6 is a study of Garcilaso's sonnets that still show strong *cancionero* characteristics and influences from Ausiàs March (Sonnets IX, III, II, XXXVIII, XIV, XXVII, and V). Chapter 7 analyzes those sonnets of Garcilaso that attempt to achieve pure Petrarchan expression (Sonnets I, VI, XX, X, and XXXII). Chapter 8 treats those sonnets in which Garcilaso seems to revolt against, or in other ways react against, the conventions of Petrarchism (Sonnets XVIII, XVII, XXV, IV, and XXVI). In addition to discussing the character of each of the sonnets, I shall trace a number of elements introduced previously, such as the lover's stance and the role of the addressee, the relation of speaker and addressee, the type of block, the nature of imitation, the idea of the lover as a model of desire and sacrificial victim, and various sound patterns that show influence of Bembo's theories of imitation.

6

Apprenticeship in the Italian Mode

As Lapesa fully documented, Garcilaso's early sonnets still show strong influence of the Spanish *cancionero* style with its love of verbal wit, polyptoton, and abstract language. It is not surprising that these are the sonnets that address the beloved as "vos" and "señora," although some of these sonnets also show later characteristics. Also treated in this chapter are the sonnets that show a strong influence of Ausiàs March. I do not argue that these sonnets are transitional or less "authentic" than the true Petrarchan imitations. To the contrary, they represent some of Garcilaso's best sonnets and an extremely original modality within the Petrarchan tradition. Within Garcilaso's Petrarchan period, there seems to be a clear trajectory (which I do not claim to be a chronology) from those poems exhibiting characteristics of Spanish *cancionero* poetry, through the Petrarchan sonnets *in pleno,* to the final stage of rebellion and originality.

In a sense, the motif of absence underlies every love poem, but some address the topic directly. The theme appeared both in the *cancionero* poetry and in Petrarch's *Canzoniere.* Several of Garcilaso's sonnets treat absence as the central theme, notably IX, III, and to a lesser extent IV. Sonnet IX has been singled out previously in this study for its marked use of the stylistic characteristics of Spanish *cancionero* poetry, and its use of heightened sound effects. In it predominate nouns and verbs, while adjectives are few and essential to the sense of the poem.

IX

Señora mía, si yo de vos ausente
en esta vida turo y no me muero,
paréceme que offendo a lo que os quiero
y al bien de que gozava en ser presente;
    tras éste luego siento otro acidente,
que's ver que si de vida desespero,
yo pierdo quanto bien de vos espero,
y ansí ando en lo que siento differente.
    En esta differencia mis sentidos
están, en vuestra ausencia, y en porfía;
no sé ya qué hazerme en mal tamaño;
    nunca entre sí los veo sino reñidos;
de tal arte pelean noche y día
que sólo se conciertan en mi daño.

Even though the poem evokes the presence of the absent señora, it in fact deals mostly with the lover's psychological state of mind. While the block (absence) is the announced subject of the poem, the lover's psychology is the topic treated. Like the *cancionero* poem, the emphasis here is on paradox. In the first quatrain, the poet exaggerates his love and assumes the paradoxical posture of wishing he could die to save face to the beloved. He states that his absence from the beloved should be sufficient cause for his death—therefore, the very continuation of his life is an offense to her. In the second quatrain he introduces a contrary thought: should he die, he would not ever be able to enjoy the mistress's presence; thus he is left vacillating, "differente," between contrary emotions. The sextet develops the struggle of the conflicting passions and senses, "sentidos," which can only agree in causing him harm. The final paradox is reached: the senses are always fighting in opposition, but this opposition leads to their agreement in causing him harm, which they accomplish by agreeing to continue their combative and conflictive natures.

The words "differente" and "differencia" signal the lover's alienation and his entrapment between alternating and conflicting passions—one bordering on a death-wish and the other the despair at the thought of never seeing the beloved again. This difference attacks his senses and leads to another sense of despair in line 11: "no sé que hazerme en mal tamaño." The despair of line 6 has been replaced by a deeper, more destructive despair that never leaves him. Girard states that a sense of alternation precedes the sacrifice of a victim, and one of the postures Garcilaso assumes in his sonnets is that of a sacrificial victim of love (*Violence* 149–56). In this context the sense of difference that attacks him as alternating (different) forces and that alienates him from others (makes him different) is an important key to understanding the posture of suffering in this and other sonnets.

I previously cited the sound patterns in this sonnet as examples of sound patterning in general, pointing out the high incidence of tonic *e*'s, especially in lines 3 to 6. The poem has other sound patterns, such as the internal rhyme of "differencia" and "ausencia" on the sixth and seventh syllables of lines 9 and 10 (which Rivers suggests is a textual corruption). Also striking is the internal rhyme in lines 4 and 8 where "siento" falls on the same syllables (6 and 7) in each rhyming line:

6	7	8	9	10	11	
sien-	to__o-	tro__a-	ci-	den-	te	(line 4)
sien-	to	di-	ffe-	ren-	te	(line 8)

Also remarkable are the five syllables closed with *n* in line 8: "y a*n*sí a*n*do e*n* lo que sie*n*to differe*n*te." Part of this sound is more than coincidental, since the form "ansí" (and "anssí") is optional and appears only six times in Garcilaso's poetry while "assí" (and "así") occurs fifty-nine times (Sarmiento). Line 12 presents an interesting variation containing one tonic *u* and three tonic *i*'s. Bembo had defined the *i* and *u* as the weakest vowel sounds, and Herrera had indicated that *a* and *o* produce a grave sound. Tonic *i*'s and *u*'s are statistically much less frequent in Spanish than the other vowels. The occurrence of four of them in one line is extraordinary. Also four of the six rhymes in the sextet have a tonic *i*, further augmenting their importance. This clearly represents a case of variety by which the poet produces relief from the tonic *e*'s of the octave. According to Bembo, variety provides balance to a poem and gives the graver parts greater intensity. The early date of this sonnet and the intensity of the sound patterns suggest that Garcilaso struggled

to achieve the melodic underlay prescribed by Bembo in imitating Petrarch.

Sonnet IX still relies heavily on the Hispanic *cancionero* tradition. The
frankness with which he expresses a hope for favors from the beloved,
"yo pierdo cuanto bien de vos espero" (7), owes more to the courtly love
tradition than to Petrarchism, which tended to find the lady inaccessible.
In this poem the poet-lover does not confront the lady's cruelty and disdain, but only her absence, which he hopes will end and result in her
favoring him. As in the *cancionero* poetry, the paradox is somewhat exaggerated and ironical. It does not yet place emphasis on the sincerity of
feeling, but still evinces a playful spirit concerning passion. The invocation of the presence of the beloved in a poem on absence not only serves
to bridge the gulf that separates them; it also adds further levels of irony
to the situation of presence and absence. The poem does not concentrate
on absence or on the beloved, but on the paradoxical emotions faced by
the lover because of the beloved's absence. It only states the paradoxical
nature of the lover's emotional distress; it does not try to re-create it nor
does it try to bridge the space of absence with tenderness or concern for
the mistress.

Sonnet III also treats the theme of absence, but with more realistic
touches, providing details that seem autobiographical, as in Canción III.
In this case, however, none are precise enough to relate them to Garcilaso's life.

III

La mar en medio y tierras é dexado
de quanto bien, cuytado, yo tenía;
y yéndome alexando cada día,
gentes, costumbres, lenguas é passado.

Ya de bolver estoy desconfïado;
pienso remedios en mi fantasía,
y el que más cierto espero es aquel día
que acabará la vida y el cuydado.

De qualquier mal pudiera socorrerme
con veros yo, señora, o esperallo,
si esperallo pudiera sin perdello:

mas de no veros ya para valerme,
si no es morir, ningún remedio hallo,
y si éste lo es, tampoco podré havello.

Even though this sonnet employs the "yo → vos (señora)" formula, the forms of address are not introduced until the first tercet. In Sonnet IX, the address and theme were announced in the first line, then the poem moved to concentrate on the lover's psychology, with the lady's presence invoked again, "vuestra ausencia" in line 10. In the case of Sonnet III the octave develops the situation and lover's psychology without invoking the attention (and presence) of the beloved. The absence in this case is realized in a more realistic fashion since the speaker has passed through different lands with strange customs and languages, distancing himself from his homeland and whatever good he possessed. Line 5 announces the problem, the loss of hope, and the rest of the quatrain develops the lover's frustrated death-wish—the only remedy he can conceive of is death, which will end all life and care.

The first tercet addresses the beloved and invokes her presence, saying that her presence would give him the strength to live through his despair. The last tercet reiterates the note of despair. He can conceive of no other remedy, other than death, and even that is not open to him. Even so, the despair in this poem seems less intense than in the previous one. The description of his travels, compressed forcefully into four lines, places more emphasis on the situation of absence than on suffering. The element of death is not a strong death-wish, but simply the only remedy he can conceive, and even that is not open to him. In spite of the form of address, the increased emphasis on descriptive elements and the unexaggerated and more realistic tone of the description place less emphasis on suffering. The poem, at least the first quatrain, seems to date from a later period, with a diminished emphasis on the rhetoric of suffering, and a fuller evocation of the visual elements. The diminished emphasis on a sound system would also suggest a later poem. Even though Herrera pointed out the "gravedad" of line 4, and the "desmayado" effect of the last lines, which he thought fit perfectly the tone of the ending, the poem does not have the intensified sound structure of the previous sonnet. The rhymes of the tercet are all grave, and the "-alla" and "-ello" are similar. In fact, however, the sound does not have the intensity of other Petrarchan poems, nor does this poem have the emotional intensity, both facts suggesting the later period of more detachment as the poet moved away from Petrarchism.

On the other hand, Sonnet II, the third of the three poems employing the "yo → vos (señora)" formula, is probably one of the most intense and violent of Garcilaso's sonnets.

II

En fin a vuestras manos é venido,
do sé que é de morir tan apretado
que aun aliviar con quexas mi cuydado
como remedio me's ya deffendido;
    mi vida no sé en qué s'ha sostenido
si no es en aver sido yo guardado
para que sólo en mí fuese provado
quánto corta una 'spada en un rendido.
    Mis lágrimas an sido derramadas
donde la sequedad y el aspereza
dieron mal fruto dellas, y mi suerte:
    basten las que por vos tengo lloradas;
no os venguéys más de mí con mi flaqueza;
allá os vengad, señora, con mi muerte!

One salient aspect of Spanish Petrarchism was to strike extreme postures of suffering and depression, as does Garcilaso in this sonnet. The first quatrain announces his certain death as he surrenders to his enemy, his mistress. The second quatrain describes that death, claiming he has been reduced to such a miserable state that he has only been kept alive to demonstrate the sharpness of the sword. Not only must he die at the hands of his beloved, but he has also been reduced to a state of deplorable suffering. The sextet changes to plant imagery. Like Apollo in Sonnet XIII, his tears have nourished an undesired effect. In this case it is the dryness and cruelty of the beloved that have thrived on his weeping. He blames his suffering on her condition, "la sequedad y el aspereza," and on his bad luck, "y mi suerte." In the last tercet he implores the mistress not to let him carry on with this suffering, but to end his life quickly, taking her vengeance not through his misery, but through his death.

Garcilaso employs two basic images, war and agriculture, both of which are paradoxical: the beloved is a victorious knight and irrigation has produced aridity. Even though each of the metaphors comes from different spheres, one from the social order and the other from the natural order, their juxtaposition is not unusual in medieval and Renaissance writing. The same combination of nature and war occurs in Sonnet XXXIII. The social order, which is a human institution and mutable, is juxtaposed with a nature image with the implicit suggestion that the social order is just as fixed and established as is the natural order. Garcilaso was a member of the lesser nobility (he did not have a title), and he sought advancement in social rank in the military and as a refined courtier (arms and letters). The property inherited by his wife in 1536 included four slaves (Gallego Morell, *Garcilaso: Documentos* 198). Garcilaso participated fully in the social hierarchy of his times, and implicitly supports its ideology in his writings.

Like the last poem, this sonnet is much more visual, but like Sonnet IX, it still has the abstract words, such as "aliviar," "cuydado," and "remedio." In this poem, however, they function as straightforward descriptive terms, rather than conceptual paradoxes typical of the *cancionero* style. This poem does not use strong emotive words, but strong images that mark the intensity of his suffering. The visual imagery in this sonnet demonstrates an important aspect of Garcilaso's Petrarchism: the replacement of the abstract conceits typical of traditional Spanish poetry with visual images in the Petrarchan mode.

In spite of the clarity of the images in this poem and the identifiable themes of the cruel mistress and suffering lover, the reality being described is somewhat unclear. Usually the sonnets refer to a key moment within the trajectory of the love affair, such as meeting, absence, general suffering, etc. This poem represents a manifest surrender of the poet-lover to the cruel mistress, but what this represents on a literal amorous level is somewhat unclear. It could hardly be that he will declare his love openly to her for the first time, for lines 9 and 10 suggest he has already made his suffering manifest to her. Line 3 denies to him the escape of complaining. The poem states he has reached the end of his ability to suffer, so he will surrender himself to her begging for death. Again this does not suggest a literal moment in a love affair. A brilliant tour de force of violence and passion, the actual literal sense of the sonnet is somewhat obscure.

Rather than refer to a literal moment in the trajectory of the love affair, this sonnet represents an extension of the Petrarchan metaphor of love as war. A number of Petrarch's poems use the metaphor of love as war because of the struggle and suffering involved. In this case rather than a metaphorical treatment of an actual event, this poem is the elaboration of an established metaphor. The fact that the poem has no experiential reference but is basically literature made out of literature does not detract from its force and effectiveness. The violence of the metaphors give the poem a sense of commitment that fits well into the Petrarchan rhetoric of sincerity. The visual imagery and the realistic horror of the images stand for the extremity of the poet-lover's commitment and passion. The evident preference for death over continued suffering and the miserable state of his existence, all stated through visual metaphors, give a force to his passion that rings true, and serves to bring his sense of sincerity to the fore, even though the poem is not describing a real event, either in its imagery or in the reality referred to by that imagery. The fact that the reality of the poem is an extension of a clichéd metaphor does not detract from the rhetorical sense of sincerity.

The presence of the mistress is invoked in line 1, "vuestras manos," and not referred to again until the last tercet, so that all the action of the poem develops from a mental space located in or before the hands of the beloved. The other images of the poem use metaphors to speak of the beloved with the effect that her presence is objectified as a cruel soldier or as harsh desert. Her real presence is invoked at the end of the poem to request pity from her cruelty. The last line seems somewhat difficult, above all, the word "allá." El Brocense commented on this phrase: "en el verso último, se lea: *Allá os vengad señora*" (B-2). Since he gives us the only known reading of the line, he must have been reaffirming against other unknown emendations the reading of the 1543 printed text. The present reading would suggest two possible emendations, either "ella os" or "aora os." In fact "allá" is a difficult reading because it defines a space not yet encompassed in the poem. Lines 1 and 2 define his surrender to the mistress as a movement into her space: "a vuestras manos é venido, / *do* sé . . ." Lines 9 and 10 also define her space as a hostile desert that he has tried to convert into a garden: "an sido derramados *donde* . . ." The difficulty arises from the "é venido" of line 1, which suggests he has already moved into her space—which signifies the end of his suffering through death. Since line 1 had already positioned the poet-lover within the space dominated by the cruel mistress, then the "allá" in reference to her space implies a sudden readjustment of the mental spaces already established in the poem, or it introduces a new space that remains undefined and disconcerting. This complexity must have been the stimulus of the unknown emendations rejected by El Brocense. The difficulty can be resolved without emendation by realizing that the mistress has remained another presence in the poem; even though the lover has submitted to her, he still considers her to be an alien force. Thus, "allá" reasserts in the parting moment the otherness of the beloved and the lack of compatibility.

This sonnet does not have the complex sound structure of some of the other sonnets, notably Sonnets IX, V, and X. Garcilaso seems to have found a viable middle register—perhaps the moderation Bembo was advocating—so that no single line strikes the reader with dominant sounds. Even though this poem employs the "yo → vos (señora)" formula, it approaches Garcilaso's full Petrarchan expression.

Only one of Garcilaso's Petrarchan sonnets has a reference to others, unlike the *coplas,* which explore the areas of rivalry. Sonnet XXXVIII mentions other competitors who have fallen seeking the beloved:

XXXVIII

Estoy contino en lágrimas bañado,
rompiendo siempre el ayre con sospiros,
y más me duele el no osar deziros
que he llegado por vos a tal estado;
    que viéndome do estoy y en lo que he andado
por el camino estrecho de seguiros,
si me quiero tornar para hüyros,
desmayo, viendo atrás lo que he dexado;
    y si quiero subir a la alta cumbre,
a cada paso espántanme en la vía
exemplos tristes de los que han caýdo;
    sobre todo, me falta ya la lumbre
de la esperança con que andar solía
por la oscura región de vuestro olvido.

Like a number of the sonnets, this poem has several traits typical of the *cancionero* style, such as abstract language, intellectual imagery, and abstract substantivized verbals, such as, "el no osar deziros" (3). The sonnet is addressed to the beloved (lines 3, 6, 7, 14). The suffering of the lover is manifest from the first lines with his weeping and sighing. Lines 3 and 4 explain the irony that his greatest suffering comes from not being able to reveal his passion to the beloved. Typical of the Petrarchan poems, the irony here is not on the language, but on the emotion itself. The central paradox is not found in the wordplays, but in the conflicting emotions.

Lines 3 and 4 also present another paradox that cannot be resolved within the poem. The poet reveals to the beloved that which he cannot reveal to her. The unity of the posture in this poem would have been better served by not having a direct address to the beloved. These lines clearly involve a conflict of artistic styles—the *cancionero* poetic posture of the lover and beloved and the ironic emotional stance of the Petrarchan lover break down in the opposition of having revealed that which he cannot reveal. The poem does not treat this paradox, but simply passes it over in silence.

The second quatrain and the first tercet examine his options. In lines 5 and 6, he looks at his present position. This type of introspection, a stepping back and evaluating the self from a more distanced point of view plays an important role in Garcilaso's Petrarchan poems, which will be discussed in Chapter 7. In lines 7 and 8 he looks back to see if he could flee, but is frightened by the trials he has left behind. When he looks to the future (lines 9–11) to see if he will continue the uphill pursuit, he is frightened by the sight of those who preceded him and fell from the ardor of the struggle. This is the only direct reference to others and to rivals in the Petrarchan sonnets, and they threaten only in the sense that they are examples whose failure suggests he too will fail. His survival hardly promises to be the type of superiority that Boscán evinces from his suffering, but it seems designed to evoke a great deal of sympathy from the reader.

The final tercet states without explanation that the poet now lacks all hope of achieving his goal. The final image of the dark region characterizing the beloved's indifference and forgetfulness is hauntingly beautiful. He has ended in despair. The "ya" of line 12 suggests a change, perhaps a change that has occurred in the process of the poem. The poem seems to be structured as a process of discovery that occurs in the last tercet. The examination of his position and his lack of options have left him in a hopeless state. The meditative course of the poem has served to disillusion him. Garcilaso's other introspective sonnets are more successful because they develop temporal trajectories that move outside the poem, which serves as a single point of convergence. Here the temporal trajectories lead to a new state of disillusionment, and the sense of change within the poem is not as successful as in other poems discussed later.

Critics have often assumed that Boscán, the Catalan, introduced Garcilaso to the works of the fifteenth-century Catalan poet Ausiàs March. The influence of March in both Boscán and Garcilaso is quite marked. Lapesa and McNerney have studied in detail the effect and importance of March's influence on Garcilaso's poetry. His influence is quite evident in a number of Boscán's sonnets and in three of Garcilaso's Petrarchan sonnets, which creates one of the distinctive variations in Garcilaso's Petrarchism. These three sonnets, V, XIV, and XXVII, show different degrees of Marchian influence. Sonnets XIV and XXVII re-create in Spanish actual metaphors from March's poetry, while Sonnet V relies heavily on Marchian elements.

Sonnet XIV consists of one long comparison whose source is usually attributed to Ausiàs March. It is an allegorical sonnet, and Garcilaso has other sonnets that are allegorical in this sense, such as Sonnets XX, XXXI and XXXII:

XIV
Como la tierna madre quel doliente
hijo le 'stá con lágrimas pidiendo
alguna cosa de la qual comiendo
sabe que ha de doblarse el mal que siente,
    y aquel piadoso amor no le consiente
que considere el daño que, haziendo
lo que le piden, haze—va corriendo
y aplaca el llanto y dobla el accidente:
    assí a mi enfermo y loco pensamiento,
que en su daño os me pide, yo querría
quitalle este mortal mantenimiento:[1]
    mas pídemele y llora cada día
tanto que quanto quiere le consiento,
olvidando su muerte y aun la mía.

Boscán has a number of sonnets with similar extended metaphors, all of which have their source in March. The last tercet of Sonnet LXXII even employs the same metaphor found in this poem, although Boscán's treatment is only three lines long.

como madre con hijo regalado,
que si le pide rejalgar llorando,
no sabe sino dalle lo que pide.

---

1. I have emended Rivers's text, removing the "a" after "quitalle" in line 11. The edition of 1543 had "quitalle a este mal mantenimiento," but the two manuscripts and El Brocense all have "quitalle este mortal mantenimiento." A. Blecua recommends accepting the variant reading because the "a" requires a reduplication of the object in line 9 (*En el texto* 59–60). Rivers seemed to accept Blecua's conclusion in his notes, but the text includes both the "a" and "mortal" (perhaps by mistake, since it represents a conflation of the two readings).

Because of the brevity of Boscán's metaphor, it is usually assumed that Garcilaso took his comparison directly from March. Garcilaso's poem has the tone of Boscán's sonnets that use extended Marchian metaphors. As Herrera noted, the comparison is established between the mother and Garcilaso (or the lover), and between the sick child and the lover's "pensamiento." This mental faculty is the one most often mentioned by Garcilaso for its uncontrollable discourse. Here he considers it as a sick beloved child whom he cannot refuse even things that make it sicker. The only reference to an addressee occurs in line 10: "os me pide," a line that has been emended by most editors. The 1543 edition read "os pide," making the first part of the line one syllable short. Two manuscript sources and the editions of El Brocense and Azara read "os me pide" (A. Blecua 56–57). El Brocense noted his emendations came from a manuscript (B-16). While modern editors have almost universally accepted the emendation, it is not a very satisfactory reading, with "os" as the direct object and "me" as the indirect object (A. Blecua 59; compare "pídemele" in line 12). In addition, the tightly structured comparisons and allegory do not easily accommodate the unexpected reference to the beloved. Another of the seven sonnets directed to the beloved has a single reference limited to an "os": "quitarme de yr a veros como quiera" (IV, 13). The reference in Sonnet IV, however, makes more sense since it is a poem on absence, and there is a certain logic in stating the cause of the suffering, and directing it to the beloved. In this sonnet, on the contrary, it is hardly the beloved that is delivered up to the suffering lover, but rather images of desire. In spite of the "os" in line 10, the poem does not seem to be addressed to a beloved. Rather, it is a poem rooted in allegorical psychology in which the presence of the beloved is extraneous to the central argument.

There are several repetitions of vocabulary, three forms of "pedir" in lines 2, 7, and 12; two forms of "doblar" in lines 4 and 8; two forms of "hazer" in lines 6 and 7; and two forms of "consentir" in lines 5 and 13. Also "daño" appears in lines 6 and 10. These repetitions do not stand out, since the concreteness of the metaphor predominates over the abstract polyptoton of the *cancionero* style.

This sonnet borrows not only its metaphor from March, but also its sickbed imagery. For March, who tried to elevate passionate love from animal desire to a pure and chaste emotion, love based on desire was a sickness—and he found the appropriate comparisons among the terminology of illness and dying. As in the central metaphor of this poem, the illness is not cured but made worse. With the metaphor comes the conception of love. It is true that Petrarch also refers to love as insanity and illness, but not with the same degree of detail and concreteness of metaphor. Thus, this poem establishes a different modality within the general trend of Garcilaso's Petrarchism.

Sonnet XXVII, a dialogue with Amor, begins with four lines translated from Ausiàs March:

XXVII

Amor, Amor, un ábito vestí
el qual de vuestro paño fue cortado;
al vestir ancho fue, mas apretado
y estrecho quando estuvo sobre mí.

Después acá de lo que consentí,
tal arrepentimiento m'á tomado
que pruevo alguna vez, de congoxado,
a romper esto en que yo me metí;

mas ¿quién podrá deste ábito librarse,
teniendo tan contraria su natura
que con él á venido a conformarse?

Si alguna parte queda, por ventura,
de mi razón, por mí no osa mostrarse,
que en tal contradición no está segura.

The question of the masculine rhymes has been treated extensively, and need not be repeated here. The first words of the poem establish a dialogue with Cupid, here called Amor (I have capitalized the second Amor), and the second line assigns provenance of the cloth to Cupid: "vuestro paño." The language shifts in the poem so that the cloth is no longer associated with Cupid, but with the lover: "esto" (8) and "deste ábito" (9). The direct address loses force throughout the poem, so that the question in the last tercet seems not to be addressed to Cupid. In fact the question no longer is asked concerning the speaker, but is generalized to include all lovers: "¿quién podrá?" (9). The poem begins invoking Love in a seeming dialogue, but by the sextet, Love seems to have abandoned the speaker, who addresses his futile question to an unspecified reader concerning any lover who has grown accustomed to the tight-

fitting clothing of love. The sextet turns on the paradox of love because
the lover, although he wishes to remove his habit, has grown accustomed
to it: "que con él á venido a conformarse" (11). The habit is contrary to
his nature, and this contrariness forms part of the "contradición" of the
last line. As usual, his commitment to love has banished reason from his
mental processes.

Commentators show a great deal of unspoken reluctance to identify
"ábito" with a religious habit. Rivers says "el sentido de una ropa metafórica" (139n). It would seem difficult to deny religious implications in
the early sixteenth century, which had fewer qualms than we in mixing
religion with secular life—in fact, the incorporation of religious language and ideas was a favorite aspect of love poetry, drawing much criticism from strict moralists. "Arrepentimiento" in line 6 seems to extend
the religious metaphor. In this sonnet the blocking element is realized
through the symbol of the tight-fitting clothing, which represents the
habitual suffering of the lover. Garcilaso has borrowed from March not
only the image, but the quatrain in which it was found, and he has constructed his own meditation on the image, developing through it the play
on religious devotion and worship of the beloved.

Sonnet V consciously exploits a good deal of religious imagery and
references using the same metaphor of a habit. It is one of the most beautiful and impressive of Garcilaso's sonnets, and has been one of the more
popular. The imagery is delicately handled and the musicality of the verse
is incredibly rich.

V

Escrito 'stá en mi alma vuestro gesto
y quanto yo escrivir de vos desseo:
vos sola lo escrivistes; yo lo leo
tan solo que aun de vos me guardo en esto.

En esto 'stoy y estaré siempre puesto,
que aunque no cabe en mí quanto en vos veo,
de tanto bien lo que no entiendo creo,
tomando ya la fe por presupuesto.

Yo no nascí sino para quereros;
mi alma os ha cortado a su medida;
por hábito del alma misma os quiero;
quanto tengo confiesso yo deveros;

por vos nací, por vos tengo la vida
por vos é de morir, y por vos muero.

The influence of March in this sonnet does not consist of direct borrowings of whole lines and images, as occurs in the previous two sonnets,
but of a subtle texture of Marchian reminiscences. The Petrarchism of
this sonnet is not always very manifest because its debts to March and
to the *cancionero* tradition are quite evident. Even so, the languid style
and visual imagery tend to mask the polyptoton in lines 1 to 3 with
"escrito," "escrevir," and "escrivistes." Rivers has commented on how
these three verbs move from the speaker to the addressee ("The Spoken"
65). The religious implications in the sonnet are quite strong. Lapesa
labels the second quatrain as "de fuerte sabor teologizante" (*Garcilaso:
Estudios* 62), and Rivers, usually reluctant to acknowledge religious imagery, comments "Todo el soneto refleja cierta hipérbole sagrada can-
cioneril" (*Obras* 76), an idea he develops in more detail in his article
"The Spoken and Written Word" (64–66). Religious vocabulary is quite
evident: "alma" (1, 10, and 11), "lo que no entiendo creo" (7), "fe" (8),
"hábito" (11), and "confiesso" (12). As Herrera noted (39), "hábito"
suggests both the cloth that has been cut to size (as in Sonnet XXVII)
for a religious habit and a habitual custom of adoration, both a profes-
sion and a daily habit. The poet-lover moves from the role of reader-
scribe to that of a religious in the church of love.

Sonnet V represents the maximum inscription of the reader into the
text. Even though the beloved is not addressed as "señora," her presence
dominates the poem. Only lines 5, 7, and 8 lack a reference to the beloved through "vos," "vuestro," and "os." She is omnipresent and omni-
potent as a larger-than-life force that the poet-lover can only understand
by reducing it to his terms. She completely dominates the lover whose
only acts are continued worship of her. With Sonnet V, Garcilaso takes
on a new metaphor that marks an important step in the relationship of
author and reader traced in this book. The sonnet reverses much of the
literary relationship of the poet-lover to the reader-beloved. Lapesa
found the metaphor of inscription or carving to be common in *cancionero* poetry, but the idea of writing to be unusual and somewhat out
of place:

Más que *escrito* hubiera sido de esperar «grabado»,
«dibujado» o «impreso»; «enprensada tu figura», dice

> Juan de Mena, desarrollando igual imagen. El que
> Garcilaso emplee *escrito* se debe a la interferencia de
> recuerdos literarios donde ese participio aparecía
> usado sin incongruencia alguna. (*Garcilaso: Estudios* 61)

Lapesa's judgment seems to rely more on sources than on the text itself, which concerns the roles of author and addressed reader, and which led to tremendous transformations in the sonnets of Boscán and Garcilaso. Sonnet V takes up directly the question of the inscription of the reader into the text, a question that was a very prominent preoccupation for Boscán and Garcilaso, and it is important that this concern becomes a topic in the poetry itself.

In Sonnet V, the addressed reader becomes the author who leaves a text for future readers that testifies to the intensity of the poet's commitment to the beloved. Not only does he become a passive victim in face of the beloved (as in other sonnets), but he is reduced to the role of passive reader of a text in which he reads the beauty of the beloved, but which is too great for him to understand on its own terms. The reader is inscribed into the soul of the lover and into the text—the text flows from her and she is the text, even though it is not capable of capturing her greatness. In a role reversal typical of courtly love poetry where the lady becomes the lord, knight, and master, and the lover becomes the servant or slave, Garcilaso conceives of the beloved, who is the addressed reader, as the writer, and the poet-lover is a reader and unfaithful scribe of the beauty of the beloved. Creating the role reversal in the arena of poet / text / reader creates new implications regarding the text. The text we are reading is an abridged version of the beauty of inspiration that the lover has copied out of the beauty of the beloved. The text has reduced the beloved to terms that the poet and we as readers can comprehend. The poet's act of reading is certainly not the same as our act of reading. The poet "reads" his text directly from the beauty of the mistress, and the text he produces is an abridged version of what he sees there. He seems in part to be a scribe who copies from the text creating a new version. Ignoring the metaphorical implications, it is difficult to specify the differences between the written text we read and the text the poet-lover copied, except that he read and copied it before we did and he is aware of a further greatness that he accepts on faith and which we can only accept on his statement. The sonnet as a parody of the processes of poetic writing and of reading does not establish a theory of writing or reading, but relies on and plays on already established commonplaces, such as poetic inspiration coming from the muse (a function that Garcilaso ascribes to the beloved, according to Rivers, "The Spoken" 66) and the act of reading as a passive receptivity. The shortness of the sonnet would not allow for the creation of a new theory of writing and reading. Garcilaso is content to shift the idea of inspiration to the beloved and to reverse the roles of the active writer and passive reader, just as the roles of master and servant had been reversed in the courtly love tradition.

I commented previously on the rich sound texture of this sonnet. In spite of Azara's dismissal of lines 5 and 9, which he labeled "durísimos" (A-3), I find line 9 to be one of the most beautiful that Garcilaso ever wrote, even though it is difficult to scan except as a purely Italianate hendecasyllable with accents on the fourth, seventh, and tenth syllables. The sound of the last tercet is quite subtly developed. The anaphora of "por vos" usually seems to explain the success of these lines, but the vowel sounds also add to the effect. All but two of the lines are based on an *e/o* assonant rhyme. Line 12 establishes it as a norm, including the reversal in "yo de-" before the final resolution: "quanto tengo confieso yo deveros." The first and third "por vos," past and future, are resolved in a short *i*: "por vos nascí" and "por vos é de morir." The short *i* at the end of metrical phrases was heard in lines 2 and 3, and in the rhymes of lines 10 and 13. Lines 13 and 14 are resolved in the *e/o* pattern, in line 13 followed by the tonic *i*: "por vos tengo la vida," and in line 14 as a dominant resolution: "y por vos muero." The subtle play of tonic *i* and *e/o* rhymes produces further melodic underpinnings for the two lines.

The poems in this chapter represent various degrees of dependence on Hispanic sources. While I have treated as a group the three sonnets that address the beloved as "vos" and "señora," these three poems do not represent the same degree of dependence on Hispanic sources. Sonnet IX clearly owes much to the *cancionero* style, while at the same time striking a new attitude regarding suffering. Sonnet II seems to belong to the group of sonnets that represents the full strain of Petrarchism, but unlike other sonnets in that group, it has no direct echoes of Petrarch. Sonnet III seems even later, with less emphasis on cruelty and suffering. Sonnet XXXVIII seems somewhat bound by its Hispanic conventions, and does not yet achieve the success of the other sonnets. Sonnets XIV, XXVII, and V all take inspiration in the poems of Ausiàs March, lending a unique element to the survey of Garcilaso's Petrarchism. These sonnets are not poorly achieved or less than successful because of their Marchian sources. On the contrary, they represent a unique modality of Spanish Petrarchism and some of Garcilaso's most successful sonnets.

7

The Petrarchan Sonnets

The limited number of Garcilaso's sonnets that fit into the Petrarchan mold suggests that Garcilaso may not have felt comfortable or perhaps even disagreed with the Petrarchan formulas (and devices) of unrequited desire and suffering. The quality of the sonnets, and of his poetry in general, demonstrates he was capable of imitating Petrarch, but the small number of such compositions suggests that he was less than eager to do so. In contrast to the far greater numbers of Petrarchan poems by Boscán, and the almost exclusive preoccupation with Petrarchism by the immediate followers of Boscán and Garcilaso, the limited number by Garcilaso could be explained by the fact that we do not have all of his poetry, but probably finds an answer in Garcilaso's constant undoing of social, intellectual, and poetic codes. As I shall suggest in Chapters 9 and 11, and in Part V, Garcilaso delighted in playing with the inherent paradoxes of accepted codes. His rejection of Neoplatonic love, studied in Chapter 10, is explicit in much of his treatment of the theme. That he rejected Neoplatonism for sensual love would infer that Petrarchism would have been more amenable to him. But the unwriting of Petrarchan formulas, as seen in the following chapters, implies a restless mind not satisfied with reproducing someone else's solutions, but always struggling to achieve its own autonomy and originality.

Because of its *cancionero* language, Sonnet I could easily have been discussed in the last chapter with Sonnet XXXVIII; however, it has also several Petrarchan features that mark it as one of the Petrarchan sonnets.

I

Quando me paro a contemplar mi 'stado
y a ver los passos por dó m'han traýdo,
hallo, según por do anduve perdido,
que a mayor mal pudiera aver llegado;
    mas quando del camino 'stó olvidado,
a tanto mal no sé por dó é venido;
sé que me acabo, y más é yo sentido
ver acabar comigo mi cuydado.
    Yo acabaré, que me entregué sin arte
a quien sabrá perderme y acabarme
si quisiere, y aun sabrá querello;
    que pues mi voluntad puede matarme
la suya, que no es tanto de mi parte,
pudiendo, ¿qué hará sino hazello?

Sonnet I is one of Garcilaso's most popular poems. It is often anthologized and has been studied in various articles. Its central image, that of a trajectory or course, is one of Garcilaso's favorites. Sonnet I is, as described by Lapesa, a work of apprenticeship and is quite close in style to the previous group of poems. Keniston recognized the debt to Petrarch in the beginning line, but judged the development to follow original ideas. He claimed the wordplays in the rest of the poem were in imitation of Petrarch's style. Lapesa maintained there was a closer connection of the beginning lines to several lines of Dante or to one of Petrarch's madrigals. More important is the debt he signals to *cancionero* poetry: "En los tercetos destacan dos rasgos peculiares de la poesía castellana anterior: la afirmación «mi voluntad puede matarme» y los insistentes juegos de palabras reiteradas" (*Garcilaso: Estudios* 77). While it is true the poem contains very clear use of the techniques and language of Spanish courtly poetry, it also has several elements that distinguish it from other poems of apprenticeship. Its beginning quotation from Petrarch, the disappearance of the avowed reader, the complete absence of any reference to the cause of his suffering and the stress placed on feeling are all elements associated with Garcilaso's Petrarchan style. Unlike Sonnet XXXVIII, which uses the same metaphor of a "camino" for meditating on the poet's present condition, Sonnet I imitates a line from Petrarch as point of departure.

Garcilaso's treatment of the Petrarchan meditative commonplace differs significantly from other treatments of the theme. Petrarch's poem is written "in morte" and focuses on his aging and the futility of love:

> Quando' io mi volgo indietro a mirar gli anni
>   C'hanno, fuggendo, i miei penseri sparsi,
>   E spento' l foco ove agghiacciando io arsi,
>   E finito el riposo pien d'affani;
> Rotta la fé degli amorosi inganni, . . .
>   (298, p. 477)

> (When I turn back to look at the years
>   which have, fleeing, scattered my thoughts,
>   and extinguished the fire where, freezing, I burned,
>   and ended my rest full of anguish;
> Broken [is] the faith in amorous deceits . . .)

Using the same point of departure, Bernardo Tasso plays with the time element almost exclusively, but also makes the love element clear in one of the sonnets from his *Libro primo* (1531), one of the poems of frank Petrarchan imitation that he deleted in the second edition of 1534:

> Quando' io mi uolgo indietro a mirar l'hore,
>   Ch'ogn'hor fuggendo se ne portan gli anni;
>   E'l poco frutto di miei lunghi affanni,
>   Ch'io colsi, & colgo in seruitù d'Amore;
>   (20)

> (When I turn back to look at the hours
>   For every fleeing hour the years have carried off,
>   And the little fruit from my long anguish
>   That I harvested, and I harvest, in service to Love;)

Lope de Vega's imitation of the Petrarchan commonplace in his *Rimas* also makes explicit the themes of love and aging and distinguishes between the suffering caused by each from the very beginning of his sonnet:

> Cuando imagino de mis breves días
> los muchos que el tirano Amor me debe

> y en mi cabello anticipar la nieve
> más que los años las tristezas mías,
>   (*Obras* 23)

These examples all imitate Petrarch in his wording and his thematic development, and they all elaborate the themes of time, love, and suffering.

Garcilaso's Sonnet I is not about aging, nor is the time element mentioned in the text. His reworking of the Petrarchan line signals the change in theme from time to condition: "Cuando me paro a contemplar mi' stado." Typical of Garcilaso's thought are the observations in the quatrains that a retrospective look produces such pain that he realizes he could be in a worse position, but when he considers his present state he realizes he is so miserable he cannot conceive of how he arrived at such an unfortunate situation. He knows only that he is dying, and his only regret is that his troubles will be extinguished with him. His poem is about his "estado," a word meaning condition or situation, but also often referring to one's legal or social status. The first tercet takes up in metaphorical terms the questions of legal status and power relations. He states "me entregué sin arte / a quien sabrá perderme" (9–10). The context of knowledge and power is evident in the following lines: "sabrá perderme y acabarme / si quisiere, y aun sabrá querello" (10–11). The relationship, not specified as to nature or to gender, is one of power in which the poet has surrendered his will: "que pues mi voluntad puede matarme" (12). There is no reference either to love or to the beloved. The phrases "a quien" (10) and "la suya" (13) do no more than indicate the power relationship in which the narrator has placed himself. It is this lack of specificity that allowed Goodwyn to conflate all of Garcilaso's biographical problems, his amorous frustrations, and his political setbacks, into the framework of the narrative "cuydado" (8). This lack of precision also marks a salient aspect of Spanish Petrarchism.

The style of the poem, as Lapesa observed, owes a great deal to *cancionero* poetry. A high number of verbs and verbal forms predominate. A majority of the lines have two or more separate actions relayed by active verb forms. The nouns are few and are symbolic: "passos" (2) and "camino" (4); or abstract, "'stado" (1), "mal" (4, 6), "cuydado" (8), and "voluntad" (12); or adverbial, "sin arte" (9) and "de mi parte" (13). There are no descriptive adjectives, only the comparative "mayor" (4) and "tanto" (6). In addition, there is a heavy use of polyptoton, although the longer Italianate lines make it less evident than in the Spanish octosyllable. Four different forms of "acabar" are used: "me acabo" (7), "acabar" (8), "acabaré" (9), and "acabarme" (10); three forms of "poder": "pudiera" (4), "puede" (12), and "pudiendo" (14); two each of "perder": "perdido" (3) and "perderme" (10); "querer": "quiere" (11) and "querello" (11); saber: "sé" (5, 6) and "sabrá" (10, 11); and "hazer": "hará" (14) and "hazello" (14). The intensity of these repetitions and the abstract nature of the verbs recall the *cancionero* style. One wonders if the ambiguity in this poem serves to obscure a relationship the author wishes to hide, or if it is a playful tease arising from the mixture of styles. Sonnet I clearly lies between the abstract intellectual Hispanic style and the sensual Italianate style, containing elegant characteristics of each. In spite of its stylistic ambiguity, the poem achieves a clear effect and its verbal reticence makes an intriguing and well-fashioned poem.

Sonnet VI, like the majority of Boscán's Petrarchan sonnets, does not directly address the beloved. Its Petrarchan themes are enhanced by direct quotations from Petrarch, and it also recalls a passage from March. In spite of the persistence of the Marchian influence, Garcilaso seems to have found with Sonnet VI and the rest of the sonnets in this chapter a truly Petrarchan mode of expression, and these sonnets represent his Petrarchism at its fullest.

VI

Por ásperos caminos é llegado
a parte que de miedo no me muevo,
y si mudarme a dar un passo pruevo,
allí por los cabellos soy tornado;
   mas tal estoy que con la muerte al lado
busco de mi bivir consejo nuevo,
y conozco el mejor y el peor apruevo,
o por costumbre mala o por mi hado.
   Por otra parte, el breve tiempo mío
y el errado processo de mis años,
en su primer principio y en su medio,
   mi inclinación, con quien ya no porfío,
la cierta muerte, fin de tantos daños,
me hazen descuydar de mi remedio.

Sonnet VI focuses on the lover's psychological state, presenting a desperation and suffering that result in his acceptance of death. It employs the metaphor of the "camino" found in other poems by Garcilaso, and as in Sonnet XXXVIII the lover is trapped by his emotions. He has arrived by a rough way and is held captive by fear and violence, for he may be yanked back by his hair. Line 4 recalls a line from Ausiàs March and another passage in the first stanza of Canción IV, where the same word clusters, "áspero" and "cabellos" occur. The second quatrain draws heavily from Petrarch. Lines 6 and 7 are direct translations. Line 5 presents death as a constant companion of his torments and an always present possibility of escape. Line 8 attributes his choice of the worse option, even though he knows better, to habit or to fate; that is, to elements that are either difficult to control or completely out of his control. This line establishes the concept of a lover's destiny fixed on the choice of suffering, whatever its cause. The sextet accumulates the elements that dispose him toward death. The phrase "el breve tiempo mío" is ambiguous, referring either to the shortness of life in general or to his own youth. The following lines do not resolve the problem. The phrase "primer principio" in line 11 seems to be an obvious redundancy; "principio" and "medio" seem to be temporal references. The insistence on the literal sense of both "principio" and "medio" recalls the other senses of the words, so that the terms can be understood both as beginning and middle of his life and as the principles and means by which he has lived. The last tercet is clear. The lover no longer struggles with his disposition or inclination, and certain death, which will end his many pains, combined with all the other elements, makes him indifferent to his remedy. Unlike other sonnets which end with a manifest death-wish, this sonnet calmly accepts death; not wishing for it, but simply viewing it as an end to his suffering.

Garcilaso furnishes a new context for the final lines of Petrarch's Canzone CCLXIV. The lines are embedded in the middle of his sonnet (lines 6–8); he has provided for them a new introduction and he draws from them further conclusions. The moral ambiguity of Petrarch's concluding lines have become the center of a new argument. The octave and sextet form two parts of his argument. "Por otra parte" in line 9, which introduces the second argument, contrasts with "a parte que" in line 2. On the one hand he is emotionally trapped either by his bad habits or destiny; on the other, general considerations on life lead him to an acceptance of death. The poem presents the reason for his despair and how his mental processes increase it, rather than relieve it. Garcilaso recreates the Petrarchan moral ambiguity, but presents it in the context of an emotional trap that will lead to a welcome acceptance of death. Poised between right and wrong, between life and death, the lover inclines toward the wrong and death.

Like so many Spanish Petrarchan sonnets that have no identified reader or beloved inscribed in the poem, this sonnet makes no explicit reference whatsoever to love. It could be read as a moral sonnet, or even as a political sonnet (as Goodwyn did with Sonnet I), but one recognizes the codes of despair and willful destruction and the intertexts from Petrarch that signal the unrequited lover. The poem focuses on the despair of the lover by assuming a posture of suffering that evokes compassion in the unidentified reader. By not naming a reader, or even the cause of his suffering, the poet-lover is isolated and maligned, ingrained in his acceptance of evil and death, a posture that evokes compassion from all readers, the beloved, friends, rivals, and critics who come to believe in the authenticity of his despair.

Sonnet XX likewise has no avowed reader and does not mention love as cause of the suffering. It also concentrates on the lover's psychological state and his death-wish:

XX

Con tal fuerça y vigor son concertados
para mi perdición los duros vientos
que cortaron mis tiernos pensamientos
luego que sobre mí fueron mostrados.

El mal es que me quedan los cuydados
en salvo destos acontecimientos,
que son duros y tienen fundamientos
en todos mis sentidos bien echados.

Aunque por otra parte no me duelo,
ya que'l bien me dexó con su partida,
del grave mal que en mí está de contino;

antes con él me abraço y me consuelo,
porque en processo de tan dura vida
ataje la largueza del camino.

Like a number of Petrarchan sonnets, this poem uses plant imagery to make its point. The imagery is allegorical in nature. The "tiernos pensamientos" are young plants killed by the cruel winds, or passions that are allied against the lover. Typical of Petrarchan pessimism, the winds and destiny join forces against the lover and cause suffering. Underlying the imagery is the irony of the allegiance of the winds, "concertados," and the implied contrary term indicating the sickness of the lover: "desconcertado." His sickness is explained in the second quatrain as a continuation of the plant allegory. As in Canción IV and the Epístola a Boscán, "pensamientos" for Garcilaso are always portrayed as the wild active part of the imagination that have free rein, able to function against reason and logic. The opposite term in this poem, "cuydados," usually refers to his depression and ultimately a death-wish. His "cuydados" remain well rooted in the senses. Even though the sextet seems to open on a note of optimism: "Aunque por otra parte no me duelo," it only leads to a grimmer and deeper pessimism. Since his good health (*bien*) left him, he does not suffer from his sickness—presumably he no longer knows any other state. The final tercet ends the poem with a death-wish. He readily accepts his suffering because it serves to shorten his life. His only consolation is death, which will relieve him from suffering.

The lack of an identified reader in this poem only heightens the poet's role as a victim deserving compassion, serving to isolate him further from human contact. He seems to fight his battle alone. There is no beloved, no reference to love, no mention of a love affair, no rivals, no friends—only the voice of the poet assailed by violent cold winds. The poem speaks from a state of isolation and only seeks compassion by implication. The brightest hope in the poem comes from the fact that his suffering will lead to death. As in the previous sonnet, the poet-lover seems to set himself apart from society and seeks help only by recounting his suffering. Unlike Boscán, who asserts his superiority as a lover and suggests his suffering makes him deserving of victory, Garcilaso strikes a posture of isolation and defeat, that privileged state of the sacrificial victim who has been unjustly harmed and must be protected from further harm as he prepares for welcomed death. It is a complex poetic stance, but one that serves to reinforce the alleged sincerity of the lover. The rhetorical stance serves to disarm readers from wishing him further harm, while the posture of suffering also convinces the reader of the seriousness of the lover's commitment to his purpose.

The imagery of the poem is visual, but allegorical in nature. The images occur because of their meaning and not for their visual or ornamental sense. The plants live and die not by their own nature, but by allegorical necessities. Not as conceptual as the purely abstract language of the early sonnets conceived in the *cancionero* style, this imagery is not as detached from morality and contrivance as later poems. Allegory almost always has moral implications, as the surface plot motivates and reveals a deeper, more substantive plot, and the inner plot often derives not only its motivation but also its moral aspects from the surface plot. Here, the tender plants freeze, but the roots continue to grow and corrupt the host. The moral sense is made more explicit by the words "mal" (5, 11) and "bien" (10). The word "duro" occurs three times, being attributed to various negative forces in the poem: "duros vientos" (2), "cuydados . . . duros" (5–7), and "dura vida" (13). While the poem moves away from the conceptual language of the early sonnets, its imagery still bears the moral sense of the poem.

Petrarch's *Canzoniere* is divided into two sections, the first consisting of those poems written within the lifetime of Laura, called "in vita"; and the second consisting of those written after her death, called "in morte." Both sections treat frustrated impossible love, differing only in that the cause of the impossibility or blocking element is different. In the first section, it is the coldness of Laura and her virtue that prevent her from responding to the poet's love; in the second, there is the physical impossibility caused by her death, which separates them. Like Garcilaso's two shepherds in Eclogue I, Salicio (who laments the loss of the treacherous Galatea) and Nemoroso (who laments the dead Elisa), Petrarch presents a double facet to the sufferings of the courtly lover. Garcilaso's sonnets also present this duality, although there is no formal division and those written "in morte" are few in number (X, IV? and XXV) in comparison to the far greater number written "in vita." Twentieth-century critics have maintained that Sonnet X refers to Isabel Freire's death.

X

¡O dulces prendas por mi mal halladas,
dulces y alegres quando Dios quería,
juntas estáys en la memoria mía
y con ella en mi muerte conjuradas!
    ¿Quién me dixera, quando las passadas
oras que'n tanto bien por vos me vía,
que me aviades de ser en algún día
con tal grave dolor representadas?
    Pues en una ora junto me llevastes
todo el bien que por términos me distes,
lleváme junto el mal que me dexastes:

si no, sospecharé que me pusistes
en tantos bienes porque desseastes
verme morir entre memorias tristes.

The sonnet has been studied extensively. I do not wish to repeat here all critical arguments, but rather to focus on those elements that relate to Garcilaso's Petrarchism. Addressed to the "dulces prendas," the poem uses the objects as a point of departure for describing the poet's paradoxical emotional reactions. The poem consists of an intricate network of verbal tenses, which relate the lover's present anguish and past pleasure, and project from both moments into a future anguish. The octave employs indefinite verbal tenses: imperfect, present, and conditional. In the octave, those actions that are definite, such as the chance discovery of the mementos, are represented by participles, rather than fixed tenses: "halladas" (1), "conjuradas" (4) and "representadas" (8). The rhymes of the octave announce the participial actions, "-adas," and the imperfect actions, "-ía." In contrast, the sextet employs definite verbal tenses: preterit, future, and imperative. The rhymes of the sextet modulate between the two preterit endings: "-astes" and "-istes." There are five preterit forms, one future, and one command. The imperfect or conditional action in the sextet is accomplished with the adverb "por términos" and two infinitives "verme morir."

In the octave, the present and the imperfect (both imperfective tenses) are contrasted. The imperfective past brought pleasure: "dulces y alegres quando Dios quería," and "quando las passadas / oras que'n tanto bien por vos me vía," while the present (often represented participially) brings only grief: "por mi mal halladas," "en mi muerte conjuradas," and "con tal grave dolor representadas." The finite preterits of the sextet are associated with both pleasure and grief, but they refer to the souvenirs, ascribing malicious intentions to them. The reference to pleasure in line 10 must recall the imperfective state of the octave and at the same time use a preterit verb to signal its termination. This is accomplished with an adverbial expression that extends the action of the preterit: "todo el bien que por términos me distes." Like Sonnets I, XXVI, and XXXIII, this poem uses verbal tenses to project the lover's emotions into the past and future. The poem is a static moment of meditation on an unexpectedly discovered souvenir, but that one moment, and the feelings that cross through it and out of it, are complex and paradoxical. The sonnet is constructed on temporal trajectories of two past experiences that come into the present, a pleasurable experience represented with the imperfect and a bitter, grievous moment represented by the preterit. The present is also indefinite in its range of suffering, while the future is projected into death surrounded by sad memories.

Like all of Garcilaso's poetry, this sonnet relies on repetitive vocabulary, but in this case it recalls less the polyptoton of the *cancionero* style and the earlier Petrarchan sonnets. The repetition of "dulces" in lines 1 and 2 is a highly effective way of emphasizing the contrast of feeling. The word "junto" (lines 3, 9, and 11) underlines the joining of opposite emotions in the same object. The terms of "bien" (lines 6, 10, and 13) and "mal" (lines 1 and 11), although typical of Garcilaso's poetry, here emphasize again the extremes of emotion arising from a single object. Likewise, the contrast of "alegres" (2) and "tristes" (14) at the opening and closing of the poem give emphasis to the same contrast. "Memoria" occurs in line 3 as a function of the brain and in line 14 as a type of thought. Both "muerte" (4) and "morir" (14) refer to the poet's suffering, although the first reference in line 4 would seem to be a poetic transference, for one expects the line to refer to the deceased mistress rather than to the poet's suffering.

The poem addresses the unexpectedly found memento that simultaneously recalls his past happiness and his present grief. The objects come to represent the poet's combined sense of longing and grief. Like the beloved in the *cancionero* tradition, the "prendas" are addressed as "vos." Not only do they represent his suffering, but they come to personify the causes of that suffering; malicious intention is even ascribed to them in the final lines. As symbols of remorse and suffering, they are personified and animated with their own will. In the same way they were conjured up with the beloved in the first quatrain, in the last stanza they are imbued with mental intentions to work evil. The strong poetic emotions portrayed in the poem animate the symbol beyond its cold, lifeless state.

Atypical of Petrarchism is the implication of happiness at a previous time. Petrarch never relates in his poetry a requited love, but Garcilaso does so here and in other poems, such as Eclogue I. Unlike the first two *canciones* and the early sonnets, Garcilaso's mature Petrarchism is more independent of purely Petrarchan ideas and topoi. He understands Petrarchism more as a model of suffering than source of details. The creation of suffering can follow any pattern as long as it carefully exploits the pathos of a given moment or situation. Here the irony of a souvenir as a stimulus of both happiness and sadness establishes a pattern of suffering, but Garcilaso does not slavishly follow the details of the Petrarchan models.

The "dulces prendas" are usually identified with the lock of hair described in Eclogue I (352–54), even though the situation in this sonnet suggesting a chance discovery does not fit the passage in the eclogue where Nemoroso says he always carries the hair in a packet near his breast, suggesting that he is continually aware of its presence. Whether the objects represent a real experience or not is not known, but the situation has obvious literary sources. The poem represents a Petrarchan commonplace of the association of objects with feelings. Castiglione explained how emotions become transferred to objects:

> Esto no puede ser menos, pues nuestros corazones naturalmente se aborrecen con todas las cosas que fueron en algunos días compañeras de nuestros enojos, y aman las que hicieron compañía a nuestros placeres. Y así acaece que un hombre enamorado huelga de ver la ventana donde alguna vez vio a su amiga, aunque la vea cerrada; y todos generalmente holgamos con una sortija, con una carta, y en fin, con toda cosa que en algún tiempo nos haya traído mucha alegría, asimismo nos alegramos con un huerto o con otro lugar cualquier que sea donde hayamos recebido algún placer muy grande; y por el contrario, nos entristecemos con un aposiento [sic], por bueno que nos parezca, si hemos estado en él alguna vez presos, o padecido algún trabajo o enojo recio, y he conocido yo hartos hombres que en ninguna manera bebieran en vaso que se pareciese a otro en que hubiesen tomado algún xarabe siendo enfermos; porque así como aquella ventana o sortija o carta al uno representa una memoria que mucho le deleita, acordándole que cualquiera destas cosas fue casi como una parte de sus placeres, así al otro el aposiento o el vaso parece que le traiga juntamente con la memoria la prisión o la enfermedad. (109)

This passage recalls the imagery of both Sonnet X and Canción III where the island prison serves for the same sort of ironical meditation as the mementos in this poem. The coincidences of vocabulary between Boscán's translation and Garcilaso's sonnet are striking: "alegría," "representa," "memoria," and "juntamente." While Castiglione describes objects that give either pleasure or pain, Garcilaso has complicated the issue by associating contrary emotions with the same object.

As Castiglione's text shows, the contemplation of things that remind one of the beloved was a commonplace. Like many such commonplaces, this one is elaborated out of love poetry, typically Petrarch's love poetry. Sixteenth-century Petrarchists re-created and readapted over and over the typical commonplaces of Petrarchan poetry. We do not know if Garcilaso wrote this sonnet in reaction to the death of Isabel Freire, nor do we know that it was inspired by the passage from Castiglione, but we do know for sure that he had read Castiglione's text, at least once in the original and at least once in Boscán's translation. Since Castiglione's treatment of the idea is a commonplace, Garcilaso need not have used this text directly for his ideas. It is clear, however, that the success of Garcilaso's sonnet lies largely in the unique way he has elaborated the basic commonplace, complicating the simplicity of love and pain by combining their source in the same object, while the subjective personal references are of little interest. The same love-hate relation that the poet-lover maintained with himself and his love affair is now re-created out of the souvenirs that remind him of his past love and present pain. Whether one accepts the idea of an anguished love of Isabel Freire or not, it is obvious that the personal element has been overemphasized and has overshadowed the importance of the poetic canons at work in the poem. Garcilaso's poetry clearly owes as much, if not more, to the poetic conventions in which he was working as to any undocumented love affair he may have had. The emphasis on the poet's undocumented sentimental biography has obscured the manner in which his poems excite us and has created a setting for understanding the poem that obscures the poetic tradition out of which it was elaborated. The poet has become for us a lover, rather than an intellectual or a reader of books, or the writer skillfully reworking the conventions of his time.

Sonnet XXXII is an allegory on the theme of indiscretion, or the perils of having incurred the wrath of the beloved by having spoken too much. It is the thematical opposite of the *coplas* and sonnets advocating silence. In this sonnet, the poet's "lengua" is not under his control, and he is surrounded by personified figures, such as "dolor," "desatino," and to a lesser degree "sufrimiento."

XXXII

Mi lengua va por do el dolor la guía;
ya yo con mi dolor sin guia camino;
entrambos emos de yr con puro tino;
cada uno va a parar do no querría:
yo porque voy sin otra compañía
sino la que me haze el desatino;
ella porque la lleve aquel que vino
a hazella dezir más que querría.
Y es para mí la ley tan desygual
que aunque inocencia siempre en mí conoçe,
siempre yo pago el yerro ageno y mío.
¿Que culpa tengo yo del desvarío
de mi lengua, si estoy en tanto mal
que el sufrimiento ya me desconoçe?

Of the sonnets attributed to Garcilaso from El Brocense's manuscript sources, this one seems less typical.[1] None of the elements, however, are unique to this sonnet. Three other works, Sonnets XXXI and XIV and Canción IV, have allegorical personifications. The forced endstops in the quatrains seem metrically awkward for Garcilaso's poetry, but are found in many of his poems. The masculine rhymes in lines 9 and 13 are also found in Sonnet XXVII and Canción II. In addition, the vocabulary does not seem typical, and the poem has certain forced expressions, such as "con puro tino." No word in this poem, however, is unique in Garcilaso's poetic production, but, curiously enough, six vocabulary items occur only twice in Garcilaso's works, once in this sonnet and once in another poem. As the following list shows, a good number of the lexical items in the sonnet occur only in Eclogue II and Canción IV. The number in parentheses indicates the number of occurrences.

guía (verb): Eclogue II (1)
guía (noun): Eclogue II (1)

---

1. Sonnet XXXII is one of the sonnets that El Brocense attributed to Garcilaso from manuscript sources. Herrera did not accept it as by Garcilaso and it was the only one of Sonnets XXX through XXXVIII that Tamayo rejected: "Ultimamente el XXXVIII, que Sánchez pone de Garci-Lasso, por ser incierto, o por haberle faltado la última lima, no me atreví a ponerle en el texto" (T-40). The sonnet has not been treated by critics (Lumsden's note on Sonnet XXXII is Rivers's Sonnet XXXVIII).

tino: Eclogue II (1), in the more common expression "perder el tino"

inocencia: Eclogue II (1)

entreambos (and *entreamos*): Eclogue II (5)

desigual: Eclogue I (1)

sufrimiento: Canción IV (1)

compañía: Sonnet XVII (1), Eclogue II (1)

desatino: Canción IV (1), Eclogue II (1); also *desatinado* appears once in each of these two poems

ley: Eclogue II (1), Canción IV (1), Sonnet XXV (1)

lengua: Sonnet XIX (1), Eclogue II (6), Eclogue III (4) (The word is ingeniously avoided in Sonnet XXXV.)

desvarío: Sonnet XXXVI (1), Eclogue I (1), Eclogue II (2), Canción II (1)

culpa: Canción III (1), Eclogue I (1), Eclogue II (5), Copla I (1), Copla II (1)

The initial impression that this poem is not typical of Garcilaso is born out in the comparison of the significant vocabulary items, six of which occur only in one other poem, two of which appear in two other poems, and four of which appear in three to five other poems. This sonnet represents a concentration of atypical vocabulary items. The rejection of a poem, however, in a writer whose works vary so tremendously, even within the corpus of Italianate verse, and one who experimented with so many modes and styles of expression, is quite risky.

The language and expressions in this sonnet are less formal than in Garcilaso's other poetry. The expression "yr con puro tino" means to find one's way by feeling or conjecture. Even though "tino" appears in Eclogue II in the more common expression, "perder el tino," it is a term more appropriate to spoken, rather than written, language, although it is found in *cancionero* poetry and Boscán's Italianate poetry. Another example of less formal language is the expression "va a parar" in line 4. Garcilaso always prefers the real future, as in Sonnets I and XXXIV, and this is the only case of the future periphrastic in all of his poetry. The whole allegory of the poem seems to be constructed on a popular phrase (that I have found only in modern literature), "la lengua va a la muela pudrida," generally meaning that one always ends up talking about personal problems (sore spots). Inherent in the phrase and in its elaboration in this sonnet is the dual sense of "lengua" as a physical organ and as speech or language. The poet makes an allegorical figure of the tongue that is no longer controlled by him ("ella" in line 7).

There is no addressed beloved in this sonnet, although her presence is felt in line 11: "siempre yo pago el yerro ageno y mío." The image of the sacrificial victim suffering for collective guilt comes clear in his claim that he must pay for his own mistakes and for those of others. The loquacious lover is accompanied by folly, which guides his tongue to various indiscretions. Rather than the presence of the beloved, there is an exaggerated presence of the speaker. "Yo" appears four times; "mi" three times; and "mí" and "me" twice each. The poet-lover and his sacrificial guilt complex are clearly inscribed in this sonnet.

Rather than a defect of tone, this sonnet probably represents a conscious effort to base the written language on the spoken language. Erasmus and Valdés both advocated the use of spoken language as a model for style (Valdés: "scrivo como hablo," 153), and both rely heavily on proverbial speech as models of correctness. Erasmus collected maxims in his *Adagia,* and Valdés constantly refers to proverbs in his *Diálogo de la lengua* as examples of correct usage. This sonnet, then, puts into practice this idea, employing a reworked proverb as a point of departure and using more colloquial expressions and vocabulary.

The clearest examples of Petrarchism in Garcilaso's sonnets are in those poems that have no identified reader and concentrate on the psychological state of the lover. The sonnets that remain closest to the beloved, either employing the "yo → vos (señora)" formula or having references to the beloved, are those that show more reliance on *cancionero* vocabulary and concepts. The lack of an identified beloved isolates the poet in his suffering from the only possible source of remedy. Communication with the beloved has ceased and no dialogue is begun. Instead, the poet displaces the cause of suffering from the beloved to his own psychological state of mind. The beloved is not blamed for not reciprocating his love; instead the poet blames himself for his situation: "y conozco el mejor y el peor apruevo" (VI, 7), and even his situation is beyond his control: "o por costumbre mala o por mi hado" (VI, 8). The disappearance of the avowed reader clearly forms part of the trajectory through the Petrarchan mode, and is a key element for understanding this movement.

The sonnets in this chapter, along with some from the previous chapter and the *canciones,* constitute Garcilaso's poetic production in the Petrarchan vein. The next four chapters study his subversion of the Petrarchan models, and his complete abandonment of Petrarchism for the classical style advocated by Bernardo Tasso. The Petrarchan sonnets include two of his most famous compositions, Sonnets I and X, and other well-wrought poems. The reception of these poems, along with other Petrarchan poems, owes much to the idea of Garcilaso as a rejected lover. Perhaps the new conception of the poet as an intellectual advocated in this study and elsewhere will place more emphasis on the lesser known sonnets.

8

Unorthodox Petrarchan Postures

As I shall demonstrate in Part V, Garcilaso seems not to have been very comfortable with received systems and codes, often perceiving the flaws in their logic and focusing on their inherent contradictions. For this reason, it is not surprising to find several sonnets that remain within the Petrarchan tradition, but subtly subvert its tenets. The sonnets studied in Part IV actually react against the Petrarchan mode, even reaching the point of treating material other than love. In contrast, the sonnets in this chapter are love sonnets, and present the typical Petrarchan situation of the unrequited suffering lover; in subtle ways, however, without abandoning the Petrarchan mode of expression, they undermine other principles of Petrarchism, such as Petrarchan observations or the central idea of continuous suffering. In all of the poems Garcilaso is aware of his Petrarchan heritage; most contain a direct quotation from Petrarch or at least several echoes of Petrarchan poems. At times Petrarchan topoi signal an eristic imitation, as Garcilaso subverts the Petrarchan quotation or strikes an unorthodox Petrarchan posture.

Sonnet XVIII actually disproves the conclusion of Petrarch's Sonnet CXCIV, although this specific example is not original and was quite popular among Italian Petrarchists, including Bembo. In this case Garcilaso does not subvert Petrarch's meaning; he openly contradicts it. Garcilaso's sonnet only takes on full meaning in light of the Petrarchan phrase that serves as an assumed intertext. Garcilaso engages in a debate with Petrarch's ideas, and his own reformulation of the Petrarchan model only comes clear through hearing both sides of the argument.

XVIII

Si a vuestra voluntad yo soy de cera
y por sol tengo solo vuestra vista,
la qual a quien no inflama o no conquista
con su mirar es de sentido fuera,

¿de dó viene una cosa que, si fuera
menos vezes de mí provada y vista,
según parece que a razón resista,
a mi sentido mismo no creyera?

Y es que yo soy de lexos inflamado
de vuestra ardiente vista y encendido
tanto que en vida me sostengo apenas;

mas si de cerca soy acometido
de vuestros ojos, luego siento elado
cuajárseme la sangre por las venas.

Both El Brocense and Herrera indicated Petrarch's line "che da lunge mi struggo, e da press'ardo" (for from afar I am destroyed and nearby I burn) as a source of the sextet (B-20; H-119). Petrarch argued that the presence of the beloved causes fire and distance causes ice, and concluded his sonnet with the epigrammatic summary line. Both commentators, and their successors, simply noted the line as if it were a source without indicating the fact that Garcilaso's argument contradicts the alleged source. The reversal of this Petrarchan line was a favorite topos of Italian Petrarchists, as seen in the notes of both El Brocense and Herrera. El Brocense quoted Bembo:

Un dinanzi al suo fuoco esser di neve,
Et tutto in fiamma andar sendo in disparte.
(B-20)

(One near his fire is of snow,
and all in flame being away.)

Herrera quoted a tercet from Ariosto which is much closer in idea, imagery and language to Garcilaso's argument:

Che certo io so, che quel che perde il core,
   lontan' arder solea per questi rai;
   e io che gli son presso, agghiaccio, et tremo.
                              (H-119)

(How certain I am that he who loses his heart
   from a distance burns by these rays
   and I who am close to them freeze and shiver.)

The conceits elaborated over the ideas of near and far were further developed by Giulio Cesare Caracciolo, the minor Neapolitan poet whom Herrera identified as the "Julio" of Garcilaso's Sonnet XIX. His sonnet, which begins "Se da lunge, e da presso ogn'hor più fiero / L'acute stral m'aggiunge" (If from afar and near the sharp arrow savagely comes to me), ends the first tercet with the lines:

E vicin son ferito, e lontan vinto,
E vedendo ardo, e disiando agghiaccio.
                        (*Il sesto* 195)

(and nearby I am wounded and from a distance conquered,
and seeing I burn, and desiring I freeze.)

In another sonnet, the first tercet plays on the same duality, striking a compromise between the extremes:

E si ti veggio, e sento al petto mio
Fiamma immortal de la beltà d'Amore
Che non meno ardo lunge che da presso.
                        (*Il sesto* 194)

(And if I see you and feel in my chest
the immortal flame of the beauty of love,
I do not burn less from afar than from nearby.)

These conceits are the type favored by the fifteenth-century Petrarchists—Bembo's example notwithstanding—centering on the continuous elaboration of new and more extreme relationships out of the opposites carefully balanced by Petrarch. Garcilaso's reworking of the Petrarchan commonplace would signify nothing more than the normal Petrarchan currency of the sixteenth century were it not for the actual rebellion against the norms of this movement later. Whether Garcilaso was copying from one of the Italian poets or not, it is clear from his phrasing and method of argument that the desire to contradict the Petrarchan phrase lies behind his poem. He maintains it is part of his experience (6) even though it seems to contradict logic (7). These allowances imply the presence of Petrarch's argument to the contrary.

Divided into two long sentences, the octave presents a question that is answered in the sextet. The poem begins with the Petrarchan topos of the mistress's eyes as suns. The poet, like wax, melts before her wish and her sight. Anne J. Cruz has suggested that the image of wax melting before the sun recalls the myth of Icarus, also treated elliptically, in Sonnet XII ("La mitología" 407–8). The re-creation of myths without naming the subject is typical of Petrarch and imitated by Garcilaso in Sonnets XII and XV and Canción IV. It seems to me unlikely in this instance because the analogy breaks down. The closer he climbs to the sun, the colder he becomes. The effect of sunlight on wax must have been a more commonly observed phenomenon before electric lights, and would not necessarily evoke the myth of Icarus. Rare in Garcilaso's sonnets is the introduction of others as point of comparison, as occurs in lines 3–4 where he maintains that anyone who was not affected by the lady would be insane. The second quatrain announces the effect he has experienced but seems counter to reason itself. The sextet then contradicts the Petrarchan idea of being destroyed from a distance and actually burned when near. Garcilaso argues to the opposite effect: from a distance he turns to fire, but at close range he turns to ice. Petrarch's conclusion is based on the normal physiological effect of an agent that causes burning: the nearer one approaches, the more one feels heat. Garcilaso's idea and image are paradoxical: the further he is from the burning agent, the more he burns, and when closer, he freezes. Each of the tercets elaborates one of these effects, terminating with the startling graphic image of the blood curdling in the veins from the chill. Even if Garcilaso did follow an Italian model, he certainly expressed the effect more vividly.

The tone of the poem is lighthearted. The colloquial flavor of the expression "fuera de sentido" is not much elevated by reversing the word order. The rough-sounding and somewhat unpoetic "cuajárseme" would not be permissible in other more elevated, more Petrarchan, sonnets, such as I or X. In line with the lightness of tone is a high number of the close vowel *i* in the rhyme words in both the quatrains and the tercets, and also on interior accents: "mí" (6), "mismo" (8), "vista" (10), and "vida" (11). There is a high degree of alliteration, above all on intervocalic *v*: "a vuestra voluntad" (1), "solo vuestra vista" (2), and "menos vezes de mí provada y vista" (6). Line 2 is rough because of the repetition of "sol": "por sol tengo solo," part of which is repeated in line 11 with "sostengo."

The poem is addressed to the mistress whose presence in the poem is necessary for the description of the effect; the poem begins praising her eyes, and her presence is clearly evoked in both tercets. Her "voluntad" and "vista" in lines 1 and 2, her "vista" again in line 10 and her eyes in line 13. The other use of "vista" in line 6 refers to the poet's own experiences. The presence of another in lines 3 and 4 tends to move the question from a direct address of the beloved to a more general reader. The poem presents an enigma: "de dó viene una cosa?" (5), based on the presence, or quality of presence of the beloved, but that she is the only person expected to meditate on this problem seems too limiting. In fact the whole question seems directed to a wider reading public, and one tends to read the question as another study of the male psychology of love rather than an experience to be shared between lovers. The total effect of the poem brings to the fore the conclusion that Garcilaso was not an uncritical Petrarchist. The poem treats, as Rivers concludes, a Petrarchan commonplace (*Obras* 115). Garcilaso hardly treats it as a commonplace, but carefully and systematically contradicts Petrarch's conclusions. The lighthearted style also contrasts with the heavy tone of Petrarchan poems. The sonnet is Petrarchan in its conception, but Garcilaso systematically contradicts Petrarch's dominant tone and concluding phrase.

Sonnet XVII does not essentially subvert Petrarchism, but elaborates its Petrarchan passages in a unique manner. The imagery of this sonnet relies heavily on direct quotations from Petrarch, but develops a new idea with extreme subtlety:

XVII

Pensando que'l camino yva derecho,
vine a parar en tanta desventura
que imaginar no puedo, aun con locura,
algo de que 'sté un rato satisfecho:

> el ancho campo me parece estrecho,
> la noche clara para mí es escura,
> la dulce compañía amarga y dura,
> y duro campo de batalla el lecho.
>   Del sueño, si ay alguno, aquella parte
> sola quês ser imagen de la muerte
> se aviene con el alma fatigada.
>   En fin que, como quiera, 'stoy de arte
> que juzgo ya por ora menos fuerte,
> aunque en ella me vi, la que es passada.

In this sonnet Garcilaso employs one of the ways of characterizing love-sickness. He presents the effects of love as the cause of a transformation of the lover's perceptions. In the eighth stanza of Eclogue I he uses the same technique, describing the shepherd's perceptions altered by love. The shepherd took pleasure in nature through his beloved and their mutual love, but now that the reciprocity is broken, he laments that nature no longer pleases him. Love made nature more beautiful and delightful, and the ugly elements, such as the black crow, were simply ignored. The rupture with the beloved has cast him into a lovesickness that has altered his perceptions.

The first quatrain of the sonnet announces the typical extremes of suffering by the courtly lover, which is so great that he cannot imagine, even in moments of folly, something that would make him happy. The next quatrain gives examples of things that no longer give pleasure because of his transformed perceptions: a wide field seems narrow, a clear night seems dark, good company is bitter and hard, and his bed seems a hard field of battle. Line 8 is a direct translation from Petrarch (Sonnet CCXXXVI). The second quatrain contains curious repetitions: the word "campo" in lines 5 and 8 and the word "dura / duro" in lines 7 and 8. The "ancho campo" in line 5 is a nature image, but in line 8 the "campo" has become a battlefield and the suggested tranquillity of nature at the beginning of the quatrain is transformed into war by the end. The word "duro" is more complex and only used tangentially in its literal sense. "Dulce" at the beginning of line 7 is negated in both its meanings by the adjectives at the end of the line. "Amarga" cancels out the primary sense of sweet and "dura" negates the suggestion of softness, but, of course, "dulce compañía" is neither literally sweet nor literally soft. Garcilaso establishes a subtextual movement in which "dulce" and "dura" are opposites and function as such, but as attributes of "compañía" neither is used literally, but in extended senses. The same occurs with "duro" in line 8. The bed as "duro campo" gives a literal sense of a hard bed, but the complete phrase "duro campo de batalla" transforms "duro" figuratively into a hard or difficult battle. Underlying this imagery are the Petrarchan poems on sleeplessness and love as war, such as "Or ch'el ciel e la terra il vento tace" (CLXIV). Garcilaso's stylistic subtleties in this quatrain in which the *locus amoenus* becomes a battlefield and words are carefully poised between their literal and figurative senses, only to be corrupted, repeat the central message on a subtextual level: to the suffering lover things are not what they seem and the plain sense of anything is easily converted into another.

The first tercet continues the quotation from Petrarch and the insomnia motif with a play on words possible only in Spanish where the two Latin words "somnium," dream, and "somnus," sleep, were fused into the same word, "sueño," with the expanded semantic field of both sleep and dream. In line 9, the phrase "Del sueño, si hay alguno," seems to indicate sleep and conversely, insomnia, one of the symptoms of lovesickness. In the passage Garcilaso is quoting, Petrarch who labeled sleep "parente della morte," dissimulating an ancient maxim, coming from Hesiod and Homer, which called sleep the brother of death, or from Ovid in *Amores* (II, ix, 41) who varied the phrase and called sleep "an image of death," meaning that the sleeper is in a state of suspension that resembles death in many respects. Garcilaso corrects Petrarch's citation by quoting Ovid. Since "sueño" has a much wider semantic field in Spanish than in Latin or Italian, the phrase "imagen de la muerte" refers to both sleep and dreams. Garcilaso has transferred the image from the sleeper to the sleeper's dreams of terror and nightmares of death. The sleeper is not, as in the ancient sense of the phrase, an image of death, but sleep brings images of terror and death to the lovesick. Garcilaso carefully exploits the full semantic possibilities of the Spanish word "sueño," with its expanded semantic ambiguity. As in the previous quatrain, things have lost their primary sense and are no longer what they seem. Petrarch is quoted, but he is corrected by citing Ovid in translation, and Ovid is simultaneously quoted and subverted as the peaceful sleeper who resembles the dead is converted into the mentally anguished lover suffering from fitful sleep and nightmarish visions of death. This is a clear example of eristic imitation in which Garcilaso announces his Petrarchan source in line 8, and proceeds to correct Petrarch and subvert Petrarch's Ovidian source.

The last tercet, as often in Garcilaso's sonnets, is conceptually so dense and elliptical that it is practically impossible to unravel the literal sense. Like the rest of the poem, it deals with impressions. The poet judges the past as less harsh than the present; yet paradoxically, he had lived in that past and was aware of its harshness. He knows from his own experience that the past was the same as the present, but he perceives himself as suffering more in the present.

The sonnet characterizes with tremendous subtlety, the state of lovesickness, placing the symptomatic changes in the lover's perceptions within the context of insomnia, a major symptom of lovesickness. Although these changes begin with nature images, the poet constructs them to end with a concentration on a single symptom of lovesickness. Unlike poems that describe the symptoms of lovesickness, this sonnet dramatizes the mental state of the lovesick person by describing the altered mental perceptions caused by depression. As a work of art it is a remarkable tour de force, the kind of work one applauds more for the virtuosity of the performance than for the sentiment expressed.

The last three sonnets to be discussed in this chapter, XXVI, IV, and XXV, are still conceived within the Petrarchan tradition, but rest uneasily in that tradition by affirming a faith, not in pessimism, but in a positive resolution of the lover's suffering. Such optimism completely contradicts the Petrarchan vision of unrelieved masochistic suffering. Sonnets XXVI and IV, first compared by Lapesa, are similar in that they affirm the power of the will over suffering and they employ the same imagery. In addition to negating the Petrarchan stance of unrelieved pessimism, both sonnets produce their affirmation in the face of a carefully constructed mental state of despair following an illusory hope. Both sonnets contain suggestions they are in response to death, but in neither case does the poem provide sufficient evidence to decide that issue definitively. Both sonnets seem to be an intentional reaction against the Petrarchan stance of despair, which usually ends in a death wish. Both are conceived in the Petrarchan mode and begin with the themes of despair and emotional impasse; they then change key and end in an affirmation of the will and life forces.

Because of its traditional ordering among the sonnets following Sonnet XXV, a poem on the death of the mistress, one tends to read Sonnet

XXVI as a poem *in morte,* although, even if it were on the death of the beloved, the moment to which it corresponds would certainly precede the moment described in Sonnet XXV. If the cause of the depression is the news of the death of the beloved, as suggested by the first quatrain, then the poet-lover has recently received it.

XXVI

Echado está por tierra el fundamento
que mi bivir cansado sostenía.
¡O quánto bien s'acaba en solo un día!
¡O quántas esperanças lleva el viento!

¡O quán ocioso está mi pensamiento
quando se ocupa en bien de cosa mía!
A mi esperança, assí como a baldía,
mil vezes la castiga mi tormento.

Las mas vézes me entrego, otras resisto
con tal furor, con una fuerça nueva,
que un monte puesto encima rompería.

Aquéste es el desseo que me lleva
a que desee tornar a ver un día
a quien fuera mejor nunca aver visto.

In the case of Sonnet XXVI, the reader does in fact lack sufficient information to decide what was the nature of the disgrace so poignantly described in the first lines. Since the cause of the dashing of his hopes is not explicit, several possibilities could be imagined, such as death of the beloved, the confirmation of jealousy (as in Sonnet XXX), or the marriage of the beloved to another, etc. Because of the Petrarchan tradition of poems *in vita* and poems *in morte,* one is inclined to read the poem as if the disaster were a death, a reading that becomes difficult in line 13 where he expresses his resolve to see her again, although Sonnet XXV expresses a similar resolve to be reunited with the dead beloved. The poem seems to contrast the two attitudes of rejected suitor and grieving lover, and it is the Petrarchan tradition that provides the basis for this contrast. The first two lines refer to the disaster that causes grief and to his previous mental state as unrequited lover. While the beloved was available and only rejected him, his life was a "bivir cansado," but her removal destroyed the possibility of a reciprocated love on which he previously sustained his faint hope and miserable existence. Lines 3–4 comment on the shortness of time for destruction and, in a line taken from Petrarch, equates the fragility of hope with the wind. Lines 5–6 express an idea not encountered previously. His imagination was quite active in producing destructive images when he was an unrequited lover; now it barely works to provide relief. "El pensamiento," the mental faculty Garcilaso most often names as a source of uncontrolled fantasies, has lapsed into idleness. He finishes the octave commenting on how his misery chastises his hope. The octave thus contrasts two types of misery, one based on unrequited love, which at least allows for hope, and another completely hopeless. It is the contrast that is fully elaborated in Eclogue I.

The sextet does not return to the theme of despair, as do Garcilaso's more orthodox Petrarchan poems, but maintains a strength of will uncharacteristic of Petrarchan suffering. In lines 9 and 10, he presents a vacillation between despair and anger, an anger so strong that it could break through "un monte puesto encima." It is likely this "monte" is not literally a mountain, but a forest, as in Sonnet IV and Elegy II. The last tercet follows on this anger, affirming it as a desire to see the beloved again. Adapting another line from Petrarch, the last line restates the paradox of the lover's two postures. He desires to see again that person who caused all his suffering. Garcilaso has over the course of this sonnet distinguished the two Petrarchan attitudes of suffering, but rather than ending on a note of despair sustained by a death-wish, he refers to an anger that will serve to overcome obstacles and result in a resolute determination to return to see her again, the very cause of all of his suffering. While the poem is obviously grounded in Petrarchan postures and incorporates three quotes from Petrarch (lines 3, 4, and 12–14), the opting for resolve over despair runs counter to the Petrarchan tradition of depression and suffering.

Sonnet IV is a poem on absence addressed to the beloved, although the octave does not refer to her and develops as a study of the psychological pessimism of the lover. The beloved is introduced, along with the theme of separation, only in line 13. Lines 5, 6, and 14 could be read to imply that death is the impediment that separates the lovers.

IV

Un rato se levanta mi esperança,
más cansada d'averse levantado,
torna a caer, que dexa, a mal mi grado,
libre el lugar a la desconfiança.

¿Quién suffrirá tan áspera mudança
del bien al mal? ¡O coraçón cansado,
esfuerça en la miseria de tu 'stado,
que tras fortuna suele aver bonança!
Yo mesmo emprenderé a fuerça de braços
romper un monte que otro no rompiera,
de mil inconvenientes muy espesso;
muerte, prisión no pueden, ni embaraços.
quitarme de yr a veros como quiera,
desnudo 'spirtu o hombre en carne y huesso.

The first quatrain speaks of the raising of hope, which cannot sustain itself and falls, leaving room for despair. The second quatrain laments this movement and ends by admonishing the heart to take courage because there is always clear weather after a storm. The Italianism "fortuna" stands out and perhaps suggests a later influence. Up to this point, the poem seems to be a conventional Petrarchan poem not addressed to a specific reader and describing emotional despair. The first tercet surprises with its turn to a positive affirmation. "Monte" refers to the thick forest he would cut through by hand. The second tercet asserts the dominance of the will and life over all types of obstacles, including death and prison. The last line, which is translated from Petrarch (with its Italian "spirtu"), explains how he will overcome even death by vowing to act in spirit. The same word cluster is found in Eclogue II when Albanio becomes mad and asks: "¿No puedo yo morir, no puedo irme / por aquí, por allí, por do quisiere, / desnudo espirtu o carne y huesso firme?" (850–53), or when he describes the loss of his soul: "Espirtu soy, de carne ya desnudo, / que busco el cuerpo mio" (919–20). Lapesa sums up the curious mixture of Petrarchism and hope: "De este modo, en una composición que debe más de la mitad de sus versos a Petrarca se ha infundido un espíritu nuevo que la hace más tensa y vibrante, aunque también más desigual y menos armónica" (*Garcilaso: Estudios* 80).

This sonnet is carefully structured in its sound system. The poem has throughout the double consonant sound "ç" praised by Bembo for its gravity. It occurs in rhyme words in the octave and sextet: "=ança" and "=aços," and occurs in the words "coraçon," "esfuerça" and "fuerça." The first three lines are grave with numerous tonic *a*'s, but the fourth line turns to a contrast with the *l*'s and close vowels. Line 9 has dominant *e* sounds; line 10, dominant *o*; and both have strong tonic vowels, while line 11 contrasts with close unaccented vowels. Line 9 provides a con-firmation that this sound system is intentionally constructed by the poet. The line is marked by three tonic *e* sounds and heavy consonant clusters. It is the only time in all of Garcilaso's poetry that he employs the alter-nate spelling "mesmo," while "mismo, -a" occurs twenty-two times (the "mesmo" in Sonnet XIX is a variant from El Brocense).

Sonnet IV is a poem on absence, but unlike the other sonnets on this theme, IX and III, it does not end with a death-wish. The poem begins in a state of real absence from the beloved, the sort of general poem without an avowed reader, like Sonnet XX. The act of will in the tercet leads finally to the affirmation of breaking the absence through force of will. In this poem we see the cause of the depression, but unlike the other general poems, this sonnet comes to give a reason for the depression and suggests ways to overcome it.

Sonnet XXV, written on the occasion of a visit to the tomb of the beloved, is a poem written *in morte*.

XXV

¡O hado secutivo en mis dolores,
cómo sentí tus leyes rigurosas!
Cortaste'l árbol con manos dañosas
y esparziste por tierra fruta y flores.

En poco espacio yazen los amores,
y toda la esperança de mis cosas,
tornados en cenizas desdeñosas
y sordas a mis quexas y clamores.

Las lágrimas que en esta sepultura
se vierten oy en día y se vertieron
recibe, aunque sin fruto allá te sean,

hasta que aquella eterna noche escura
me cierre aquestos ojos que te vieron,
dexándome con otros que te vean.

Garcilaso addresses a fate, the one who puts into effect the sentence, probably a reference to the third fate who cuts the thread of life. "Cor-taste," at the beginning of line 3, reinforces this identification, although it turns out to be a tree that is cut, not the thread of life. "Executar" did not mean "to execute" in Garcilaso's time. Even the eighteenth-century *Autoridades* calls it a rare usage. Rather it meant "to put into effect."

The adjective "executivo" signified a person or thing that acts quickly and decisively. Beyond the literal meanings, Garcilaso is probably punning on the fixed expression: "executar en los bienes," which signified the legal confiscation and sale of personal property to cover outstanding debts. The Fate confiscated his "bien," his beloved, from his power. The legal sense of the expression is reinforced with "leyes" in line 2, although the word metaphorically refers to death. The second quatrain also has a density of imagery, although not so complex as the first quatrain. The sense of containment is clear from the "poco espacio" which holds both his love and beloved, and all his hope in worldly affairs ("de mis cosas"). The ashes of the beloved treat him with cold disdain, being deaf to his laments and cries. The Latinism "clamores" provides a sense of classical, unmoderated grief. Even without the fuller references of the sextet, the image of the poet-lover, moved, weeping and vociferous before the lifeless tomb that is in no way affected by his passion presents a striking contrast.

The sextet is brilliantly constructed over a series of spatial and temporal contrasts that underline the opposition of life and death. The word "ésta" in line 9 defines a here and now, the confined space of line 5, that is in opposition to the "allá" of line 11. The "oy" of line 10 establishes a present that contrasts with the future implied in "te sean" and "te vean." The "oy" is marked by the present "se vierten" and the past "se vertieron." Perhaps the phrase "en día" would read better separated by commas to distinguish it from the modern common expression "hoy en día." In this poem, "en día" signifies a time that contrasts with "noche" in line 12. In line 10, the present is now "oy" and well-lighted "en día," while line 12 is limitless "eterna" and at night and dark "noche escura." The speaker is identified by "ésta," "oy," "en día," and "aquestos." The addressee is characterized by "allá," "aquella," "noche," and "otros." The speaker is identified with the present and past tenses: "se vierten," "se vertieron," and "te vieron," while the addressee is identified with the subjunctive "te sean" and "te vean," indicating probability and future. The lover becomes reduced to a here and now, confined by time and space like the ashes of the beloved in the sepulcher. The beloved is an other, a limitless there: "esta sepultura" will become the "allá"; the precise "oy en día" will become "aquella eterna noche escura"; "aquestos ojos" will become "otros"; the precise tenses of this world will become the timeless tenses of the other world. The eyes that wept the tears and saw the beloved will become others that can look on the spirits of the dead. The meditation on death, on the confines of the here and now, produces the image of the other, the there and beyond.

The metaphor based on the expression "sin fruto" is very complex, but all the same easily understood, and provides an echo of the exclamation in line 4. The metaphorical use of "fruto" as that which one gains from an enterprise is more rhetorical than visual, and is nearly a cliché. Garcilaso breathes new life into the figure by having it result from his tears. The fruit produced by the tears would be understanding and compassion. Since the mistress is dead, his pleas will not be heard or rewarded. But tears are also a liquid element that could be thought of as providing moisture for irrigation, as do Apollo's tears in Sonnet XIII. The metaphor of fruit takes on a new life by the reintroduction of the literal sense. Garcilaso takes two phenomena, "tears = compassion" and "irrigation = fruit," and crosses them, at the same time denying the comparison: "tears do not produce fruit," a construct explained by Gracián as a conceit of proportion or analogy.

Sonnet XXV presents a difficulty in identifying the addressee. Usually, the brevity of the sonnet prevents more than one addressee. Garcilaso's Sonnet XXXVII has two addressees, but they are clearly distinguished by different forms of address "tú" and "vos." Sonnet XXVI has apostrophes within the sonnet, but the apostrophe does not present a difficulty in interpretation. Sonnet XXV consistently uses "tú" throughout as the form of address, but it seems clear from the context that we are to understand different addressees in the first quatrain and in the sextet. The first addressee is named as the "hado" or fate that cuts the thread of life, in this case the tree of life. The addressee of the sextet does not seem to be the fate of the first quatrain. The grieving speaker laments that his tears cannot benefit the person addressed: "aunque sin fruto allá te sean." Rivers identifies the second addressee as the sepulcher mentioned in line 9. While that identification can fit with line 11, it seems impossible that it can be made to fit with line 14, where the speaker expresses the hope of seeing the addressee in a future afterlife. It would seem most logical, as Snell states (188), that the second addressee is the dead beloved. This identification is also problematical because Garcilaso always addresses the beloved as "vos." The only uses of "tú" in his sonnets is limited to animals or children. The beloved "señora" is always called "vos" as are Cupid in Sonnet XXVII and his friends Boscán (XXVIII and XXXIII) and Julio (XIX), even though Boscán is addressed as "tú" in Elegy II. It is clear from the versification (not to mention the sound of the lines) that "te" in lines 11, 13, and 14 is not a mistake for "os." In conclusion, there is no completely satisfactory explanation of the problem. Reading the sextet as a continuation of the addressee from the first quatrain is possible, but complicated by the idea in the second tercet that night will close his eyes, not the fate; it is difficult to imagine how he saw her in this life or will see her in the afterlife. The most reasonable explanation from the context is that the addressee changes in the sextet and in fact is the dead beloved whom he hopes to see in the afterlife, in spite of the difficulties presented by the unsignaled change of addressee in the sextet and the familiar form of address for the beloved.

This sonnet can be dated as late, not because it supposedly refers to Isabel Freire's death, but because of the borrowing from Sannazaro in line 4. The imagery is quite dense and is often used on several levels simultaneously, such as the "hado secutivo," which refers to the third fate, and is reinforced with the verb "cortaste," but is also a legal image reinforced by the expression "en mis dolores" and the word "leyes." The abstract emotional expressions are notably missing. Line 2 limits itself to the simple expression "sentí," with no further plays on other forms of "sentir," "sentido," or "sentimiento," typical of the earlier style. The word "esperanza" in line 6 forms part of the visual imagery, since it lies with his love confined to the small space of a sepulcher. The sextet presents all of its ideas through concrete imagery. Unfortunately, the poem is not often presented for the beauty of its imagery or measured expression, but as a key moment in his love affair for Isabel Freire, a visit to her tomb. Not only do the complex images, half-imagery, half-allegory (for example, the line "esparziste por tierra fruta y flores") make it one of Garcilaso's most interesting poems, but like several other contemplative poems it also represents a concentration of idea and thought that projects out of the poem along various temporal trajectories. The brevity of the sonnet captures the poignant moment that looks to a past of suffering and to a future reunion. The present in the poem is a point that projects from a defined here and now into eternity. The problem of the brevity of form is superseded by multiple lines projecting backward and forward. The "poco espacio" of line 5 is like the brevity of the poem itself, short and contained, but its significance radiates from historical to cosmic levels.

This sonnet is late enough and has sufficient sources outside of Petrarch to suggest Garcilaso's classical style. This idea is reinforced by the density of the imagery and some of the classical touches, such as the custom of placing a vial of tears in the sepulcher and the references to ashes, suggesting the ancient custom of cremation. The Latinism "clamores" recalls ancient public rituals of grief. Added to these elements is the unusual aspect of the two addressees and the form "te" used to address the beloved. Above all, the restraint of expression and lack of moral outrage suggest a later style. On the other hand, the poem recalls several Petrarchan topoi and corresponds well to Petrarch's *in morte* poems, above all the poems in which he mentions Laura's tomb (CCCIV, CCCXXVI, CCCXXXI, and CCCXXXIII). It is, however, the only poem discussed in this chapter that does not have a direct translation of a line or phrase from Petrarch. Conceived within the framework of Petrarchism, the quiet and determined optimism of the ending undercuts the pessimism of the typical Petrarchan resolution. In addition, the poetic discourse seems to correspond to Garcilaso's later forms of expression, especially the sense of the distancing of the subject from his emotional grief—the sense of observing grief rather than living it or re-creating it in the work of art. The sense of detachment, above all, suggests the beginnings of the movement away from the heavy emotional involvement of Petrarchan expression (Rivers, "Pastoral Paradox").

Garcilaso's Petrarchism could hardly be called orthodox or servile. The early attempts are heavily imbued with characteristics of the *cancionero* style. A number of the sonnets rely on material elaborated from Ausiàs March. As soon as he has adapted the Petrarchan style he begins to undermine it, either by contradicting Petrarchan observations or ascribing a note of optimism in place of the gloomy death-wishes of the model. None of these sonnets has achieved the acclaim of the Petrarchan sonnets, even though their wit and subtlety make them very interesting poems. Their complex use of intertexts and rejection of convention make them more difficult to appreciate than those poems that adhere more closely to the simpler conventions of the Petrarchan courtly lover. Perhaps some of the sonnets discussed in this chapter could be viewed as reactions against Petrarchism, such as Sonnet IV with its bold assertion of the strength of the will; or Sonnet XXV, which places Petrarchan despair in a classical setting and maintains a quiet affirmation of hope in face of adversity. Yet it seems that these poems found their stimulus in the Petrarchan mode and in a Petrarchan posture of despair rather than in a reaction against Petrarch, as do the sonnets in Part IV. The lack of a large number of purely Petrarchan sonnets and the development of unorthodox Petrarchan postures in poems that have direct quotations from Petrarch suggest one of two possibilities: either many Petrarchan poems have been lost or Garcilaso was not very comfortable in the Petrarchan mold and by his own efforts before he met (or read) Bernardo Tasso, he was struggling to free himself from the Petrarchan burdens of psychological oppression, moral ambiguity, and gloomy pessimism relieved only through recourse to a death-wish.

IV
Anti-Petrarchan Postures
in the Sonnets

THIS SECTION COMPLETES the study of the sonnets with an examination of those sonnets that can be classified as anti-Petrarchan. In these sonnets Bernardo Tasso's mandate to imitate the classics comes to the fore, and close analogies with various elements of classical Neo-Latin poetry can be noted, such as the use of mythology, the diminished emphasis on anguish, the imitation of the classical epigram (and an increased reliance on paradoxical situations), the treatment of Neoplatonic love motifs and the introduction of more personal themes (typical of Neo-Latin poetry). In all these sonnets Garcilaso abandons the Petrarchan postures of unrequited love and anguished suffering. Death-wishes and outright moralizing are replaced with delicate paradoxes elaborated out of nonamorous situations. The relationship between narrator and addressed reader in the anti-Petrarchan and classical sonnets undergoes further transformations from the Petrarchan models. The twenty-one sonnets discussed in the following three chapters show two major tendencies. One is an increased use of the "tú" form of address, seen previously only in Sonnet XXVI which is judged to be late and shows several classical influences. There are two possible reasons for a general shift from "vos" in the early sonnets to "tú" in the later sonnets. As the poetry moved from the courtly and Petrarchan conventions, the formal "vos," used to address the lady as lord and master, may have seemed less appropriate. Also, as he began to imitate Latin and Greek models, the lack of a formal form of address in the classical languages led him to place more emphasis on the "tú" form. Accepting the latter explanation, Rivers labels the "tú" form of address "el tuteo clásico" ("El problema" 55).

Another tendency noted in the sonnets in this section is the use of a named or specified addressee, an aspect of Italian poetry introduced into Spanish by Garcilaso. Four sonnets address male friends of the poet, XXXIII and XXVIII (Boscán), XXXV (Mario), and XIX (Julio). Two of these employ "vos" (XXVIII and XIX) and the other two use no personal pronouns or second-person verb forms. Two other sonnets address historical persons without identifying them, XXI (Clarísimo marqués) and XXIV (Ilustre honor del nombre de Cardona); both use the formal "vos." In total, nine of the sonnets employ the "vos" form (XXXVII, XI, XXIII, XXII, XXVIII, XXI, XIX, and XXIV), but only two are addressed to a mistress (XXII and XXIII), although the mistress in Sonnet XXIII is quite different from the lady in Petrarchan and courtly love poetry. Five of the sonnets employ the "tú" form: XXXVII (el can), XXXIX (celos), XXXI (nieto-celoso temor), VII (Amor) and XVI (Parténope). Six of the sonnets have no form of address at all. Another modification occurs in the distancing and even the disappearance of the narrative "yo." In Sonnets XIII and XXIX, there are no first-person verb forms, although there is a commentator on the action in Sonnet XIII. Sonnet XXIX has only a narrative voice and no implied "yo." In Sonnet XVI, the "yo" of the poem represents the voice of the poet's deceased brother. In general, there are several tendencies in the later sonnets that break with the structures of poet-lover and addressee established in the Petrarchan sonnets. None of the later sonnets concentrates on the lover's psychology of suffering, as did the early sonnets, and there is a larger variety of addressees: a dog, nymphs, jealousy, suspicions, and various male friends.

I have divided the analysis of the anti-Petrarchan sonnets into three chapters. Chapter 9 traces the various innovative directions taken in Garcilaso's love sonnets following Bernardo Tasso's suggestions of new poetic material (Sonnets XII, XXXVII, XV, XI, XIII, XXIX, XXXIX, XXX, XXXI, XXXIII, XXXV, and XXIII). Some employ myth-fabula, while others addressed to male readers strike different postures concerning the suffering of the courtly lover. One group of sonnets introduces the theme of jealousy. Chapter 10 analyzes the Neoplatonic love themes found in five of the sonnets (Sonnets VIII, XXII, VII, XXXIV, and XXVIII), treating them separately because Neoplatonism offered a radically different theory of love to the Renaissance poet. Chapter 11 discusses the epigrammatic and encomiastic sonnets (Sonnets XIX, XVI, XXI, and XXIV). In these sonnets Garcilaso has abandoned the theme of love entirely, and each of the sonnets is more personal and biographical. Even though the sonnet of praise did not achieve importance until the seventeenth century in Spanish poetry, the study of Garcilaso's initiation of the theme provides an interesting point of departure and a fitting conclusion to the trajectory traced in his sonnets.

9

Love Sonnets in a New Mode

Garcilaso's sonnets demonstrate clearly both his apprenticeship in the Petrarchan mode and his later movements toward more classical modes of expression. The sonnets in the new style by Tasso and Garcilaso remain unchanged in form, but are infused with new poetic material and new modes of expression, breaking away from the Petrarchan material and manner. One aspect of the introduction of classical material is seen in the use of mythology. Tasso advocated the use of "fabula" and digressions to exemplify the thematic material, and Garcilaso employed myth as a basis for Sonnets XII, XV, XI, XIII, and XXIX. Petrarch had incorporated many classical references into his poetry, but he tended to dissimulate the allusions by not naming the mythological figures. Two of Garcilaso's sonnets, XII and XV, follow this pattern of oblique mythological reference, and in both sonnets the myth is used more to make a moral point than to elaborate the theme, making them more typically medieval in tone than the sonnets in which he names the central figure (Seznec 96, 134).

The first two sonnets discussed, XII and XXXVII, may not spring from Tasso's idea of the use of fable, but probably relate to emblematic traditions. Even though Sonnet XII is dated in the last period, the octave is Petrarchan in tone and language, while each tercet, however, presents a mythological story, the first of the fall of Icarus and the second the fall of Phaeton:

XII

Si para refrenar este desseo
loco, impossible, vano, temeroso,
y guarecer de un mal tan peligroso
que es darme a entender yo lo que no creo,
    no me aprovecha verme qual me veo,
o muy aventurado o muy medroso,
en tanta confusión que nunca oso
fïar el mal de mí que lo posseo,
    ¿qué me á de aprovechar ver la pintura
d'aquel que con las alas derretidas,
cayendo, fama y nombre al mar á dado,
    y la del que su fuego y su locura
llora entre aquellas plantas conocidas,
apenas en ell agua resfrïado?

Dated by critics as late, this sonnet seems to be Petrarchan in inspiration, discussing desire through veiled myths, but the style seems more mature and confident. The quatrains discuss fear and daring—emphasizing that desire always results in daring. Line 4 opposes conviction and faith to understanding, implicitly claiming that reason cannot be effective in changing one's inner convictions. In the second quatrain the poet argues that if his state of confusion and the frustration of his desire do not serve as sufficient warning to alter his belief, then it does little good to try to change his emotional state through rational argument. In the sextets, he then asks rhetorically what good can it do to see depicted the moral examples of the falls of Icarus and Phaeton, two mythical figures famous for the punishments of their daring. Like many passages in Petrarch's *Canzoniere,* the myths remain unnamed, forming a puzzle for the reader. The sonnet is constructed as a logical syllogism:

1. Reason cannot alter faith.
    Proof: Knowledge of mental anguish does not alter faith.
2. Mythological moral examples persuade through reason.
3. Hence, they are useless in altering one's inner faith.

Since no paired paintings of Icarus and Phaeton in existence during Garcilaso's lifetime have been discovered, other than the two obscure Sebastiano del Piombo frescoes of Icarus and Phaeton in Rome (Hirst 34–37), critics have tended to follow Herrera's suggestion that the depiction is poetic, but can be considered painting because both poetry and painting are simply analogous expressions of the same artistic impulse: "Debió ver la pintura de Icaro y Faetón, o sea la pintura o la historia, porque la poesía es pintura que habla, como la pintura poesía muda, según dijo Simónides" (H-85). Sonnets by Sannazaro and Tansillo have been suggested as sources for the Icarus motif, but the Italian poems have little similarity to Garcilaso's sonnet. Tansillo did join both myths in a madrigal (Turner 55), but the poem has so little relationship to Garcilaso's poem that Turner concludes "it is impossible to say with any certainty which single poem provided the immediate inspiration to the Spaniard" (59).

Ciocchini suggested that this mythological sonnet, as well as Sonnets XIII and XVIII, are emblematic in form ("Garcilaso" 125–26). Following up this suggestion, I propose as a likely source for Garcilaso's outburst against moralizing myths Alciati's book of emblems, the second edition of which, issued in Paris in 1534, does indeed depict Icarus and Phaeton falling from the sky. Not so the first two editions of 1531 and 1534 (printed in Cologne), which use an astrologer for the emblem "In astrologos" and a drawing of Phaeton seated calmly in his chariot for the emblem "In temerarios." The second edition illustrates the "In astrologos" with an engraving of a nude Icarus falling to the sea surrounded by loose plumage (Fig. 1) and the "In temerarios" with an engraving of Phaeton falling from the chariot to a barren landscape relieved by a river, a cliff, and two trees (the suggestion for the plants and water in Garcilaso's lines 13 and 14) (Fig. 2). These two engravings not only provide the details with which Garcilaso illustrates his text, but they are also presented with the didactic intent he finds so offensive. Like so many later critics, Garcilaso seems to have found the emblem a rather superficial genre. Seznec characterizes this reaction to the "banal character of the emblems. . . . The disappointed reader, finding nothing but commonplaces clothed in transparent dress, begins with good reason to wonder at the presumption which placed such futilities under the patronage of the Sphinx" (102). The two emblems in question address serious problems of ambition and emotion with rather well-known and trivial moral examples. The designation of engravings as "pintura" (lines 9 and 12)

Fig. 1.   Icarus, from Alciati's *Emblematum liber*
(Paris, 1534)

In Temerarios.

Aspicis aurigam currus Phaëtonta paterni
Igniuomos ausum flectere Solis equos:
Maxima qui postquàm terris incendia sparsit,
Est temere insesso lapsus ab axe miser.

Fig. 2.   Phaeton, from Alciati's *Emblematum liber*
(Paris, 1534)

might seem to argue against the identification of Alciati's engravings as the source of these depictions of the mythological examples. Alciati's texts, however, often refer to the engravings with the words "pinxit." The poems for the emblems "In illaudata laudantes," "In Statuum Bacchi" and "Amor virtu" refer to the engravings with the word "pinxit," and "In Deo laetandum" uses the word "pictor." Garcilaso clearly takes offense at the simplistic nature of the emblems as solutions to complex human emotions.

In Sonnet XII the myths do not adorn the text nor do they serve as a story or digression out of which arises paradoxical observations. Rather, they are evoked as moral examples, typical of the medieval method of treating Ovidian stories as more important for their moral lessons than for the delight of the story. These two myths continued to exist through the Renaissance as moral examples, while others were less exemplar. Garcilaso's other sonnets avoid the use of myth for didactic purposes. The use of mythology in this sonnet probably does not arise from Tasso's suggestion of the use of "fabula," but rather is a sudden reaction, a stylized outburst, against the superficiality of a new Renaissance genre, the emblem. While the myths in this sonnet do not signal the type of reaction against Petrarchism that will be studied in this chapter, the sonnet is important for its use of mythology and its reaction against a known literary genre. Critics have tried to identify in the text references to one or the other of the "known" loves of Garcilaso (Garcilaso, Obras, 1981, 98). In this case, as in many others, Garcilaso's poetry springs not from his personal emotional experiences, but from his reading of books. As I shall repeat throughout this study, Garcilaso was a probing, even bookish poet whose sources are often intellectual rather than experiential. Even though he argues in this sonnet for the primacy of desire over reason, his arguments were inspired by a written text and printed engraving, and they treat the question as a series of logical propositions. The text is an expression of his mind—not his heart—and the search for clues to his love life distorts both the sources of his inspiration as well as misconstrues our understanding of the text.

Sonnet XXXVII is difficult to fit into any trajectory of Garcilaso's poetry. Ciocchini pointed out the emblematic nature of this sonnet ("Garcilaso" 125), and, even though it is not related to a known emblem, the use of "fabula" in this sonnet corresponds more closely to an emblem than to any other genre. Devices were popular among Italian nobility in the sixteenth century, and it is possible that this sonnet is the description of a particular device (it could even serve as Garcilaso's own personal device). The setting is barren, and has been called Dantesque, but it also resembles the sparsely sketched emblems in early emblem collections.

XXXVII

A la entrada de un valle, en un desierto
do nadie atravesava ni se vía,
vi que con estrañeza un can hazía
estremos de dolor con desconcierto:
    aora suelta el llanto al cielo abierto,
ora va rastreando por la vía;
camina, buelve, pára, y todavía
quedava desmayado como muerto.
    Y fue que se apartó de su presencia
su amo, y no le hallava, y esto siente:
mirad hasta dó llega el mal de ausencia.
    Movióme a compassión ver su accidente;
díxele, lastimado: «Ten paciencia,
que yo alcanço razón, y estoy ausente».

The octave describes the dog alone in a desert at the entrance to a valley. Line 2 reports the absence of people, with a forceful play on "vía" and "vi" (lines 2 and 3). The first tercet explains why the dog suffers so greatly, and the poet directs a commentary to a general reader, addressed as "vos." In the last tercet the poet relates his compassion and directs a commentary to the dog, addressed as "tú." Ciocchini observes that the last sentence could easily serve as the epigraph for the "emblem" or "device" described in the octave. The implication is that the poet suffers more than the animal, even though rational beings should be better able to control their passions.

The inspiration of this sonnet is probably the double context of Tasso's mandate to employ "fabula" to present poetic material, and, as in the case of Sonnet XII, the newly invented genres of emblems and devices. In addition Bernardo Tasso used the same extended image to a different point in one of the "poemi aggiunti" of the *Libro primo* (41v). In Tasso's sonnet the dog, despised by its master, seeks a new master, just as the disdained lover may seek a new beloved. Even though Tasso's faithful dog abandons its master, several phrases recall Garcilaso's poem, such as the first quatrain:

> Come fido animal, ch'al suo signore
> Venuto à in odio, hora si fugge, hor riede;
> Et se ben fero grido, o uerga il fiede
> Non uorria uscir del dolce albergo fuore.

> (Like a faithful animal who has come to be hated
> by his master, now he flees, now he returns;
> and if he cruelly shouts or whips him, the faithful dog
> will not want to leave the sweet household.)

and the first tercet:

> Cos'io temendo di Madonna l'ire
> Tristo fuggo, & ritorno, & importuno
> Cheggio a la sua pietate humile aita . . .

> (Thus I, fearing the wrath of my lady,
> sadly flee, and return and annoyingly
> I beseech her pity for humble help.)

Even if Garcilaso did imitate Tasso in this sonnet, it is important to note that there are no direct coincidences of phrasing, only that Garcilaso has reworked the central idea to apply to a new situation.

Garcilaso's sonnet moves away from the involved suffering narrator typical of the Petrarchan poetic stance. The image of the dog externalizes the idea of suffering, and only at the end, in a rather ironical tone, does the speaker imply his own participation in suffering. Fewer are the adjectives of emotional care. In their place are the observable movements of the dog. The suffering of the poet is objectified and he presents himself as a detached observer who can sympathize because of his implied greater suffering, which he only mentions in parting.

Sonnet XV, which recounts various episodes of the myth of Orpheus without naming the pagan god, is still dependent on the Petrarchan tradition of the lover's lament, but it uses the myth in a more conceptual and less moralistic way than the previous sonnet. It is also considered to be from Garcilaso's last period.

XV

Si quexas y lamentos pueden tanto
que enfrenaron el curso de los ríos
y en los diversos montes y sombríos
los árboles movieron con su canto;
    si convertieron a escuchar su llanto
los fieros tigres y peñascos fríos;
si, en fin, con menos casos que los míos
baxaron a los reynos del espanto:
    ¿por qué no ablandará mi trabajosa
vida, en miseria y lágrimas passada,
un corazón comigo endurecido?
    Con más piedad devria ser escuchada
la boz del que se llora por perdido
que la del que perdió y llora otra cosa.

The first quatrain describes Orpheus's powers to stop rivers and move forests of trees with his song. The first two lines of the next quatrain continue the description of the poet's supernatural powers with the pacification of the tigers and the animation of cliffs. Orpheus represents the ability to animate lifeless nature through poetry, even things that have no innate senses, such as trees and cliffs. The last two lines of this quatrain play on the verb "bajar" to recount his descent to and victory over the underworld to save his wife from death. For the first time, the sonnet becomes personal as the poet compares his suffering with that of Orpheus, finding that he has suffered more than the pagan god. Such a comment would suggest on the first reading a poem "in morte," following the division Petrarch made in his works. The first sextet, however, makes clear that the poem corresponds to the "in vita" series, as the poet questions why his soft lament does not soften his beloved's heart hardened to his suffering and weeping. The final tercet continues stating that his voice, crying because he is irrevocably lost, should be heard more than that of the mythical god who weeps not because he himself is lost, but because he lost another. The understated paradox, so different from the exaggerated postures of anguish in the Petrarchan poems, is typical of the classical Greek epigram. In spite of the supernatural powers and dramatic suffering of Orpheus, Garcilaso prefers to draw a mild paradoxical observation from the situation. The rhyme scheme of the sextet delays the rhyme of "trabajosa" until the last line, the furthest separation possible in a sonnet. Bembo had recommended against a delay of more than five lines, but had left the final judgment to the poet. In this case, the delayed rhyme is like the lost Eurydice whose presence is sought but withheld.

The sonnet consists of one long comparison of the mythical powers of the poet to transform nature, and his own limited powers that cannot even impress the hard heart of his beloved. The intertwining of the two poetic postures, and the final comparison of the two voices and their effects make the myth less moralistic. The sonnet is addressed to the reader through the rhetorical question. The poem, however, clearly draws a comparison between the myth and the lover, while Garcilaso's other mythological sonnets leave the comparison implicit in the description. Another moralistic note may lie in the reference to Orpheus's voice. The medieval moralizer Fulgentius had given the etymology for Orpheus as "golden voice" (as if the word were "orea" + "phone," that is, "pure voice"; 96–98). In spite of the heavy moralizations and Christian allegories in the Middle Ages, the myth of Orpheus remained a favorite among Renaissance philosophers and mythographers, and, as a poet and creator, the character is also one of Garcilaso's favorite comparisons.

Another sonnet that re-creates the world of pagan mythology is Sonnet XI. The river nymphs are not famous mythological heroes, but a type of rustic pagan deity that inhabited springs, rivers, ponds, and other bodies of water.

XI

Hermosas nymphas, que en el rio metidas,
contentas habitáys en las moradas
de reluzientes piedras fabricadas
y en colunnas de vidrio sostenidas,
   agora estéys labrando embevescidas
o texendo las telas delicadas,
agora unas con otras apartadas
contándoos los amores y las vidas:
   dexad un rato la labor, alçando
vuestras rubias cabeças a mirarme,
y no os detendréys mucho según ando,
   que o no podréys de lástima escucharme,
o convertido en agua aquí llorando,
podréys allá d'espacio consolarme.

The octave describes the nymphs and their world and occupations. In the first tercet the speaker requests them to give him their attention as he passes. He says he will not occupy their attention for long, since either they will not be able to hear his tale because of their suffering through compassion, or he will through tears dissolve into water in which state they will be able to console him at their leisure. From the commentaries of El Brocense and Herrera to Mele and Lapesa numerous sources for this sonnet have been suggested, including Petrarch, Sannazaro, Virgil, and others. One hardly needs to add further sources, but the tradition studied in Chapter 5, beginning with the *Greek Anthology* and passing through the Neo-Latin poets and Tasso, suggests a long tradition behind this poem. This sonnet is obviously inspired in Bernardo Tasso's two classicizing sonnets addressed to nymphs, quoted in Chapter 5. In both of Tasso's sonnets the nymphs are in a river and they are asked to listen to, or told they have listened to, the poet's love laments. In the sonnet in *Libro primo* the nymphs, while not telling each other love stories, are "amiche d'Amore, & de pietate" (friends of Love and mercy). The first tercet recalls most Garcilaso's poem:

> Aprite al pianto mio l'humido seno,
>   Et queste amare lagrime chiudete
>   Nel piu secreto uostro herboso fondo.
> (52v)

> (Open to my weeping your humid heart
>   and close these bitter tears
>   in the most secret part of your grassy deep.)

The first quatrain of the sonnet from the *Libro secondo* treats the same motif:

> Nimphe, ch'al suon de la sampogna mia
>   Souente alzando fuor le chiome bionde
>   Di queste si correnti & lucid' onde,
>   Vdiste il duol, ch' amor dal cor mi apria.
> (53)

> (Nymphs, who to the sound of my reed-pipe
>   often raising your blonde tresses

212 Anti-Petrarchan Postures in the Sonnets

out of the running and so lucid waves,
you heard the pain that love opened from my heart.)

Like all correspondences of texts between Tasso and Garcilaso, it is impossible to ascertain from coincidences of phrasing that Garcilaso actually used Tasso as a source for his poem.

Garcilaso's sonnet relies on various understood contrasts, the obliqueness of the counterelements signaling a major departure from the Petrarchan joy of explicit antitheses. The major contrast is between the nymphs and speaker. They are numerous, female, beautiful, and happy; the speaker is alone, male, pitiful, and miserable. They live in water; he walks on land—although the phrase "según ando" in line 11 is not only a literal traversing of the land; it refers figuratively to his condition and emotional state. He does not state the cause of his suffering, but a clue is given when the nymphs relate their loves (line 8), and the reader of sixteenth-century poetry is familiar with the causes of suffering whether they are stated as amorous or not. The activities of the nymphs are related in the present with the word "agora" that begins both lines 5 and 7, and which serves as an either/or construction. The address of a person otherwise occupied recalls the dedication to the duke of Alba in Eclogue I, while the weaving of the delicate cloths recalls the activities of the four nymphs in Eclogue III. The sonnet does seem to pertain to the late period with its descriptive elements, such as "reluzientes piedras," "colunnas de vidrio" and "rubias cabeças." While the nymphs are captured in a present that, although variable, seems to be eternally pleasant, the speaker always projects himself into a foreshortened future: "no os detendréys mucho," "no podréys . . . escucharme," and "podréys . . . consolarme," as he stops to relate his unfortunate past. They live in an eternally static present of diverse and pleasant activities, while the speaker, burdened by his past, projects himself into a hopeless future.

Garcilaso does not draw a moral, but states obliquely the great suffering of the lover. As in Eclogue III, the point is made through classical distancing and understatement. The tone is sentimental as we imagine the great grief of the speaker, but unlike the Petrarchan mode, which searches for explicit and graphic ways of describing that suffering, this poem simply states that his grief is so great that the happy nymphs could not bear to hear it, or, if they chose to listen, he would dissolve with weeping. The grief is born in silence by the speaker. As readers we are not even told the cause of it, nor do we know if the nymphs consented to listen. As Rivers points out ("Pastoral Paradox"), citing an anecdote retold by Boscán, the greatest passion is that which we cannot talk about and remains unstated. The emphasis in the poem has shifted from the suffering of the lover to the contrast of his great but unstated pain with the happy and trivial activities of the river nymphs.

Two other sonnets, XIII and XXIX, also employ mythological figures, but in these poems, the central figure is named, and the first-person narrative voice disappears. Sonnet XIII describes the transformation of Daphne into a laurel tree, a description that resembles a similar passage in Eclogue III.

XIII

A Daphne ya los braços le crecían
y en luengos ramos bueltos se mostravan;
en verdes hojas vi que se tornavan
los cabellos quel oro escurecían;
   de áspera corteza se cubrían
los tiernos miembros que aun bullendo 'stavan;
los blancos pies en tierra se hincavan
y en torcidas raýzes se bolvían.
   Aquel que fue la causa de tal daño,
a fuerça de llorar, crecer hazía
este árbol, que con lágrimas regava.
   ¡O miserable 'stado, o mal tamaño,
que con llorarla crezca cada día
la causa y la razón por que llorava!

Mary Barnard has emphasized the grotesque elements in the description of the transformation in the octave, placing them in the context of Renaissance mannerist art (*The Myth* 110–30). The first tercet develops a paradox from the situation: the tears from Apollo, weeping for the loss of the nymph, served only to water the tree and make it grow. Thus, the weeping, which Apollo hoped would make the nymph repent, in fact served to produce the opposite effect. The last tercet simply underlines the paradox, saying how lamentable it is. The rhymes in the octave are plural imperfect endings "-ían" and "-avan." The loneliness of Apollo is underlined by the repetition of the same vowels in the sextet, but as singular imperfects "ía" and "ava." Obviously, the implication is that the poet himself suffers in a similar paradoxical way, his tears causing his mistress to become entrenched in her rejection of him. Important to note is that the personal voice of the narrator occurs only in line 3 as the unstated subject of "vi." The narrator never refers to himself personally, but one assumes that the reason for lamenting the "'stado" of line 12 is that the poet and speaker of the poem know it only too well. The poem does not extract an exemplar course of action from the myth, but simply observes a paradox that is then repeated in a way that suggests it has a deeper application: lamenting may produce undesired results. The emphasis in the poem has changed. The interest is on the descriptive elements, which are prolonged and savored, and the sonnet concludes without drawing a moral or explicit personal observation. Tasso had observed that the ancients could begin a poem or end it without the formal rhetorical parts required for prose. Although this poem does not actually end without a sense of closure, at the same time, it does not make its point evident, nor does it try to draw a moral. Unlike Sonnet XII with its moralistic myths of Icarus and Phaeton, Sonnet XIII uses its myth to present a suggestive example, but leaves the actual inferences unstated.

Sonnet XIII, with its strong paradox and the absence of a moral, seemed to approach the spirit of the classical epigram. Sonnet XXIX, the famous sonnet on Leander, is a reworking of an epigram by Martial on Leander, which, like the sonnet, simply states a paradox without drawing a moral:

XXIX

Passando el mar Leandro el animoso,
en amoroso fuego todo ardiendo,
esforçó el viento, y fuésse 'mbraveciendo
el agua con un ímpetu furioso.
 Vencido del trabajo pressuroso,
contrastar a las ondas no pudiendo,
y más del bien que allí perdia muriendo
que su propia vida congoxoso,
  como pudo, 'sforçó su boz cansada
y a las ondas habló d'esta manera,
mas nunca fue su boz dellas oýda:

«Ondas, pues no se 'scusa que yo muera,
dexadme allá llegar, y a la tornada
vuestro furor essecutá en mi vida».

In transforming Martial's four lines into a fourteen-line sonnet, Garci-laso had to add other elements not found in the original and to expand certain phrases. The first quatrain develops a play of the four elements, where Leander (a land creature out of his element) is burning in amorous fire and is assailed by the other two elements, wind and water. According to Renaissance mythographers, Musaeus, the Greek author of the fable of Hero and Leander, was not a late Hellenistic writer, but was one of the early theologians who had studied in Egypt with Moses (D. C. Allen 9). Renaissance Neoplatonists maintained that many myths contained inner mystical and even Christian teachings. We note in this case that Garcilaso has provided a physical interpretation of the myth, converting the opening into a battleground of the four elements in much the same way that mythographers from classical times onward had interpreted the myths as allegories of physical processes (Seznec 37–83; D. C. Allen 53–59). The second quatrain develops a minor paradox on the way to Martial's final one. Garcilaso claims Leander fears more for losing his beloved through his own death than he fears losing his own life (similar to the paradox in Sonnet I). None of line 11, "mas nunca fue su boz dellas oýda," with its ironical futility follows from suggestions in the original. In addition to the added elements, there is a tendency to expand single words or word groups into whole phrases. Where Martial says Leander was seeking "dulces amores," Garcilaso expands these two words into a full line: "en amoroso fuego todo ardiendo," recalling Ariosto: "tutto infiammato d'amoroso fuoco" (*Orlando furioso*, XIX, 26). Garcilaso expands Martial's phrase "dicitur undas" into two lines: "como pudo, 'sforçó su boz cansada / y a las ondas habló d'esta manera." Typical of some sonnets that reproduce epigrams, the pithiness of style in the original succumbs to languid padding. The sonnet usually develops a more complex and substantial idea; thus, this poem seems rather light and superficial. Not so to Garcilaso's successors, however, who imitated and glossed this poem many times (Alatorre, "Sobre"). Like the previous poem, and like the epigram in general, this sonnet does not make a moral point, but rather leaves the implications of the final paradox unstated. The personal "yo" has disappeared completely. In Sonnet XIII on

Daphne, the speaker was the one who suffered and the implications were personal and probably amorous. In this poem, the content is again amorous, but the application of the paradox could be more metaphysical than amorous. The paradox relates it to the larger issues of the four elements of the physical world and the forces of fortune and fate on human destiny, rather than purely love emotions.

All five of the mythological sonnets re-create myths of settings from the Greek and Roman pagan world. The myth, or "fabula," as Tasso called it, is used to objectify the poet's feelings. Rather than concentrating on allegories and paradoxes of sentiment, typical of the Petrarchan mode, Garcilaso in these poems uses a myth in order to arrive at an implied message. In much of Garcilaso's late poetry, the moral message and heavy sentiment recede in the face of more fully developed examples of classical material and form. The distancing of poetic voice even to the point of the disappearance of an identifiable involved narrator from the message approaches the classical spirit and abandons the style of the medieval courtly love lyric with the involvement of poetic voice and sentiment. Although several of these poems mention the poet's suffering, the general movement is away from the typical posture of the lovesick poet toward a more objectified and less personally involved poetic message.

Another class of sonnets moves toward the presentation of new attitudes concerning love. The mythological sonnets, in one form or another, present the figure of the suffering lover, such as Orpheus, Apollo, and Leander. Other sonnets present different attitudes toward love, and may actually reject the "dolorido sentir" of the courtly and Petrarchan lover. The important theme of Neoplatonic love will be covered in a separate chapter. Here I shall deal mainly with new or unorthodox attitudes toward love.

One such new attitude to love was the exploration of the passion of jealousy. Garcilaso has two, possibly three, sonnets on the theme of jealousy (XXXIX, XXX, and XXXI); he also treats the theme extensively in Elegy II and in Salicio's lament in Eclogue I. The development in the elegy is experiential and autobiographical, and in the eclogue it is supposedly autobiographical and related to Isabel Freire, although there are few personal indications other than the name Salicio, the setting in Spain (192–93) on the banks of the Tagus (113), and the reference to the longevity of the love affair (68). Critics have related the jealousy of the elegy with the "dark lady" of Naples based on the details given in the poem (lines 37–42). The treatment of the theme in the two sonnets is philosophical, developing the psychology of jealousy in Sonnet XXX and the nature of it through allegory in Sonnet XXXI. The two sonnets have been related to the Neapolitan period and the love of the "dark lady." They are abstract and philosophical in tone, and they have been related to the sentiments expressed in Elegy II and not to those in Eclogue I, although there is no particular reason for doing so, except that critics have seldom employed the term jealousy to describe the sentiments expressed in the eclogue. According to Williamson, jealousy as a theme for lyric poetry was first developed in the sixteenth century (*Bernardo* 44–45). It is clearly not a Petrarchan theme, since Petrarch envisioned Laura in such a way that it would have been impossible for him to experience jealousy because of a rival suitor. Her perfection precluded her reciprocating the love of another person. Petrarch expressed in his *Canzoniere* Laura's coldness and disdain, but never could he imagine the treason related by Garcilaso in Elegy II and Eclogue I. In both poems the lover relates a previous period of reciprocated love, another condition inconceivable in Petrarchan love. In Elegy II he simply imagines her infidelity, whereas in Eclogue I the perfidy is complete and he rails against the unnaturalness of her passion for the rival.

Jealousy as a poetic theme differs greatly from that of love. Human love resides in a marvelous space between happiness and despair. Associated with human desire, it can, if fulfilled, produce ecstasy; but if frustrated, it can produce prolonged and miserable suffering. Its ability to produce happiness and suffering, depending on its use, is one of the elements that makes it so adaptable as a poetic theme. Jealousy, on the other hand, is a completely negative emotion that can never produce happiness or joy, but only suffering or bitter satisfaction at the demise of the rival. Garcilaso had numerous examples stretching from the classics to the medieval poets as models of how to handle amorous passion in poetry, whereas jealousy was a recent theme that could only be dealt with in a negative manner. The marvelous ability to shift from joy to suffering in love poetry gave the love themes great adaptability, while jealousy was a theme to be shunned as a personal reference, for the shame it could bring. It had to be treated in a negative, abstract manner that avoided too close a personal relationship. The theme of jealousy in Garcilaso's sonnets is closely related to Sannazaro's Sonnet XXIII, one of whose

translations has been attributed to Garcilaso as his Sonnet XXXIX. Herrera mentioned Sannazaro's sonnet as a source for Garcilaso's Sonnet
XXX.

XXXIX

¡O celos, de amor terrible freno
quen un punto me buelve y tiene fuerte;
hermanos de crueldad, deshonrrada muerte
que con tu vista tornas el çielo sereno!
¡O serpiente nacida en dulçe seno
de hermosas flores, que mi esperança es muerte:
tras prósperos comienços, adversa suerte,
tras süave manjar, rezio veneno!
¿De quál furia infernal acá saliste,
o cruel monstruo, o peste de mortales,
que tan tristes y crudos mis días heziste?
Tórnate al infierno sin mentar mis males:
desdichado miedo, ¿a qué veniste?,
que bien bastava amor con sus pesares.

Sannazaro's sonnet is a series of metaphors that disparages jealousy as
an ugly passion that affects one beyond control. Like love, it is impossible
to escape and it holds its victim tight. It is related to death in terribleness
and in its power to cause human misery. Line 4 presents the familiar
storm image from love poetry. The second quatrain compares jealousy to
a serpent among flowers, which ends up in killing hope (5); in addition, it
kills the pleasure of love (7–8). Jealousy comes as bad luck or poison, a
metaphor that nicely turns on the serpent image. The sextet compares
jealousy to an infernal fury, a monster or a plague sent from Hell. In the
last lines the poet returns to a comparison with love, and he states he
found love bad enough without the addition of jealousy, which is much
worse. In the sonnet, jealousy is addressed, but not personally identified
with the speaker other than as an exterior force, like a fury or plague,
that attacks him and destroys his pleasure. Although it is compared to
love, it is not like love, a passion the author embraces. Jealousy is a passion he can only disparage and distance from his person and being. This
sonnet sets the tone for Garcilaso's sonnets on jealousy, which are abstract, even allegorical (recalling the "hermanos de . . . la muerte" in line
3) and philosophical in nature.

Sonnet XXX is not about jealousy per se, but about "sospechas," the suspicions that precede jealousy. The metaphor is one of war in which the poet concedes to the victorious suspicions.

XXX

Sospechas que, en mi triste fantasía
puestas, hazéys la guerra a mi sentido,
bolviendo y rebolviendo el afligido
pecho con dura mano noche y día:
    ya se acabó la resistencia mía
y la fuerça del alma; ya rendido,
vençer de vos me dexo, arrepentido
de averos contrastado en tal porfía.
    Llevadme a aquel lugar tan espantable
que, por no ver mi muerte allí esculpida,
cerrados hasta aquí tuve los ojos.
    Las armas pongo ya, que concedida
no es tan larga defensa al miserable:
colgad en vuestro carro mis despojos.

The sonnet depends on a strict distinction between suspicion of infidelity and jealousy itself, which occurs if the suspicions are confirmed. Jealousy is never mentioned in the poem, unless one interprets "muerte" (line 10) as the suffering caused by jealousy after confirmation of the suspicions. The poem sets up a psychological framework. The suspicions reside in the fantasy, one of the scholastic minor faculties responsible for conceiving images. From the fantasy they make war on his "sentido," which used in the singular suggests an ellipsis for "sentido común," the faculty that combined the impressions received from the five exterior senses. Affecting this faculty, the suspicions would distort and magnify any fault perceived by any of the five senses. The extended metaphor is of war, and the vigilance the lover must maintain to prevent jealousy from conquering his inner psychological faculties. The phrase "bolviendo y rebolviendo" recalls the use of the same words in Sonnet XXXIII: "buelve y rebuelve Amor mi pensamiento." None of the commentators or editors has explained the phrase, "volver el pecho con la mano," an expression that is rather obscure. Perhaps it is a variation of the Spanish expression "meter la mano en su pecho," which *Autoridades* defines as "Phrase con que se advierte á alguno que reprehende á otro, como avisandole que se reconozca, y hallará acáso en sí la misma culpa que condena." It could also be related to the Italian expression "Darsi nel petto," which is a self-accusatory act of accepting guilt by beating the chest. Poliziano's use of the expression is interesting in this case because it includes the phrase "tre volte" (three times), which recalls Garcilaso's verb *volver*: "Datti tre volte con le man nel petto" (*Tutte* 88). Garcilaso's expression seems to indicate a self-incriminating examination of the conscious.

In the second quatrain he announces his surrender in rather repetitious phrases. The first tercet presents the confirmation of the suspicions. Since he has surrendered, he asks the suspicions to take him to that frightful place. "Espantable" in line 9 seems to suggest death even before it is mentioned in line 10. The image, a cemetery in which the speaker has a vision of the epitaph of his own tomb, portrays the effect of the confirmation of his suspicions. He had wrestled with suspicions, preferring to live in doubtful agony, but now he has surrendered to them and is willing to accept the greater agony (muerte) of jealousy. The effect of this tercet is both dramatic and chilling. The eerie and indeterminate "aquel lugar" which is subsequently associated with fright and death stimulates the chill caused by these lines in which the poet discovers his own epitaph. In the last tercet he again repeats his surrender. Laying down his arms, he orders the suspicions to display the spoils on their triumphal chariot, another echo of the dedicatory epigrams in the *Greek Anthology*. Unlike the war metaphor in the Petrarchan sonnets that glory in suffering and the possibilities of death, the language of this sonnet does not strike an ambivalent attitude toward the negative. The narrator has resisted the passion and only in despair does he accept it. Jealousy is painted in the darkest of terms as frightening and repulsive. There is no glory for the victim as there was in Sonnet II. He does not achieve the status of sacred victim, but has succumbed to an ugly, unbecoming passion, which is portrayed, following Sannazaro, as a grim aspect of death.

Sonnet XXXI is an allegory in which the poet bears a beautiful son, love, who in turn bears a monstrous son, jealousy.

XXXI

Dentro en mi alma fue de mí engendrado
un dulze amor, y de mi sentimiento
tan aprovado fue su nacimiento
como de un solo hijo deseado;
    mas luego dél nació quien ha estragado
del todo el amoroso pensamiento;

en áspero rigor y en gran tormento
los primeros deleytes ha tornado.
   ¡O crudo nieto, que das vida al padre
y matas al agüelo!, ¿por qué creces
tan desconforme a aquél de que has nacido?
   ¡O celoso temor!, ¿a quién pareces?,
que aun la invidia, tu propia y fiera madre,
se espanta en ver el monstruo que á parido.

Lapesa expresses disdain for the allegorical nature of this poem: "su imaginación se pierde en enrevesadas alegorías. . . . Extraña encontrar estas
personificaciones en época tan avanzada del arte garcilasiano. . . . Ade-
más no son la única muestra, aunque sí la menos feliz, de alquimia intel-
ectualista en obras escritas durante la madurez del poeta" (*Garcilaso:
Estudios* 150). Indeed, the allegory of this poem is one of the least successful, and cannot compare with the brilliance of Canción IV, for example. The poem does seem to be from Garcilaso's late period in
the use of descriptive adjectives: "aprovado," "deseado," "amoroso,"
"áspero," "crudo" (Italianism for "cruel"), and "fiera." Garcilaso was
approaching a new theme in lyric poetry, and the materials at hand for
imitating included Sannazaro's sonnet with its image of jealousy as the
brothers of death. Tansillo also employed the imagery of familial ties in
one of his sonnets on jealousy: "O di buon genitore, e di rea madre / Fera
malnata, infame orribil figlia" (Oh base-born beast, infamous horrible
daughter, from a good father and criminal mother) (27). As with other
passages in which Tansillo and Garcilaso echo each other, it is impossible
to determine whether one is imitating the other or if they have each elaborated a common source.

    Emphasizing Garcilaso's distance from Petrarch, it is noteworthy that
his love was reciprocated at the beginning (line 3). Line 7 encapsulates
his suffering: "en áspero rigor y en gran tormento." Within the allegorical structure, Garcilaso notes that love (el padre) thrives on jealousy, but
the lover (el agüelo) is destroyed by it. The last tercet makes two important observations. In the phrase "celoso temor," jealousy is related
to fear, one of the inward retentive passions. In the last two lines he
distinguishes jealousy from envy, finding jealousy to be much worse, and
even frightful to envy herself, portrayed as the mother of jealousy. He
again employs the concept of fright and proclaims the dreadful offspring
to be a monster. Finally, the language of primitivism is found in the

words "áspero" and "fiera." While he does not place great emphasis on this aspect, it is clear Garcilaso relates jealousy to those uncivilizing forces in society, as he does with love in Canción IV. Garcilaso's favorite way of treating barbarity in human nature and society is through allegory. Again, Sannazaro's sonnet provided indications for the development of this allegory. He had characterized jealousy as the sister of cruel and horrible death. The attempt to present jealousy as an abstract hostile force completely alien to the good nature of the poet-lover, who is unexpectedly and almost innocently assailed by the negative force, is realized in various allegories and attempts to distance the guilt from the suffering host.

Other changes in attitudes toward love are seen in the four love sonnets addressed to male friends. As documented previously, a new direction in Spanish Petrarchism as practiced by Garcilaso and Boscán consisted of poems addressed to the general reader, rather than to the beloved, either by implication, or indirectly through inanimate objects or personifications. Petrarch had addressed poems to named male readers, and the practice in Italian poetry was fairly common, but it did not form part of Garcilaso's and Boscán's Petrarchan stance. Therefore, there is a certain novelty in the four love sonnets that Garcilaso addresses to particular male readers. The shift from poems addressed to the beloved to a general unspecified reader implied that the readers of the poems were also male. The naming of a known male friend foregrounds the male-centered world of Renaissance poetry. In these poems the male bonding that had begun to replace the amorous bond in Petrarchan poetry is completed. In this chapter I shall discuss two of the sonnets addressed to specific male readers, and leave the other two for subsequent chapters where they fit better thematically.

Sonnet XXXIII, addressed to Boscán, is written from Africa and is one of the most interesting sonnets of the late period. The juxtaposition of two planes of history that constitute the "fabula" with which Garcilaso illustrates the point of the poem recalls the intermingling of past, present, and future in Sonnets X and XXV:

XXXIII

A Boscán desde la Goleta
Boscán, las armas y el furor de Marte,
que con su propria fuerça el africano
suelo regando, hazen que el romano

imperio reverdezca en esta parte,
   han reduzido a la memoria el arte
y el antiguo valor italïano,
por cuya fuerça y valerosa mano
Africa se aterró de parte a parte.
   Aquí donde el romano encendimiento,
dond' el fuego y la llama licenciosa
solo el nombre dexaron a Cartago,
   buelve y revuelve Amor mi pensamiento,[1]
hiere y enciend' el alma temerosa,
y en llanto y en ceniza me deshago.

The "fabula" in this sonnet is both personal and historical. It refers to the Roman victory over Carthage and Charles V's campaign to Tunisia in 1535, in which Garcilaso participated. The complete destruction of Carthage by the Roman general Scipio, a feat that earned him the surname Africanus, is compared to the new Holy Roman Emperor's victory at La Goleta, a fortress near the site of ancient Carthage. In Elegy II, Garcilaso uses the epithet César Africano to refer to Charles V. The comparison of antiquity and the Renaissance was hardly new. In imitation of the Roman punishment of Carthage by razing the city and sowing salt in the earth, Charles implied such a comparison when he ordered the destruction of the "casa solar" of the *comunero* Padilla family in Toledo (located very near Garcilaso's own house), and the sowing of salt in the ground (Seaver 349). The comparison would be purely symbolic, since the Romans had had the practical end of destroying the land for agriculture and habitation, while the sowing of salt in a vacant lot could only be symbolic with no agricultural purpose. In Garcilaso's poem, the African soil is being irrigated by blood, itself salty, to make the empire flourish again in Africa. The destruction of the soil for vegetation by the Romans is now countermanded through the bloody irrigation of war to create a new flowering of the empire in Africa. The parallel nature of the two wars is also emphasized in the repetition of "fuerça" in both descriptions. In line 2 it refers to Mars's fury and arms, and in line 7 to the valor of the Italian armies. Herrera replaced the first "fuerça" with "sangre" to clarify the metaphor. Later editors eliminated this emendation as capricious. The repetition of lexical items is one of the techniques

---

1. I have capitalized the personified Amor.

employed by Garcilaso in the late period to unify seemingly unrelated items or to establish parallels between two events. Here he obviously placed the word in both descriptions to emphasize their parallel natures.

Both military campaigns are compared obliquely in the last tercet to the poet's own love situation. As history repeats itself in the two military campaigns, so too does love render its struggle eternal in the suffering of the poet. Again, unlike the Petrarchan mode, the comparison in this sonnet is not drawn out, but is simply left to the reader to relate the various points. The basic metaphor is Petrarchan; in fact, it is a Petrarchan cliché: love is war. Petrarch's use of this metaphor is quite different from Garcilaso's method here. In Garcilaso's Sonnet II, which employs the war metaphor, the metaphor is constructed in order to describe the situation and is subjugated to it. Sonnet II uses the image of defeat in war, rather than struggle, and the image of war is used to explain the horror of the poet's situation, defeated in the war of love. In Sonnet XXXIII, however, the metaphor exists in its own right, independent of the situation. In both sonnets, war is horrible, but in Sonnet II it is a metaphor structured to reveal the poet's emotional intensity. In Sonnet XXXIII, it is a realistic fable taken from history, which is compared obliquely to the sufferings of love and serves to objectify the poet's inner feelings. War is horrible because it is described realistically and independently of the poet's emotional situation. Curiously, both sonnets employ a secondary agricultural metaphor. Perhaps this is not coincidental, since war has the effect of destroying agricultural production, either incidentally or purposefully as in the case of the Romans. Both sonnets elaborate a traditional metaphor of courtly and Petrarchan love poetry, but in completely different ways. Sonnet II uses war imagery to re-create the personal anguish of the lover, while Sonnet XXXIII relates love in general to two specific wars, developing the theme in an objective non-Petrarchan manner.

The two themes of Sonnet XXXIII, war and love, are governed by different gods, Marte (line 1) and Cupid (Amor, which I have capitalized, in line 12). The comparison and contrast of love and war in Garcilaso's poetry is a major theme, and is often presented as governed by opposing gods. I shall return to duality in the discussions of Canción IV, Elegy II, and Ode ad florem Gnidi. In Sonnet XXXIII Garcilaso does not explicitly equate the two gods, but carefully constructs the argument and language of each part in order to facilitate a comparison. Thus line 12, "buelve y rebuelve Amor mi pensamiento," returns to line 5 and the image of the emperor with Italian troops bringing to memory the Roman conquest of Carthage. Line 13 where love also "hiere y enciende 'l alma temerosa" recalls previous elements of the wars. "Hiere" refers to "el furor de Marte" in line 1 and the blood spilled on African soil in line 3. "Enciende" refers to the fires of love in lines 9 and 10, which are meant, especially with their adjective "licenciosa" to refer in general to the poet's passion (and possibly Dido's suicide). The "llanto" and "ceniza" of the last line recall in their parallel position and sense the wounds and fires of the previous line, as well as the previously stated historical elements. In love as in war, the wounds and suffering produce tears and fire, and the fires and fury of war and of love produce ashes and destruction. In addition to these carefully constructed points of comparison, several details of the last tercet invite comparison with the preceding descriptions of war. The tears of line 14 recall the only other liquid element in the poem: the blood that irrigates the African soil in line 3. Both liquids, both salty in nature, are the result of wounds and suffering. The ashes of line 14 recall the destruction of Carthage referred to in line 11. The fire imagery of lines 9 and 10 leads naturally to a comparison with the lover's passion, and the ashes to which he and Carthage are reduced. Also "rebuelve" of line 12 probably recalls the cyclical nature of the historical examples. History repeats itself as do the sufferings of love. The comparison of these elements does not, however, lead to a clear-cut message about his love and passion, as do more typically Petrarchan poems that draw an explicit message from the comparison. Here the poet strategically slants each description in order to lead to the final comparison, but neither element is subordinated to the other.

There are references to Ariosto in this poem, even though Chevalier specifically denied any influence of Ariosto in Garcilaso's sonnets: "on ne trouve pas de réminiscence sûre du *Roland furieux* dans l'oeuvre de Garcilaso en dehors des *Eglogues*" (*L'Arioste* 63). Herrera noted that the "llama licenciosa" in line 10 comes from *Orlando furioso*, XXVII, 24, 3: "licenziosa fiamma arde." Evidently Chevalier considered this to be coincidental and insignificant. This sonnet, however, has another line that unequivocally comes from *Orlando furioso*, reinforcing Herrera's observation. Line 5 with its curious Latinism "reducido" is modeled on the first line of stanza 24 of Canto XIX: "Revocando a la memoria l'arte" (a borrowing not noted by any commentators). The verbs employed by each author are parallel in meaning: "revocare" is literally "to call back" and "reducir" is used literally by Garcilaso to mean "to lead back." These two references, plus others in Elegy II, recall *Orlando furioso* and suggest that on this military campaign Garcilaso was reading the third edition of the Italian epic, which had been published in 1532 (Brand 165–83).

This line recalls the Renaissance popularity of the art of memory. Frances Yates explained that the art of memory consisted of placing mental images, which represented the things to be remembered, on other images of a series of places that the author knew. Thus a journey or the memory of rooms in a building could serve to recall the sequence of items represented by images. Not only is this poem constructed over two historical moments that are said to be parallel, but the last two tercets also relate place and mental image. Line 9 begins "Aquí donde . . ." and describes the site of Carthage where the poet suffers from the passion of love. The images of war, the spilling of blood, the incendiary destruction, the licentious flame, and the unmitigated suffering are also images of love and of the poet's own suffering. Thus, the two wars, one of which recalls the other in one's memory, are eternal images of the suffering from love. The unity of place and image recall the art of memory obliquely referred to in line 5.

This sonnet clearly shows the full powers of Garcilaso's poetic art. As in Sonnets X and XXV, Garcilaso as a sonneteer seems best when he is balancing and harmonizing contrasts and antitheses along separate temporal planes. In this way the sonnet is not a closed system, but points outwardly along various trajectories, and continually passes in and out of itself as it moves back and forth over its underlying comparisons and antitheses. The complexity of this sonnet with its multiple planes of history and personal references—a locus pointing back to the power of the Roman Empire and suggesting the suffering of a lovesick poet—makes it one of Garcilaso's most impressive sonnets.

Like Sonnet XXXIII, Sonnet XXVIII is also addressed to Boscán. Discussed in Chapter 1 in its relationship to sincerity, it will be studied again in the chapter on Neoplatonic love. It is mentioned here because it is a love sonnet that is addressed to a male friend. Unlike the previous sonnet whose final tercet recalled the suffering lover, this sonnet strikes other unorthodox attitudes toward Petrarchan love, expressing optimism and joy upon falling in love.

Sonnet XXXV also strikes a non-Petrarchan attitude toward love. The Mario to whom it is addressed is, according to all commentators, Mario

Galeota, the supposed lover in the Ode ad florem Gnidi and the "Marius meus" of the second Latin ode.

XXXV

A Mario, estando, según algunos dizen,
     herido en la lengua y en el braço
Mario, el ingrato Amor, como testigo
de mi fe pura y de mi gran firmeza,
usando en mí su vil naturaleza,
qu'es hazer más ofensa al más amigo,
     teniendo miedo que si escrivo y digo
su condición, abato su grandeza,
no bastando su esfuerço a su crüeza,
ha esforçado la mano a mi enemigo;
     y ansí, en la parte que la diestra mano
govierna y en aquella que declara
los concettos del alma, fuy herido.
     Mas yo haré que aquesta offensa cara
le cueste al offensor, ya que estoy sano,
libre, desesperado, y offendido.

Only three of Garcilaso's sonnets have titles (XVI, XXXIII, and XXXV). There is no evidence that he wrote any of the titles, and this one is clearly by an early editor or copyist since it refers to speculation over the situation of the sonnet. In this case, the title is not really necessary; the poet makes clear the situation in the first tercet. Unlike Petrarchan poems which vaguely make reference to a personal situation—often left to be re-created in the reader's imagination—this poem is quite clear even without its title. The wounds referred to in the title were historical. A letter from the battlefield, dated 22 June 1535, stated: "Garcilaso received two lance wounds; the one in the mouth was trifling and the other in the arm was fairly serious, but they are not dangerous" (Keniston, *Garcilaso* 134–35).

This sonnet clearly breaks with the courtly love tradition. Addressed to a male friend, it uses a lighthearted playful tone to speak of love. The sufferings of love have become a competition between the lover and the personified Cupid who incited the lover's enemies with sufficient zeal for them to wound him (I have capitalized Amor in line 1). Desire and violence—in face of the bond of male friendship—have been relegated to games and light play, as the poet makes sport of his desire and the wounds he received in battle. The first quatrain refers to his love poetry, and how it continually rails against love and the lover's condition. He pretends that since Cupid feared that Garcilaso's poetry would destroy his reputation, he continued his custom of doing harm to those who were most faithful to him and stimulated Garcilaso's enemies in war to wound him in those physical functions that govern communication—the right hand and the tongue. The central incident is biographical and particular but the elaboration is fanciful and playful, recalling the lighthearted Hellenistic epigrams on Cupid in the *Greek Anthology*.

As in other late poems by Garcilaso, there are repeated words in the text. Lines 7 and 8 repeat different forms of "esforçar" in reference to Cupid's powers: first, his innate powers, second, his powers of subterfuge. "Ofensa" in line 4 is picked up again in line 12, and varied in lines 13 and 14, where the poet calls Cupid "offensor" and himself the "offendido." This wordplay, typical of the *cancionero* poetry, here strikes a lighthearted tone. The last tercet again assumes an unusual posture, swearing vengeance on Cupid. In the context of the sonnet, his vengeance will take the form of further amorous poetry from his pen. The playful tone of this poem probably does more to discredit Cupid and love than the descriptions of masochistic suffering and ambiguously stated warnings against love found in more traditional love poetry.

Sonnet XXIII, perhaps the most famous of all the sonnets, also strikes a heterodox attitude toward the canons of courtly love. The theme is patently classical and unrelated to the courtly tradition. Garcilaso does not attack the Petrarchan tradition, but he expands the poetic love material to the point that the poem no longer relates to the medieval codes of love.

XXIII

En tanto que de rosa y d'açucena
se muestra la color en vuestro gesto,
y que vuestro mirar ardiente, honesto,
con clara luz la tempestad serena;

y en tanto que'l cabello, que'n la vena
del oro s'escogió, con buelo presto
por el hermoso cuello blanco, enhiesto,
el viento mueve, esparze y desordena:

coged de vuestra alegre primavera
el dulce fruto antes que'l tiempo ayrado
cubra de nieve la hermosa cumbre.
Marchitará la rosa el viento elado,
todo lo mudará la edad ligera
por no hazer mudança en su costumbre.

Herrera's variant for line 4, "enciende al coraçón i lo refrena," is found
in most editions until those of Keniston and Rivers. Blecua has argued
that both versions of line 4 are by Garcilaso, but that critically we can
accept only the 1543 version in order to avoid contaminating the text
with later reworkings by the author. Since both versions may be by Garcilaso, I shall consider both lines in my discussion of the poem, pointing
out the advantages of each. The 1543 reading introduces a storm symbolic of passion, which recurs in various references to breezes, "el viento
mueve" (8) and "viento elado" (12), and in a winter storm "que'l tiempo
ayrado" (10). Herrera's reading works better within the first quatrain,
the verbs "enciende" and "refrena" following the adjectives "ardiente"
and "honesto" from line 3, and the symbols of the rose and lily from
line 1.

In many ways, Sonnet XXIII is one of Garcilaso's most impressive
poems, and it has found favor with anthologizers and critics alike who
have studied it extensively. El Brocense, betraying his love of punning,
noted that this poem is clearly related to Bernardo Tasso's "Mentre che
l'aureo crin v'ondeggia intorno," one of the "poemi aggiunti" of the
1531 edition (*Libro secondo* 65): "Este florido soneto es sacado del
Tasso" (B-24). This attribution has been accepted by all commentators.
Herrera traced the whole *Carpe diem* theme, and concluded by noting
the relationship to Tasso's sonnet: "Bernardo Tasso hizo un soneto al
mismo argumento . . . que si no me engaño, [Garcilaso] lo tradució; y
vean la ventaja que hizo el uno al otro en algunas cosas" (H-137). Tamayo de Vargas repeated the attribution of source: "El XXIII, es excelen-
tísima imitación del Tasso, como observó Sánchez" (T-27). Azara repeated the identification, but confusedly attributed Tasso's sonnet to
Petrarch (A-13). Stanton has analyzed in depth Garcilaso's debt to Tasso,
and has agreed with Herrera that Garcilaso's sonnet is far superior:
"[Garcilaso] has imitated the formal beauty of the Italian's sonnet, but
he has also vertebrated its loose, boneless structure, activized and made
more concrete the language and images, dropped the sentimental chaff,

softened the destructive part of the theme, and omitted overt reference to the non-beautiful" (203). As in previous cases in which Garcilaso treated a similar image or theme as Tasso, Garcilaso has not translated the source poem, but has completely reworked the material in his own fashion.

Stanton has analyzed the poem in depth, pointing out that the rose and lily are symbolic of passion and chastity, and are subtly developed throughout the poem, forming a symbolic subtext in the sonnet. Traditionally, the red rose was associated with Venus and the white lily with the Virgin. The meaning of the symbols is defined in line 3: "ardiente, honesto," and best developed in Herrera's variant for line 4, where the rose inflames the lover's breast and the lily holds it in check. The 1543 line makes the same distinction, but less effectively, since the rose (passion) is rendered with a substantive "la tempestad" and the lily (chastity) with a verb "serena." The same idea can be continued throughout the poem. The "buelo presto" (6) and "viento" (8) recall the storm of line 4, while the "cuello blanco, enhiesto" (7) resembles in its whiteness and uprightness, symbols of chastity. In the sextet the whiteness of the lily becomes a winter snow which represents the change of the golden hair of lines 5 and 6 to the white hair of old age. The rose will wither with the winter cold, but the whiteness of the lily (chastity and purity) remains as a permanent attribute. The fact that the rose alone withers and the lily tacitly remains intact makes the symbolism of the flowers obvious. The rose and lily function both as metaphors and as symbols. Metaphorically they represent the complexion of the mistress, white skin with red cheeks, and symbolically they are the interior psychological conflict of passion and chastity. As metaphors they describe; as symbols they represent abstractions.

The poem is addressed to the beloved. The traditional theme, as implied in the phrase "carpe diem," requires a direct address to the lady. Garcilaso employs the "vos" pattern established in the *coplas,* which permits a play on the sound pattern *est:* "vuestro" (2, 3, 9), "muestra" (2), "gesto" (2), and "tempestad" (4), which figures so prominently in Sonnet V. Even though the "vos" derives from the Spanish *cancionero* tradition, the mistress is addressed from a different perspective. The classical tradition of *carpe diem* involves a posture quite contrary to the frustrated desire found in courtly and Petrarchan love poetry. Love (and sex) were not for Petrarch lighthearted matters, and he certainly never urged his beloved to cede her virtue, an act that would have destroyed her perfection. Garcilaso's classicizing comes to perfection in this sonnet as he assumes a theme from antiquity, and one that incidentally breaks completely with medieval courtly love. The last two lines were first criticized by Herrera for their abrupt change of tone. The poem consists of delicate imagery up to the last two lines, which take on the tone and force of an epigram. Rather than a reversion to the *cancionero* style, it is probable that Garcilaso concluded the poem in imitation of the classical epigram. It is the type of ending that had been used occasionally by Petrarch. Rather than imitate the epigram throughout the sonnet, as Garcilaso did in other poems, this sonnet established through its imagery and symbolism a context for the epigrammatic conclusion.

The sonnets discussed in this chapter show significant departures from the strict canons of love and suffering implicit in the close imitation of Petrarch. As argued in Chapter 5, Tasso's proposed new sources of imitation implied a significant departure from the attitudes and postures of courtly love encoded in the Petrarchan mode. Some of the sonnets follow Tasso's specific suggestions for the incorporation of myth into the lyric. Garcilaso's mythological sonnets also show significant shifts of attitude regarding the expression of love and suffering. The other sonnets in this chapter break significantly with Petrarchism in the presentation of new attitudes regarding love. All the sonnets deemphasize the re-creation in the poem of the emotional suffering of the lover, and abandon the rhetoric of suffering identified in earlier chapters as a salient aspect of Petrarchism. In all the sonnets that employ myth and history, Garcilaso uses the fable to objectify the emotional suffering of the lover. Other sonnets explore the darker emotions of jealousy or assume playful attitudes toward love and seduction. The evidence of the classical spirit is seen in most of these poems, whether in the myths, the history of Rome, the imitation of Hellenistic allegories on Cupid, or in the *carpe diem* theme. Bernardo Tasso's revolution, which few have deemed newsworthy, was indeed significant for the transformation of Garcilaso's poetry in his last years, providing the stimulus for the radical shifts in thematic material and attitudes toward love.

10

Neoplatonic Themes in the Love Sonnets

Garcilaso's treatment of Neoplatonic themes in his sonnets is less developed than that of Boscán, whose fourteen sonnets in the new Platonic mode introduced several important themes into Spanish poetry. Even in comparison with Garcilaso's other works, Neoplatonism in the sonnets is less significant. Royston O. Jones pointed out the importance of Neoplatonism in Eclogue II, which dramatizes the sharp distinction between sensual love with its passionate frenzy and pure love with its emotional calm. As I shall show in Chapter 13, Elegy II also contrasts stormy sensual love with tranquil intellectual love. Critics have been reluctant to identify Neoplatonic themes in the sonnets. Only in Sonnets VIII and XXII has the presence of Neoplatonic ideas been suggested. In this chapter, after presenting for reasons of comparison some aspects of Boscán's treatment of Neoplatonic love in his sonnets, I shall, in addition to analyzing Sonnets VIII and XXII, discuss in Sonnets VII, XXXIV, and XXVIII Neoplatonic themes that have previously been explained as autobiographical. Several sonnets by Boscán and Bernardo Tasso will serve to confirm and clarify the Neoplatonic aspects of Garcilaso's sonnets.

Renaissance Neoplatonic love, first codified by Marsilio Ficino in his commentary on Plato's *Symposium*, was introduced to Italian poetry by Pietro Bembo in his dialogue *Gli asolani* (1505), and was further codified and popularized with Castiglione's *El cortigiano,* published in 1528 and translated several years later by Boscán at the urging of Garcilaso. In the last half of the fourth book, Castiglione presents as a character in the dialogue the same Pietro Bembo who begins a description of Neoplatonic love, presented under the courtly question of how the mature courtier can love and still retain his dignity. Undoubtedly, Castiglione chose Bembo as the spokesman because of his previous explanation of Neoplatonic love in *Gli asolani.* Unlike courtly love and Petrarchism, Neoplatonic love, as described by Castiglione, offers a system of requited love freed from the torments of frustrated desire:

> Desta manera será nuestro Cortesano muy aceto a su Dama, y así ella se conformará siempre con la voluntad dél y le será dulce y blanda y tan deseosa de contentalle cuanto de ser amada dél, y las voluntades de entrambos serán honestas y conformes, y por consiguiente vivirán vida bienaventurada. (384)

This picture of harmony contrasts with the horrors of the ordinary lot of the courtly lover:

> . . . nunca otra cosa se siente sino afanes, tormentos, dolores, adversidades, sobresaltos y fatigas; de manera que el andar ordinariamente amarillo y afligido en continas lágrimas y sospiros, el estar triste, el callar siempre o quexarse, el desear la muerte, y, en fin, el vivir en estrema miseria y desventura, son las puras calidades que se dicen ser proprias de los enamorados. (373)

Neoplatonic love is peaceful and requited as opposed to courtly love, which is sensual and frustrated. The acceptance of the Neoplatonic system of love introduced significant transformations into Renaissance love poetry.

Because of Garcilaso's limited treatment of the theme, a better understanding of Neoplatonism in his sonnets is gained from a discussion of its fuller treatment in Boscán. Neoplatonism presented a serious challenge to Renaissance poets, for Platonic love had never been celebrated in poetry. The introduction of a totally new system of love required renovation of the existing modes of expression with new and appropriate imagery and vocabulary. Naturally the poets looked to the language, myths, and imagery in the Platonic writings to express the mysteries of mystical love. Boscán's fourteen Neoplatonic sonnets (LXXVII–XC), probably the first extended collection in Spanish, present new themes and new attitudes toward love. Crawford maintained that these sonnets described Boscán's marriage and the peace that it produced for him. In his monograph *Juan Boscán,* David Darst demonstrated the relationship of these sonnets to the ideas expounded at the end of *El cortesano* (52). Boscán's obvious familiarity with this text and his use of Neoplatonic imagery and ideas in the sonnets makes Darst's explanation more probable. As in Garcilaso, the source of Boscán's poetry is often found in ideas and not in his experiences.

Boscán's sonnets waver between condemning the old courtly love and extolling the new love as a victory. Simply defining the new love in contrast to the old allows him recourse to the old familiar courtly and Petrarchan imagery of suffering, sadness, weeping, prison, storms at sea, sickness, darkness, and bestial sensuality. At times the contrast is briefly referred to in order to pass to the description of the new love. Other times, the old imagery dominates, as in Sonnet LXXXIII, which dwells on sadness and savagery until the last tercet. Since condemnation of sensual love and the suffering it caused formed part of the courtly love tradition—albeit as part of the glorification of love—Boscán barely needed to change the focus of the poem to achieve a Neoplatonic point of view. He simply continues to condemn love, and simply adds a celebration of the new love. At times the new love is no more than the opposite of the old: good health after sickness (LXXXVII and XC), a port after the storm (LXXIX), light and freedom after imprisonment (LXXXIX).

Remarkable in the poems, and certainly their most innovative aspect, is the optimism and celebration of life. In his first sonnet, Boscán had warned his readers of the pessimism of his verses: "O vosostros que andáis tras mis escritos, / gustando de leer tormentos tristes" (9–10). The Neoplatonic poems are freed from sad torments. A great deal of his imagery is new to love poetry. Love is not the old dissonant song of courtly love, but a new melodious song that reflects the music of the spheres and the harmony of the heavens (LXXVII). His new love is requited (LXXVIII); it is a triumph (LXXIX), a victory (LXXXIII), a miracle (LXXIX and LXXX), the arrival in paradise, be it the pagan Mount Olympus (LXXXVIII) or a vaguely Christian Heaven (LXXXII). He distinguishes the old burning from the new spiritual fires awakened in him now that his soul has been prepared for them (LXXXV). Essential to these poems is the new attitude to love, and its relationship to Platonic imagery and philosophy. This love is new—not only in object, but in manner: "Un nuevo amor un nuevo bien me ha dado" (LXXXI). It has produced a new type of poetry: "Agora empieza amor un nuevo canto" (LXXVII). The new love is good in nature: "Amor es bueno en sí naturalmente" (LXXXIV), and is constructed over the good: "Dulce placer fundado sobre bueno" (LXXXII). The new love is chaste "El casto amor" (XC), and it is requited "y soy amado" (LXXVIII). The new love is a function of the reason, an intellectual love of spirit instead of the body: "Razón juntó lo honesto y deleytable" (LXXVII). Love is spiritual and a part of the soul: "resucitando el mortal velo, / resucitó también la inmortal alma" (LXXIX). Like a mystic (the final aspiration of the Platonic lover), the poet is assumed into Paradise and removed from the things of the world:

> Dulce pensar que estoy en paraíso,
> sino que en fin me acuerdo que soy hombre,
> y en las cosas del mundo tomo aviso.
> (LXXXII)

Boscán here uses the same imagery of mystical absorption that Fray Luis de León (Ode III) and San Juan de la Cruz would employ in their religious and mystical poetry.

Another striking type of imagery employed by Boscán in his Neoplatonic sonnets is the references to Christianity and New Testament miracles. These Christian references clearly correspond to the syncretic nature of Renaissance Platonism. Not only did the Renaissance Neoplatonists argue that the pagan world was simply a veiled Christianity; they also conceived of Christian mysticism as part of Platonic mysticism. Ficino's condemned *Theologia platonica* was an attempt at syncretism. His formulation of Neoplatonic love, his *De amore,* had tended to Christianize Plato's *Symposium:* "Greek gods and demons are transformed into Christian angels; Socrates' instructress in the meaning of love, Diotima, is said to be inspired by the Holy Spirit" (Nelson, "Platonism" 510). The syncretism of the Renaissance Platonists—the Christianization of pagan antiquity and the paganizing of Christianity—derived from deeply rooted beliefs in the resolution of opposition in the world into the unity and harmony of the abstract celestial forms.

While it is unlikely that Boscán's syncretism springs from such deep philosophical motivations, it is evident that he follows current fashions of synthesizing Christianity and paganism into his amorous vision. In Sonnet LXXXVIII he arrives at the peak of Mount Olympus. The Christian references are more striking. The sound of his new poetry in this vein is "sabroso y santo" (LXXVII). His conversion from sensual love to Platonic love was a "milagro" (LXXIX and LXXX). God appears in three sonnets: "a Dios ya yo no pido, / sino que me conserve en este estado" (LXXXI); "hasta que Dios con su absoluto mando / mi guerra convirtió en tanta vitoria" (LXXXIII); and "El casto amor, que Dios del cielo envía" (XC). Two of the sonnets refer directly to Christ's miracles. In Sonnet LXXXVII, he relates that those who witnessed his cure from sensual love must have been like the Jews astounded by the blindman who regained his sight: "como al ciego miraron los Judíos / espantados de velle como vía" (13–14). Sonnet XC, which closes the cycle, refers to Christ's cure of the man at the pool of Bethsaida (John 5:5–12), actually paraphrasing the Evangelical phrase: "Toma tu lecho acuestas, y haz tu vía" (8). The final tercet closes the series, addressing the power of God:

> ¡O poder eternal y soberano!
> ¿quién sanará con propia diligencia,
> si la salud no da tu larga mano?

Boscán strikingly incorporates into his Neoplatonic sonnets various Christian concepts and references, an intellectual habit typical of Renaissance Neoplatonists in general.

Important in Boscán's Neoplatonic sonnets is the introduction of others who are neither rivals nor suitors, but those who are indifferent to— yet commenting upon—him as a sensual lover. Instead of the romantic triangle typical of Boscán's Petrarchan poetry, where the poet's desire is displaced by his attempt to outdo his rival in romantic sensitivity, the Neoplatonic sonnets show that the love is peaceful and requited and that the threat of violence from rivalry has disappeared. In distinguishing Platonic love from Petrarchan love, Boscán often portrays his former Petrarchan self as a spectacle and social outcast. His character and physiognomy as a sensual lover were so transformed that he could not hide his condition from the rest of society: "en mi rostro se muestran mis locuras" (LXXXIV), and it frightened others who saw him:

> Gran tiempo fui de males tan dañado,
> por el dañado amor que en mí reynaba,

> que a sanos y a dolientes espantaba
> la vista de un doliente tan llagado.
>   (LXXXVII)

They saw him and disapproved, and began to gossip about his condition, magnifying it and inventing new elements. Such a person would implicitly lose his reputation in society: "Con cuánto lamentar fui escarmiento, / Para toda la gente que me vía! / Hablilla fui . . . / Y entre lenguas se mejoraba el cuento / Que a su placer cada uno le decía" (LXXXIX). The newly transformed lover witnessed his own new self: "Víme sano después en un momento" (LXXXVII), and "Volví luego á mirarme, y víme sano" (XC). The others in whose presence this drama was played out also noted the change in him: "Y vueltos en placer los males míos, / Miraban todos esta salud mía" (LXXXVII), and in their estimation, he gained self-respect: "ahora libre entre todos me contemplo" (LXXXIX). He is assured that his transformation is noted by all: ". . . mi mal sanó con gran renombre" (LXXXII), and that he will gain their admiration: "Celebrado seré en toda la gente, / llevando en mí triunfo para el cielo" (LXXIX). The presence of other members of society who have noted and condemned his previous condition dependent on sensual desire, and who witness and celebrate his miraculous transformation, is explicit, rather than implied, as in the case of the rival in the Petrarchan poetry. They are an important factor in the description of the transformation, providing a judicial norm that permits the precise description and judgment of his former self in comparison with the transformed self. Even though the transformation of the sensual lover to a Platonic lover is at times realized with Petrarchan language and imagery, the philosophical basis of the conversion is carefully delineated.

Garcilaso's sonnets do not develop to such a high degree the concept of a reformed and transformed Neoplatonic lover. Like his Elegy II, which contrasts Boscán's successful transformation with his own entrapment in sensual love, the sonnets employ Neoplatonic imagery, but often only to return the lover to cycles of frustrated suffering. Three of the sonnets do celebrate a conversion and freedom from sensuality, but these are the only indications of a change. As such, they are far from Boscán's extended and systematic development of Platonic themes. Only Garcilaso's Sonnet VIII has been claimed to be fully Neoplatonic in inspiration:

VIII

De aquella vista pura y excellente
salen espirtus bivos y encendidos,
y siendo por mis ojos recebidos,
me passan hasta donde el mal se siente;
    éntranse en el camino fácilmente
por do los mios, de tal calor movidos
salen fuera de mí como perdidos,
llamados d'aquel bien que 'stá presente.
    Ausente, en la memoria la imagino;
mis espirtus, pensando que la vían,
se mueven y se encienden sin medida;
    mas no hallando fácil el camino,
que los suyos entrando derretían,
rebientan por salir do no ay salida.

The Golden Age commentators had related this sonnet to Dante because of the metaphor of the spirits. Rivers, however, has identified in this sonnet the Neoplatonic doctrine of spirits and argued convincingly that this poem is based on a passage in *El cortesano* ("The Sources").

In medieval medical terminology, spirits are airy vapors that circulate through the body (as opposed to humors, which are liquid substances in the body). They are defined in *El cortesano* as "unos delgadísimos vapores hechos de la más pura y clara parte de la sangre que se halle en nuestro cuerpo" (387). They serve as mediators between the soul and body and are the means by which the soul maintains and governs the body. The metaphor of agitated spirits entrapped in the body has been adopted from Plato's metaphor in *Phaedrus* of the soul sprouting feathers and wings for its flight to the heavens. Socrates' description is quite graphic:

> When in this condition the soul gazes upon the beauty of its beloved, and is fostered and warmed by the emanations which flood in upon it . . . it wins relief from its pain and is glad; but when it is parched by separation the openings of the passages where the feathers shoot close up through drought and obstruct the development of the new growth. Imprisoned below the surface together with the flood of longing . . . , each embryo feather throbs

like a pulse and presses against its proper outlet, so that the soul
is driven mad by the pain of the pricks in every part, and yet
feels gladness because it preserves the memory of the beauty of
its darling. (58)

Even the distinction between presence and absence has carried over to
Garcilaso's poetry. In Renaissance Neoplatonism, this description is applied to the generation of spirits as does Castiglione in *El cortesano:*

. . . mas [los espíritus], hallando los pasos cerrados, hállabanse
sin salida y porfían cuanto más pueden por salir, y así encerrados
no hacen sino dar mil espoladas al alma, y con sus aguijones desa-
sosiéganla y apasiónanla gravemente, como acaece a los niños
cuando les empiezan a nacer los dientes; y de aquí proceden las
lágrimas, los sospiros, las cuitas y los tormentos de los ena-
morados. (388)

Garcilaso follows the Platonic idea quite closely. In the presence of the
beloved, the spirits flow freely, but when absent, they find no channel for
escape and cause discomfort. The success of this poem relies to a great
degree on the image of the spirits being heated and contained to the
point of explosion.

Unstated, but central to this poem, are two other Platonic ideas. First
is the preeminence given to sight in Neoplatonic philosophy. Ficino made
a radical separation among the five senses. Sight and hearing are elevated
senses by which one can achieve mystical levels. Taste, smell, and touch
are corporal and bestial and serve to destroy spirituality. For this reason
the beloved's vision is described as "pura y excellente," recalling the Platonic doctrines of the spiritual superiority of sight. Also important in
Platonic philosophy is the memory, which, when it sees the beauty of the
beloved, begins to recall the celestial beauty of its primal origin. Socrates
presents a long digression on memory when describing the process of
falling in love in *Phaedrus.* While the memory here is solely of the beloved, its presence reinforces the Neoplatonic context.

Even though the poem treats the theme of the beloved's absence (contrasted with her presence), it is not addressed to the beloved. Like the
Petrarchan sonnets without a designated reader, this poem delves into
the lover's psychology—this time on the basis of Neoplatonic imagery.
The beloved is another presence: "la imagino" (9) and "mis espirtus . . .

la vían" (10). Identified by gender in absence, her presence was signaled with the phrase "aquel bien" (8). Like the Petrarchan poems, the beloved is secondary to the description of the effects of love. Her presence and absence are simply conditions necessary for describing the psychological effects.

As in all of Garcilaso's sonnets, the success of the poem depends on oppositions and parallels. The violent juxtaposition and contrast of "presente / Ausente" in lines 8 and 9 is very effective. The Italianism "espirtus" occurs twice, first as her spirits (2) and second as his (10), and is replaced twice, once by "los míos" (6) and once by "los suyos" (13). Other words are repeated: "encendidos" (2) and "movidos" (6) are repeated in the phrase "se mueven y se encienden" (11). The words "salir" and "entrar," essential movements in the poem, recalling implicit descent and return, recur frequently: "salen espirtus" (2), "éntranse" (4), "entrando" (13), and "salir do no ay salida" (14). Lines 4 and 12 are strikingly similar, even though conceptually opposite:

éntranse en el camino facilmente (4)

mas no hallando fácil el camino (12)

Also contrasted are the antitheses "mal" (4) in reference to his pain and "bien" (8) in reference to the beloved.

Even though constructed over basic Neoplatonic imagery, and incorporating other Neoplatonic ideas, such as the superiority of sight or the importance of memory, the poem is essentially not Neoplatonic in meaning. The narrative "yo" in Garcilaso's poetry never achieved the calm that Boscán relates in his sonnets, or that Garcilaso attributes to him in Elegy II. Even Neoplatonic imagery and ideas for Garcilaso relate to perturbed emotion and illness ("mal" in line 4) characteristic of sensual love. In *Phaedrus,* Socrates speaks of the mixed pleasure and pain caused by the absence of the beloved, coupled with his/her presence in the memory. Garcilaso has chosen to dramatize this moment of suffering. Instead of celebrating the victory or triumph of a peaceful requited love as does Boscán, he chooses to portray the painful process of falling in love. Even when inspired by Neoplatonic ideas, his vision of love is tortured and painful.

Garcilaso's Sonnet XXII also relates an unsuccessful attempt to sublimate desire. The sonnet has always been recognized as one of his most enigmatic texts, and only recently have Rivers and Snell suggested an interpretation that is both logical and, incidentally, based in Neoplatonic philosophy. Criticized in the sixteenth and seventeenth centuries for the quotation of a line in Italian from Petrarch, the poem was considered to be written for a specific unknown occasion and it still lacks a coherent interpretation. El Brocense indicates that the text was frequently discussed and interpreted even in the sixteenth century: "Más fácil sería en este Soneto refutar *lo que otros han dicho*, que decir cosa cierta: porque no se sabe el intento a que fue hecho" (B-23; italics mine). In addition to this disclaimer, El Brocense began his interpretation with "Parece que . . ." (B-23). Herrera said: "El argumento de esto soneto es caso particular, y por eso difícil de inteligencia. Parece que . . ." (H-129). He then offers three different explanations. Only Tamayo spoke with confidence, saying the poem was less difficult than the other commentators had made it (T-26). Azara did not offer an explanation, but rejected the interpretations of El Brocense and Herrera: "Las circumstancias con que lo visten Herrera y Sánchez son conjeturas que no satisfacen" (A-12). Modern commentators have expressed the same doubts about this poem. Navarro Tomás repeated the suggestions of the early commentators, beginning "Parece que . . ." (224). In his edition, Keniston accepted Brocense's solution qualified by a double negative: "The explanation of [Brocense] is the least unsatisfactory" (270), but he presented it without qualification in his study (214–15). Rivers also finds the poem difficult, but does offer a new interpretation, typically prefaced in terms of doubt: "Quizá más verosímil sea . . ." (123). Except for Snell, Garcilaso's critics have eschewed the difficulties of this sonnet, and only those who were forced to deal with it in their commentaries or editions have offered explanations. These solutions, always couched in terms of doubt, usually begin with the idea that the poem cannot be fully understood because we cannot reconstruct the situation which inspired it.

Even the date of the sonnet has been difficult to resolve. Lapesa finds it uncertain, although he assumes, because of the quote from Petrarch, that it was written in Italy, but he could not decide, either on internal evidence or through stylistic characteristics whether it pertained to the 1529–30 or the 1532–36 period (*Garcilaso: Estudios* 187). Stylistically, the poem seems somewhat early because of its abstract language and intellectual imagery, more characteristic of the *cancionero*-style poetry than of Garcilaso's late classical poetry, which often presents more concrete imagery. The text, metrically correct, presents no critical variants, and its straightforward style does not suggest the need for emendation.

XXII

Con ansia estrema de mirar qué tiene
vuestro pecho escondido allá en su centro
y ver si a lo de fuera lo de dentro
en apariencia y ser igual conviene,
    en él puse la vista, mas detiene
de vuestra hermosura el duro encuentro
mis ojos, y no passan tan adentro
que miren lo que'l alma en sí contiene.
    Y assí se quedan tristes en la puerta
hecha, por mi dolor, con essa mano,
que aun a su mismo pecho no perdona;
    donde vi claro mi esperança muerta
y el golpe, que en vos hizo Amor en vano,
non esservi passato oltra la gona.

All critics, assuming that the poem corresponds to a particular situation, have tried to reconstruct the circumstances for which it was written. Brocense suggested that the lady saw the poet staring at her naked breasts, and in trying to cover them, pricked herself with a pin. This explains the "duro encuentro" (6), the idea "que aun a su mismo pecho no perdona" (11), and "el golpe" (13). Herrera offered three different possibilities: one based on Brocense's naked breasts (although he eliminated the pin-prick), another that is based on revealed underclothing that served as a door (the explanation Tamayo accepted), and a third one based on the transference of love from the breast to the hand as the object of love (H-129). These interpretations failed to consider the intertextuality of the line from Petrarch. Rivers suggested an interpretation based on Neoplatonic ideas of love: "Quizá más verosímil sea un sentido figurativo: su hermosura carnal era de por sí una cruel barrera para los ojos del poeta, quien quería verle el alma" (123). Snell expanded on this idea, labeling the ideas in the octave as Neoplatonic, but returning to El Brocense's interpretation for the sextet. The imagery of the octave corresponds, as does Garcilaso's Sonnet VIII, to the ideas expounded by the character Pietro Bembo in Castiglione's *El cortegiano,* where the imagery of external beauty and internal virtue are made clear. Bembo states that external beauty is but a step in the process of Platonic love. It should remind the lover of the internal beauty and goodness of the mistress, which in turn reminds him of beauty in general and finally of celestial beauty:

> . . . y con esto acaece pocas veces que una ruin alma está en un hermoso cuerpo, y de aquí viene que la hermosura que se vee de fuera es la verdadera señal de la bondad que queda dentro; y en el cuerpo de cada uno es imprimida, en los unos más y en los otros menos, una cierta gracia casi como un carácter o sello del alma por el cual es conocida por de fuera, como los árboles que con la hermosura de la flor señalan la bondad de la fruta. (377–78)

He further equates goodness and beauty, explaining their appearance in the same person in whom beauty is a sign of moral goodness:

> . . . y puédese bien decir que lo bueno y lo hermoso en alguna manera son una misma cosa, en especial en los cuerpos humanos, de la hermosura de los cuales la más cercana causa pienso yo que sea la hermosura del alma, la cual, como participante de aquella verdadera hermosura divina, hace resplandeciente y hermoso todo lo que toca, especialmente si aquel cuerpo donde ella mora no es de tan baxa materia que ella no pueda imprimilla su calidad. (380)

In the first quatrain, the poet claims to try to look inside the mistress's bosom to see if her internal virtue corresponds to her external beauty. The second quatrain states that the lover was unable to penetrate past the physical beauty of the mistress, because her external beauty was such that it impeded his vision.

Herrera must have understood this interpretation for he gives a long discourse on the Platonic idea of beauty for the word "hermosura" in line 6, but in the overall interpretation of the poem he was misled by El Brocense. Herrera anticipated this commentary in his long article on Neoplatonic love, which he wrote as a commentary to Sonnet VII. In this commentary he distinguishes three categories of love: physical, moral, and mystical. He says these correspond to three types of vision, and three types of beauty:

> Y aunque todo amor nace de la vista, el contemplativo sube de ella a la mente. El activo y moral, como simple y corpóreo, pára en la vista, y no pasa más adelante; el deleitable desciende de ella al tocamiento. A estas especies responden otras tres suertes de belleza, como se verá en el Soneto 22. (H-50)

And in a commentary on Sonnet XXII, he explains the three types of beauty and their function in the system of Platonic love:

> ... hay tres suertes de belleza: de entendimiento, de ánima, de cuerpo. La del entendimiento, por la mente roba y arrebata la ánima a gozar de él solo. La del alma, por la vista sola, o por el oído, o por ambos. La de cuerpo, por todos los sentidos, por los cuales la belleza misma puede pasar a la ánima. (H-130)

Herrera follows this with the succeeding comment on the phrase "Y no pasan" (7) which draws upon the Platonic ideas of the previous commentary: "Paró en la belleza exterior, yendo a la contemplación de la celestial del espíritu" (H-131). The correspondence of Garcilaso's ideas with the language of *El cortesano* would suggest that this is a more plausible interpretation than the contrived literal situations suggested by the early commentators. In this case, El Brocense clearly misled his readers, and most future readers, by stating that it had a hidden literal meaning: "porque no se sabe el intento a qué fue hecho." Rather than constructed over some unknown incident, "algún caso particular que sucedió a Garcilaso" (Azara), the sense of the poem is clearly stated in the octave, and in essence contains no hidden literal references to the poet's biography. Of course it involves a paradox. The "duro encuentro" is not a pinprick or blow, but "el duro encuentro de vuestra hermosura." Castiglione proposes and extols a new way of loving that is far superior in its ethics to the older courtly love, which was based on sensuality and the suffering from frustrated passion. He soundly condemns courtly and Petrarchan forms of love as inferior and bestial, while extolling the excellence of Platonic love. Garcilaso, almost with tongue in cheek, tries literally to stare at his mistress's breast in order to interiorize his vision and see the internal beauty of her heart and soul. The matter-of-fact method of expression and the feigned innocence contrasted with the implied sensuality produce an amusing paradox.

Perhaps this would have been understood from the beginning if the tercets, especially the first one, were not so difficult. Line 9 simply restates the conclusion of the octave: "Y assí se quedan tristes [los ojos] en la puerta." One must of course understand "puerta" as an intellectual image (more typical of *cancionero* poetry than of the Italianate style), meaning that his eyes could not enter the room or bosom, but stayed on the outside, as Herrera said, stopped in the process of seeking the soul.

Castiglione had also used the image of the door, but in an opposite sense in which intellectual love closed the door on sensuality: "[el fuego] debe luego proveer en ello con presto remedio, despertando la razón y fortaleciendo con ella la fortaleza del alma, y tajando de tal manera los pasos a la sensualidad y cerrando así las puertas a los deseos, que ni por fuerza ni por engaño puedan meterse dentro . . ." (383). If Garcilaso took his image of the door from this passage, the irony in this sonnet indeed runs deep, for the door that closes out sensuality has become a door that shut out the access to pure Platonic love, closing the door forever on his hopes of the happiness from requited love. It is lines 10 and 11 that seem to have impossible references, and which required the fabrication of particular situations to explain the poem: ". . . en la puerta / hecha, por mi dolor, con essa mano, / que aun a su mismo pecho no perdona." The commentators assumed, as seems logical from the syntax that the hand belonged to the mistress, and that the door in some way was a covering for her body, reinforced by the "gonna" of the last line. Brocense adduced the pinprick to explain how the hand wounded its own bosom.

I would suggest a completely different interpretation of these verses, one that comes from a rereading of the intertext indicated in the last line: the second stanza of Petrarch's Canzone XXIII "Nel dolce tempo de la prima etade." In this stanza the poet explains how love assaulted him and produced those changes that characterize his old age.

> I' dico che dal dì che 'l primo assalto
> Mi diede Amor, molt'anni eran passati,
> Sì ch'io cangiava il giovenil aspetto;
> E d'intorno al mio cor pensier gelati
> Fatto avean quasi adamantino smalto
> Ch'allentar non lassava il duro affetto;
> Lagrima ancor non mi bagnava il petto,
> Nè rompea el sonno; e quel che in me non era,
> Mi pareva un miracolo in altrui.
> Lasso! che son? che fui?
> La vita el fin, e 'l dì loda la sera.
> Chè, sentendo il crudel di ch'io ragiono
> Infin allor percossa di suo strale
> Non essermi passato oltra la gonna,
> Prese in sua scorta una possente donna,
> Vèr cui poco già mai mi valse o vale

Ingegno o forza o dimandar perdono.
Ei duo mi trasformaro in quel ch'i' sono,
Facendomi d'uom vivo un lauro verde,
Che per fredda stagion foglia non perde.

(133)

(I say that since the day when Love made
the first assault on me many years had passed,
so that I was changing my youthful aspect;
and around my heart frozen thoughts
had made an almost diamond hardness
which my stiff demeanor did not allow to melt;
no tear yet bathed my breast
nor broke my sleep, and that which was not in me
seemed to me a miracle in others.
Alas, what am I? what was I?
The end glorifies life, the evening, the day.
For the cruel one of whom I speak,
sensing that no blow of his arrows
had yet passed through my garment,
took in his company a powerful lady,
against whom not wit nor force nor asking
pardon has been of any benefit.
Those two [eyes] transformed me into what I am,
making out of me, a living man, a green laurel
that loses no leaf through all the cold season.)

This stanza, like Garcilaso's principal image, deals with the nature of the interior heart, and Petrarch's line adapted by Garcilaso refers to Cupid's arrows not entering the poet's breast, which has been fortified against love. The poet (Petrarch) as a young man had resisted the temptation to fall in love until Cupid in frustration presented Laura to him, the cause of all his changes. Metaphorically, Cupid's arrows had not even penetrated his gown. Beginning with Garcilaso's last two lines and moving backward, we understand from the intertext that the "golpe" is not a pinprick, but Cupid's arrows that did not penetrate even the gown of the mistress:

> donde vi claro mi esperança muerta
> y el golpe, que en vos hizo Amor en vano,
> *non esservi passato oltra la gona.*

Garcilaso changes Petrarch's "essermi" to "esservi" to describe the mistress's resistance to his advances. Clearly "Amor" must be capitalized because it is, as in Petrarch and Garcilaso's Sonnets VII, XXVII, XXXIII, XXXV, the personification of Cupid. Garcilaso again plays with the idea of sight. The lover, blinded by the exterior beauty, could not see the interior virtue of the mistress, and in fact, in this external beauty he "sees" his hopes die: "donde *vi* claro mi esperança muerta." These hopes are not the courtly desire of conquest, but the Platonic desire of an intellectually requited love. His love of sensual beauty and his inability to enter the door signify the death of Platonic love, further indicated by the fact that his love has not been reciprocated. Cupid's arrows have not passed the gown of the mistress, in the same way his vision, struck by her sensual beauty, could not pass the covering of the body.

Continuing backwards, we see that the hand of line 10 belongs to Cupid, not to the mistress, and the phrase "que aun a su mismo pecho no perdona" is a definition of the owner of the hand, rather than a reference to some unknown circumstance. The conceit of Cupid's being wounded by his own weapons recalls the myth of Cupid's love for Psyche, a late Roman myth not found in the Greek mythographers. There is, however, the idea of Cupid in love in the *Greek Anthology:* "One shall burn fire with fire, Love has touched Love to the quick" (V, 309). The idea of the fires of love not sparing even Cupid himself occurs in a poem "Cupido Amans" in the so-called *Latin Anthology:* "hic meus est ignis: meus est, qui parcere nescit" (this fire is mine: it is mine that knows not how to spare) (Duff and Duff 2:542). Another source of the wounded Cupid comes from Poliziano's translation of Moschus's poem "Amor fugitivo," which is found both in the *Greek Anthology* and in a separate manuscript. In the poem, Venus complains that her naughty son, who has hidden, does not spare even her from his arrows of love: "Upon his back a quiver gilded o'er / Holds bitter shafts that often wounded me" (Chamberlin 5). Poliziano translated the Greek poem into Latin, adding that Cupid not only wounded his mother Venus, but, recalling the Latin myth of Cupid and Psyche, also himself:

Sunt et amari intus calami, quibus ille protervus
Me quoque saepe ferit matrem; sunt omnia saeva,
Omnia, seque ipsum multo quoque saevius angit.

(Poliziano II, 526)

(Moreover bitter are the arrows with which that insolent child
Often injures me his mother; they are cruel in all things,
All things, and he quite cruelly wounds even himself.)

Poliziano's close friend Girolamo Benivieni translated his version into
Italian:

& contro à me talhora
Madre el protervo arcier suoi strali intende.
Crudele è in tutto, e più crudele anchora
Se stesso afflige.

(Benivieni 121v)

(And against me at times
His mother the insolent archer aims his arrows.
He is cruel in everything, and more cruelly yet
He wounds himself often.)

A more elaborate version by Thomaso Castellani, whose verb "perdona"
is closer to Garcilaso's text, was published in 1545:

La terra, il cielo, & l'infernal palude
Con l'aspre punte sue siede, & tormenta.
Ferito ha Giove, & me sue madre spesso;
Et l'empio non perdona anchora se stesso.

(Rime 53)

(Earth, Heaven and the infernal morass
He besieges and torments with his sharp arrows.

> He has wounded jupiter, and me his mother often,
> And the cruel [child] does not forgive even himself.)

This version was translated into Spanish by Hernando de Acuña:

> la tierra, el cielo y la infernal laguna,
> todo para sus tiros está abierto;
> a Júpiter hirió y a mí apasiona,
> y es tal, que aun a sí mismo no perdona.
> (Acuña 348)

Minturno in his *L'Amore innamorato* describes Cupid's enduring the pain he usually inflicts on others: "Amore, che dall'arme sue stesse ferito" (Love, who was wounded by his own arms) (25). Fulgentius comments: "and it was as if the proud archer had pierced himself with his own arrows" (88). The "pecho" of line 11 relates to the arrows not passing the gown of the mistress and recalls the "vuestro pecho" of line 2, that is, the mistress's bosom that is fortified against the poet's gaze and against the arrows of love. Paradoxically, even Cupid, as well as the poet, suffer from the arrows and pangs of love, but the mistress has never felt love; in fact, the arrows have never even pierced her gown. The phrase "por mi dolor" then takes on the added sense of the suffering of unrequited love.

The sonnet is an involved play on the various meanings of "pecho" as heart, soul, and breast—the first indicating his love, the heart pierced by Cupid's arrows, the second being the soul of the beloved contemplated by the lover in a mystical sublimation of the senses, and finally the physical breast, a sensual motif that prevents the poet from sublimating his senses and passions and enjoying a pure love. His failure condemns him to "dolor," and signals the death of hope for liberation from the sufferings of sensual love. Instead of the liberating Platonic love outlined by Bembo in *El cortesano,* the poet is condemned to the frustrated unrequited love of the medieval poets. Again he employs Neoplatonic imagery to relate sensual passionate love, and narrate the failure of Neoplatonic love, focusing on the moment of struggle and pain, rather than the moment of liberation.

Garcilaso has two sonnets that celebrate freedom from love, and another that describes falling in love at a mature age. Even though Neoplatonic elements have not been identified in these sonnets none of them has proved to be problematical to the critics, other than the difficulty of determining the references to the poet's love affairs. Sonnets VII and XXXIV treat the theme of liberation from love. Sonnet VII speaks of a new love and a new kind of love, but there are few indications in the poems themselves to link them to Neoplatonic love. Critics have traditionally related them to the mysterious lady of Naples, and the new love of Sonnet VII is explained as sensual. The text sheds no light on the circumstances of why the poet is freed from love, or what type of love is the new one, although the attitude seems to be non-Petrarchan. Sonnet XXXIV hardly seems to be Neoplatonic, and in fact it contains no explicit Platonic reference. Its joy and sense of liberation, however, compare to similar poems that are clearly Neoplatonic.

Sonnet VII relates a new love affair that is both against the poet's resolve and out of his control:

VII

No pierda más quien ha tanto perdido;
bástate, Amor, lo que á por mí passado;
válgame ora jamás aver provado
a deffenderme de lo que as querido.

Tu templo y sus paredes é vestido
de mis mojadas ropas y adornado,
como acontece a quien ha ya escapado
libre de la tormenta en que se vido.

Yo avia jurado nunca más meterme,
a poder mio y a mi consentimiento,
en otro tal peligro como vano:

mas del que viene no podré valerme,
y en esto no voy contra el juramento,
que ni es como los otros ni en mi mano.

Addressed to the god of love (I have capitalized Amor, line 2), the poet claims he has suffered sufficiently from his previous loves. In the second quatrain, the poet dedicates his wet clothes, as if he had escaped from a storm of love, as a votive offering in the temple of love. Herrera traced the motif of the votive offering to Virgil and Horace (H-53). It was also a popular motif in the *Greek Anthology* and in Renaissance Neoplatonic poetry. Printed third from last in the "poemi aggiunti" section of the

1531 edition of Bernardo Tasso's *Libro primo* is a sonnet celebrating Platonic love.

> Questo spezzato giogo et questo laccio,
>   Che con si stretto nodo mi tenea,
>   Hor c'ho da l'alma mia suelto la Idea
>   Di lei, che mi fe un tempo, foco et ghiaccio,
> Appendo in alto al tuo gran tempio et faccio,
>   O bel figliol' de la piu bella Dea,
>   Quel, che promesso t'ho mentre ch'io ardea
>   S'usciva fuor di si gravoso impaccio.
> Tua merce, hor lieto in libertà mi godo
>   Con si tranquilla et riposata pace
>   Che pareggia el passato empio dolore:
> Sempr'io t'adorero, sempr'in honore
>   Havrò gli aurei tuoi strali, et la tua face,
>   Le tue catene, e'l tuo tenace nodo.
>
>   (56)

> (This broken yoke and this bond
>   that with such a tight knot constrained me,
>   now that I have freed from my soul the idea
>   of her, who was at one time for me both fire and ice.
> I hang on high in your great temple, and I fulfill,
>   oh beautiful child of the most beautiful goddess,
>   that which I had promised when I was burning,
>   should I escape such a grave entanglement.
> Your grace, now happily in liberty I rejoice
>   With such tranquil and restful peace
>   That the godless past equals pain.
> I will always adore you, always in honor
>   I will hold your golden arrows, and your torch,
>   Your chains and your tenacious bonds.)

In the 1560 edition of his complete works, Tasso titled this poem "A Cupidine." The sonnet, like the octave of Garcilaso's poem, celebrates freedom from love, presented here as a yoke and bond, and characterized with the typical Petrarchan antithesis of fire and ice. In the second quatrain he presents as a votive offering in the temple of Cupid his former instruments of subjugation. Like Garcilaso, Tasso is not clear about why he was liberated from love. In line 12 he promises to adore and honor Cupid forever and the instruments by which he creates love. The implied contradiction of celebrating freedom from love and at the same time pledging love and respect to the god of love creates an ambiguity that can only be resolved by understanding a conversion from sensual to Platonic love. The lover's stance in the poem clearly does not correspond to a Petrarchan topos, for Petrarch never celebrated freedom from love. The only celebration allowed within the Petrarchan corpus is a joy at more suffering meted out by the beloved. The only model for such a celebration of freedom from the constraints of desire is the Neoplatonic philosophy of love that was popularized in various treatises. Perhaps the word "Idea" (capitalized in the original) recalls the Platonic doctrines of the eternal idea. Also the "tranquilla e riposata pace" in line 10 is another echo of the emotional calm promised by the Neoplatonic theory of love.

Boscán's Sonnet LXXXIX, which also celebrates freedom from love and employs the same image of the votive offering, presents no ambiguity because it is placed within the series of fourteen sonnets that develop various aspects of Neoplatonic love. Boscán celebrates freedom from his former passionate frustrated love:

LXXXIX

¡O monte levantado en el alma mía,
en la cumbre del qual agora siento,
con quánto lamentar fui escarmiento,
para toda la gente que me vía!

Hablilla fui que en mí se componía,
de lástima y dolor y de tormento;
y entre lenguas se mejoraba el cuento,
que a su placer cada uno le decía.

Sé que es así, no sé cómo se ha hecho,
que ahora libre entre todos me contemplo,
de la fuerte prisión do fui envuelto.

Y así agora en memoria de un tal hecho,
colgando estoy los hierros en el templo,
adonde amanecí, despierto y suelto.

Taken in isolation, Boscán's sonnet presents the same ambiguity as that of Tasso. In the octave the reformed lover, having risen above the storm, is on a mountain top, looking back and regretting the social degradation he suffered through love, which is only mentioned in line 11 as a "fuerte prisión." The whole thrust of the octave is on how his former lovesickness made him a social outcast. The first sextet presents his freedom, "libre entre todos," from his former prison. In the last tercet he offers his chains as votive offerings in the temple where he awoke free from the fetters. Unlike Tasso and Garcilaso, Boscán does not specify which temple, but the position of this sonnet within the Neoplatonic sonnets makes clear its intention of celebrating freedom from sensual love.

These three sonnets celebrate the victory of freedom from the bondage of love, and employ the image of the votive offering; although, since each one presents the enslavement to love in different terms, the votive offering, symbolic of the past suffering, is different in each poem. Tasso's yoke and bonds recall the bestial nature of desire through the image of animal servitude. Boscán's image of the chains and prison corresponds to certain realities of the period. On the Isabelline church of San Juan de los Reyes in Toledo (constructed during Garcilaso's infancy) are seen the chains of Christian prisoners who were freed from Moorish captivity. Even though Boscán's prison was metaphorical, the image of the votive offering is taken from a well-known custom of the period. Garcilaso's image is classical in nature and perhaps has classical sources, even though the dangers of the storm obviously symbolize the emotional trap of frustrated love. In spite of its classical sources and the obvious symbolism, Garcilaso's image of the votive offering of wet clothing seems to belong in this case to a newly established topos of Neoplatonic love poetry.

Given the topos of the octave and its close relationship to the sonnets by Tasso and Boscán, one can only identify the enigmatic new love of the sextet of Sonnet VII with Neoplatonic love, as did Herrera in his commentaries (H-50). The poet says he had sworn never to place himself willingly in similar danger again. In spite of this, in the last tercet he states he is falling in love again, but he assures his reader, who no longer seems to be Amor, that this love is not like the others nor is it in his control. Previously identified as the sensual love of Naples, it seems to be the new Platonic love that does not present dangers because it is requited and produces great spiritual calm.

Garcilaso's Sonnet XXXIV also celebrates the freedom from love, but it focuses on the situation of the others who are still subjected to sensual love:

XXXIV

Gracias al cielo doy que ya del cuello
del todo el grave yugo he desasido,
y que del viento el mar embravecido
veré desde lo alto sin temello;
    veré colgada de un sutil cabello
la vida del amante embevecido
en error, en engaño adormecido,
sordo a las vozes que le avisan dello.
    Alegraráme el mal de los mortales,
y yo en aquesto no tan inhumano
seré contra mi ser quanto parece:
    alegraréme como haze el sano,
no de ver a los otros en los males,
sino de ver que dellos él carece.

Like Boscán's Sonnet LXXXIX in which the poet examines his former self and his relationship and alienation from society, Garcilaso's sonnet looks at the sensual courtly and Petrarchan lovers—in this case, others, not the poet himself—and rejoices in his liberation from error. He uses three metaphors to describe the Petrarchan lover: (1) the yoke that subjugates the neck (like Tasso's "spezzato giogo"); (2) the storm that threatens the sea; and (3) illness. The most striking image is that of the life of the lover suspended and sustained like Damocles' sword by a single hair. In line 4, where the poet surveys from above the storms that wrack the existence of the sensual lover, Garcilaso recalls a similar image from Boscán's Sonnet LXXXVIII where the Neoplatonic lover, elevated to the heights of Mount Olympus where no storm nor wind (understand passion) can reach, surveys his tumultuous past. Like Garcilaso's lovers, Boscán also lived in error:

Miro de allí do estaban los amores,
que perdido en el mundo me traían;
y miro por quál arte sus errores.

The first quatrain of Garcilaso's sonnet is adapted from the first four lines of Book II of Lucretius's *De rerum natura,* where the poet sees the storm from land rather than "lo alto." Herrera emended the phrase to correspond to Lucretius's text, replacing "lo alto" with "la tierra." While this makes clear the hiatus required between "lo" and "alto" for purposes of scansion, El Brocense's reading relates better to the Neoplatonic situation than does Lucretius's text. Undoubtedly, Garcilaso saw the ability to "imitate" Lucretius to his own purpose of exalting his freedom from the storms of sensual love. Like Tasso's and Boscán's sonnets, this sonnet does not make clear its commitment, but simply states the lover's future joy of freedom from the yoke, storms, and illness of sensual love, themes common to Boscán's sequence of Neoplatonic sonnets. The love sonnet often incarnates a single moment or simply one emotion or one part of the complete love situation. Garcilaso's two sonnets, VII and XXXIV, along with Tasso's and Boscán's sonnets, celebrate freedom from love as a lyric moment of victory, simply assuming that the rest of the circumstances are evident. Boscán's cycle of sonnets on Neoplatonic love serves to isolate a number of the moments from the complete situation. The relation of Sonnet LXXXVIII to Garcilaso's two sonnets and Tasso's sonnet makes evident their intention. In light of these four sonnets it is clear that a new lyrical motif must be defined in early sixteenth-century poetry: the celebration of the freedom from sensual love, without explaining how the freedom came about, or what type of love has replaced it. Clearly, the sense of liberation of the will from frustrated desire forms an emotion strong enough to warrant its own celebration, isolated from the circumstances that caused it, creating a sort of victory ode that celebrates the victory without naming the contest.

Sonnet XXVIII, which was discussed previously as problematical for the concept of sincerity, seems to correspond to another of these moments in the course of Neoplatonic love.

XXVIII

Boscan, vengado estáys, con mengua mía,
de mi rigor passado y mi aspereza,
con que reprehenderos la terneza
de vuestro blando coraçón solía;
    agora me castigo cada día
de tal selvatiquez y tal torpeza,
mas es a tiempo que de mi baxeza
correrme y castigarme bien podría.
    Sabed que'n mi perfeta edad y armado,

con mis ojos abiertos, m'he rendido
al niño que sabéys, ciego y desnudo.
De tan hermoso fuego consumido
nunca fue coraçón; si preguntado
soy lo demás, en lo demás soy mudo

As explained previously, the sonnet presents problems for the sentimental trajectory traced by the critics, for the poet claims never to have been in love previously. This problem disappears if he is thought of as referring to Platonic love, considered as real love in opposition to frustrated desire, often mistakenly identified as love. The Neoplatonic theorists of love clearly distinguish between sensual love (not called love, but bestial desire) and real love, by which they mean the Neoplatonic intellectual love. The phrase "vuestro blando coraçón" in line 4 recalls Boscán's repetition of the epithet in another of his Neoplatonic sonnets: "Antes terné que cante *blandamente* / pues amo *blandamente* y soy amado" (Sonnet LXXVIII). These word clusters suggest a relationship between the two poems.

The sonnet depicts the sensual lover, opposed to the Platonic lover, as uncivilized and barbaric, summarizing the traditional courtly idea of the nonlover as barbarian. The word clusters are highly significant. Garcilaso as a sensual lover in the past suffered from "rigor," "aspereza," "selvatiquez," and "torpeza," emphasizing the animal characteristics of roughness, wildness, and slow-wittedness. Line 7 claims that all of this is more appropriate for the lower classes: "bajeza." It is through shame ("correrme y castigarme") of his past condition that he rises to a higher station. In the past he had mocked Boscán's "terneza" and "blando coraçón." The division between the sensual and Platonic lover could not be clearer. As a nonlover or sensual lover Garcilaso demonstrated characteristics of a rude barbarian or beast.

The sextet is full of very subtly developed series of correspondences and oppositions. Garcilaso sets up three pairs of oppositions between his condition and that of Cupid. The poet is mature, he is armed, and he has his eyes wide open. Cupid is a child, he is naked, and he is blind. The irony is complete, for the poet as a mature, armed, and aware person should not have to submit to a naked and blind child. These characteristics of Cupid seem to be adapted from epigram V, 309 in the *Greek Anthology*:

> Love may justly be called thrice a brigand.
> He is wakeful, reckless, and he strips us bare.[1]
> —Diophanes of Myrina

The reference to the lover's age, a necessary part of the paradox of a mature man submitting to a child, could also be a reference to the fact that Neoplatonic love, as presented in *El cortesano* is a love for older courtiers who have passed the fires of youth; at the same time, nonetheless, Bembo makes clear that the courtier must not be too old: "Hase de entender con todo, cuando aquí digo viejos, que no es mi intención decillo de los que no son tanto que estén ya tan gastados y caídos, que el alma, por la flaqueza del cuerpo, no pueda ya aprovecharse en los de sus potencias" (374).

Even though the "tan hermoso fuego" of the last tercet has often been interpreted as a reference to the sensual beauty of the Neoplatonic lady, it probably has its origin in Neoplatonic philosophy. Pico de la Mirandola discusses the conception of fire in his *Heptaplus*:

> Therefore, whatever is in the lower worlds is also in the higher ones, but in a more refined (superior) form; similarly, what is found in the higher worlds can be seen also in the lower ones, but in a deteriorated condition and with a somewhat adulterated nature, so to speak. Among us, heat is an elemental quality: in the celestial world it is a calorific power [virtue]; in the angelic minds, it is an idea of warmth. I shall speak more clearly: among us, fire is a physical element; the sun is fire in the sky, the celestial world; in the region above man, fire is the seraphic intellect. But see how they differ: the elemental fire burns, the celestial fire enlivens, the super-celestial fire loves. (24)

Boscán devotes a whole sonnet to a discussion of the ennobling flame that carries the soul aloft. In Sonnet LXXXIV Boscán had detailed his misuse of the noble element of fire in his sensual longings, and then in Sonnet LXXXV he describes the ennobling fire and its effects, providing a philosophical context for Garcilaso's "hermoso fuego":

---

1. Hutton (*Greek Anthology*) does not list any imitations of this epigram, nor have I been able to locate any Neo-Latin epigrams that treat the theme, which clearly corresponds to the Hellenistic elaborations on the allegories on Eros.

LXXXV

Este fuego que agora yo en mí siento,
es puro y simple, y puesto allá en su esfera;
y quando acá desciende su hoguera,
es porque tal materia le presento,
    que en su calor revivo y me caliento,
templando todo el ayre en tal manera,
que do quiera que estoy, es primavera,
con flores y con fruto en un momento.
    Su luz al derredor do estoy presente
alumbra en un instante quanto veo,
mudándolo en color claro y luciente.
    Si esse tal fuego hurtara Prometeo,
quando quiso alegrar la mortal gente,
tuviera gran desculpa su deseo.

Boscán echoes precisely the language of Pico who states that the celestial fire "enlivens," while Boscán uses the verb "revivir" to describe the descent of the fire into his purified soul. Platonic love, which is a fire that in heaven is love and in the sky is warmth and light, has descended to his purified soul and changes his perception of the world. It is a mystical light that gives him special illumination (9–11). In the last tercet, referring to the myth of Prometheus, he says the desire of the mythical hero could be forgiven if it was a desire to enjoy this mystical fire. These passages from Pico and Boscán provide a philosophical context for interpreting Garcilaso's phrase "hermoso fuego" as a spiritual yearning and mystical desire.

There is a difficulty in the last line of Garcilaso's sonnet. The printed edition reads "soy lo que más," which every editor has emended to "soy lo demás." This creates a difficulty in that the word "demás" has exactly the same meaning in both expressions, which makes the line rather unpoetical. A further emendation could alleviate this problem. In Garcilaso's handwriting, it would have been possible to read "soy" for "por," if one imagines "soy" written with a long "s" and an "i" in place of the "y." This produces, to my mind, a superior reading: "si preguntado / por lo demás, en lo demás soy mudo." The first "lo demás" is understood as other people as well as other things, providing a richer poetic texture; whereas, "soy lo demás" can mean only other things. The addition of "mudo" to "ciego" completes the irony of the senselessness of the mature man both blind and speechless.

The love sonnet often incarnates a single moment or simply one emotion or one part of the complete love situation. Garcilaso's two sonnets, VII and XXXIV, along with Tasso's and Boscán's sonnets, celebrate freedom from love as a lyric moment of victory. Sonnet XXVIII celebrates the new love as the only real love, associating his past with nonlove and animal passions. The study of Neoplatonic ideas and imagery in Boscán's and Garcilaso's sonnets reveals that several of Garcilaso's sonnets that had proved difficult to explicate in light of the poet's biography become more comprehensible in the context of the philosophy of love systematized by Ficino and popularized by Bembo and Castiglione. As in other aspects of Garcilaso's poetry, the best tool for explication is the intellectual ambience of his time, rather than fabricated pseudoexperiences used to explain the poems. The conviction held by twentieth-century critics, inherited from Romanticism, that all good poetry comes from the heart and feelings, rather than the head and ideas, has led Garcilaso's critics into games of supposition, rather than investigation of the cultural ambience in which the poet lived, learned, and wrote.

The study of Neoplatonism in the poetry of Boscán and Garcilaso confirms the idea they were definitely in the vanguard of literature in the early sixteenth century. Previously admired for the renovation of Spanish metrics and poetry, one sees in the study of their Neoplatonism that they were introducing into Spanish the very trends that were being introduced into Italian poetry at the same time. Employing sources printed in the late twenties, and having before them poets published in the early thirties, both writers brought to Spanish poetry the new imagery and themes based on Neoplatonic love, and presented them in new and original ways. Boscán's systematic treatment of Neoplatonic themes in Sonnets LXXVII to XC provides one of the first systematic uses of Platonism as a theory of love in poetry in any language. Garcilaso's highly individual reaction to Neoplatonic theory of love provides an interesting glimpse of the poet no longer trying to actualize in his poetry the ideas and emotional responses of literary models, but using these models as points of departure to describe his own individual reactions. The attempts to read these poems as biographical love stories, which often began in the sixteenth century, mislead critics into a failure to see the philosophic thesis that lay behind the poems. The poets' unexpected participation in the literary vanguard of their time left commentators and critics searching for biographical sources for poems that turn out to be clearly philosophical in inspiration.

11

The Dedicatory Sonnets

A final group of sonnets from the late period eschews amorous themes entirely and introduces subject matter from other poetic traditions. The sonnet becomes, as it will even more in the following century, a vehicle for other types of material, such as epitaphs, poems of praise, and moral and philosophical themes. The four sonnets studied in this chapter represent the culmination of Garcilaso's attempts to distance the speaker of his poems from the involved unrequited lover of the courtly and Petrarchan love traditions. In these sonnets the theme of love disappears completely and the poems become more personal and biographical in content. This chapter focuses on the ways in which the sonnets of praise assume new poetic postures and incorporate biographical, that is, documentable biographical facts, into the poetry. In the cases of Sonnets XXI and XXIV, the biographical information becomes important in understanding Garcilaso's patronage and poetic goals in the last years of his life.

In the usual interpretation suggested by El Brocense, Sonnet XIX is not a dedicatory poem, but is a love sonnet addressed to a male friend, identified by Herrera as Giulo Cesare Caracciolo. In suggesting a different interpretation, I have placed the poem among the sonnets of praise.

XIX

Julio, después que me partí llorando
de quien jamás mi pensamiento parte
y dexé de mi alma aquella parte
que al cuerpo vida y fuerça 'stava dando,
    de mi bien a mí mesmo voy tomando
estrecha cuenta, y siento de tal arte
faltarme todo'l bien que temo en parte
que á de faltarme el ayre sospirando.
    Y con este temor mi lengua prueva
a razonar con vos, o dulce amigo,
del amarga memoria d'aquel día
    en que yo comencé como testigo
a poder dar, del alma vuestra, nueva
y a sabella de vos del alma mía.

The poem apparently caused problems even for sixteenth-century readers. El Brocense recognized the difficulty and offered a solution which has sufficed for successive readers: "La dificultad que tiene al fin este Soneto, parece que se puede soltar diciendo que Garci-Lasso llegó donde estaba el alma (que es la dama) de Julio, and Julio quedó donde estaba la de Garci-Lasso" (B-23). This interpretation has become the norm; even Herrera accepted it. The standard interpretation depends not only on El Brocense's interpretation of the confusing last tercet, but also of "quien" in line 2 as a beloved. It is also possible that "quien" refers to the same friend, Julio, named in line 1. This interpretation makes easier the solution of the last tercet in which the two friends have exchanged souls, and hence can communicate through their own soul, which has remained with the other. This sonnet places more emphasis on friendship than the other three addressed to male friends, and in the alternate interpretation I suggest, its sole message is friendship.

Herrera identified Julio as the Neapolitan poet Giulio Cesare Caracciolo (dates unknown). Giulio was not a common name among poets in the sixteenth century, but there exists no confirmation of Herrera's identification in the published poetry of Caracciolo, which contains no poems addressed to Garcilaso. Caracciolo became politically active in opposing the policies of the viceroy Pedro de Toledo, who introduced the Inquisition in Naples, and several of Caracciolo's sonnets reflect his political views. He belonged to the Accademia degli Ardenti, which was founded in 1546 and suppressed in 1547 by the viceroy (*Dizionario* 19:395).

The poem develops over a distance caused by separation, reiterated by "partí" and "parte," as well as "dexé" signaling further separation. The anxiety of separation is an absence of a "bien" (6 and 7), such that the poet fears he will suffocate. Through his fear he gains extrasensory powers, which suggests the effects of melancholy caused by fear. Melancholics suffered from fantastic delusions that at times were considered to be prophetic (Klibansky 36). Thus, fear has given him heightened powers of perception. The memory of the day they parted also bridges the chasm of absence. While the friend is "dulce," the memory of separation is "amarga"; both terms of the antithesis define and mark the gulf of separation.

Only in Sonnet XXVIII, in which Garcilaso compares his love life to that of Boscán, does the person addressed play an important role. In the other two sonnets addressed to male readers, the person addressed is incidental to the poem. In Sonnet XIX, the importance of Julio is far greater, and the role ascribed to friendship is much more important. Even El Brocense's interpretation, in which the two friends are so close that they are able to communicate about their unrequited loves through their transferred souls, places more emphasis on the themes of friendship and male bonding. The idea that the person missed is the friend Julio is not completely farfetched, since with the introduction of Neoplatonism, the exaltation of friendship became an important theme. Garcilaso himself exalts his friendship with Boscán in his Epístola, and Neoplatonic poets, such as Aldana, and writers like Erasmus, produced hyperbolic and sentimental praises of friendship in quite casual circumstances. In this sonnet the anxiety of separation from his friend comes to dominate the poem. The cause of the anxiety is presented so enigmatically that the separation from the friend assumes a central position in the poem. Even if the veiled allusions to an absent "bien" refer to the mistresses of the speaker and addressee, the allusions are so enigmatic and marginalized that the theme of friendship comes to be central to the sonnet. The subordination of the love theme, if one exists at all, represents a final step in the trajectory of distancing of the narrative voice from the posture of the unrequited lover of the Petrarchan tradition.

Tasso's exhortation to imitate the best Greek and Latin poets would have led Garcilaso to the *Greek Anthology*. There is no evidence that Garcilaso was able to read Greek, although Cienfuegos (49a) and Fernández de Navarrete (13) claimed he did. Fernández de Navarrete's phrase suggests more fiction than truth: "Hablaba el griego más culto y ático." Even if he could not read Greek, he could have read imitations of the Greek epigrams by Navagero, Fracastoro, Flaminio, Bembo, Scipione Capece, and Minturno, among hosts of others. Along with other poems (Rothberg 77–85), the two sonnets that Boscán composed on Garcilaso's death and Garcilaso's sonnet on his brother's death serve as ample proof of their induction into the circle of admirers of the recently published collection of Greek epigrams. Like Boscán's sonnets on the death of Garcilaso, Garcilaso's Sonnet XVI, on his brother's death, seems detached and unfeeling:

XVI

Para la sepultura de don Hernando de Guzmán
No las francesas armas odïosas,
en contra puestas del ayrado pecho,
ni en los guardados muros con pertrecho
los tiros y saetas ponçoñosas;
no las escaramuças peligrosas,
ni aquel fiero rüido contrahecho
d'aquel que para Júppiter fue hecho
por manos de Vulcano artificiosas,
pudieron, aunque más yo me ofrecía
a los peligros de la dura guerra,
quitar una ora sola de mi hado;
mas infición de ayre en solo un día
me quitó al mundo y m'ha en ti sepultado,
Parthénope, tan lexos de mi tierra.

As the title indicates, Sonnet XVI is part of the genre of the sepulchral epitaphs of which a great number are found in the *Greek Anthology*. In Garcilaso's sonnet the dead soldier, brother of the poet, speaks through the epitaph on his tomb. He departs from tradition by addressing not the passerby reading the inscription, but Parthenope, the legendary siren who is buried in Naples. The siren represents the city of Naples where the body of the speaker is buried. The quatrains list the elements that did not kill him: not French arms, not arrows, not a dangerous skirmish, not explosives (and firearms), the last presented in mythological dress as the thunderbolts of Jupiter. In the first tercet he asserts his bravery in battle and repeats the information that in the midst of so much danger he was not harmed in the least. The last tercet reveals the cause of his death: the plague, which was considered to spread not through invisible germs but by a general corruption or infection of the air issuing from the mouths of the sick and dead. The only emotion in the poem is attached to the last line—and that only by implication. The fact that the speaker states he is buried far from his native land seems to imply sadness, but in no way does the poem lament the fact or show grief over the soldier's death.

The three parallels in the *Greek Anthology* indicated by Rothberg present soldiers who are dying of disease and commit suicide to avoid a disgraceful death (84). The soldier in 9.354 says: "Pierce my heart then, sword, for I will die like a valiant soldier, beating off disease even as I did war" (III, 191). Poems 7.233 and 234 describe Aelius, a Roman captain, who also impales himself on his sword. Apollonides has him say: "I am vanquished of my own will, lest Disease boast of the deed," and Philippus of Thessalonica places emphasis of the final speech on cowardice: "Men perish by the sword, cowards by disease" (II, 133). All three epigrams contain two implications that Garcilaso must skirt. The classical indifference to suicide, which neither fits the facts nor squares with Christian morality, is avoided because the brother died of disease. The implication of a cowardly death by disease is confronted and contradicted directly in lines 9 and 10 by alluding to the brother's bravery in war: "aunque más yo me ofrecía / a los peligros de la dura guerra." As Rothberg suggests, it is possible Garcilaso modeled his poem on the epigram of Minturno, which combines elements from both 7.233 and 234. Garcilaso would have had to know it in manuscript, since it was not published until 1564.

DE AELIO.

Palladis Ausoniae cùm iá decus omne clueret,
    Aelius insignis munere militiae;
Extremo affectus morbo, ne gloria morbo
    Vlla foret, sese uulnere diripuit:
Atque, sui haudquaquá oblitus, sic denique dixit:
    Marte viri, morbo turba misella cadunt.

(Poemata 2)

(Aelius, an Italian follower of Minerva, when he
    was declared

famous by all and decorated with military awards,
was near death by disease, and so that his glory
    not be pierced by disease, he fatally wounded himself,
    and in no way forgetting his honor, he said at the end:
    "Men fall by Mars, the miserable mob by disease.")

Much closer to Garcilaso's sonnet is the freer version of 9.354 by Giorgio
Anselmo (1470–1525), published in 1526 in Parma:

Quem non hostiles debellavere phallanges,
    Nunc intestino languidus hoste premor.
Quin eat in pectus prius hoc Aedapsius ensis,
    Hoste velut, pulsa Febre, perire iuvat.
                                    (Hutton 173)

(I whom the enemy troops had not felled,
    now withered, am done in by an internal enemy.
Why not let the sword of Aedapsius enter this breast first?
    As it did the enemy, it can destroy this attack of fever.)

While Garcilaso's sonnet seems closer to 7.233 and 234 than to 9.354,
it is much closer to Anselmo's rendition of 9.354 than Minturno's rendition of the epigrams on Aelius. Anselmo's version, like Garcilaso's sonnet, plays on the fact that he whom the enemy did not destroy is now
destroyed by disease. He also ameliorates the issue of suicide by reducing
it to a hypothesis, rather than an actual deed.

As in Boscán's sonnets on the death of Garcilaso, Garcilaso's sonnet on
the death of his brother avoids all references to sentiment and develops a
simple paradox. Boscán's Sonnet XCI concludes that Garcilaso must be
destined for fame because, like Achilles, he always exceeded in everything, his trials were well known, and he died young. In Sonnet XCII,
Boscán, like Nemoroso in Eclogue I, wonders why his dead friend has
not taken him with him in death and has left him "Acá en esta baxeza"
(8). Boscán's sonnets at least associate grief with death. In XCI, Achilles'
mother laments his death and in XCII Boscán ponders his loneliness and
abandonment. Like many of the Greek epigrams on death, Garcilaso's
Sonnet XVI has no allusions to grief. It develops the paradox that a per-

son so exposed to danger and death was killed by an illness. This detachment from grief is surprising in the context of the exaggerated suffering inscribed in the love sonnets of the two poets, which try to move the reader to compassion—to feel what the unrequited lover feels for an unnamed beloved. The reader of the love poetry by both poets, above all Garcilaso's famous poems on death: Eclogue I, Sonnets X and XXV, and Elegy I, is surprised to find in their epitaphs on the death of a dear friend and a brother an absence of grief, coupled with a studied sense of detachment and a concentration on trivial paradoxes in the face of events that should elicit great grief. This detachment goes beyond that pointed out by Rivers in his article "The Pastoral Paradox of Natural Art," where he studies those moments in which the poet refers to grief, but does not try to portray it or make the reader empathize with it. The influence of classical art, above all the Greek epigram, has carried them to great and paradoxical lengths. In their love poetry they present exaggerated postures of suffering, perhaps, as Castillejo claimed, for a nonexistent woman. In Sonnets XCI and XCII and Sonnet XVI, Boscán and Garcilaso present the deaths of real people who were close to them, but they studiously avoid all references to any personal or emotional involvement.

Sonnet XXI is a poem of praise to a previously unidentified marquis:

XXI

Claríssimo marqués, en quien derrama
el cielo quanto bien conoce el mundo,
si al gran valor en que'l sugeto fundo
y al claro resplandor de vuestra llama
arribare mi pluma ý do la llama[1]
la boz de vuestro nombre alto y profundo,
seréys vos solo eterno y sin segundo,
y por vos inmortal quien tanto os ama.
    Quanto del largo cielo se desea,
quanto sobre la tierra se procura,

---

1. I have emended Rivers's reading by adding an accent mark to "y" (line 5). The conjunction "y" makes little sense, while the adverb of place "ý" makes the passage coherent. Keniston notes two adverbial uses of "ý" in the early sixteenth century (*Syntax* 82).

> todo se halla en vos de parte a parte;
> y, en fin, de solo vos formó natura
> una estraña y no vista al mundo idea
> y hizo igual al pensamiento el arte.

Nearly all critical interest in the poem has focused on the identification of the marquis. Because of the Renaissance habit of not titling poems, even sixteenth-century readers were not certain which marquis was indicated. The identification of the addressee in this sonnet has been a question since 1580 when Fernando de Herrera stated the marquis was either don Pedro de Toledo, Marqués de Villafranca and viceroy of Naples, or don Alfonso Dávalos, Marqués del Vasto, and according to Herrera, a friend of Garcilaso. Most twentieth-century editors, Navarro Tomás, Keniston, Rivers, and Labandeira, among others, have opted for don Pedro de Toledo because of Garcilaso's close ties to the family of the viceroy and the personal favors he received from him. Eclogue I is dedicated to the viceroy and most critics believe Eclogue III is dedicated to his wife. In spite of the preference given to the viceroy, it seems most probable that the sonnet is dedicated to the Marqués del Vasto. The weak metaphor in line 4, "vuestra llama," indicating the patron's soul, is so contrived that it seems to be a veiled reference to the marquis's coat-of-arms or a device. The Marqués del Vasto did have such a device. Paolo Giovio in his treatise on devices describes several designed for the Marqués del Vasto, one of which represented the eternal flame of the temple of Juno as a symbol of the marquis's constancy in love. This would be the device to which Garcilaso refers with the phrase "vuestra llama." The references to the Italian poet Antonio Epicuro and the Academy in Naples place the composition of the device among Garcilaso's circle of friends in Naples:

> El dicho Señor Marques [del Vasto] traxo otra [empresa] harto galana en materia de amores hecha por Antonio Epicuro, Varon de grandes letras, y erudicion en la Academia Napolitana: la qual fue el templo de [J]uno Lacinia, que sosteniendo unas columnas, tenia en medio un altar, sobre'l qual estaua encendido el fuego, que jamas no se apagaua por ningun viento, aunque'l templo estaua abierto al derredor por los espacios que hazian las dichas columnas, queriendo dezir a una Dama a quien gran tiempo hauia que amaua, y seruia, y ella se quexaua sin razon; porque'l fuego

de su amor era eterno, y que no se podia apagar, como el del altar
del templo de Iuno Lacinia; y sirviole de mote el titulo del dicho
templo, que por la parte de dentro estaua puesto abraçando la
redondez del, que dezia Ivnoni Lacinie Dicatvm. Y esta empresa
fue muy galana, aunque tuvo nessecidad de algun sabio que de-
clarasse la Historia a los que no la sabian. (81–82)

Also the marquis's title, Vasto, would fit the idea described in line 6:
"vuestro nombre alto y profundo." His name is "alto" because it is high-
sounding and expresses greatness, and "profundo" because it has the
deeper meaning that describes the character and learning of the marquis.

Born in 1502, the Marqués del Vasto was about Garcilaso's age, and
had advanced at the age of twenty-three to the position of "Capitán general de la infantería española e italiana del ejército de Italia, como recom-
pensa a sus servicios militares, principalmente en Pavia" (Martínez Fernando 22). Even though the Marqués del Vasto was an important
general, headed the successful expedition to Tunis and the disastrous
campaign in Provence, and later was governor of Milan, there exists no
full-scale biography of him. The short biography in the *Dizionario biografico degli italiani* (volume 4) states that the marquis displayed a temperamental personality and was plagued by rivalries and jealousy: "ini-
micizia dovuta soprattutto al carattere suscettibile e alla grande ambi-
zione dell'A[valos], il quale considerò sempre come rivali tutti i capitane
e i funzionari imperiali che gli furono vicini con qualche autorità" (en-
mity owing above all to the temperamental character and great ambition
of Avalos, who always considered as rivals all captains and imperial officers who were near to him with any authority) (613). Unable to bear
insults, his sensitivity dominated his character: "La sconfitta inflitta agli
imperiali . . . e, più, le beffe degli assediati vittoriosi, misero l'A[valos]
in tale stato di furore che con un gesto tipico del suo carattere debole e
morbosamente orgoglioso abbandonò la guerra e se ne ritornò a Napoli"
(The defeat inflicted on the imperial troops . . . and, moreover, the insults
of the victorious besieged, put Avalos in such a state of anger that with
a typical gesture of his weak and morosely proud character he abandoned the war and returned to Naples) (613).

Alfonso Dávalos, second marquis of Vasto, was, along with Vittoria
Colonna, one of the most celebrated and aggrandized figures in poetry
and painting in the sixteenth century. It is probable that the marquis
rewarded these tributes generously, as was the custom of the period,

which would account for the great number of them. Dávalos was tradi-tionally thought to be the subject of three Titians. In the *Allocution of Alfonso d'Avalos, Marchese del Vasto,* in the Prado, Titian portrays a moment when the marquis calmed riotous troops with an oration. An-other portrait is found in a private collection in Paris. Panofsky has ar-gued that Titian's *Allegory of Alfonso d'Avalos, Marchese del Vasto* in the Louvre portrays another subject (*Problems* 126). He is also portrayed on a medal in the National Gallery of Art in Washington, D.C. (C. Wil-son 103), and in the series of tapestries celebrating the victory of Pavia (Anelli 28–31).

The marquis was also the subject of numerous poems in Latin, Italian, and Spanish. Honorato Fascitelli (1502–64), to whom Bembo wrote mentioning Garcilaso, treats the marquis in the first of his *Carmina,* ti-tled Alphonsus (Sannazaro, *Poemata* 234–40). There exists in the New-berry Library a Latin poem of 1280 hexameters by Johannes Baptista Soterinus celebrating the marquis. The manuscript was probably a pre-sentation copy as it is in a professional hand. The praise is extremely hyperbolic throughout, as the marquis is compared with Scipio, Her-cules, Alexander, and Achilles, among others. Francesco Franchini (1495–1554) dedicated two epigrams to the marquis (30–32) and wrote an epitaph for his tomb (74). In Ranutius Gherus's vast collection of Neo-Latin poetry in Italy there are three epigrams on the death of the marquis: one by Parthenius Paravicinus (II, 181) celebrates his victories; another by Gabrielis Faernus (I, 943) is a lament on his death, and one other mistakenly attributed to Giovio Giovanni Pontano (II, 486), who died before the marquis was born, is a sepulchral inscription. The collec-tion of Giovanni Matteo Toscano printed an epigram by Antonio Tebal-deo (I, 228v–229).

The marquis was well celebrated by his fellow Italian poets. Bernardo Tasso dedicated four sonnets and one ode to the marquis (*Libro secondo* 35v, 39, 39v; *Libro terzo* VIII, XXII). Other poets addressed works to him in Italian: Ferrante Carrafa (*Rime di diversi* 85, 88), Angelo di Cos-tanzo (*Rime di diversi* 102), Scipione Capece (144–45), Giulio Camillo (Muzio 151–52), Bernardino Rota (1508–75; 80–83), Giulio Cesare Caracciolo (the "Julio" of Garcilaso's Sonnet XIX; *Il sesto* 55), and the most prolific in this area, Girolamo Muzio (1495–1576), much of whose poetic output is addressed to the marquis. He wrote to him thirty-eight sonnets and twenty long verse epistles, and was answered in several of them by his patron. Phrases in two sonnets by Muzio recall Garcilaso's imagery and phrasing:

AL SIGNOR MARCHESE DEL VASTO.
Valoroso Signor, se le mie rime
    Si potesser leuare à tanta altezza,
    Chi pareggiasser l'immortal bellezza
    Di lei, ch'eternamente in uoi s'imprime:
                                    (48)

(Valiant Lord, if my rhymes
    could rise to such a height,
    that they appeared to be the immortal beauty
    of him, who eternally is imprinted in you.)

O s'io potessi un giorno hauer le piume
    Da leuarme Signor a quella altezza,
                                    (56)

(Oh, if I could some day have the feathers (pens)
    to raise me, Sir, to that height,)

In the same poem, Muzio refers to "Vostro alto nome," recalling Garcilaso's "Vuestro nombre alto y profundo." Muzio did not become attached to the household of the marquis until after Garcilaso's death, and it is doubtful he would have known Garcilaso's sonnet. A better explanation of the coincidences is that they both drew from the same extensive catalogue of conceits available to poets for extolling the virtues, or lack thereof, of the many possible patrons in Renaissance society. Also other works, in which the marquis was not the subject, were dedicated to him. Pietro Aretino dedicated several works to him, and Iacopo Nardi dedicated his translation of Livy to the marquis (*Dizionario* 4:615).

The Spanish poet Hernando de Acuña (1518–80) dedicated three sonnets of praise to the marquis (257–59) and composed four sonnets on the death of the marquis (240–44). He probably did know Garcilaso's sonnet, because he paraphrased the last line in a poem of praise to a mistress:

> y vemos obra que, para formarse,
>   convino por razón que fuese el arte
>   igual al pensamiento, y la natura
>   al mundo lo mostró en vuestra figura.
>   (340)

Several elements in addition to the emblem of the eternal flame point to the Marqués del Vasto as the addressee of Sonnet XXI. It would be unlikely that he would address the viceroy as "marqués," when he had other higher titles, and the host of dedicatory poems addressed to the marquis, both in life and in death, would make it likely, even without the additional proof, that Garcilaso also addressed his sonnet to the same popular patron.

Reexamining the documents from the last years of Garcilaso's life in light of the identification of the marquis in this sonnet sheds new light on Garcilaso's biography during the last three years of his life and the importance of his relationship to the Marqués del Vasto. Keniston (and Rivers, who follows him) concluded that Sonnet XXI was written to don Pedro de Toledo, the viceroy of Naples, because the viceroy was instrumental in securing Garcilaso's release from the island imprisonment in the Danube and restoring him to favor with the emperor. In spite of this help, his influence on Garcilaso from 1534 on seems to have waned in preference to that of the Marqués del Vasto. On 15 September 1534, the viceroy wrote to Charles V requesting that Garcilaso be named to the position of chatelain of the castle of Reggio degli Abruzzi. He did not shy away from mentioning Garcilaso's past troubles with the emperor: "aunque ha dado algunos enojos a V. M., en el tiempo que era razon servir con su persona" (Gallego Morell, *Garcilaso: Documentos* 161). The viceroy also envisions reuniting Garcilaso with his family, whose absence the poet laments in the second Latin ode and in Sonnet III: "y con hazerle V. M. esta merced hare que traya a su muger y se arraigue aca" (161). The viceroy assures the emperor that Garcilaso will defend the castle and will be different from others with such charges: "porque no hara lo que los otros castellanos han hecho" (161). Lumsden has pointed out the importance of this document for Garcilaso's biography, and how it, along with the letter of 31 October 1534, appointing Garcilaso to the position, shows how Garcilaso regained the emperor's good graces. It is doubtful that Garcilaso ever occupied the position, for barely five months later he participated in the campaign to Tunisia, and on 19

March 1536, one year and four months later, he renounced the position in favor of Diego Gaytan (Gallego Morell, *Garcilaso: Documentos* 170–71). Three days later the emperor named Diego Gaytan the new chatelain of Reggio (Martínez Fernando 114; Gallego Morell, *Garcilaso: Documentos* 172–74).

Even though Pedro de Toledo had provided him with a stable position and income and the possibility of relocating his family from Spain, Garcilaso chose to renounce the position and its security for more war campaigns. The documents seem to indicate that he passed from the protection and patronage of the viceroy to that of the Marqués del Vasto. Many points correspond between the lives of Garcilaso and the marquis. The marquis was in charge of the expeditions to Tunisia and in Provence. Two documents grant sums of money to Garcilaso in name of the marquis (del Guasto)[2] for the purpose of paying soldiers (Gallego Morell, *Garcilaso: Documentos* 187–89). In the letter that Pietro Bembo sent to Honorato Fascitelli concerning the ode Garcilaso wrote him, Bembo praises the ode and comments on Garcilaso's relation to the marquis: "Non mi maraviglio se il S. Marchese del Vasto l'ha voluto seco, et hallo carissimo, come mi narra il Padre Maestro" (I am not surprised that the Marquis of Vasto has wanted him with him, and holds him very dear, as the father teacher tells me) (Gallego Morrell, *Garcilaso: Documentos* 167). Finally, it would seem that Garcilaso had begun to seek favor with the marquis by imitating the military daring of the marquis himself whose rise to fame and fortune came from a daring and risky maneuver that resulted in the capture of Francis I at the battle of Pavia in 1525. Garcilaso's recorded conduct on both campaigns to Tunisia and Provence was dangerously dashing. Before the battle at La Goleta, Garcilaso engaged the enemy and was wounded in the right hand and mouth: "The Emperor is insistent that none of the gentlemen shall engage in skirmishing. Garcilaso received two lance wounds; the one in the mouth was trifling and the other in the arm was fairly serious, but they are not dangerous" (Keniston, *Garcilaso* 134–35). In Provence he engaged in an impromptu assault on the tower of Le Muy and was fatally wounded (Keniston, 155–56).

The sonnet employs a number of hyperbolic conceits. "Claríssimo" is a title conceded by certain Italian governments to a marquis. Garcilaso

---

2. Fernández de Oviedo calls Alonso Dávalos the "marqués del Guasto" (134), as if his name were Dutch (Wast) rather than Italian.

could be using the term in a laudatory and hyperbolic manner, but it is in all likelihood a reference to a literal title. *Autoridades* gives both a metaphorical and precise definition: "Se toma tambien por mui illustre, nobilissimo, celeberrimo, y a todas luces insigne y famoso," and "Es tambien renombre y título honorífico con que en algunas repúblicas, y especialmente en la de Venecia, se distinguen algúnas familias o sugetos de conocida nobleza." I have found no evidence that the marquis received such a title, but it would seem likely that he received many honors after the successful expedition to Tunisia. The dichotomy "cielo/mundo" (line 2) is expanded in lines 9 and 10 where the marquis achieves perfection in both realms. The last tercet approaches the same idea with a new conceit based on Platonic doctrine of forms and ideas. The marquis of this poem is an exception to Plato's rule that everything in the world is an inferior copy or example of its one perfect form, which resides in the realm of ideas or the heavens. In this case heaven formed the idea, unique and rare on the earth rather than in the heavens, and unlike other earthly beings, the marquis was created on earth with the perfection of a heavenly form or idea.

Garcilaso's Sonnet XXI belongs to a genre that has not attracted the interest of subsequent readers, being the praise of a patron with the implied lack of sincerity. The sonnet of praise was a well-cultivated genre in Italian, where it has met the same cold critical reception. Williamson said of Bernardo Tasso's sonnets of praise: "substantially all of his court poems are empty of interest" (*Bernardo* 35). Gracián alone lauded the poem, believing that its subtlety made up for the lack of worth in the object praised: "Déjase algunas veces llevar el discurso de la grandeza del objecto, y aunque no haya tanto fundamento, lo suple la sutileza de la ponderación. Así en este soneto, el más canoro cisne del Tajo . . ." (341). It is probably the first sonnet of praise written in Spanish. While Garcilaso clearly knew how to praise, the poem itself does not have the interest that the genre would attain in the seventeenth century when conceits and counterpraise would create a dynamic poetic tension. Garcilaso does, however, mark the path in this direction, for he introduces complicated conceits based on Neoplatonic philosophy. The "pluma" in line 5 is not only a pen, but a feather, or by metonymy a bird, that will achieve poetic flight, the same image used by Girolamo Muzio. The flight of the soul will produce poetic rapture and poetry worthy of the marquis, and will produce the poetic flight that will grant immortality to the poet. In spite of its rather awkward terms of praise, it is interesting as the forerunner of a genre, and for the way it playfully and conceptually reaches its goal. It is also one of the late poems in which Garcilaso directly addresses the question of writing. While these allusions give the poem a self-consciousness of expression, the reference is indeed interesting and the solution to the problems of praise through literary conceits initiates in Spanish a long tradition of laudatory poetry addressed to the nobility. Like the sonnet on his brother's death, this sonnet, whose biographical importance has remained hidden, moves away from all references to love and desire. As previously discussed, the unstated goal in the *coplas* and other love poetry may have been the social advancement of the poet. This poem abandons the traditional thematics of unrequited love and passion and addresses the patron directly, praising his intelligence and character—the unstated goals of social favor and recompense remain unstated.

Sonnet XXIV is one of the most interesting poems of praise, and an important document concerning Garcilaso's literary circle and poetic ideals. In it he discusses the goals for his poetry within the context of Spanish literature.

XXIV

Illustre honor del nombre de Cardona,
décima moradora de Parnaso,
a Tansillo, a Minturno, al culto Taso
sujetto noble de imortal corona:
    si en medio del camino no abandona
la fuerça y el espirtu a vuestro Lasso,
por vos me llevará mi osado passo
a la cumbre difícil d'Elicona.
    Podré llevar entonces sin trabajo,
con dulce son que'l curso al agua enfrena,
por un camino hasta agora enxuto,
    el patrio, celebrado y rico Tajo,
que del valor de su luziente arena
a vuestro nombre pague el gran tributo.

The poem is supposedly addressed to the poet María de Cardona. Apparently none of her poetry survives, although she was a well-known literary figure in the sixteenth century, and Garcilaso celebrates her for her poetry. Moreover, I have not been able to locate the poems that the three poets named in line 3 supposedly addressed to her.[3] On the other hand, the naming of the three poets gives us concrete proof of Garcilaso's association with these three writers. The three poets stand as dative of interest to the subject, and the epithet "culto" referring to Tasso suggests his use of antiquity as a model for his poetry. There is a paradox between the literal sense of "sujetto" and the fact she is noble and crowned. In the second quatrain, Garcilaso suggests that with her inspiration he too will be able to reach the sacred heights of Helicon. Typical of Garcilaso is the image of "camino," which in this case suggests the poet himself had his own personal literary trajectory, not a love trajectory, but one based on the absorption of classical models in his poetry. Addressing the poem to a great lady recalls the type of intellectual love for courtiers recommended by Bembo in Castiglione's *Cortigiano*. Here the intellectual love allows the poet to reach new heights of poetic inspiration, even suggesting his path is daring: "osado passo," and figuring himself in the rhyme scheme of the quatrains. The sextet not only reiterates Garcilaso's identification with the Tagus, the river of his native land, but also passes critical judgment on previous Spanish literature, in this case, poetry in particular. It is surprising that no commentator has brought into focus the remarkable line 11: "por un camino hasta agora enxuto." The Tagus will take a new course with Garcilaso's poetry, one that had to the present been dry. Like the commentary in the dedicatory letter to Boscán's *Cortesano* that condemns previous writing in Spanish, this line, in its fullest sense, discredits his predecessors in Spanish poetry. I would believe that he does not simply mean that he is setting a new course that has never been tried for Spanish poetry, but rather that Spanish poetry, to this point, had been dry and sterile, and he, at last, was bringing Castilian waters to this unused channel. His confidence in Tasso's rebellion against sixteenth-century Petrarchism provides the basis for his poetic renovation of Spanish letters, a goal that he realized historically. The Renaissance break with the Middle Ages often consisted of a disparaging hostility to barbaric styles developed during the millennium after the fall of Rome, and Garcilaso participates in that attitude here. Line 10 seems to be elliptical for a longer expression, such as: "con dulce son que [produce el río cuando] el curso al agua enfrena." The last tercet turns the wordplays on the waters of the river back to the lady addressed, saying

3. There is a brief biography of María di Cardona in the *Dizionario biografico*. Along with numerous other writers, Tasso and Tansillo did dedicate poems to Maria d'Aragona, wife of the marquis of Vasto, who may be a better candidate for the "María" of Eclogue III.

the gold from the sands of the Tagus will render a great tribute to her worth.

Sonnet XXIV is a well-focused and clearly achieved sonnet of praise, which, along with the Second Latin Ode, is one of the works that provides a glimpse into Garcilaso's literary circles and his ambitions as a writer. Since few of the facts concerning the figure addressed can be verified and the autobiographical interest is so fascinating, the pretext of praise in the poem takes secondary interest to the poet's inscription of his creative self into the poem. In the sonnet Garcilaso refers to his goals as a poet, prophetically announcing the mission of changing the course of his national literature. Set in this context, the poem indeed renders true praise to his subject.

The four sonnets discussed in this chapter complete Garcilaso's trajectory of breaking away from the posture of the unrequited courtly lover as codified by Petrarch. In Sonnet XIX he subordinates the love theme to the theme of friendship (or he suppresses it completely). The imitation of the Neo-Latin epigram comes to the fore as Garcilaso distances himself from portraying grief and spins a paradox out of the circumstances of his brother's death. Like the Neo-Latin epigram, all the sonnets in this chapter become more personal and autobiographical. One needs to know the circumstances in each case in order to interpret the poem. Sonnet XIX remains elusive because we do not know the events to which Garcilaso is referring, but the poem is clearly personal as it addresses a named friend and refers to events experienced by them. The circumstances surrounding his brother's death are the focus of Sonnet XVI. Finally, the two sonnets of praise are instrumental as keys to Garcilaso's last years in Naples. The correct identification of the marquis in Sonnet XXI allows us to reinterpret the events and understand the change of patronage in the last years of the poet's life. It even provides a clue to understanding his daring, and temerity, in war and battle. Sonnet XXIV proclaims the poet's own goal as a writer hoping to change the course of his national literature. The four sonnets discussed in this chapter are unlike the earlier love sonnets, which employed an inconsequential biographical moment as a point of departure, such as the chance discovery of mementos, a moment of retrospective reflection, or a reference to absence. In the earlier poems the biographical event is vague and nonspecific, serving as a stimulus for the real subject of the poem, the lover's meditation on his emotional state. In the early love poems Garcilaso relates the initial experience (which may be imagined) to universal emotional responses. The nondocumentable experience is a pretext for the poet to explore human psychology. The later poems employ biography in a more realistic fashion. They refer to known people and to historic events. Like the Neo-Latin epigram, these sonnets are both personal and biographical in a way that is foreign to the decorum of medieval and Renaissance poetry in the vernacular.

The sonnets discussed in the last chapters clearly document Garcilaso's participation in Tasso's new conception of imitating classical, instead of medieval, subject matter in native meters and forms. The thematic material and style of Garcilaso's sonnets move quickly from the confining subject matter and anguished expression of the Petrarchan love sonnet. Significantly, there are no quotations or imitations of Petrarch in these poems; rather, the direct borrowings come from Ariosto, Sannazaro, and classical and Renaissance writers. In the love poems in the new style Garcilaso employs myth or "fabula" to distance the speaker from the love situation, finally achieving in his famous Leandro sonnet the complete suppression of all personal voices and references, that of the lover and the beloved. Other sonnets address a male friend rather than the beloved, foregrounding male bonding as an aspect of the love relationship. Other love poems treat the Renaissance theme of jealousy or the classical theme of *carpe diem*. Even though the Neoplatonic sonnets are programmatic in treating a set philosophical theme, in each case Garcilaso pays less attention to the exposition of the philosophy than to the inscription of his own personal reaction into the poem. Unlike Petrarchism, which Garcilaso adopted as a personal mode, presenting Petrarchan postures and observations as his own personal experiences, Neoplatonism remains elusive in Garcilaso's poetry. Either he uses the ideas of the philosophy to present his own differing emotional response or he refers to his acceptance of the philosophy as a victory, without specifying the contest or the defeated. Finally, he introduces new subject matter that is not related to love and focuses on his own life in a personal manner. As in his other poems in the new style introduced by Tasso, the later sonnets display a self-consciousness regarding composition and the role of the poet. Garcilaso's sonnets traverse a huge distance from medieval courtly love in the Castilian and Catalan styles through an intensive period of formation in Petrarchism to less involved poetic postures of classical poetry and even the complete rejection of love as a theme of poetic discourse.

V
Code and Paradox

GARCILASO'S FAME RESTS MORE on his longer poems, both in the Petrarchan and classical styles. His Petrarchan *canciones,* like his longer poems in the classical style, show his wit and love of paradox. The imitation of antique styles proposed by Bernardo Tasso included the revival of several longer genres. Garcilaso did not undertake, so far as we know, the epic or the fable, but he did introduce into Spanish several of the longer lyrical forms, such as the literary epistle, the elegy, eclogue, and ode. In the longer poems Garcilaso displays a fuller development of his wit and a structural complexity impossible in his shorter poems. The *coplas* and *villancicos* depend on wit that, because of the brevity of the poem, manifests itself in rhetorical devices rather than structural patterning. Much the same could be said for the sonnets, which usually develop on a single clear paradox. The longer forms reveal Garcilaso as a poet challenging the ironies and paradoxes of the received ideas of his age, a keen and probing philosophical wit undercutting and challenging the comfortable clichés of Renaissance thought.

In this section I shall discuss two longer poems, one Petrarchan *canción* and an elegy, one of the classical genres introduced by Tasso. In both poems, one sees the same basic structural patterns (such as repeated vocabulary and underlying subtextual unities of concept and symbol) and incisive wit. Chapter 12 analyzes a poem from the Petrarchan period, Canción IV, with the intention of showing how Garcilaso brought the overall vagaries and underlying paradoxes of courtly love into sharp focus. Chapter 13 analyzes Elegy II in order to show how even the most sacred of the ancient maxims, the idea of the Golden Mean celebrated by Aristotle and Horace and fundamental to Christian morality, does not hold up under Garcilaso's close, ironical scrutiny. These two poems have usually been neglected by the critics. Canción IV, enigmatic and difficult, is often thought to be an artistic failure, and the elegies have been little studied. Both of these works present aspects of Garcilaso's poetry that are seldom brought to the fore, but that inform all of his works: a subtextual thematic unity combined with a deep ironical questioning of the thematic material.

12

Mars and Venus Shamed: The Paradox of Love and Civilization

Courtly love involved an inherent paradox. In its initial stages, it had been called "fin amours" and was recognized as a civilizing element in society. The lovers sublimated their desires, which raised them above lust and brutality and made them more sensitive and refined courtiers (Lewis 2–3). Early troubadour conceptions of love place emphasis on joy and freedom (Topsfield 43–44). Only the noble and refined were capable of the sensitivity necessary to be lovers, in contrast to the lower classes who could only experience animal desires and pleasures. Medieval physicians derived "heroes," a technical term for lovesickness, not from Greek "eros," or love, but from Latin "herus," lord or master, justifying this etymology with the explanation that only the noble-born were susceptible to such a malady. They described love as a sickness and disease, but ironically a disease exclusively for the elegant and refined (Lowes 497).

As the poetic posture of the lover came to make a claim for the aptness of the poet as role model for the best lover, the poetic stance placed more and more emphasis on the poet-lover's rights through suffering, and less on his nobility. With the final transformation within the courtly love tradition from the lover as poet-wit to sincere tormented being, the last vestiges of elegance and joy were replaced in the poetry of the European Petrarchists and Ausiàs March with images of suffering, sickness, torture, death, and suicide, even at times employing technical terms from medicine and sickness (Heiple, "'Accidens'").

Garcilaso's Sonnet XXVIII, discussed in Chapter 10, depicts the non-lover (probably the sensual lover, in contrast to the Platonic lover) as uncivilized and barbaric. Even though it does not refer specifically to courtly love, the poem summarizes traditional ideas of the nonlover as a barbarian. The word clusters in the sonnet are highly significant. The nonlover suffered from "rigor," "aspereza," "selvatiquez," and "torpeza." The animal characteristics of roughness, wildness, and slow-wittedness are evident. The word "bajeza" suggests that this conduct is more appropriate for the lower classes. Through shame of his past condition he was able to rise to a higher station. In the past he had mocked Boscán's "terneza" and "blando coraçón," the characteristics of the refined courtier and lover. The division between the courtly and noncourtly are clear. As a nonlover, or non-Platonic lover, Garcilaso demonstrated characteristics of a rude barbarian or beast. Important in the vocabulary are the words denoting primitivism such as "selvatiquez" and "aspereza," which refer to a Renaissance concept of primitivism revived from antiquity.

The orthodox Christian view looked to the Garden of Eden and the paradise humans enjoyed before the Fall as the beginning of civilization. The pagan myth of the golden age paralleled Christian thought in this respect, even to the coming reign of justice and return of the golden age (De Armas, *The Return* 1–17). Any other explanation would seem to impinge upon Christian orthodoxy. There did exist, however, another classical tradition that described the beginnings of civilization as a rise from primitivism. Lucretius, in Book V of his poem on Stoical philosophy, *De natura rerum* (Garcilaso adapted four lines of Book II in Sonnet XXXIV), described in detail the state of primitive humans and the steps that occurred in the subsequent process of civilization (Lovejoy and Boas 222–42). The Roman architect Vitruvius, describing why humans first built shelters, summarized Lucretius's arguments (Lovejoy and Boas 374–75). The ideas of the primitive development of humanity, the so-called hard primitivism, were available to Renaissance humanists in respected texts from antiquity. Panofsky, tracing the development of these ideas during the Middle Ages and Renaissance, commented on their unorthodoxy: "By inserting this long passage from Vitruvius into his *Genealogia Deorum,* Boccaccio has lent authority to a doctrine which was not only un-Christian, but positively anti-religious" ("Early History" 39).

Panofsky speculated that the myth of Vulcan is central to this process. Vulcan was the pagan god of the forge—hence the first to convert natural elements to the artificial creations enjoyed by humans. Vulcan was the creator of lightning bolts for Jupiter, forged in his workshop in Mount Etna. Garcilaso renders homage to this Vulcan in Sonnet XVI, the epitaph for his brother's tomb:

> ni aquel fiero rüydo contrahecho
> d'aquel que para Júppiter fue hecho
> por manos de Vulcano artificiosas.
>
> (6–8)

Vulcan had also been the first to introduce buildings in primitive society; hence he represented the first major step in the process of civilization, and in addition was the first artist (Panofsky, "Early History" 40–49). The painter Piero di Cosimo (1462–1521), who for other reasons was probably very influential on Garcilaso's poetry (Porqueras Mayo), was intrigued by the concept of primitivism and painted a number of canvases on primitive civilization. The theme allowed him to paint the curious forms and abnormalities that so fascinated him (Vasari 2:176–83). Panofsky suggested a trajectory in the paintings and proposed the following reconstruction of their meaning:

> . . . a remarkable series of pictures which describe the first steps of human civilization as the transition from an *aera ante Vulcanum* to an *aera sub Vulcanum;* they depict the rise of mankind from an age when human beings fought with animals on equal terms, and cohabited with them so as to produce such monsters as human-faced swine, to an early form of civilized life contingent upon the control of fire. (180)

In Eclogue II Garcilaso also celebrated Vulcan as the first among artists:

> El arteficio humano no hiziera
> pintura que esprimiera bivamente
> el armada, la gente, el curso, el agua;

> y apenas en la fragua donde sudan
> los cýclopes y mudan fatigados
> los braços, ya cansados del martillo,
> pudiera assí exprimillo el gran maestro.
>
> (1616–22)

Missing from the Piero di Cosimo series is the picture of Mars and Venus trapped in the net with Vulcan looking on. Panofsky conjectured that this is also a key moment in the process of civilization. Vulcan catches his wife in adultery with Mars and makes a public spectacle of the two. He thus introduces shame into the world, the important step in the process of civilization that prevents random human copulation with other humans and with beasts, which produces the hybrid monsters seen in Piero di Cosimo's *Primitive Hunt* (Fig. 3) and the *Return from the Hunt* (Fig. 4). In the former, which depicts the violence of the primitive age, half the figures are satyrs. In the *Return from the Hunt,* there is a satyr and a centaur, all evidence of the interbreeding of humans with animals. Piero di Cosimo's *Vulcan and Eolus* (Fig. 5) could be an illustration of Vitruvius's description of the process of civilization. In the lower left two men work at a primitive forge. In the front center is a man sleeping without a cover on the ground, and slightly behind and to the right of him is a second family unit. Behind them, four men construct a building of rough timbers. In the background on the left is a small edifice inhabited by a family unit. The landscape is inhabited by a giraffe, an ostrich, and various small animals, birds, and insects typical of Piero's delight in the exotic. The painting serves as an exposition of the evolution of humanity from primitivism to civilization.

Hernando de Acuña in a remarkable sonnet compares love to the human primitive state in a way that recalls Piero's paintings:

> Cuando era nuevo el mundo y producía
> gentes, como salvajes, indiscretas,
> y el cielo dio furor a los poetas
> y el canto con que el vulgo los seguía,
>   fingieron dios a Amor, y que tenía
> por armas fuego, red, arco y saetas,
> porque las fieras gentes no sujetas
> se allanasen al trato y compañía;
>   después, viniendo a más razón los hombres,

Fig. 3. Piero di Cosimo, *Primitive Hunt*. New York, The Metropolitan Museum of Art

Fig. 4. Piero di Cosimo, *Return from the Hunt.* New York, The Metropolitan Museum of Art

Fig. 5.   Piero di Cosimo, *Vulcan and Eolus*. Ottawa, National Gallery of Canada

> los que fueron más sabios y constantes
> al Amor figuraron niño y ciego,
>   para mostrar que dél y destos hombres
> les viene por herencia a los amantes
> simpleza, ceguedad, desasosiego.

(248)

The poem divides the iconographical symbols of Cupid into two groups, claiming they were invented by two different types of poets for two different stages of civilization. When the world was primitive and poets were divinely inspired, they portrayed Cupid as armed in order to frighten uncivilized beings who could only understand force. The first two lines portray well Piero di Cosimo's primitivism in his *Primitive Hunt* and *Return from the Hunt*, where he portrays the hybrid monstrosities that result from primitive savages given to indiscreet fornication and bestiality. Acuña states they were "salvajes" (2) and "fieras gentes" (7) not subject to human social customs and discourse. He says, however, that later poets living in a civilized society governed by reason presented Cupid as a blind child to remind people of love's simple primitive roots. Like Garcilaso's Sonnet XXVIII, Acuña uses the iconography of Cupid as a point of departure to present the paradoxical nature of love as both a civilizing and barbarizing force. Garcilaso characterized the nonlover as a barbarian and lowborn who, mature, wide-eyed, and armed, paradoxically surrenders to a blind and naked child. Acuña treats love differently, locating it between primitivism and civilization. For the primitive, it was a civilizing element that by threat of arms brought primitive beings to civilized conduct, ensuring the survival of the species. For an already civilized society, however, love is a disruptive and destabilizing element that returns humankind to the first stages of civilization when people were characterized by simplicity, blindness, and unrest. Violence lies at the heart of this view of primitivism, as seen in Piero di Cosimo's paintings and Acuña's description of Cupid's weapons. Several Renaissance paintings focus on violence and slaughter of humans by other humans, such as Piero's *Battle of the Lapiths and Centaurs* (Bacci, *L'Opera* XXXVI–XL) and Pallaiollo's engraving *The Battle of the Nudes* (Levenson 66, 69).

Garcilaso's Canción IV re-creates the ancient pagan concept of primitivism as an allegorized state of the lover. This poem undertakes through complex allegories the characterization of the psychology of lovesickness, developed as a conflict of primitivism and civilization and explained with physiological and mythical allegories. Written in dense allegories the poem has not found a receptive audience among modern critics. Keniston concluded that "the composition seems to-day oversubtle and artificial" (*Garcilaso* 191). Margot Arce also expressed dissatisfaction with the poem: "Los cambios bruscos, la falta de seguridad, el análisis psicológico detallista, que pone de relieve los encontrados sentimientos del poeta, hace de esta canción un conjunto exagerado y retorcido, tanto en la forma como en el conjunto" (*Garcilaso* 131). She concludes that Garcilaso was unable to dominate his material, creating "el producto de un sentimiento más vehemente, de una menor elaboración de estilo, de un imperfecto dominio de los elementos poéticos" (Garcilaso 135). Lapesa finds a lack of unity in the work: "Más que una sola acción, es la trama una sucesión de invenciones alegóricas no congruentemente enlazadas, cada una de las cuales se inicia antes de que terminen las anteriores" (*Garcilaso: Estudios* 73). He views the imperfection of the work as the result of the conflict between Garcilaso's native Hispanic formation and the new Petrarchan modes that the poet was trying to dominate: "A nuestro modo de ver, en la canción IV no hay sólo conflicto psicológico, sino también artístico" (*Garcilaso: Estudios* 73).

In marked contrast to modern critical reservations and outright disparagement are the enthusiastic praises showered on the poem by Herrera and Tamayo. Herrera found it unique in Garcilaso's poetry, a noble dramatization of the conflict of reason and appetite:

> Sola esta canción muestra el ingenio, erudición y grandeza de espíritu de G. L.; porque es tan generosa y noble y afectuosa y llena de sentimentos, y declara tan bien aquella secreta contienda de la razón y el apetito, que oso decir que ninguna de las estimadas de Italia le hace ventaja, y que pocas merecen igualdad con ella. (H-217)

Herrera's praises are exceeded only by those of Tamayo:

> La IV es tal que, a mi ver, no tienen todas las lenguas juntas cosa más culta: y así es la primera de las obras de Garci-Lasso . . . porque si se mira la poesía, es cuidadosa; si la materia, importantísima; si la disposición, estremada; si la dificultad de la mucha filosofía que en sí encierra, reducida con suma claridad a lo que sólo el ingenio capacísimo de Garci-Lasso podía comprehender, no otro. (T-49)

The difference of opinion between modern critics and the Golden Age commentators could not be more striking. The disparity of judgment is so great and the praise so extreme that it must derive from more than Counter-Reformation morality. Obviously the critics and commentators start from different aesthetic bases. Tamayo praises the complexity of the philosophical thought and Garcilaso's ability to reduce it to clarity.

The revealing reference to Garcilaso's "ingenio capacísimo" marks the difference of aesthetic bias. Modern critics praise the sincerity of Garcilaso's sentiment; for them, poetry must consist of feeling and emotion and give adequate expression to the poet's passions. At the basis of Tamayo's praise lies an appreciation of the philosophical and intellectual values of poetry.

Lapesa's observation that the poem is composed of various unrelated allegories and sudden shifts of thought will provide the key for structuring the discussion of this complex poem. Garcilaso provides a complex unity based on repetition of key concepts and terms. I shall begin by discussing each of the allegories stanza by stanza and conclude with a broader discussion of the unifying elements and characteristics of the overall structure of the poem. The first stanza announces the purpose of the poem and deals primarily with the image of the lover as a barbarian captured by another and dragged by his hair over rocky ground:

> El aspereza de mis males quiero
> que se muestre también en mis razones,
> como ya en los efettos s'á mostrado;
> lloraré de mi mal las ocasiones,
> sabrá el mundo la causa por que muero,   5
> y moriré a lo menos confesado,
> pues soy por los cabellos arrastrado
> de un tan desatinado pensamiento
> que por agudas peñas peligrosas,
>   por matas espinosas,   10
> corre con ligereza más que el viento,
> bañando de mi sangre la carrera.
> Y para más despacio atormentarme,
> llévame alguna vez por entre flores,
> adó de mis tormentos y dolores   15
> descanso y dellos vengo a no acordarme;
> mas él a más descanso no me espera:
> antes, como me ve desta manera,
> con un nuevo furor y desatino
> torna a sequir el áspero camino.   20

The first three lines announce the purpose of the song. The poet and lover wants "el aspereza" which has previously been seen in his composure to be seen in his discourse (razones). This poem has the intent of making manifest in his writings that which had only been seen in his person. "Aspereza" is the theme of the poem. It opens the first stanza and closes it in line 20 with the phrase "el áspero camino," framing the first stanza with the concept of "aspereza," one of the words used in Sonnet XXVIII to characterize the unrefined lover. "Razones" is a good example of how words in this poem are employed ambiguously, or even ironically. As well as being the plural of "razón," or reason, it also means discourse or utterance. Both concepts are evident in line 2. The poet wishes to make evident in his discourse, or poetry, a harshness that had only been seen previously in his "efettos."[1] Even though "razones" clearly refers to spoken discourse, here understood as poetry, and has lost nearly all of its literal sense as a plural of "razón," in fact, "la razón" is an important allegorical element in this poem. For this reason, it is not surprising that "razones" functions with both meanings of discourse and reason. Lines 2 and 3 repeat different forms of "mostrar." Repetition as a stylistic device continues throughout the poem. While such close repetition of different verbal forms is typical of the *cancionero* style, these repetitions, and others throughout the poem, are not specifically highlighted in the same way as in the *cancionero* tradition. Perhaps this was the reason Lapesa sensed a conflict of artistic styles in this poem. I shall point out other close repetitions in the course of discussing each stanza, but shall reserve for later a fuller treatment of repetition as a theme identifier.

The next three lines continue the reflection on the nature of this song. In it he will announce to the world the cause of his suffering, the word "causa" contrasting with "efettos" in line 3. Herrera criticized the religious implications of "confesado." It does, however, allow Garcilaso one further play on the literal and figurative sense of "morir," first as suffering and second as dying. Lines 7–12 introduce the first allegory. Like a savage, the poet-lover is dragged through a rugged landscape, recalling the landscapes of Piero di Cosimo's primitive paintings. He is dragged by an allegorically personified thought, and bloodied, and only occasionally allowed to see the flowers. "El pensamiento" is clearly one of the most

---

1. A careful examination of the first three lines of this poem suggests that "efettos" may be an error for "afettos," which not only makes more sense in the passage, but also forms a clear opposition to "razones." "Efettos" does not contrast very well with "causa" in the next sentence, and the term "efettos" seems less effective. "Afettos" on the other hand contrasts nicely with the literal sense of "razones" and makes a nice parallel between emotions and reasons, although the latter has a different sense in the plural.

explosive of the human mental faculties in Renaissance psychology. Garcilaso presents his thought in the Epístola a Boscán as free and wandering. Calderón always presents the allegorical figure of "El Pensamiento" as a "loco." The association of thought with freedom and random movement is clearly established in Garcilaso's two poems and Calderón's *auto* texts. Lines 13–17 present a calm in his suffering in which he is allowed to see the flowers instead of the brutal craggy cliffs. This momentary and fleeting relief only increases his pain by allowing him to realize the extent of his suffering. Garcilaso continues the repetitions: "atormentarme" (13) and "tormento" (15); "descanso" (16 and 17, used in separate senses; "desatino" (20) echoes "desatinado" from line 8.

Lines 9–10 and line 13 reflect the kind of sound patterning outlined by Bembo. Lines 9 and 10 are marked by a rhythm of single consonants with the *p, g,* and *s* standing out:

> que por agudas *p*eñas *p*eligro*s*as
> *p*or mata*s* e*sp*ino*s*as.

Line 13 then turns grave with four tonic *a*'s and four double consonants: "y *p*ara *m*ás de*sp*acio ato*rm*enta*rm*e." In spite of the *p*'s and *t*'s, the line seems to show "gravità" in contrast to the fast-moving lines 9 and 10. The sudden change shows the type of musicality recommended by Bembo, which works effectively to mark the even graver danger represented by pleasant surroundings and a cease of torture.

The first stanza introduces the theme of the poem, love, which is characterized as an uncivilized, barbaric element. The next two stanzas describe the process by which his reason was barbarized by his thought (*pensamiento*). The second stanza sets the stage for his submission to passion.

> No vine por mis pies a tantos daños:
> fuerças de mi destino me truxeron
> y a la que m'atormenta m'entregaron.
> Mi razón y jüizio bien creyeron
> guardarme como en los passados años   25
> d'otros graves peligros me guardaron,
> mas quando los passados compararon
> con los que venir vieron, no sabían
> lo que hazer de sí ni dó meterse,

que luego empeçó a verse   30
la fuerça y el rigor con que venían.
Mas de pura vergüença constreñida,
con tardo passo y coraçón medroso
al fin ya mi razón salió al camino;
quanto era el enemigo más vezino,   35
tanto más el recelo temeroso
le mostrava el peligro de su vida;
pensar en el dolor de ser vencida
la sangre alguna vez le callentava,
mas el mismo temor se la enfrïava.   40

Lines 22 and 23 contain the clearest reference to a destiny or predestina-
tion in Garcilaso's works. These are forces that hand him over to one
single force ("a la que"), which I assume, in contrast to Rivers, functions
as an ambiguous reference to the "fuerças" in the previous line and signifies the appetite the poet is so reluctant to name, and perhaps secondarily
to the mistress, whom Rivers identifies as Isabel Freire. Within the allegory, the force that will torment him is his appetite or desire—not named
until the sixth stanza (line 105). Garcilaso's expression in this poem, as
we shall see, relies on ambiguity, a faithful reflection of the ambiguities
of feeling in courtly love itself. There is a direct reference later in the
poem to the mistress where she is labeled as "aquella tan amada mi
enemiga" (146), a further ambiguous phrase. Thus, "la que" is a vague
reference to the allegorical force that defeats his reason and perhaps to
the beloved, the primary cause that gives his appetite ascendancy. His
reason and judgment (line 4) are allegorical figures that try to defend
him against the mysterious unnamed force. This force, which will defeat
his reason, is not identified, but simply alluded to as a "peligro" (lines
25 and 37). His reason and judgment should protect him, but they are
frightened by the terrifying aspect of the force, and they do not know
where to hide or how to act. Finally, forced by shame, his reason comes
to his aid, but with fear and already too late. This reference to shame
(22) is the first reference to a theme that will assume importance only
later in the poem. The poem does not yet describe a fight, but such terms
as "guardar" (25 and 26), "peligros" (26 and 37), "medroso" (33),
"enemigo" (35), "recelo temeroso" (36), and "vencida" (38) suggest a
presence to be feared and combated. The last three lines of the stanza
present the lover's change of humors that will lead to his being defeated.

The thought of defeat at times heats his blood, producing a choler that will let him fight, but the fear cools it, producing melancholy and depression. The physiological references will also become important later in the poem when cold melancholy will produce fear and sadness in his emotional state, the two emotions associated with melancholy (Klibansky 15). Thus, this stanza establishes the allegorical scene of reason preparing to defend the lover in battle from a fearful danger, one that predisposes the humors of the lover to defeat.

There are notable repetitions in the text. "Fuerça" first refers to destiny, then in the phrase "la que" equivocally to the passion that dominates him. In line 30 it takes on new meaning in the reference to the manner of attack. Lines 25 and 26 have different forms of "guardar." Lines 28 and 30 repeat different forms of "ver," with different senses. "Peligro" first occurs in line 25, a line showing "gravità" with its double consonants based on *r*, which is continued in line 26 with tonic *a*'s:

>   d'*otros graves* peli*gros* me gu*ar*d*a*ron,
>   m*a*s qu*a*ndo los p*a*ss*a*dos comp*a*r*a*ron

"Peligro" recurs in line 37. These repetitions underline the close-knit allegory and the density of thought and texture.

The next stanza presents the defeat of his reason:

>   Estava yo a mirar, y peleando
>   en mi defensa, mi razón estava
>   cansada y en mil partes ya herida,
>   y sin ver yo quién dentro me incitava
>   ni saber cómo, estava desseando   45
>   que allí quedasse mi razón vencida;
>   nunca en todo el processo de mi vida
>   cosa se me cumplió que desseasse
>   tan presto como aquésta, que a la ora
>   se rindió la señora   50
>   y al siervo consintió que governasse
>   y usase de la ley del vencimiento.
>   Entonces yo sentíme salteado
>   d'una vergüença libre y generosa;
>   corríme gravemente que una cosa   55

tan sin razón uviesse assí passado;
luego siguió el dolor al corrimiento
de ver mi reyno en mano de quien cuento,
que me da vida y muerte cada día,
y es la más moderada tiranía.   60

This stanza, continuing with the same studied ambiguity, presents the
allegorical defeat of the lover's reason. Reason, fighting in the lover's defense, was tired and wounded. The lover had a sudden wish to see his
reason defeated, and this single wish was sufficient to cause his reason
to surrender. Garcilaso only alludes elliptically to the force that causes
him to wish for the overthrow of his reason. In line 44, he states he could
not see who or what (*quien*) stimulated the desire in him to see the defeat
of his reason. The same vague allusion recurs in line 58 where the victor
is "quien cuento," undoubtedly both his appetite and the beloved. The
moment of victory and surrender are contained in the general word
"cosa," in line 48 (repeated in line 55 with the same meaning). The ambiguity is duplicated in line 50 where he describes the surrender of reason
with a phrase that suggests a completely different meaning: "se rindió la
señora." Entwistle actually interpreted this line as Garcilaso's disdain of
a Neapolitan lady of easy virtues ("Loves" 384). Probably the most
shocking line in all of Garcilaso's poetry because of the ambiguous play
on "señora," which seems to indicate the seduction of the beloved, but
actually refers to the allegorical reason.

The stanza is dominated by images of war, defeat, and government.
The confluence of violence and desire become manifest in the allegory
of the poem. Line 51 describes the effect of the surrender of the will in
terms that recall Saint Augustine's definition of lust: "the love of those
things which a man can lose against his will" (10). Garcilaso, however,
continues the military metaphor instead of the theological material, referring to the plight of the conquered in a battle. Lines 53–55 introduce
the second reference to shame, a theme that is developed later in the
myth of Mars and Venus. The reference to the conquered is picked up in
the metaphor of kingdom, government, and tyranny, as he develops the
idea that the rightful party, his reason, was unjustly and unreasonably
(Garcilaso makes the same pun in line 56) ousted.

This stanza has the highest number of repetitions in all the poem. "Razón" appears three times, first (line 42) as the allegorical figure engaged
in battle. The second reference (46) seems to lie between the allegorical

sense and the literal sense of the word. The third reference, "tan sin razón" (56), has few vestiges of the allegorical figure, and is in effect a pun on a fixed expression using the word. The ambiguous "quien" appears twice (44 and 58). The defeat of reason is a "cosa" (48 and 55). The idea of shame occurs in "corríme" (55) and "corrimiento" (57), as well as "vergüença" (54). In addition, the metaphors are reinforced with various words concerning government, such as "governasse" (51), "reyno" (57), and "tiranía" (60), the strength of the latter undercut by "moderada." "Libre," paired with "generosa," suggests a Latinism meaning freeborn, and contrasts beautifully with "siervo" (51) and "tiranía" (60). The Petrarchan antithesis "vida y muerte" (59) takes on new resonance amidst the metaphors of birth, class, defeat, and enslavement. This stanza is the most contrived verbally with many repetitions, contrasts, and poised ambiguities, developing the allegory of the defeat of reason in the process of love. The stanza not only develops in detail the defeat of reason, but it also presents the poet's reaction to the event, all carefully couched in studied ambiguities of not naming the cause (the victor) of reason's defeat, of playing with the sense of "señora" (50), and concluding with "moderada tiranía," a phrase that brilliantly captures the horror of his entrapment and the irony of his acceptance of it.

The fourth stanza explains the same event, employing scientific terminology from chemistry and physics; that is, Renaissance science, which made use of many ideas that we now associate with the occult sciences.

> Los ojos, cuya lumbre bien pudiera
> tornar clara la noche tenebrosa
> y escurecer el sol a mediodía,
> me convertieron luego en otra cosa,
> en bolviéndose a mí la vez primera   65
> con la calor del rayo que salía
> de su vista, que'n mí se difundía;
> y de mis ojos la abundante vena
> de lágrimas, al sol que me inflamava,
> no menos ayudava   70
> a hazer mi natura en todo agena
> de lo que era primero. Corromperse
> sentí el sosiego y libertad passada,
> y el mal de que muriendo estó engendrarse,
> y en tierra sus raízes ahondarse   75

tanto quanto su cima levantada
sobre qualquier altura haze verse;
el fruto que d'aquí suele cogerse
mil es amargo, alguna vez sabroso,
mas mortífero siempre y ponçoñoso.   80

The fourth stanza begins with one of two references to the beauty of the beloved—here a praise of the eyes and at the beginning of the sixth stanza a praise of the hair. As Lapesa notes, they are two very rare instances of praise of the mistress's beauty in Garcilaso's poetry. A closer reading reveals that neither is in reality a praise of the beloved because the elements of beauty become part of the allegorical structure of the poem. Lines 1–3 elaborate the power of the eyes in their ability to turn dark night into day and to shadow the noonday sun. The finality of this comparison is not praise, as it is in Petrarch, but a scientific description of the transformation of his physiology: "me convertieron luego en otra cosa" (64). The heat emanating from the luminous eyes, "la calor del rayo" (66), combined with the dehydration he experiences through weeping, produces a fundamental change in his humoral composition. The four humors corresponded to four basic characteristics: choler = heat, blood = humidity, phlegm = coldness, and melancholy = dryness. Basic humoral medicine posited a body and its functions, called natural things, which were affected by food, drink, sleep, eliminations, etc., called nonnatural things. Diseases that could result from an excess of one of the humors were called counternatural things. The action of the humors was simple. A cold draft produced a chill in the body producing phlegm, and a condition we still call a "cold" or "resfriado." In this poem, the lover's tears produce a drying of the body, resulting in melancholy; the heat from the mistress's eyes then burns the melancholy and other humors producing a dry ashlike humor called "melancholia adusta," or burnt melancholy, considered to be especially pernicious (Babb 21–22). Combined with the weeping which would dry out his body, a cold dry humor—melancholia—would come to predominate. Each of the effects changed him "ayudava / a hazer mi natura en todo agena / de lo que era primero" (70–72).

The word that finishes line 72, "Corromperse," moves the argument from the field of medicine to physics, in this case to the theories of transmutations, which were believed to occur as a natural process in nature and which alchemists hoped to reproduce at accelerated pace in the laboratory.[2] The earth was thought to be like a huge chemical flask that slowly nurtured and produced gold, the most perfect of substances, from chemical mutations. Since gold was the most perfect of metals, all chemical processes strived to produce gold, which was believed to grow in mines (Shumaker 195). Garcilaso refers to this theory in Eclogue III when he says that the gold that is found in the Tajo is grown in the bottom of the river:

> del oro que'l felice Tajo embía,
> apurado después de bien cernidas
> las menudas arenas do se cría.
> (106–8)

Important among the alchemical steps were corruption and generation, referred to by Garcilaso in line 72, "corromperse," and line 74 "engendrarse."

The number of alchemical processes along with the symbols to represent them varied from treatise to treatise, and even though it is impossible to establish a composite overview, it is possible to outline the basic theory to arrive at an understanding of Garcilaso's metaphor. The concepts of corruption and generation come from Aristotle's treatise *On Generation and Corruption,* where he explains natural life processes and how death and corruption produce new material from which new life forms can be engendered. In alchemy, it was necessary to produce a corruption of the elements in the flask to their basic constituents of matter and form from which the alchemist could recombine them into higher levels of perfection with new forms. Gold would be produced from the generation of new life from the corruption and destruction of the old elements. Generation was variously portrayed in alchemical symbolism. It could result from the death of the old elements and the copulation of the primal matter with a new form. Certainly prominent in these theories was the generation of the philosophical tree, which is obviously the allegory that Garcilaso uses in this stanza. According to Coudert the image of the tree was very important:

> The image of the tree was ideally suited for the philosopher's stone as well, for, like a tree, it continually bore new fruit. "Our stone,"

---

2. Using some of the material from this chapter I made this point with more examples from the alchemical tradition in an article in *The Hermetic Journal* ("[Al]chemical Imagery").

writes Nicholas Flamel, "turned into a true and pure tree, to bud abundantly, and afterwards to bring forth infinite little sprigs and branches." In the *De Alchimia,* a tree grows out of the body of a dead man lying in his coffin. The coffin symbolizes the alchemical vessel, and the corpse, the seed which must die before it can germinate. . . . Seeing trees in alchemical vessels is not as absurd as it might appear. Isaac Newton, a meticulous alchemical experimenter, saw almost exactly what Flamel had seen. (121–24)

From the corruption of "el sosiego y libertad passada" (73) was produced the sickness that grew in him like a tree. Garcilaso's allegory of the tree recalls the biblical tree of the knowledge of good and evil and the tree of life. Garcilaso clearly refers to the former, since the fruit from the tree produces a deadly poison, an evil that at one time was thought to be desirable. The allegory of the tree of good and evil fits perfectly into the symbolism of the poem. It allows him to use an alchemical metaphor to finish off his medical description of falling in love, and the tree itself produces a series of comparisons that add depth to the allegory. The fruit from the tree of the knowledge of good and evil seemed to be a good, as the primal parents were tempted, but turned out to be evil and introduced death and pain in the world. The eating of the fruit from the tree is at times conceived of as a sexual act, an interpretation suggested by the shame that Adam and Eve felt after the act and the need to cover their sexual organs. In the same way Garcilaso's love—even though not a physical act—produced a change in him and an awareness of sexuality. The theme of shame, already introduced, will be developed in stanza 6.

The fruit from the tree of good and evil engendered a sickness in the world, and distempered the elements and produced seasons and death. It was humankind's primal loss of innocence from which it would never recover. Calderón always presents the effects of the eating of the fruit in Paradise as a poisoning of human nature that will produce death. The biblical injunction makes clear that the expulsion from Paradise produced pain and death, which had not existed previously. The allegorical tree, representing good and evil, which turned out to be apparent good and real evil, is a perfect symbol for the ambiguous nature of love that Garcilaso is developing. From the primal corruption of innocence and generation of evil comes sensual love, which is an incurable sickness leading to death, resulting from the chemical imbalances introduced into the body.

The shift in allegory has allowed Garcilaso to return to the concept of primitivism, the moment of the expulsion from Paradise. He does not mention Paradise, but concentrates on the description of the fruit from the tree that seems beneficial, but produces sickness and death. Courtly love, not sexual love, produces a fall from grace, the sickness, suffering, and death that corrupt the lover. Not only is love a primitive element in society, as seen in the beginning stanzas, but it is also related to that other concept of creation, the golden age from which the first humans fell. In either conception of human development, love is the primitive destabilizing element. Garcilaso has referred to two contradictory conceptions of human development and posited love as a key element in each.

This stanza illustrates the use of allegory in the poem. As noted previously, Lapesa adduces as a criticism of this poem its multiple allegories that overlap. Whether one appreciates allegory or not is a different question from understanding its nature and particular powers. The nature of allegory is such that the fable is the element that produces interest and movement in the literary work, but it is the hidden meaning, the matter beneath the cortex, that really counts. For this reason, the surface allegory can shift, end, or overlap without producing a major break in the sense of the work. Garcilaso's allegories are a tour de force of subtlety and interaction. The fourth stanza describes in essence the same process covered in the first three stanzas. While the previous stanzas described love as a mental process in which the mind is returned to a primitive state, this stanza describes it as a physical process, employing metaphors and symbols from medicine and alchemy. Even the description of the beauty of the mistress's eyes forms part of the allegorical process. The first allegory of primitivism comes to interact with the new allegory of the fall from Paradise; two contrary myths of human development are employed to describe the same mental process.

Having passed from the description of the process by which he surrendered to love, or appetite, the fifth stanza focuses on the effects of continuous unfulfilled desire.

> De mí agora huyendo, voy buscando
> a quien huye de mí como enemiga,
> que al un error añado el otro yerro,

y en medio del trabajo y la fatiga
estoy cantando yo, y está sonando   85
de mis atados pies el grave hierro.
Mas poco dura el canto si me encierro
acá dentro de mí, porque allí veo
un campo lleno de desconfiança:
    muéstrame'l esperança   90
de lexos su vestido y su meneo,
mas ver su rostro nunca me consiente;
torno a llorar mis daños, porque entiendo
que es un crudo linaje de tormento
para matar aquel que está sediento   95
mostralle el agua por que está muriendo,
de la qual el cuytado juntamente
la claridad contempla, el ruido siente,
mas quando llega ya para bevella,
gran espacio se halla lexos della.   100

The fifth stanza, the midpoint in the poem, turns to the question of a solution to the problem, looking for a way out of the dilemma by discussing the role of the song and the torments of unachieved desire. The concept of flight (*huir*) is introduced and will be referred to later in the poem. Flight is an impossibility since the poet is bound by chains, and the idea of flight becomes as elusive as tormenting desires of unattainable things. The poet is poised in a situation between the impossible actions of neither being able to consummate his desire nor being able to escape from the desire imposed on him. Since flight is impossible, its reference in the poem produces a negative structure, emphasizing the lover's containment and bondage. Lines 84 through 87 refer to the poem itself—his singing—accompanied by the sounds of his chains of bondage. But his containment—the inability to flee—will also cause his song to die and be contained within him: "mas poco dura el canto si me encierro / acá dentro de mí" (87–88). The rest of the stanza develops the torment of continual unsatisfied desire, based on the myth of Tantalus. In a field of despair (89–92), an allegorical Hope shows her gown and walk, but never shows her face, an enticement to the lover to continue his pursuit. Lines 93–100 develop the myth of Tantalus's suffering in the underworld, dissimulating the myth by not naming its subject. Like the even greater torment alluded to in the first stanza, this torment consists of tempting the sufferer with pleasure and gratification, while constantly placing at a remove the source of temptation. Of note is the Italianism "crudo," meaning cruel in line 94. "Linaje" is also a curious word that seems to mean caste or kind. The myth of Tantalus is fully developed with all its sensual qualities so that the emotive effect of such suffering can be communicated to the reader. Thus, he describes both the sight and sound of the water: "la claridad contempla, el ruido siente" (98). The word "lexos" is used in line 91 to refer to his vision of hope and repeated in line 100 to describe the waters receding as Tantalus stoops to drink. Garcilaso enters into a representation of the effects of unfulfilled desire, re-creating the frustration encountered by the sensual lover.

The sixth stanza develops the role of shame and the poet's rejection of civilization.

> De los cabellos de oro fue texida
> la red que fabricó mi sentimiento,
> do mi razón, rebuelta y enrredada,
> con gran vergüença suya y corrimiento,
> sujetta al apetito y sometida,   105
> en público adulterio fue tomada,
> del cielo y de la tierra contemplada.
> Mas ya no es tiempo de mirar yo en esto,
> pues no tengo con qué considerallo,
>   y en tal punto me hallo   110
> que estoy sin armas en el campo puesto,
> y el passo ya cerrado y la hüida.
> ¿Quién no se espantará de lo que digo?:
> que's cierto que é venido a tal estremo
> que del grave dolor que huyo y temo   115
> me hallo algunas vezes tan amigo
> que en medio dél, si buelvo a ver la vida
> de libertad, la juzgo por perdida,
> y maldigo las oras y momentos
> gastadas mal en libres pensamientos.   120

This stanza returns to the apparent theme of the praise of the lady's outstanding features, but as with the eyes in the fourth stanza, the description of the hair in this stanza begins a new allegorical reference. The purpose of the "cabellos de oro" is not the praise of the lady, but the introduction of the myth of Mars and Venus. The motif of the praise of the lady is converted into an allegory based on the myth of Mars and Venus trapped in the act of sexual intercourse by the finely woven, invisible mesh net constructed by Venus's husband Vulcan. In this myth, Mars and Venus were trapped in the lascivious act and the other gods were invited to look on and ridicule them. As in the previous stanza with Tantalus, Garcilaso does not mention any of the pagan figures, but the structure of the myth is obvious, even though Garcilaso has invented a new allegorization of the myth. The beauty of the mistress's hair allowed his feeling (*sentimiento*) to weave a net from the hair that captures his reason in copulation with his appetite. This is the only time Garcilaso names the allegorical "apetito," who must have been the victorious party in the duel in the beginning stanzas. His reason and his appetite are caught in public adultery and viewed by both heaven and earth. This is a further step in the allegory. Previously, his reason and appetite dueled and reason was vanquished. Now both have been caught in illicit fornication and exposed to ridicule and shame.

If Panofsky was correct in his suggestion that Vulcan represents a turning point in human development from primitivism to advanced civilization, then this is a key moment in the Vulcan myth representing the introduction of shame into society and social progression from indiscreet fornication to laws of monogamy. Panofsky did not speculate on the meaning of the lost Piero di Cosimo painting *Mars and Venus with her Cupids, and Vulcan,* described by Vasari (quoted by Panofsky, "Early History" 56), but one can imagine that Vulcan's exposure of his wife and her paramour in the act of adultery would represent a further step in the civilization of humankind from primitive beast cohabiting and indiscreetly fornicating with animals and other humans to a stage of marriage and fidelity that would assure purity of species and bloodlines. In Garcilaso's allegory, the Vulcan figure is represented by his "sentimiento," that is, his own feeling, which produces the public sense of shame. Rather than imposed by a superior pagan god, his own psychological faculties are capable of producing a sense of shame, which is represented in the text: "con gran vergüença suya y corrimiento" (104).

The lover in this allegory does not abandon his primitive state. Lines 108–9 reject the feeling of shame, saying the lover cannot take advantage of this opportunity and does not have the ability to make this transformation: "Mas ya no es tiempo de mirar yo en esto, / pues no tengo con qué considerallo." Like Garcilaso's Sonnet XXII, this poem brings the lover to a crucial moment of transformation, but he does not advance to a new stage of the program. Innate human sense of shame, allegorized in the myth of Mars and Venus, has led the lover to the point of redemption, which he considers unacceptable and rejects. Instead he finds himself in another military situation (110–12), and as previously introduced in stanza 5, he is trapped, unable to progress and unable to flee: "y el passo ya cerrado y la hüida" (112). Lines 113–20 begin the development of the idea that he chooses his suffering and refuses to leave it. Having brought himself to the point of rejection, he now reasons that he must have chosen his suffering as torture rather than for any good it might have promised. Line 115 returns to the concept of flight, but in the rest of the stanza he rejects his past liberty, judging it as lost time. "Libertad" and "libres" repeat the rejected concept of freedom in lines 118 and 120. Also interesting in this context is the word *hallar*, which refers less to a sense of discovery than to a situation of being placed or controlled by others. The lover as a suffering Tantalus had found himself far from the waters in the last line of the previous stanza: "gran espacio se halla lexos della" (100). In the sixth stanza, the poet-lover also finds himself placed in an impossible situation: "y en tal punto me hallo" (110), just as his love of his situation is also imposed from without. Finally he finds himself befriending his pain: "é venido a tal estremo / que del grave dolor que huyo y temo / me hallo algunas veces tan amigo" (114–16). Such casual repetitions reinforce the concept of helplessness and inability to control his own destiny.

The seventh stanza returns to the allegories of the mental faculties and the technique of multiple repetitions of individual vocabulary items prevalent in the earlier stanzas.

No reyna siempre aquesta fantasía,
que en imaginación tan varïable
no se reposa un ora el pensamiento:
viene con un rigor tan intratable
a tiempos el dolor que al alma mía   125
desampara, huyendo, el sufrimiento.
Lo que dura la furia del tormento,
no ay parte en mí que no se me trastorne
y que en torno de mí no esté llorando,
de nuevo protestando   130

que de la via espantosa atrás me torne.
Esto ya por razón no va fundado,
ni le dan parte dello a mi jüizio,
que este discurso todo es ya perdido,
mas es en tanto daño del sentido   135
este dolor, y en tanto perjüizio,
que todo lo sensible atormentado,
del bien, si alguno tuvo, ya olvidado
está de todo punto, y sólo siente
la furia y el rigor del mal presente.   140

Lines 121–26 form a complex sentence and intricate thought. Garcilaso
names three mental faculties: "fantasía," "imaginación," and "pensamiento." It is difficult to understand exactly which system of mental faculties he is referring to and the relationship he wishes to establish between them. Most philosophical and medical descriptions of the mental
faculties, conceived of as real physical organs having a fixed seat in the
brain, are imprecise in delimiting functions. Furthermore, there is little
standardization among them: some present many faculties, some combine them into a few faculties with various names. In general, the brain
was thought to have three ventricles: front, middle, and posterior. Each
ventricle housed a separate faculty: the posterior ventricle held the memory; the middle ventricle the reason, variously called judgment, ra-
tiocinio, or reason; and the front ventricle housed the imagination, but
other faculties were also assigned to it, such as the will, fantasy, appetite,
and common sense (the faculty for combining the various exterior sense
perceptions). Ordinary mental functions conceived of the imagination as
receiving the sense perceptions and forming an image of them. The reason then passed judgment on these images and sent them to the memory
for storage. Garcilaso probably means to indicate that the reason, the
middle judging faculty, has submitted to the appetite, the faculty from
the front ventricle or lower soul that expresses desire and that reason is
supposed to control. Since the reason has submitted to the faculty that
it is supposed to control, it is incapable of controlling the thoughts that
are formed in the imagination or form judgments concerning the images
passed from the imagination. The explosive nature and randomness of
thought was commented on previously. Only now the poet-lover is unable to control or judge the quality of those thoughts. Also significant is
the fact that medical writers often indicated types of madness (although

they did not assign names to them) resulting from a lesion of one or two of the faculties, with the remaining ones still functioning.

Garcilaso claims thought so often presents such visions of cruelty that the soul is alienated from the body because it cannot bear the pain. This is, of course, the final step of madness resulting in the alienation of the soul. A common definition of madness in medical treatises is "alienatio animae." Garcilaso describes a process of madness caused by the loss of reason (with a still active, but uncontrolled imagination) that leads to the loss of all governing faculties and the alienation of the soul. He labels this madness "furia" (127 and 140).

Garcilaso continues the discussion of the faculties in lines 132–34, punning again on the now triple sense of "razón" as an allegorical figure, as a faculty of the mind, and as an expression in the phrase "por razón." Reason is lacking in both senses in these mental functions. Nor is any of this communicated to his judgment (another name for the middle ventricle and faculty): "ni le dan parte dello a mi jüicio" (133). This "discurso" of the mind is simply lost since it is not passed to the judgment and memory. Garcilaso's opening thesis was to pass his suffering from his emotions to his writings. This movement (*discurso*) of the mind is lost and does not become written discourse. The mental imagery and pain damage the senses, which come only to feel pain of suffering. Elaborating on the opening lines, love affects his manner and personality, but does not pass its imagery to his writings. The written form of this suffering consists of a series of overlapping and interrupted allegories, the external writing reproducing the inner turmoil of the imagination.

The seventh stanza contains many repetitions of words. "Furia," already mentioned, names the resultant mental state and is repeated in lines 127 and 140. "Rigor" occurs in lines 124 and 140 in reference to the strength of the random thoughts. "Dolor" (125) recurs in line 136. Different forms of "tornar" dominate lines 128–31. Everything in his being is affected: "no ay parte en mí que no se me trastorne" (128). The next line uses the expression "en torno." The next two lines end with another use of "tornar," to turn back. Also, the subtle play of sounds between the two rhyme words is worthy of note: "se me trastorne" (128) and "atrás me torne" (131). Not only does Garcilaso employ different forms of "tornar," but he also plays with the sound of the two phrases. The last lines of the stanza introduce different forms of "sentir": "sentido" (135), "sensible" (137), and "siente" (139). This stanza, even more so than the previous, plays with different forms of various repeated words. This stylistic affectation occurs mainly in those passages that describe mental processes rather than those that make use of myth. This poem clearly employs different styles in different parts for different effects.

The eighth stanza describes the only comfort he receives from this impossible situation.

> En medio de la fuerça del tormento
> una sombra de bien se me presenta,
> do el fiero ardor un poco se mitiga:
> figúraseme cierto a mí que sienta
> alguna parte de lo que yo siento   145
> aquella tan amada mi enemiga
> (es tan incomportable la fatiga
> que si con algo yo no me engañasse
> para poder llevalle, moriría
>   y assí me acabaría   150
> sin que de mí en el mundo se hablasse),
> assí que del estado más perdido
> saco algún bien. Mas luego en mí la suerte
> trueca y rebuelve el orden: que algún ora
> si el mal acaso un poco en mí mejora,   155
> aquel descanso luego se convierte
> en un temor que m'á puesto en olvido
> aquélla por quien sola me é perdido,
> y assí del bien que un rato satisfaze
> nace el dolor que el alma me deshaze.   160

The comfort comes from the relief he feels when he remembers that his beloved must also feel something of his suffering: "figúraseme cierto a mí que sienta / alguna parte de lo que yo siento / aquella tan amada mi enemiga" (144–46). This feeling serves to moderate his "fiero ardor," another phrase that recalls the primitive, even savage, nature that his desire takes. "Tormento" (141) and "presenta" (142), with their near rhymes, set up the stanza for the juncture of "sienta" and "siento" (144–45) in neighboring rhyming positions, but not as rhyme words. Critics have paid particular attention to the sources and paradox of the phrase "aquella tan amada mi enemiga." This paradox summarizes perfectly the ambiguities and paradoxes developed throughout the poem, and it is a perfect touch to finish the poem with the only clear reference to the be-loved—as an insoluble paradox. The poet parenthetically confesses that he needs this comfort in order to bear the pain. Otherwise he would die—and curiously enough his preoccupation with dying concerns not death but dying without recognition: "y assí me acabaría / sin que de mí en el mundo se hablasse" (151–52). The announced intention was to bring his "aspereza" to his writing, and in these lines he fears dying without being remembered. The poem, which serves to externalize his inner emotions, is also a means of achieving fame. The idea of fame—being remembered—must also be associated with the theme of shame, the option to civilization that the lover rejected previously. Thematically, fame and reputation are related, the word "fama" signifying both con-cepts in Spanish Renaissance usage. The stanza returns to and ends on a note of despair. As he comes to the realization that his beloved may have forgotten him, he again falls into depression. The body of the poem ends on a final paradox—his only sense of satisfaction leads him back to his suffering: "y assí del bien que un rato satisfaze / nace el dolor que el alma me deshaze" (159–60).

The only repetitions in this stanza are of partiality and otherness. Dif-ferent forms of "alguno" appear throughout: "alguna parte" (145), "algo" (148), "algún bien" (153), and "algún ora" (154). "Aquella" ap-pears twice in reference to the beloved: "aquella tan amada mi enemiga" (146) and "aquella por quien sola me é perdido" (158). Otherness is also attributed to the satisfaction he described at the beginning of the stanza, but he has lost at the end: "aquel descanso" (156) no longer belongs to him, hence its otherness. These repetitions give a sense of only partial satisfaction and alleviation from the beloved and from pleasure and rest. The sense of alienation, first ascribed to his soul, now encom-passes him and his exclusion from happiness. Noteworthy is the repeti-tion of the "ue" in lines 153–54, adding to the impression that this is one of Garcilaso's most carefully constructed poems.

The final partial stanza is, following the genre, addressed to the poem itself.

> Canción, si quien te viere se espantare
> de la instabilidad y ligereza
> y rebuelta del vago pensamiento,
> estable, grave y firme es el tormento,
> le di, que's causa cuya fortaleza   165

es tal que qualquier parte en que tocare
la hará rebolver hasta que pare
en aquel fin de lo terrible y fuerte
que todo el mundo afirma que es la muerte.

The envoi, directed to the poem, describes the amorphous nature of the poem. The poet steps out of his role as lover willingly conquered and subjected to his appetites, and comments on the nature of the composition itself. He notes the variable tone of the poem, due in part to the abrupt and numerous changes from one allegory to another. This observation clearly agrees with Lapesa's criticism of the poem, but Garcilaso introduces the idea in order to defend the poem. He counters the criticism of the instability and lightness of the poem with the observation that his suffering is stable and serious. His wandering thought causes the disruptive elements; pain produces the stable elements. The "rebuelta" nature of the poem duplicates the wandering of this thought. As discussed in Chapter 4, the central pair of words, "ligereza" and "grave," recall Bembo's critical vocabulary of "piacevolezza" and "gravità," and Garcilaso has used Bembo's observation to create a sound pattern reinforcing the semantic text in these lines. Line 162 has three short i's and three l's, and only one consonant cluster, while line 164 has two accented a's and seven consonant clusters, especially with r. In spite of the tonic i in sixth position, the double consonants add a weight and length to the line that contrast with the lightness of line 162.

Garcilaso defends the rambling nature of the poem by stating that its strength (*fortaleza*) is that no matter where one begins reading (*tocare*), the poem revolves to end on the theme of death, "revolver" in line 167 reiterating the term "rebuelta" in line 163, and the verb "parar" recalling the adjective "firme" in line 164. Even though the poem has many turns (*rebuelta*) of thought, it all turns on the word "muerte," emphasizing its negative pessimistic vision of love as a tortured state leading to a finality of doom.

The preceding analysis of the various allegories in Canción IV has touched on and in some cases discussed fully the major themes of the poem. From this analysis the broad outlines become clear. The poem describes the effects of unrequited love on the human psyche—especially highlighting the ambiguous nature of those effects, such as the loss of reason, the pleasure in suffering, and the will to destruction. As in other long poems, but to a lesser degree, Garcilaso has used key words throughout to unify the various "moments" of the poem. This effect occurs less in this poem for several reasons. First, the poem has no clearly defined sections or unified passages. The different allegories flow from one to the other, overlap, or take on mythic proportions without clear breaks of tone and idea. Unlike the other poems, Canción IV does not change levels of discourse to signify the changes in idea and section. Second, Garcilaso was obviously trying to create a complex surface structure of interwoven allegories used to describe from various points of view the passion of love. As he says in the envoi, the basis is always constant—torment and death—but the surface movement is full of shifts and fickle changes. The surface of Garcilaso's poem recalls from the visual arts Isabelline architectural style that covered all the surfaces with complex and intertwined webs of decorations, such as the interior of San Juan de los Reyes, newly constructed in Toledo a few blocks from Garcilaso's house during his infancy. The unrelenting need to proliferate architectural surface ornament recalls the surface complexity of this poem. The poem is intended to have a central core of idea that is solid and constant, but the surface gives the impression—like the effect of love—of nervousness, sudden changes, and intertwined strands of emotion. For these reasons, the unity of the poem is to be found in the central core of the idea and not in the undulating surface structure composed of shifting allegories and myths.

There are, as in other long poems by Garcilaso, certain words repeated throughout the poem to mark the major themes, such as the important theme of shame woven into the fabric of the poem. The word *vergüença* recurs throughout (32, 54, and 104), and various forms of *correrse* appear in the same sections (55, 57, and 104). Other words, such as *dolor* (15, 38, 57, 115, 125, 136, and 160), which is carefully spaced throughout the poem, *rigor* (31, 124, and 140), and various forms of *tormento* and *atormentarse* (13, 23, and 137) simply refer to the central core of the poem. They provide a sense of unity in the constancy of their references.

Other words suggest a sense of unity through their repetition, but their meaning and point of reference change throughout the poem, so that they in fact provide examples of the constantly shifting surface structure. I commented previously on the word *razón* that first refers to the poem itself (2), then to the armed and bellicose allegorical figure (24, 34, 42, and 46), and which is converted in the subdued, but armed and bellicose figure of Mars in line 103. In other passages, *razón* is used in various expressions that pun on the allegorical meaning established in the poem and the idiomatic sense of the expression: "que una cosa / tan sin razón uviesse assí passado" (55–56) and "Esto ya por razón no va fundado" (132). The word *grave*, which probably takes on additional resonance from Bembo's ideas on imitation, suffers similar changes. At first it signifies the seriousness of the danger: "graves peligros" (26). Next it refers to the depth of his feeling: "corríme gravemente" (55). The next reference is more ambiguous because it refers to the weight of his chains, but at the same time, these chains are producing a sound, so the word seems to function as a misplaced epithet and refer to the sound as well: "y está sonando / de mis atados pies el grave hierro" (85–86). In addition, Herrera noted the "gravedad" of this line (H-232). The next reference is more straightforward: "grave dolor" (115). Finally, the word seems to recall Bembo's ideas even more, being placed in a line that is grave, and in a position that contrasts it with "ligereza": "estable, grave y firme es el tormento" (164). The word not only refers to the seriousness and weight of the pain, but also to the sound of the poem.

The word *ligereza* (which occurs only in Garcilaso's late poetry, the eclogues, and Sonnet XXXIII) is used only twice, but it suffers the same transformation. In the first stanza, it refers to the speed with which the allegorical "pensamiento"—as crude barbarian—drags him over crags and brush: "corre con ligereza" (11). It only appears at the end of the poem in the envoi, where "pensamiento" now refers ambiguously to the allegorical force and the surface level of the poem itself. "Ligereza" is no longer speed and lightness, but it is the fickleness of the poem itself: "de la instabilidad y ligereza / y revuelta del vago pensamiento" (162–63). The lover's uncivilized thoughts have been transferred to the poem itself so that the unstable thought that led to his falling in love and suffering unrequited love has come to characterize the structure of the poem itself. The word "ligereza" that referred to his thoughts at the beginning has now come to refer to the structure and sound of the poetic composition. The poet's stated intention of transferring to his writings the passions of his being has been realized not only in the ideas, but also in the form of writing.

Other words appear throughout the poem, but they serve as negative theme identifiers. In the same way that Garcilaso uses "razón" to avoid naming the appetite as the destructive force, so too are the various forms of "huir" and "libertad" repeated, not because the poet is fleeing or because he is free, but quite the contrary, because he is enslaved and detained. The words signify the absence of their opposites. This adds to the ambiguous nature of the poem by producing elusive and convoluted forms of expression. In lines 80 and 81, the poet is fleeing from himself and his mistress flees from him, but by line 86, he refers to his chained feet and says his poem turns back inside him. "Huir" always refers to the inability to escape: "el passo ya cerrado y la hüida" (112). Even though he pretends to flee from his suffering "del grave dolor que huyo" (115), in fact he is trapped by the situation. Finally the soul flees the body (126) to escape the pain, and the only successful flight in the poem is one that results in the final alienation of the lover.

Liberty is a similar concept, a positive term used to express its opposite, a negative situation. At first it refers to the station and nobility of the shame that besets him. Paired with "generosa" (noble), it recalls the Latin sense of freeborn: "una vergüença libre y generosa" (54). In line 73, he recalls his "libertad passada"; later he sees his former liberty from afar: "si buelvo a ver la vida / de libertad, la juzgo por perdida" (117–18); and he curses his former freedom: "y maldigo las oras y momentos / gastados en libres pensamientos" (119–20). The poem seldom refers to enslavement, but the constant references to liberty as an unattainable state, serve through negative definition to describe the situation of the lover.

The repetitions in Canción IV clearly serve a different purpose than in other poems. In the Canción there are fewer of them and they tend to be clustered in single passages. Those that do extend throughout the poem are even fewer in number and do not show consistency, either by changing meaning or point of reference , or by referring negatively to the real unstated opposite. The repetitions form part of the deceptive, constantly shifting surface texture arising from the torments that characterize his love passion.

Whether one disparages the poem along with twentieth-century critics, or agrees with the Golden Age commentators in the appreciation of it, one has to admire its structural complexity, the use of profound allegorical association and myth, to reproduce in the structure of the poem the very nature of the love passion itself. Twentieth-century critics, searching for feeling and sincerity in the poem, have failed to appreciate Canción IV for its deep thought, constant turning, and redefining of the same issues—in essence, its highly intellectual approach to its subject matter. It is a deep, brooding poem, abstracting thought processes in convoluted allegories and myths.

By way of conclusion it might be useful to look at Garcilaso's use of allegory within the context of the prejudices of twentieth-century sensibility. Undoubtedly, one of the problems faced by the modern critics is the lack of appreciation of allegory itself. In his theoretical study of allegory, Fletcher discusses the twentieth-century appreciation of symbol and image (and one could now add metonymy to the list) and a deep distrust and dislike of allegory (and to a certain extent metaphor). Fletcher senses that part of this prejudice comes from the fact that there lies at the heart of allegory a certain predictability. Once the process of allegory begins generating new characters or situations or concepts, then the reader knows that the process will continue throughout. Furthermore, allegorical figures have a predictability about them. Sin as an allegorical figure can only act in certain ways. The distrust of allegory and the belief in its artistic inferiority began in the nineteenth century with the Romantic reaction against intellectual art forms and was further reinforced during the vogue of realism. The mimetic mode of fiction could only view allegory as superficial and artificial. Undoubtedly, that belief lies behind the condemnation of Garcilaso's Canción IV by twentieth-century critics.

As noted by Lapesa, Garcilaso's allegories are not predictable, nor are they singular. Garcilaso employs many allegories to describe the same event. In this way, he avoids the trap of predictability. As he claims in the envoi, the poem gives many turns, but they all turn on the same thematic center. Another way of avoiding predictability is the use of ambiguity and paradox. Fletcher discusses this type of development as an artistic plus, since the author not only avoids a simplistic sense of mechanical creation, but gives depth and resonance to the allegory. I have discussed in detail numerous levels of ambiguity in this poem, from the reluctance to name the victorious force and refer to the mistress to the ambiguous use of language and terms. The ambiguity and veiled manner of expression create an effect of complexity of thought. Garcilaso does not generate allegories according to a simplistic pattern of correspondences, but presents them veiled in a web of complexity that gives them depth and interest. In like vein, Garcilaso's allegories are not simple correspondences, but are based on traditional associations and myths that provide wide areas of comparison and establish an almost cosmic depth to some of the associations, such as the use of primitivism to characterize the loss of reason.

Fletcher also discusses the importance of magic in the construction of allegory. Since allegory uses one plot and set of characters to tell another story that is in fact the matter of importance, there is a sense in which the elements of the surface story seem to be contrived and motivated solely by the inner allegorical plot. They are not free to generate a random surface plot, but must necessarily generate the deeper allegorical plot; at times the surface plot loses its sense of independence and realism, and its motivating forces seem contrived. In this sense, magic becomes important as the characters are motivated by hidden occult causes. In the same way, Garcilaso introduces occult imagery, such as chemical and alchemical transformations and references to well-known myths, to provide parallels to the surface action and to show parallel causes. The myths serve the same function of imposing an exterior action that functions on the surface of the poem as a motivation for the plot that in turn signifies a deeper inner level.

Twentieth-century critics have found the poem difficult and problematical because of its style of expression. The problem lies more in their approach to the poem than in its inherent problems. Garcilaso has focused in a highly intellectual way on one of the most paradox-ridden codes of his time—the conception of love. He has re-created in the poem the process of falling in love and the basic paradox of the lover beset by an ennobling passion that turns him into a barbarian. The poem not only describes these processes, but also re-creates in its very nature the disturbed thought process of the lover. The constant use of ambiguity, such as the unforgettable line "se rindió la señora" (50), moves away from the casual and almost incidental use of paradox through antitheses and oxymora in the courtly and Petrarchan love poetry and comes to expose the profound paradox at the center of the conception of love itself. Garcilaso goes to the heart of the paradox, re-creating in allegorical form the primitive states of society and the lover's inability to accept shame and move to a more civilized and healthy state of being. The code of courtly love has not been undone, but its central paradox has been exposed. The lover may be a warrior and heroic, but he is defeated. Love may be a civilizing force for the noble of mind, but it produces sickness and returns the lover to a primitive state. The lover may be a Mars bolstered by reason, but Mars submits to Venus and loses his power. Love may be a good or "bien," but it attacks humans as a sickness or "mal." When Garcilaso has finished his poem, little coherency remains in the code, as the paradoxes come to dominate its conception.

In this poem, Garcilaso's allegories take on a depth of subtlety that can only be admired for its dexterity and profundity. Rather than a fault, the multiple allegories produce a rich texture of resonance of references and levels of meaning. The core of the allegory remains constant, and its description moves forward methodically. The surface fables, or allegories, are introduced as best suits the purpose of understanding the real matter of the poem. Again, a critical approach based on realism and sincerity will fail to appreciate this poem and the richness of its texture and thought. Undoubtedly, Herrera's and Tamayo de Vargas's high praises of the poem came from a real appreciation of the art of allegory, rather than a confused set of values. Perhaps only Dante and Calderón can compare in complexity and depth of meaning and poetic expression with Garcilaso in this poem.

13

Mars Dominant: Jealousy and the Difficulty of Moderation

One aspect of Garcilaso's poetry has barely surfaced in critical studies: Garcilaso the antipreceptist, or, if it is not too strong a term, Garcilaso the iconoclast. Often called the "poeta del dolorido sentir," Garcilaso has always been associated with profound emotional feeling and sincere expression—with the tacit assumption that such qualities do not allow for profundity of thought or for critical thinking. His *cancionero* poetry and that of his last period, however, show a delight in wit, and even a keen sense of humor. Only in the middle Petrarchan period does his poetry show the heavy, passionate seriousness that has come to characterize him as a poet. Still to be studied is his delight in setting up and unraveling hallowed commonplaces of thought. The naturalness of Garcilaso's style, however, often masks the deep critical attitudes with which the poet undermines some of the most highly valued precepts of his time. In this chapter I study how Elegy II, whose major theme is jealousy, undermines the Aristotelian and Horatian ideals of the golden mean.

Jealousy as a poetic theme achieved importance only in the Renaissance. It had not entered in a major way as a theme in Petrarch's poetry, but is found in the lyric poetry of sixteenth-century Neapolitan poets. Edward Williamson emphasized the novelty of this theme for the Renaissance in his study *Bernardo Tasso* (44–45). As discussed previously, Garcilaso treats the theme of jealousy allegorically in Sonnets XXXIX (a

translation of a sonnet by Sannazaro on jealousy attributed to Garcilaso), XXX, and XXXI, and passionately in Salicio's lament in Eclogue
I, which has been traditionally construed as expressing Garcilaso's grief
upon the marriage of Isabel Freire. While Garcilaso does use Petrarchan
elements in Salicio's song of lament, he also employs other recourses,
such as a section recalling Dante's *Rime petrose,* an *ubi sunt* of medieval
tradition and a long section on jealousy. There are important differences
between Petrarchan attitudes and those expressed in Garcilaso's eclogue.
Petrarch speaks of Laura's cruelty, hardness, and aloofness, but implicitly
all of these characteristics come from her perfect virtue. And, deep down,
Petrarch would probably not want her any other way. Petrarchan love is
a trap. The lover must choose a lady so perfect in her virtue that she
would never concede favors, but he must constantly request favors from
her, and accuse her of cruelty for not granting those things that would
mar her perfection, the very things that would make it impossible to love
her because she had conceded them. The Petrarchan lover constructs a
perfect circular trap in which he poeticizes every type of suffering and
despair imaginable in the closed circle of his desire. This, however, is not
the situation of Salicio in Eclogue I, who suffers from jealousy because
he was abandoned by his beloved. The poem implies that their love was
requited until she left him for another. Neither requited love nor jealousy
are at all Petrarchan. In fact, Eclogue I corresponds more to the anonymous *Questión de amor,* which is a debate over which type of abandoned
lover suffers more: the one who is rejected or the one who loses his beloved in death.

Eclogue I was considered to be the only poem on jealousy that relates
to Garcilaso's supposed love for Isabel Freire. All the other poems on this
theme are thought to concern the mysterious lady from Naples who figures so prominently in Elegy II. It has been concluded from the last line
of Sonnet VII, "[el amor que viene] ni es como los otros ni en mi mano,"
that the Neapolitan affair was a sensual love affair in which his mistress
probably betrayed him, thus his anger and jealous reaction. As I have
suggested in Chapter 10, the new love mentioned in Sonnet VII is probably Neoplatonic love rather than a sensual passion for the Neapolitan
lady. The jealousy motif in Garcilaso's Sonnets XXX, XXXI, and the
attributed Sonnet XXXIX is so heavily indebted to Sannazaro and Tansillo that one would be hard-pressed to ascribe precise biographical details to it. The theme of jealousy in Elegy II is set within a context of
obvious autobiographical circumstances. The narrator speaks of a love

he had left in Naples and details his suffering over imagining her infidelity. Unlike other biographical details that have been extracted from Garcilaso's poetry, the biographical element in Elegy II leaves no room for doubt nor presents any difficulty of interpretation. Garcilaso names himself (line 27) and refers to details of his return from the campaign in Tunisia. The poem unequivocally refers to a love affair in Naples and his jealousy over the imagined infidelity of his mistress. This poem is of course different from Garcilaso's other poem on another return trip to Naples written one year previously (October 1534), the Epístola a Boscán, in which he asserts he left nothing there: "no abiendo dexado allá enterrado algún thesoro" (77–78). In Elegy II (written August 1535) he states he has left a beloved in Naples and he worries that in his absence she has found another: "Allí mi coraçón tuvo su nido / un tiempo ya" (40–41). His imagination runs wild with jealousy and the theme of the rival is explicitly stated: "porque me consumiesse contemplando / mi amado y dulce fruto en mano agena, / y el duro possessor de mí burlando" (106–9). These lines recall the similar expression in Eclogue I: "y cierto no trocara mi figura / con esse que de mí s'está reyendo" (179–80). Elegía II is clearly autobiographical, while the sonnets on jealousy are abstract and the pastoral poems have fictionalized the circumstances, but all of them may refer to the same personal events.

These supposedly biographical elements do not constitute, however, the main thrust of the poem; rather they are subordinated to other thematic elements. In order to make of Garcilaso a poet of the heart, critics have by and large sacked his Elegy II for its biographical information and have left its intellectual content untouched and unappreciated. Keniston first commented on the poem's sincerity: "he laments at the effects his long absence is sure to have, expressing his fears in a tercet which rings with a sincerity rare in his later works" (*Garcilaso*, 212). Keniston also stated that no work "is so rich in its revelation of his personality" (232); he concluded his remarks criticizing its artistic merit, its "lack of logical coherence," but praising its natural expression (236). Lapesa appreciates the aesthetic beauty of the poem, but following Keniston, he judges it to consist of a "variedad de temas" (*Garcilaso: Estudios* 151). More recently, a broader appreciation of the formal aspects of the poem has been suggested by Claudio Guillén ("Sátira"). He discusses how this poem in its structure and content corresponds to the Italian *capitolo*, which develops several themes simultaneously. Like Garcilaso's other longer poems, however, this elegy is more tightly constructed, in this case

presenting a central paradox that the poet first introduces as a serious
theme, and then develops as a paradoxical situation which he finally
leaves unresolved as a painful and insoluble dilemma.

The paradoxical nature of Garcilaso's thought is evident from the beginning. Lines 1 through 6 celebrate Charles V's African campaign:

> Aquí, Boscán, donde del buen troyano
> Anchises con eterno nombre y vida
> conserva la ceniza el Mantüano,
>   debaxo de la seña esclarecida
> de Caesar affricano nos hallamos
> la vencedora gente recogida:

The poem is addressed to Boscán who comes to figure into the poem
only much later. The complex syntax and classical allusions of the opening lines create a style worthy of later "culteranos." Azara criticized the
difficulty of this tercet, calling it "confusísimo" (A-56). The sense of the
first tercet is that Virgil, the Mantuan, has preserved the ashes of Anchises with such fame and renown that the poet does not need to name
the place, Trapani in Sicily, from which he is writing. It is necessary to
make a complete break between the first and second tercet so that the
ashes of Anchises are not preserved under the bright sign of Charles V.
The second tercet relates the circumstances of the poem, and gives the
clue for dating it. The troops of Charles V, returning from the victorious
campaign in Tunisia, are stationed in Trapani. The campaign to Tunisia
has been so successful that Charles V will be known in the future as
"Caesar affricano," just as Scipius received his sobriquet "Africanus"
from his successes in the campaign against Carthage. Herrera said succinctly: "Por la proximidad de la antigua ciudad de Cartago, destruida
por Scipio 'Africanus,' al nuevo conquistador de Túnez le dieron el
mismo título" (H-359). Like Sonnet XXXIII, which was written in reference to the same event, the poem seems to conflate the stature of Charles
V with the glories of the Roman past. The comparison is, however, curiously incomplete. One would expect the poet to round it off by saying
that in the same way that Virgil has bestowed eternal fame on Anchises
and the place of his burial, so shall he, Garcilaso the poet, preserve the
memory of Charles V. The body of the poem, however, seems to find
great disillusionment in war, and this motif is announced in the ambiguity of line 6, which curiously undermines the heroic stature of the first

five lines. While not antitheses, "vencedora" and "recogida" certainly present an opposition, the first referring to the victory of the imperial troops in Tunisia and the second to their encampment in Sicily. "Recogida" suggests timidity and inwardness in contrast to the heroics and outwardness of victory, and both of these epithets are used in reference to the same soldiers. Surely, Charles V would not find his Virgil in Garcilaso. The tension of line 6 anticipates the type of irony and paradox that characterize this poem as a whole and foreshadows the later presentation of war as cruel, rather than glorious.

The soldiers are huddled into camp, strangely positioned between bravery and timidity, and as the next lines indicate, their thoughts are far from noble:

> diversos en estudio, que unos vamos
> muriendo por coger de la fatiga
> el fruto que con el sudor sembramos;
> otros (que hazen la virtud amiga
> y premio de sus obras y assí quieren
> que la gente lo piense y que lo diga)
> destotros en lo público difieren,
> y en lo secreto sabe Dios en quánto
> se contradizen en lo que profieren.
>   (7–15)

All are looking for the spoils of war, although some may maintain the pretense of not caring for their own gain. "Estudio" is a neologism used in its Latin sense of zeal. The adjective "diversos" (line 7) indicates contrary opinions. Lines 7–9 present war as fatigue and sweat sown for profit. The poet identifies with the first group ("vamos muriendo") but not the second ("otros que hazen . . . y assí quieren").

"Diversos" and the idea of opposition are essential parts of the theme that is fully announced in the next six lines:

> Yo voy por medio, porque nunca tanto
> quise obligarme a procurar hazienda,
> que un poco más que aquéllos me levanto;
> ni voy tampoco por la estrecha senda
> de los que cierto sé que a la otra vía
> buelven, de noche al caminar, la rienda.
>   (16–21)

In spite of having identified with those eagerly and crassly seeking gain, the poet now renounces desire for remuneration, choosing instead the middle course of moderation. The theme of moderation, the golden mean, presented as an untenable position between extremes, will dominate the rest of the poem. This theme is one of the most celebrated of classical and Christian thought. Aristotle in his *Nicomachean Ethics* devotes the last part of Book II to extolling the virtues of the mean, and the idea of moderation is a predominant theme in the odes of Horace. It was also adapted from Aristotle to Christian ethics by the scholastic philosophers. Garcilaso knew Aristotle's *Ethics* very well; he paraphrased several passages of it in his Epístola a Boscán, and his admiration for Horace will be documented in Chapter 14. The poet strikes a middle course, neither desiring gain nor pretending to disdain it.

As he characterizes the hypocrisy of those who appear to spurn wealth, he suddenly finds he has left his middle course by entering into satire, and he rebukes himself for his lack of moderation:

> Mas ¿dónde me llevó la pluma mía?,
> que a sátira me voy mi passo a passo,
> y aquesta que os escrivo es elegía.
> Yo endereço, señor, en fin mi passo
> por donde vos sabéys que su processo
> siempre á llevado y lleva Garcilaso;
> (22–27)

Ironically in the same passage that the poet proclaims he will take a middle course, he falls into an excess of criticism. This is one of five places in the poem where Garcilaso steps out of character to address himself or his reader (also 85–87, 97–98, 109–10, and 169–71). On another of these occasions he reprimands himself for an excess. Since moderation or its lack is the central idea of the poem, the device of self-censure serves well to emphasize it. Claudio Guillén ("Sátira" 210–11) cites this passage as part of Garcilaso's struggle with the broader genre of the Italian *capitolo* and the use of satire.

The next lines, which describe the soldiers' encampment in the forest, express the idea in such a way as to reinforce the theme of moderation:

> y assí, en mitad d'aqueste monte espesso,
> de las diversidades me sostengo,

no sin dificultad, mas no por esso
   dexo las musas, antes torno y vengo
dellas al negociar, y varïando,
con ellas dulcemente me entretengo.
   Assí se van las oras engañando;
assí del duro afán y grave pena
estamos algún ora descansando.

(28–36)

"Mitad" (28) refers more to the concept of "among" rather than its literal sense of "in the middle of," but the literal sense again introduces the concept of middle and moderation, contrasted with "diversidades" of the following line. "Monte" in Garcilaso refers to forest rather than mountain, but it usually carries a metaphorical sense of difficulties and trials, as in Sonnet IV where it has the same adjective "espesso": "Yo mesmo emprenderé a fuerça de braços / romper un monte que otro no rompiera, / de mil inconvenientes muy espesso." The "diversidades" refer to the two extremes referred to previously and the meetings he attends, suggested by the verb "negociar." Not only is the poet sustained between two opposing groups, one self-seeking and the other full of hypocrisy; he is also torn between two activities, on the one hand, political and business negotiations, and on the other, the composition of poetry. The poet does not strike a middle course in this case, rather he interchanges the two, "varïando." Poetry allows him to rest from the work involved, although "duro afán y grave pena" sound more like suffering from un-requited love than actual business (See Goodwyn, "Una teoría"). The references to writing are part of the informality of style that allows for the introduction of the personal as well as formal.

Continuing in the same vein, the poet announces the goal of their trip to be Naples, famous in antiquity for relaxation and love, and where the poet also hopes to find relief from his work. The topic of love also allows him to enter into the details of his own personal love life:

D'aquí iremos a ver de la Serena
la patria, que bien muestra aver ya sido
de ocio y d'amor antiguamente llena.
   Allí mi coraçón tuvo su nido
un tiempo ya, mas no sé, triste, agora
o si estará ocupado o desparzido;

> d'aquesto un frio temor assí a desora
> por mis huessos discurre en tal manera
> que no puedo bivir con él un'ora.
>
> (37–45)

Garcilaso celebrates Naples as a city for relaxation, because it was known in antiquity as a vacation city from the work city of Rome. With regard to the theme of relaxation in Naples, Herrera quoted a contemporary of Garcilaso, Firenzuola, who was not published until 1549, but whom Rivers supposes Garcilaso knew and used as a point of reference in this poem: "ne la bella Parthenope, ch'un nido / fu gia di cortesia, d'amore un seggio" (in beautiful Parthenope, which was a nest of courtesy, a seat of love) (*Garcilaso: Obras* 246). It is not necessary to posit a direct influence of Firenzuola on Garcilaso since both poets are playing on the name of one of the sections of Naples, called Il Seggio del Nido. Strangely enough, none of the commentators on Garcilaso has noticed this equivocal reference, even though all have explained the reference to Nido in the Ode ad florem Gnidi. The striking phrase "Allí mi coraçon tuvo su nido" is a pun in which Garcilaso refers simultaneously to the mistress and the section of the city in which she lived. The nest imagery then continues in the following lines, naming two disastrous options for the lover: "o estará ocupado o desparzido" (also recalling the nest imagery in Eclogue I, lines 164–65, 326–27). The language of the last tercet of this section is more medical, referring to a cold fear that grips his body. Fear and coldness were causes of melancholy, and of other negative emotions, such as sadness and despair, concepts that Garcilaso will develop later in the poem.

Following the description of Naples and the love he left there, the emotion that accompanies the memory of that love is expressed as an extended complex metaphor, comparing absence from the beloved to the diverse effects of water on fire in a blacksmith's forge:

> Si, triste, de mi bien yo estado uviera
> un breve tiempo ausente, no lo niego
> que con mayor seguridad biviera:
>   la breve ausencia haze el mismo juego
> en la fragua d'amor que en fragua ardiente
> el agua moderada haze al fuego,

la qual verás que no tan solamente
no le suele matar, mas le refuerça
con ardor más intenso y eminente,
    porque un contrario, con la poca fuerça
de su contrario, por vencer la lucha
su braço abiva y su valor esfuerça.
    Pero si el agua en abundancia mucha
sobre'l fuego s'esparze y se derrama,
el humo sube al cielo, el son s'escucha
    y, el claro resplandor de biva llama
en polvo y en ceniza convertido,
apenas queda dél sino la fama:
    assí el ausencia larga, que á esparzido
en abundancia su licor que amata
el fuego que'l amor tenia encendido,
    de tal suerte lo dexa que lo trata
la mano sin peligro en le momento
que en aparencia y son se desbarata
                        (46–69)

A little water, like a short absence, makes the fire burn brighter because, as Garcilaso explains, the fire burns with more vigor to conquer its opposite, water. On the contrary, a lot of water, like a long absence, douses the flame and extinguishes the coals. Rivers comments that this type of extended imagery, taken from the mechanical arts, is typical of the *cancionero* style. Garcilaso obviously introduced this comparison in this poem because it allows him to speculate on moderation and the struggle of contraries in nature, the very battle he feels in himself trying to find the just mean. He chooses vocabulary that keeps the theme constantly before the reader. A small amount of water is within the limits of moderation: "una moderada agua," and the struggle of fire and water is the struggle of contraries, the extremes within which one should find the just mean: "porque un contrario, con la poca fuerça / de su contrario, por vencer la lucha / su braço abiva y su valor esfuerça" (55–57). This extended metaphor, developed over the course of twenty-one lines, serves to introduce the struggle of real contraries, the elements. Since each of the four elements has double characteristics (dry and cold, cold and humid, etc.), the elements form partial and complete opposites. Earth (dry and cold) and air (humid and hot) are complete opposites as are water (cold and humid) and fire (hot and dry). Nature is composed of a war of the elements in which a balance is achieved from the constant struggle between the opposites. While Garcilaso's metaphor serves to dramatize the effects of absence in a love affair, it also allows him to extend and develop an important part of the theme: the struggle between elemental contraries in nature.

The next section develops another series of paradoxical arguments:

> Yo solo fuera voy d'aqueste cuento,
> porque'l amor m'aflige y m'atormenta
> y en el ausencia crece el mal que siento;
>   y pienso yo que la razón consienta
> y permita la causa deste effeto,
> que a mí solo entre todos se presenta,
>   porque como del cielo yo sujeto
> estava eternamente y diputado
> al amoroso fuego en que me meto,
>   assí, para poder ser amatado,
> el ausencia sin término, infinita
> deve ser, y sin tiempo limitado;
>   lo qual no avrá razón que lo permita,
> porque por más y más que ausencia dure,
> con la vida s'acaba, que's finita.
>
>   (70–84)

Garcilaso slowly modulates into an expansion of his thematic arguments in this section. He begins by saying that he does not fit the analogy presented in the previous twenty-one lines. That is to say, long absences do not kill his passion, but make it more severe. He believes this occurs because he has always been inclined to be in love, in fact, so inclined by the heavens. The early commentators disputed the orthodoxy of this tercet. One can only admire the way Garcilaso steers a middle course between determinism and freedom, saying first he is the subject of the heavens, and second, that he places himself in their hands. He then argues that in order for an absence to kill passion, it must be limitless, but since he knows his absence will cease with death, it cannot, then, be limitless.

The next tercet introduces the theme of fortune, which will be interwoven into the rest of the arguments of the poem:

> Mas a mí ¿quién avrá que m'assegure
> que mi mala fortuna con mudança
> y olvido contra mí no se conjure?
> (85–87)

Posed in a rhetorical question, he wonders if fortune is operating from
a change and forgetfulness. Fortune is, of course, another type of destiny,
recalling the previous tercet on fate. But Fortune, with its opposing faces
of prosperity and adversity, is a destiny of contraries and sudden
changes. It is the war of the elements moved to the realm of weather and
chance accidents in human affairs.

In the next tercet, the poet's fear, a cold retentive emotion, begins to
pursue his hope and overpower his desire, a hot expansive emotion. The
suggestion of fixed fate and an angry pursuant Fortune makes him lose
hope and fall into despair:

> Este temor persigue la esperança
> y oprime y enflaquece el gran deseo
> con que mis ojos van de su holgança;
> (88–90)

Human emotions, which were also classified as contraries, some being
inward and others outward, were thought to be caused by the humoral
complexion of the body and the spirits engendered in the heart. Cold,
damp humors produced inward negative emotions, such as fear and depression, while hot, dry humors produced outward and aggressive emotions, such as anger, hope, desire, etc. In traditional science, the four
elements corresponded to the four humors. With these verses Garcilaso
begins to move the battle of the elements presented in lines 46–69 into
the body and to the battle of the humors and their corresponding contrary emotions.

In the next tercet, the poet resigns himself to the struggle:

> con ellos solamente agora veo
> este dolor que'l coraçón me parte,
> y con él y comigo aquí peleo.
> (91–93)

The verb "parte" suggests not only pain and suffering, but also the duality that dominates his poem. The word "peleo" which he uses to characterize his struggle against pain and the struggles of adversaries in him causes him to digress on the powers of the pagan god of strife and war, Mars:

> ¡O crudo, o riguroso, o fiero Marte,
> de túnica cubierto de diamante
> y endurecido siempre en toda parte!,
>   ¿qué tiene que hazer el tierno amante
> con tu dureza y áspero exercicio,
> llevado siempre del furor delante?
>   (94–99)

Mele and Rivers comment on the opposition of Mars and Venus in this passage, although Venus is not named but only implied in the phrase "tierno amante." Garcilaso's invocation of the pagan god must be understood within the cosmological system that equated the microcosm with the macrocosm. The poet had previously mentioned the positioning of the stars in his destiny, so here he does not address a pagan god, but the planet Mars that incarnated the characteristics of the pagan god and could by its positioning in the heavens make the warlike characteristics of the god manifest on the earth. Garcilaso had stated previously that he had been destined to be a lover by the heavens: "porque como del cielo yo sujeto / estava eternamente y diputado / al amoroso fuego en que me meto" (76–78). In the heavens, the planet Mars exercises influence as a malevolent force. Garcilaso names three characteristics of Mars the god and the planet: he is cruel, severe, and bestial. Lines 95–96 place emphasis on the hardness of Mars and his armor, and this hardness contrasts with the "tierno amante" in line 97. Lines 98–99 return to the hardness and fury of the god. The contrast of Mars with the lover is effected through a rhetorical question, like the previous questions the poet makes to himself and to his reader. The reason that Venus is not mentioned in this passage, and is only represented by the single phrase "tierno amante," is because the astrological Mars is dominant here and has in effect effaced the power of Venus. The rhyme scheme in this passage and the placement of "Marte" and "amante" is significant for their opposition. Both words are the middle of the three rhyming words; each is placed at the end of the first line of a tercet; and the contrasting rhymes in this passage nearly rhyme with each other, ending in "-arte" and "-ante." Thus, Mars stands directly over the subjugated lover in the text. This passage transports the previously announced battle of contraries from the physical world of the elements and humors to the heavens where the hot and dry Mars subjugates the cold and humid Venus.[1]

Also important in these two tercets are the broader political implications. The poem began with Virgil and the fame of Anchises as a setting for the victorious, but hardly nobly motivated, troops of Charles V huddled together in the dense thick forests. Lines 94–99 rail at the cruelty and hardness of Mars, and, in other words, war. Even though the theme of Mars was introduced by the metaphorical "peleo" in reference to emotions and the passage is directed to the lover overcome by Mars, the extended vituperation against war seems to follow naturally from the poet's previous ambiguity concerning the troops and the victory of Charles V. While ambiguity does not constitute explicit criticism, the lack of an all-out praise of the emperor's war policy and the ambiguous phrasing in which he couches it would imply a hesitancy in giving support.

The next three tercets show the effect of Mars on the lover:

> Exercitando por mi mal tu officio,
> soy reduzido a términos que muerte
> será mi postrimero beneficio;
>   y ésta no permitió mi dura suerte
> que me sobreviniesse peleando
> de hierro traspassado agudo y fuerte,
>   porque me consumiesse contemplando
> mi amado y dulce fruto en mano agena,
> y el duro possessor de mí burlando.
>   (100–108)

Under the influence of Mars, the lover is plunged into war, which, combined with his love passion, produces a longing for death. He imagines that his "dura suerte" has saved him from death so he can suffer the

---

1. One would expect Venus to be hot and humid, but her planet was always associated with water, which is cold and humid.

worse fate of seeing his beloved in the hands of another. The ambiguously worded phrase "possessor de mí" indicates how the rival has come to dominate the emotions of the poet. The rival is not only laughing at him, but also controls his emotional responses. The effect of Mars on the lover has been to produce jealousy. The cold inward emotion of fear, first introduced in line 88, has now come to full force, producing mental alienation.

> Mas ¿dónde me trasporta y enagena
> de mi propio sentido el triste miedo?
> A parte de vergüença y dolor llena,
>   donde, si el mal yo viesse, ya no puedo,
> según con esperalle estoy perdido,
> acrecentar en la miseria un dedo.
>   Assí lo pienso agora, y si él venido
> fuesse en su misma forma y su figura,
> ternia el presente por mejor partido,
>   y agradeceria siempre a la ventura
> mostrarme de mi mal solo el retrato
> que pintan mi temor y mi tristura.
>   (109–20)

Melancholy caused by fear and sadness (first associated in a Hippocratic aphorism on melancholy, Klibansky 15) can lead to madness, and the poet sees in these images the first steps. For the second time the poet reproaches himself with a critical question. Just as his satirical vein had carried him from his middle course of neither seeking nor falsely disdaining the rewards of victory, so too had his jealousy (the perversion of desire, a hot, outward emotion) mixed with fear (a cold inward emotion) produced frightening images uncharacteristic of the well-balanced mind.

Lines 121–45 develop the opposition of emotions by presenting a different set of contraries, the possible responses to a dying man: either to tell him he will die, or to let him believe he will survive:

> Yo sé qué cosa es esperar un rato
> el bien del propio engaño y solamente
> tener con él inteligencia y trato,
>   como acontece al mísero doliente
> que, del un cabo, el cierto amigo y sano

le muestra el grave mal de su acidente,
   y le amonesta que del cuerpo humano
comience a levantar a mejor parte
el alma suelta con bolar liviano;
   mas la tierna muger, de la otra parte,
no se puede entregar al desengaño
y encúbrele del mal la mayor parte;
   él, abraçado con su dulce engaño,
buelve los ojos a la boz piadosa
y alégrase muriendo con su daño:
   assí los quito yo de toda cosa
y póngolos en solo el pensamiento
de la esperança, cierta o mentirosa;
   en este dulce error muero contento,
porque ver claro y conocer mi 'stado
no puede ya curar el mal que siento,
   y acabo como aquel que'n un templado
baño metido, sin sentillo muere,
las venas dulcemente desatado.

                                        (121–45)

The phrases "del un cabo" (125) and "de la otra parte" (130) mark the
extremes. The extended image in these lines concerns death. A good
friend may tell his sick friend that death is imminent, while a loving wife
may spare his grief by hiding the fact from him. Garcilaso accepts the
latter option, the sweet illusion that he will recover while in fact he is
dying, and he imagines his death as a Stoical suicide, calmly expiring
while peacefully bleeding to death in a warm bath.

The text tercets reintroduce Boscán to whom the poem was addressed
in line 1. While the address at the beginning seemed superfluous and
confused the syntax even more, the reference here assumes great relevance. He is here addressed as "tú," while in lines 25–27 he was addressed as "Señor" and "vos."

Tú, que en la patria, entre quien bien te quiere,
la deleytosa playa estás mirando
y oyendo el son del mar que en ella hiere,
   y sin impedimiento contemplando
la misma a quien tú vas eterna fama

> en tus bivos escritos procurando,
>   alégrate, que más hermosa llama
> que aquella que'l troyano encendimiento
> pudo causar, el coraçón t'inflama;
>   no tienes que temer el movimiento
> de la fortuna con soplar contrario,
> que el puro resplandor serena el viento.
>
> (145–56)

Line 145 draws a complete contrast with the situation of Garcilaso. Boscán is in the homeland, Garcilaso in a foreign land. The forced position of "entre" in the phrase "entre quien bien te quiere" makes the point that Boscán is with and accompanied by someone who loves him, perhaps even surrounded by loving friends, while Garcilaso is between warring contraries. The strained context of "entre" in reference to Boscán recalls and contrasts clearly with Garcilaso's strained position between contraries. Boscán is on the shore looking at the sea and hearing the sound of the waves, the humid climate tempering his hot dry thoughts. Garcilaso is in a thick mountain forest. Boscán enjoys a requited love, probably the domestic tranquility he describes in his Octava rima (393ff.). His love seems to have a tranquil Platonic base, for his poems will give his beloved eternal fame. This seems to be a reference to the same Neoplatonic love based in beauty whose tranquility Boscán celebrates in his sonnets. The beauty of his beloved inflames his heart with a more beautiful flame than Helen could cause in Troy. The love and abduction of Helen would represent the excesses of sensual love that result in the destructive burning of Troy; whereas Boscán's love produces a more beautiful flame that fires his heart. These references to types of fire recall Pico della Mirandola's classification of elemental, celestial, and intellectual fire in his *Heptaplus* (24). The Neoplatonic theme is reinforced with the poet's statement that he need not fear a change of his situation because his love is based on beauty. The reference to Fortune and its sudden reverses prepares for the shift back to Garcilaso, especially the word "contrario," which recalls the thematic thread of the poem. The friend Boscán serves in this poem as a contrast with the passionate jealous love that destroys the equilibrium of the emotions.

The poet now sees himself as a soldier of fortune, a paid mercenary whose only will is that of his employer:

Yo, como conduzido mercenario,
voy do fortuna a mi pesar m'embía,
si no a morir, que aquéste's voluntario;
    solo sostiene la esperança mía
un tan débil engaño que de nuevo
es menester hazelle cada día,
    y si no le fabrico y le renuevo,
da consigo en el suelo de mi esperança
tanto que'n vano a levantalla pruevo.
                              (157–65)

The comparison strikes close to home, but is far enough removed from
the truth to serve as a metaphor, and an apt one at that, in a poem dominated by the force and power of Mars. Garcilaso was a soldier who was
involved in the tiring negotiations of rewarding the soldiers and officers
after the campaign in Tunisia, but he was far from being a soldier for
hire. The metaphorical degradation of his actual position indicates a
change in his amorous psychology. The text is clear: "*como* conduzido
mercenario"; like a mercenary he suffers in the battle of love with only
the two options, either continuing to struggle or dying. In the war of
love, he has lost his will (hence a mercenary) and is led on by his hope
and sustained by a weak deception that, if he did not reinforce it daily,
would simply expire. The metaphor in this passage should not be mistaken for biographical information. Garcilaso chose the metaphor of the
mercenary because it presents a situation of limited options, just as jealousy also closes options, making his rival "el duro possessor de mí"
(108). The effect of Mars on the lover is the cause of a mixture of cold
and heat that produces the outwardly aggressive, but inwardly biting
passion of jealousy. Thus, the metaphor fits perfectly to characterize the
jealousy that dominates the will and circumscribes his powers.

His faithfulness causes a rare constancy that prevents Fortune from
making its usual change. Thus, Garcilaso is condemned to his suffering
without the possibility of reprieve.

Aqueste premio mi servir alcança,
que en sola la miseria de mi vida
negó fortuna su común mudança.
                              (166–68)

This passage again recalls the two faces of Fortune and the contraries she introduces, but here she shows, as in Boscán's Sonnet VI, an unusual constancy in suffering. It may also refer to the rewards being distributed in Sicily as booty.

In verse 169, the poet again questions in an aside where he could flee.

> ¿Dónde podré hüir que sacudida
> un rato sea de mí la grave carga
> que oprime mi cerviz enflaquecida?
>   Mas ¡ay!, que la distancia no descarga
> el triste coraçón, y el mal, doquiera
> que 'stoy, para alcançarme el braço alarga:
>   (169–74)

There is great irony in these lines very important for understanding jealousy. Alienated from himself, the poet has no space to occupy. He is dominated by other forces, and any attempt to exercise his will only serves to recall his subjugation to his passion and the will of others. His natural instinct to flee from the problem and uncomfortable situation encounters the difficulty that he has already fled; in fact, absence is his problem, and it is impossible to flee from jealousy and absence. His problems can reach him wherever he flees, whether to hot regions or to frozen lands. He devotes one tercet to each clime.

> si donde'l sol ardiente reverbera
> en la arenosa Libya, engendradora
> de toda cosa ponçoñosa y fiera,
>   o adonde'l es vencido a qualquier ora
> de la rígida nieve y viento frío,
> parte do no se bive ni se mora,
>   (175–80)

The two climes recall the contrast of climes in the first stanza of Canción I, imitated from Petrarch and Horace. Their significance here is quite different. In Canción I the extremes of opposite climes are trials of the lover's fidelity—no matter how far or how severe the clime, the poet-lover will remain faithful. In Elegy II, the climes represent the contraries that continually struggle for control of the poet.

The concluding lines of the poem return to the theme of Fortune, the pagan force of contrary destinies, and bring about the final transformation of the contraries, converting the opposing climes into the opposing passions described earlier.

> si en ésta o en aquélla el desvarío
> o la fortuna me llevasse un día
> y allí gastasse todo el tiempo mío,
>   el çeloso temor con mano fría
> en medio del calor y ardiente arena
> el triste coraçón m'apretaría;
>   y en el rigor del yelo, en la serena
> noche, soplando el viento agudo y puro
> que'l veloce correr del agua enfrena,
>   d'aqueste bivo fuego, en que m'apuro
> y consumirme poco a poco espero,
> sé que aun allí no podré estar seguro,
> y assí diverso entre contrarios muero.
>   (184–94)

Even in a hot, desert clime he would be beset by the cold fear of jealousy, and even in an arctic clime the heat of his passion would overcome him and consume his vital forces. In the final line—an admirable synthesis of the long development of contraries—the poet establishes an untenable middle ground where he is slowly destroyed. The Renaissance concept of the correspondence of the microcosm and macrocosm has permitted the struggles of the jealous lover to range from earthly moral philosophy and elemental science to a struggle of cosmic forces. The theme of amorous rivalry, which Garcilaso seemed to control in his *coplas,* has led to the horrible suffering caused by jealousy, a new theme in Renaissance poetry explored by the Neapolitan lyricists. Garcilaso relates jealousy to the concept of the golden mean which he introduces early in the elegy, first in its proper sense of reference to the domain of moral moderation. He then applies the same concept to love and absence, which he presents with the involved struggle of the contrary elements of fire and water in a blacksmith's forge. The elements constitute a struggle on the physical level of the microcosm, for the same struggle occurs on a medical level in the lover's humors and emotions. These struggles in the microcosm are reflections of the great astrological struggles of the pagan gods and goddesses in the name of their planetary forces with Mars dominating

Venus, the love passion turned to hateful aggressive jealousy. After further developing the medical struggle of emotions, he returns to the struggle of contraries in earthly climates. The opposition of hot deserts and frozen polar regions recalls the Petrarchan language of Garcilaso's Canción I, but here it reinforces the imagery between contraries that is developed as the major theme of the poem, moving from the moral theme of the golden mean to the struggle of contraries in the cosmos, in nature, in one's own physical being, and in the earth's geography. Garcilaso has subverted and converted the Aristotelian and Horatian ideal into a paradoxical middle ground between warring contraries, a ground that is impossible to hold and defend. The conversion of a moral precept into emotional strife and a moral dilemma is nothing less than the subversion of an established precept. The moral truth of classical moderation has become a paradoxical untenable position where the poet expires besieged by contradictory passions and warring elements.

With great irony Garcilaso, at the height of his powers and in a period and in a specific movement that exalted the classics, actually undermines one of the major themes of classical thought, an idea expounded in Aristotle's *Ethics*, a book he knew very well, and a recurrent theme of Horace, one of his favorite classical writers. The middle course he takes with regard to the greed of the other soldiers sounds very virtuous. Little does the reader anticipate that the poem will actually turn on the concept of a middle course concluding with the poet expiring between warring extremes. Close readings of Canción IV and Elegy II present a new Garcilaso, not the old poet of the "dolorido sentir," but a new figure, the master of paradox and irony.

VI
Mars in the House of Venus: The Ode ad florem Gnidi

14

Garcilaso's Ode and the Classical Tradition

The study of the Ode ad florem Gnidi is divided into two chapters. The first examines the reception and formal structure of the poem and the second analyzes the mythological context of the poem. The present chapter covers several historical aspects of the poem, its relationship to Tasso's conception of the ode, Garcilaso's own study of Horace in Naples and the reception of the ode in different periods. The last part of the chapter undertakes a formal analysis of the structural unity of the poem, revealing the subtextual construct elaborated by Garcilaso to balance the seemingly chaotic shifts and juxtapositions that characterize the classical ode.

As argued in Chapter 5, Garcilaso's Ode ad florem Gnidi obviously owes much to Bernardo Tasso's adaptation of the Horatian ode to the vernacular. In the early 1550s, when Tasso was preparing for press his *Libro quarto* (which contained eighteen new odes) with the reedition of the first three books, he often mentioned his odes in his correspondence. In one letter of 1553, he spells out his debt to Horace in the vernacular odes:

> Vi mando ... tre Ode alla Oraziana; alla Oraziana dico, non quanto a' numeri del verso (perchè questa nostra lingua non lo sopporta) ma quanto alle altre parti dell'artificio. Io passo talora

la clausula lunga d'una Stanza nell' altra: talora la faccio breve,
come meglio mi pare: faccio talora il construtto pieno d'una lu-
cida oscurità, come fa ancor' Orazio: alle volte esco alla materia
principiata con la digressione, e poi ritorno: alle volte finisco nella
digressione, ad imitazione de' buoni poeti Lirici. (*Delle lettere*
2:125)

(I send you . . . three odes in Horatian style; I say Horatian not in
reference to the rhythm of the verse (because our language does
not support it), but regarding the other parts of artifice. I some-
times continue a long sentence from one stanza to the next; some-
times I make it short, however seems best to me; other times I
make the structure full of a lucid obscurity, as Horace did. At
times I leave the theme I began in the digression and then I return;
other times I finish in the digression, in imitation of the good
lyric poets.)

Tasso's description of the Horatian ode concentrates on the formal
structure, and the freedom allotted the poet in structuring the material.
Unlike the *canzone* in which each stanza is a discrete syntactic unit, the
classical odes of Horace and Pindar at times continue the sentences from
stanza to stanza. The structure of the Horatian ode is not fixed in form;
it may employ any one of a variety of metrical forms or the material may
be arranged in a seemingly haphazard way. Other aspects of the Horatian
ode also influenced Tasso and Garcilaso. The Horatian ode was always
concerned with the social good, rather than the poet's personal feelings:
"Being moral and preaching the morality of the sane and civilized pagan,
the Horatian ode is, naturally enough, largely concerned with other
people. We are always aware of a social background. The poet is always
a member of society addressing his fellow men" (Maddison, *Apollo* 25).
Another important difference in the Horatian ode concerns the use of
imagery:

The characteristic development of the Horatian *carmen* is
through image to aphorism. The thoughts that agglomerate about
a particular idea are communicated concretely through specific
illustrations; with the poet we repeat the experience and observation; then we are led to the same general reflections. In the place
of the propositions, there are pictures, in place of the arguments,

illustrations. Even in didactic passages Horace prefers the specific example to the abstract generalization. (Maddison 30)

Tasso's debt in the formation of the vernacular ode extends also to Pindar, whose odes are somewhat more capricious than those of Horace, especially in the disposition of the materials. Tasso commented in the introduction to the 1531 edition of *Gli amore* that in their lyrics the ancients were freed from the structures required by prose composition: "non curavano de dargli quelle parte che quel della prosa ricerca" (they did not worry about giving it those parts that one seeks in prose). Yet these differences were great enough, that upon sending an ode to a friend in 1553, he saw the need to give him advance warning:

> ed eziandio ch'io sappia che sappiate, e forse meglio di me, la natura, e l'artificio dell'Ode, non mi rimarrò però di ridurvi a memoria questo poco, Che el Lirico, cominciata la materia principale che s'ha proposta di trattare, e uscendo poi con la digressione, alle volte ritorna nella materia principiata, alle volte finisce il suo Poema nella digressione; il che si vede in Pindaro, e in Orazio in moltissimi lochi. (*Delle lettere* 2:123)

> (and even though I know you know, and perhaps better than I, the nature and artifice of the ode, it is not out of place to recall this little bit: The lyric poet, once the principal material that he proposes to treat has been commenced, and emerging then into the digression, sometimes returns to the material with which he began, other times finishes his poem in the digression, which is seen in Pindar and in Horace in very many places.)

He believed this warning necessary so that readers not judge him bereft of reason:

> Questo ho voluto ricordarvi, perchè, mostrandola a persone di minore guidicio, che voi non sete, non si pensino ch'io mi sia dimenticata la strada da tornar a casa.

> (I wanted to recall this to you, so that, showing it to people of lesser judgment, which you are not, they do not think I had forgotten my way on returning home.)

In addition to the formal structures of the stanza and the parting envoi, the *canzone* presents an argument with its opening, burden, and conclusion. The author of the ode, as conceived of by Tasso, could indulge in digressions and willful and abrupt changes, and simply end the poem without a formal return to the central argument.

Maddison comments on this aspect of Pindar's odes: "Themes are not treated consecutively, but various ideas are interwoven, so that each thread runs throughout, but only occasionally appears on the surface" (*Apollo* 14–15). Central to every Pindaric ode is a myth that must be "related to the games or to the hero or to the city" (Maddison 6). The myth, however, was not a simple narration, but was often presented only in part or through allusion: "Pindar recounted only the high point of a myth, the parts that he felt relevant to his immediate purpose" (Maddison 7), and the ordering of the material does not follow narrative sequence: "The myth, in its arrangement, preserves the original order of thought. Ideas are set down as they occurred to the poet's mind, not as logical principles of narration would arrange them" (Maddison 15). Also important in Pindar, as in Horace, is the use of imagery: "Pindar is the most visual and concrete of poets. Nothing is left to the vague, abstract word. Everything is clearly pictured" (Maddison 18). From these classical models and from Neo-Latin odes by his humanist contemporaries, Tasso developed his own odes, which, according to Maddison, resemble those of Horace most closely:

> Tasso was classically inspired and, of the ancient poets, he is most like Horace. He writes on similar themes, political events of the day and personal and private conduct, in a somewhat similar fashion, with natural metaphors and classical allusions. However his range is much narrower than Horace's. (*Apollo* 174)

In spite of Garcilaso's debt to Tasso in the formal aspects of his ode, the poem clearly corresponds as well to Garcilaso's own passionate interest and study of Horace in the last years of his life. Lapesa recognizes the Horatian influence, but finds it to be less than that of Virgil's bucolic poems (*Garcilaso: Estudios* 94). Garcilaso's two elegies and the Epístola a Boscán represent other adaptations of Horatian genres to Spanish. In addition, he wrote a number of odes in Latin, of which three have survived. It is impossible to determine if the study of Horace had attracted him in his youth, but the interest in and study of Horace permeated the ambience of Naples in the 1520s and 1530s. In his second Latin ode, Garcilaso describes his literary associations in Naples. Apparently he attended meetings of the Accademia Pontaniana, one of the earliest and most illustrious of the formal organizations created by humanists for the discussion and divulgence of their studies and ideas. These groups often had constitutions of incorporation, employed strict rules, and existed as important Italian cultural institutions from the Renaissance to the twentieth century. Rivaling in importance the Accademia Platonica of Florence and the Accademia Pomponiana of Rome, the Accademia of Naples was founded by Alfonso of Aragon in 1442 after he conquered the city. Its most common name, the Accademia Pontaniana, comes from its most famous member, the humanist Giovanni Pontano (1426–1503), who participated in its gatherings. The meetings were held in the house of Jacopo Sannazaro, from 1503 until his death in 1530. From then until 1543, the meetings were held in the house of Scipione Capece. In the second Latin ode, Garcilaso describes the meetings in Capece's house, and Capece's high regard for Garcilaso is seen in his dedicating to Garcilaso his edition of Donatello's commentaries on Virgil's *Aeneid*. When, in 1543, Capece, who was very religious and influenced by Valdés, fell under suspicion of heresy and in disfavor with the viceroy Pedro de Toledo, the Accademia was closed in its one hundred and first year (Maylender 4:327–37).

In the second Latin ode, as in certain of his Spanish poems, Garcilaso plays on the topos of presence and absence. He juxtaposes things he left in Spain with the description of his literary friends and their reunions in Naples. He concludes by saying that the advantages of his life in Naples outweigh the pleasures of home, family, and domesticity. Addressed to Antonio Telesio (c. 1482–c. 1534), known in Latin as Thylesius, he refers to Telesio's play *Imber aureus* (first published 1529). According to Hutton, Telesio arrived in Naples in 1531, and, not finding the support of a patron, returned to Cosenza the following year (*Greek Anthology* 188). His departure in 1532 and his death in 1533 or 1534 would serve to fix the date of Garcilaso's poem as most probably 1532.

The Latin ode is one of Garcilaso's most autobiographical poems. He mentions his wife (*pace* Keniston, *Garcilaso* 67) and family, his imprisonment in Austria, and his friends in Naples. He describes Seripando's orations in the Academy and mentions by name his friends Mario Galeota and Placido di Sangro. Even some of the topics referred to may relate to his life, such as Seripando's explanation of how the sins of parents are visited on children. This topic, clearly related to the cycles of family curses and vengeances in Greek drama, may also have been viewed in light of Seripando's Christian ideas on justification of faith. It could also have had personal meaning for Garcilaso whose political career was always seriously affected by his brother's espousal of the *comunero* cause against the emperor. Undoubtedly, Garcilaso's interest in Seripando's topic would have gone beyond the purely academic. Garcilaso's friendship with Seripando must have been intense. The only personal letter of Garcilaso's that survives is addressed to Seripando and is found among his papers in Naples. Seripando remembered Garcilaso in a letter to Placido di Sangro (the same friend mentioned in Garcilaso's second Latin ode):

> Di queste due modi d'interpretare non voglio dir piu, ricordandomi d'haverne scritto pure assai anni sono, quando ero posto in questi studdi, a quel honoratissimo et virtuosissimo cavaliero Garcilasso della Vega amico nostro commone, richiesto da lui (che come sapete, era studiosissimo d'Horatio and l'imitava nei suoi scritti felicemente) come io m'intendessi quel passo "Nec verbum verbo curabis reddere fidus interpres," ove m'ingegnai esporre Horatio con questa distintione di M. Tullio contra l'openione di molti. (Jedin 88)[1]

> (I do not wish to say more about these two kinds of translation, remembering that I wrote about them a number of years ago when I was involved in these studies to that most honorable and virtuous gentleman Garcilasso de la Vega, our common friend. Asked by him [for as you remember, he was very keen on Horace and he imitated him felicitously in his writings] how I understood that phrase "Do not try to render each word with another word as a faithful translator," where I endeavored to expound Horace with this distinction from Tully against the opinion of many.)

That Garcilaso questioned Seripando about a line from Horace's *Ars poetica* and Seripando remembered Garcilaso as an imitator of Horace is interesting in light not only of Tasso's molding of the Horatian ode in

---

1. Jedin quotes this passage and cites an Oration, while Mele ("Las poesías latinas" 135) quotes it in translation and cites Seripando's correspondence. I have quoted from Jedin, but assumed that Mele gives the correct citation.

the vernacular, but also for the intense study and appreciation of Horace by Garcilaso and his Neapolitan friends. The line that Seripando explicated to Garcilaso concerns translation, and recalls Garcilaso's own commentaries on Boscán's method of translating Castiglione:

> Fue demás desto muy fiel traductor, porque no se ató al rigor de la letra, como hazen algunos, sino a la verdad de las sentencias, y por diferentes caminos puso en esta lengua toda la fuerça y el ornamento de la otra. (Garcilaso, *Obras completas con comentarios* 489)

Other studies of Horace were also appearing. Antonio Telesio, to whom the second Latin ode is addressed, had delivered an oration in Rome on Horace's odes, *In odas Horatii Flacci auspicia ad iuventutem romanam,* which was published in the 1520s. Aulus Ianus Parrhasius published in Naples in 1531 his commentary on Horace's *Ars poetica.*

In spite of Garcilaso's involvement in the study of Horace and the debt to Horace in his Ode ad florem Gnidi, the Horatian nature of the Spanish ode was obscured by Fernando de Herrera's editing of the text. Garcilaso's title unequivocally identifies the genre: Ode ad florem Gnidi. The Latin of the title recalls its classical sources (Dunn 301), and critics have recognized its Horatian inspiration. Menéndez y Pelayo discussed it in his study on Horace in Spain, and Lapesa labels the poem as a new genre in Spanish. Elias Rivers argues in the introduction to his critical edition that the ode was conceived of as different from the preceding sonnets and *canciones,* which correspond to Boscán's Book II and represent Garcilaso's Italianate period when he first began to use Italian verse forms. The forms and expression in the four *canciones* and in some of the sonnets have their roots in Italian medieval forms and Petrarchan anguish and unrequited love. The ode, with the elegies, epistle, and eclogues, represents the new style, Garcilaso's third period when he began to imitate classical genres and modes of expression. These poems correspond to Boscán's Book III which also contains classical and Italianate genres: *fábula, capítulo, epístola,* and *octava rima.*

Unlike Boscán's formal arrangement of his poetry into three books, Garcilaso's poetry was published as a whole in Book IV. The editor, presumably Boscán, did order the poems (except the sonnets) to indicate the various periods of poetic production. In his critical edition with commentaries of 1580, Fernando de Herrera, in spite of his great learning in

Spanish, Italian, and classical poetry, misunderstood the significance of the ordering of the poems; instead of treating the ode as a new departure from traditional Petrarchan themes and forms, he grouped it with the *canciones*. He suppressed the original 1543 title, Ode ad florem Gnidi, and retitled it simply as Canción V. In line 12 where Garcilaso repeats the pun of the title on the place name Gnido, he eliminated the pun, reforming the spelling to Nido. In his commentaries he failed to distinguish between the ode and the other *canciones*, even though this poem looks different from the other *canciones* because of its shorter stanzas and the lack of an envoi at the end.

Although Herrera's edition became the basis for all future editions until 1922, not everyone agreed with his emendation. In his observations, Prete Jacopin did not chastise Herrera for the change, but notes it so his readers will not mistake the composition: "En la quinta *Cancion,* que es la Oda ad florem Gnydi . . ." (Herrera, *Controversia* 14). Tamayo noticed Herrera's emendation, but was willing to leave the poem without a title: "La V, que tiene por título Ad Florem Gnidi Ode, en los más impresos, y Herrera la pone sin ninguno, en el Escorial no le hallé, en otros sí: yo la continuaría sin él con las demás" (T-54). Manuel Faria e Sousa, however, in the introduction to volume 3 of his own collected poetry, made scoffing references to Herrera's retitling of the poem:

> Es composicion que quiere singulares elevaciones, i pensamientos, i grabedad. De Garcilasso permanece una [oda] que absolutamente es la mejor de Castilla. Siguese desto que pudiera Fernando de Herrera escusar la mudança que hizo del titulo de la de Garcilasso, que el mismo la diò; si lo hizo por huir de la voz Oda, que dizen algunos suena otra cosa indecente (observación muy de los modernos) tendrele por ridiculo, aviendole tenido antes por solo impertinente.

In spite of such ribbing (Did Faria e Sousa really believe Herrera had associated "oda" with the imperative of *joder*?), Herrera had clear precedents for failing to recognize the differences between the *canción* and the ode as devised by Bernardo Tasso. Poets and preceptists of Herrera's generation generally dismissed the importance of the introduction of the ode as a genre separate from the *canzone*. Girolamo Muzio's *Arte poetica* in verse, published in his *Rimas* of 1551, criticizes the introduction of neologisms into Italian and he ridicules those who import useless words into the language.

> Alcuni son, che forse troppo amanti
> D'ogni cosa d'altrui, lor rime noue
> Chiaman con gli stranieri antichi nomi:
> Ode, epigrammi, et inni, et elegie.
>   (Muzio, "Dell'Arte" 172)

> (There are some, perhaps too much lovers
> of everything that belongs to others, who label
> their new poems with strange ancient names:
> Odes, Epigrams, Hymns, and Elegies.)

After railing against the pretentiousness of adopting unneeded foreign customs, and expressing concern for the demise of the sonnet, *canzone*, *terza rima*, and *octava*, he concludes his argument by attacking the name *ode* and defending the dignity of the *canzone*:

> Et per Dio, chi dice "oda", che dice egli
> Se non dice "canzone"? In questa rima
> Chiuse' l Petrarcha il suon de' suoi sospiri, . . .
> E cantò de la Dea l'eterne lode
> Cosi soaue, & cosi alteramente,
> Che ben dourebbon gli intelletti sani
> Non sentir voglia di straniero cibo.
>   (172–73)

> (And by God, he who says ode, what is he
>   saying
> if he is not saying *canzone*? In this genre
> Petrarch enclosed the sound of his sighs, . . .
> and he sang eternal praises of the goddess
> so smoothly, so loftily
> that sane intelligences should not feel
> the need of foreign fare.)

Minturno, one of the poets mentioned by Garcilaso in his Sonnet XXIV, explained that he had written two odes in honor of Charles V, following the fashion of Alamanni, but instead of the terms *ballata, contraballata,* and *stanza* to name the triadic form, he employed *volta, rivolta,* and *stanza.* He explains in great detail the other Pindaric effects of these odes, but he minimized their essential difference, calling them "canzone Pindarica" (*L'Arte poetica* 182). In another passage, when the interlocutor questions him about the madrigal and the Horatian ode, he maintains they are simply a type of *canzone:*

> "Se la composizione sia d'una volta, o d'una Stanza, qual nome haurà: percioche Horatio compose Oda d'una Volta?" [MIN-TURNO]: "Qual' altro, che di Canzone? Percioche di sua natura riceuer più Stanze simili alla prima potrebbe: ma di più la materia né è capace." (186)

> ("If the composition is of one turn, or of one stanza, what name should it have, for Horace composed an ode with one move-ment?" [MINTURNO]: "What other but *canzone?* Because if it were to receive from its nature more stanzas, they would be simi-lar to the first, but the material does not allow for more.")

This passage was translated and incorporated literally by Francisco de Cascales in his *Tablas poéticas.*[2] In his treatment of the *canción* in gen-eral Herrera tends to distinguish between the classical and the vernacular lyric, but he does combine both in the same discussion. He concedes in conclusion that the omission of the envoi in the *canción* "no será error, pues consta bien y se sigue la imitación griega y latina" (H-187). In addi-tion, in his own poetry, Herrera does not make essential differences be-tween the *canción* and the *lira,* as do other poets, such as Francisco de la Torre, nor does he distinguish them by title. Herrera clearly was not sensitive to the innovative thrusts of the lyric poets of the 1530s. Part of his insensitivity is explained by the fact that he tended to regard literary

---

2. PIERIO.—Y si la canción no tiene más que una estancia (como Horacio, que compuso odas de sola una estancia; y como las balatas y madrigales, que por la mayor parte no tienen más que una estancia), ¿cómo se llamará?

CASTALIO. ¿Cómo se a de llamar sino canción? Pues de su naturaleza puede recibir otras estan-cias semejantes a la primera, y por no ser la materia capaz de más o por ser el uso en contrario, como lo es en las balatas y madrigales, no se estiende más" (237–38).

values as universal rather than particular and historical. In applying the "universal" rule, he not only failed to comprehend an important aspect of Garcilaso's poetry, but, by renaming the ode, he also passed that misconception on to future generations.

Herrera's classification became standard. His edition was the basis for most "new" editions up to 1922, when Keniston produced a new critical edition based on the first edition of 1543. Even so, in his edition, the ode is presented in its proper place, but with its title in large capitals as "CANCION V," and the real title following in smaller capitals below as a subtitle. Rivers in his edition with commentary explains in the introduction that the ode represents a classical genre, and is not really the last *canción* because it was meant to begin a new section of works inspired in classical forms. In the text, however, the title "CANCION V" is given in square brackets, unlike other variants that appear only in the notes, such as the famous fourth line in Sonnet XXIII. In addition, the running heads on pages 205, 207, 209, 211, 213, and 215 are "CANCION V" instead of "ODE." This is clearly the longest surviving of Herrera's emendations because editors have been unwilling to suppress it. Rivers's recent article on genres goes even further in rectifying this misunderstanding ("El problema").

Such an error could easily be dismissed as a curious bit of trivia had it not so adversely affected the critical evaluation of the poem. Not only was the ode misclassified and renamed as a *canción*; in addition, modern critical judgments of it come from applying the criteria of the *canción* to the poem, and its alleged defects are said to stem from its lack of conformity to the sincerity of the *canción*. The ode was introduced in order to break out of the mold of the intensely personal and emotionally bound *canción*, and it is unfortunate that Garcilaso's most successful poem in breaking these bounds should have been adversely judged precisely because it failed to stay within those bounds. Lázaro Carreter has recently stated this paradox succinctly: "El que siga en el volumen a cuatro canciones, ha hecho que se clasifique entre ellas, como una quinta canción, cuando—es lo que intentaremos probar—constituía un experimento dirigido precisamente contra ese género" (109). Garcilaso's ode has not fared well with post-Romantic critics. Up to the late nineteenth century, the ode was often singled out as one of his great creations, and the form of the *lira* enjoyed a popularity among Garcilaso's successors that is difficult for us to understand. The belief in the sincerity of Garcilaso's poetic expression, however, produced an adverse critical reaction to the Ode ad florem Gnidi. Assuming that Garcilaso was at his best when he was most sincere, that is, when he expressed his frustrated passionate love for Isabel Freire, critics found the Ode ad florem Gnidi a lesser effort because in it the poet makes an appeal on behalf of a friend. This stance, according to the criterion of sincerity, must perforce be inauthentic. Although critics found the poem exquisite, they felt it necessary to withhold full approval because of its supposedly trivial content. Menéndez y Pelayo (*Horacio*) had high praise for the poem, calling it "una de las más lindas y primorosas imitaciones de la lírica clásica" (13) and found the stanzas "modelos de ligereza y de gracia" (13) but his reservations over the triviality of the content were summed up with the phrase "aquel precioso juguete" (14).

Dámaso Alonso expressed the same enthusiasm, labeling it "una indudable belleza," but reproached its lack of sincerity: "Hablaba por un amigo, y su voz no tiene aquí esa suave y melancólica veladura que tiembla cuando habla de doña Isabel Freire" (*La poesía de San Juan* 191). Lapesa shows the same dichotomy of judgment. He described the poem as having "marmórea perfección" (*Garcilaso: Estudios* 146), but agreed with Menéndez y Pelayo that it was a game: "en efecto, posee la gracia y finura del puro juego" (146), and agreed with Dámaso Alonso that it was not "el mejor momento de Garcilaso" (147). In the end he arrived at the same conclusion as Dámaso Alonso: "Es obra, en fin, hermosa, de antológica maestría y de relevante importancia histórica; pero no logra cautivar al lector que ansía remansarse en el alma, dulce y honda, del poeta" (147). Both critics supported this thesis by faulting the excess of adjectives (as discussed in Chapter 1). The criterion of sincerity clearly informs these judgments, and the critics expect the poet's creations to reveal his soul to the reader. These judgments employ the criteria of the *canción*, not of the ode, which uses a public voice and presents practical morality based on the *demos*, or social utility. Most critical judgments have completely overlooked the nature of the Renaissance ode.

The structure of Garcilaso's ode takes its lead from the form of the classical ode as practiced by Bernardo Tasso. The innovations introduced by Tasso consisted not only of a change of narrative voice and stanzaic form; they also signaled other differences of form and material. The *canzone*, which took its form from the Provençal *canso*, corresponded to medieval rhetorical structures that had been unknown to the ancients. As Dunn has carefully documented, Garcilaso imitates two separate odes by Horace, but employing the imitative strategies of the Renaissance

Neo-Latin poets. Dunn concludes that Garcilaso's imitation of Horace's Odes I, vi and I, viii in this poem ingeniously incorporates his borrowed sources, by adapting them to new ends: "Garcilaso does nothing to hide his sources. They show transparently through his poem, but are given a new colour. . . . He has used the two Odes of Horace for purposes which are different from Horace's purposes, but without any sense of violence in the adaptation" (307). This is a clear case of eristic imitation as practiced by the Neo-Latin humanists.

Structurally, Garcilaso's ode can be discussed from many points of view, since it is one of his richest works. In the conclusion of this chapter I wish to examine how Garcilaso combines the traditional form of the ode, characterized by surprising juxtapositions, with a tightly structured subtextual unity. Like a number of poems in the late period, the ode begins discussing style, as the poet rejects the martial style of the epic and settles into a persuasive mood. The lady is introduced as the main topic, and the harm she has caused to the poet's friend is described. The digression or fabula, the myth of Anaxarete who refused to correspond the love of Iphis and was turned into stone serves as a moral example to remind the mistress of the consequences of not corresponding his friend's love. The poem concludes repeating the moral admonishment to the lady. The first two stanzas describe the mythic powers of the poetry and music of Orpheus:

> Ode ad florem Gnidi
> Si de mi baxa lira
> tanto pudiesse el son que en un momento
> aplacase la ira
> del animoso viento
> y la furia del mar y el movimiento,
>
> y en ásperas montañas
> con el süave canto enterneciesse
> las fieras alimañas,
> los árboles moviesse
> y al son confusamente los truxiesse:
>
> (1–10)

In the next two stanzas, he rejects the martial themes of epic poetry, describing the horror of the conquered in war:

> no pienses que cantado
> sería de mí, hermosa flor de Gnido,
> el fiero Marte ayrado,
> a muerte convertido,
> de polvo y sangre y de sudor teñido.
>
> ni aquellos capitanes
> en las sublimes ruedas colocados,
> por quien los alemanes,
> el fiero cuello atados,
> y los franceses van domesticados;
>
> (10–20)

The next three stanzas identify the true theme of the poem, the powers
of the beloved over the lover, who becomes a captive galley slave in
Venus's conch shell:

> mas solamente aquella
> fuerça de tu beldad seria cantada,
> y alguna vez con ella
> también seria notada
> el aspereza de que estás armada,
>
> y cómo por ti sola
> y por tu gran valor y hermosura,
> convertido en vïola,
> llora su desventura
> el miserable amante en tu figura.
>
> Hablo d'aquel cativo
> de quien tener se deve más cuidado,
> que 'stá muriendo bivo,
> al remo condenado,
> en la concha de Venus amarrado.
>
> (21–35)

The next five stanzas describe the transformations effected in the lover.
The anaphora of "por ti," which begins four of the stanzas, successfully
unites them in structure and meaning. Each of the four stanzas describes
a different area in which the lover has lost his natural vigor. In the first
he has lost his desire to conform to the natural order of his person:

> Por ti, como solía,
> del áspero cavallo no corrige
> la furia y gallardía,
> ni con freno la rige,
> ni con bivas espuelas ya l'aflige;
> (36–40)

In the second, he has lost his passion for arms:

> por ti con diestra mano
> no rebuelve la espada presurosa,
> y en el dudoso llano
> huye la polvorosa
> palestra como sierpe ponçoñosa;
> (41–45)

In the third, he has lost his passion for letters:

> por ti su blanda musa,
> en lugar de la cíthera sonante,
> tristes querellas usa
> que con llanto abundante
> hacen bañar el rostro del amante;
> (46–50)

In the fourth and fifth, he has willfully destroyed his friendship with the poet:

> por ti el mayor amigo
> l'es importuno, grave y enojoso:
> yo puedo ser testigo,
> que ya del peligroso
> naufragio fuy su puerto y su reposo,
>
> y agora en tal manera
> vence el dolor a la razón perdida
> que ponçoñosa fiera
> nunca fue aborrecida
> tanto como yo dél, ni tan temida.
> (51–60)

The next eight stanzas retell the Ovidian myth of the transformation of Anaxarete into stone because of her refusal to accept the love of Iphis, who hanged himself. The first stanza admonishes the Neapolitan lady to avoid the fate of Anaxarete:

> No fuiste tú engendrada
> ni produzida de la dura tierra;
> no deve ser notada
> que ingratamente yerra
> quien todo el otro error de sí destierra.
> (61–65)

The next stanza summarizes the narrations within the context of the warning to the haughty lady:

> Hágate temerosa
> el caso de Anaxárete, y covarde,
> que de ser desdeñosa
> se arrepentió muy tarde,
> y assí su alma con su mármol arde.
> (66–70)

Garcilaso chose to present the myth, not as a narrative, but as the description of an unmoving plastic image. He represents one emblematic moment in the story in which neither figure moves. Unlike his source Ovid, who is also describing transformations, Garcilaso does not present a narrative sequence, but focuses on the moment that Anaxarete sees her dead lover:

> Estávase alegrando
> del mal ageno el pecho empedernido
> cuando, abaxo mirando,
> el cuerpo muerto vido
> del miserable amante allí tendido,
> (71–75)

The image is an emblem of Anaxarete's disdain and haughtiness. The narrative leaves her "abajo mirando" and shifts to a description of her lover Iphis (not named) who has hanged himself:

> y al cuello el lazo atado
> con que desenlazó de la cadena
> el corazón cuytado,
> y con su breve pena
> compró la eterna punición agena.
>
> (76–80)

The narrative shifts back, without break, to Anaxarete who has not moved, and remaining immobile, she slowly changes into marble, remaining fixed in the same posture forever:

> Sentió allí convertirse
> en piedad amorosa el aspereza.
> ¡Oh tarde arrepentirse!
> ¡Oh última terneza!
> ¿Cómo te sucedió mayor dureza?
>
> Los ojos s'enclavaron
> en el tendido cuerpo que allí vieron;
> los huessos se tornaron
> más duros y crecieron
> y en sí toda la carne convertieron;
>
> las entrañas eladas
> tornaron poco a poco en piedra dura;
> por las venas cuytadas
> la sangre su figura
> iva desconociendo y su natura,
>
> hasta que finalmente,
> en duro mármol buelta y transformada,
>
> (81–97)

Finally she herself is converted into a subject of wonder and amazement to the people.

> hizo de sí la gente
> no tan maravillada
> quanto de aquella ingratitud vengada.
>
> (98–100)

Garcilaso's narration has centered around one unmoved plastic image. The narrative details move forward and backward from the haughty lady caught in one brief moment that freezes and captures her image for eternity. The last two stanzas draw a moral from the story, and serve as a final warning to the haughty mistress:

> No quieras tú, señora,
> de Némesis ayrada las saetas
> provar, por Dios, agora;
> baste que tus perfettas
> obras y hermosura a los poetas
>
> den inmortal materia,
> sin que también en verso lamentable
> celebren la miseria
> d'algún caso notable
> que por ti passe, triste, miserable.
>
> (101–10)

Since the appearance of the sixteenth-century commentators, Garcilaso's ode has been purported to refer to specific people. El Brocense claimed the two figures were Fabio Galeota and Violante Sanseverino, and there is a love poem by Fabio Galeota addressed to this lady (B-45). Herrera reacted sharply to this identification, claiming the two figures were Mario Galeota, Garcilaso's friend, and Catalina Sanseverino (H-246). Accepting, somewhat illogically, a compromise of the two commentaries, modern critics maintain that the title of the poem and its translation in stanza 3, "hermosa flor de Gnido," refer to a Neapolitan lady, Violante Sanseverino, whose family lived in the Seggio di Nido district of Naples; hence she is the flower of Nido. Her first name is recalled in the sixth stanza where her suffering admirer has been changed into a "viola." For the lover they have substituted Mario Galeota, to whom Garcilaso addressed Sonnet XXXV and who is mentioned in the second Latin ode as "Marius Meus." This identification is somewhat illogical, attempting to reduce Garcilaso's circle of friends to those already known. Everyone had agreed, even Herrera, that the lover's last name is referred to in the poem through wordplay in stanza 7, where Garcilaso puns on his last name Galeota and "galeote," a galley slave in the shell of Venus.

As the Spanish critics have so often pointed out, in the Ode ad florem Gnidi, Garcilaso speaks on behalf of a friend. The poet enters into the poem from the beginning, when he refers to "mi baxa lira." He reiterates his presence in lines 11 and 12: "no pienses que cantado sería de mí." In lines 20 through 25, where the poet identifies the true theme of the poem, he again uses the passive voice, but does not refer to himself. In lines 51 through 60 the speaker identifies himself as a friend of the simpering lover. He says the lover can no longer stand the presence of "el mayor amigo" (51), and that the poet is a witness of this fact, since "fuy su puerto y su reposo" (55) after the shipwreck of his emotions. And now, in the unnatural state of affairs of the sick lover, the friend is more abhorred by the lover than a poisonous beast. The speaker pleads and argues on behalf of a stricken friend. In this unusual poetic posture, the speaker is not the lover, but a friend of the lover who comments on the disrupted social order that the hard-heartedness of the beloved has caused. Like the voice of the *demos* in the choral odes of classical tragedy, Garcilaso argues on behalf of the social good. He does not present the lover as the most desirable of suitors, but argues that the beloved's coldness has caused grave social ills that will in turn come to affect her person unless remedied. From the point of view of the speaker and the arguments he presents, Garcilaso's ode corresponds perfectly to the classical ode in its view of society and the social good.

The addressee in the poem is unusual from several aspects. Although she is the beloved, she is not the beloved of the speaker. Her historical presence is conflated with the identity of Venus, and even though she is identified with a deity, she is addressed with the less formal "tú" form. The transition from the concept of the lady as lord in courtly love poetry to a real person could result in the change from the formal "vos" to the informal "tú." In addition, the classical influence (Latin has only the "tu" form) could be a determining factor, with the result that, even though deified, the lady is not addressed with "vos" as are other mythological figures.

The addressee plays a large role in the poem, with more than a dozen references to her and her beauty: "hermosa flor de Gnido" (12), "aquella fuerça de tu beldad" (21–22), "tu gran valor y hermosura" (27), and once her harshness is noted: "el aspereza de que estás armada" (25). As subject of the verb, the lady is often addressed with command forms: "no pienses" (11) and "no quieras" (101), or is the object of an imperative form: "Hágate temerosa" (66). The two indicative forms refer to her harshness "estás armada" (25) and her breeding "No fuiste tú engendrada / ni produzida de la dura tierra" (61–62). In nearly half the references, the addressee is referred to as the object of the pronoun "por," with the intention of casting blame on her hard and cold rejection of the lamentable lover. The "por ti," which initiates in repetitive style four separate stanzas (lines 36, 41, 46, and 51), first occurs in line 26: "y cómo por ti sola," and is specified in line 27: "y por tu gran valor y hermosura." It recurs in the last line of the poem, as the poet reminds the lady that she does not want to be remembered for the hardness of her character, nor would she want poets to celebrate her for the misery she has caused "d'algún caso notable / que por ti passe, triste, miserable" (109–10). The lady in this ode is not the exalted recipient of a flattering message, but of commands and object forms that impute to her the blame of grave social ills.

The Ode ad florem Gnidi integrates many diverse elements, stories, and arguments that form a brilliant, scintillating surface texture. Rather than strive for surface unity, Garcilaso works to unify the poem on sub-textual levels. One of the methods of unifying the poem concerns the theme of conversion. Garcilaso solves the problem of the transformations in a variety of ways. The first metamorphosis, the transformation of nature through the effects of poetry, simply recalls the myth of Orpheus; since Garcilaso merely expresses a wish to possess such powers, he needs only describe the effects of the mythical poetry without positing a specific cause. The second transformation, that of the warrior into a weak-willed lover, is accomplished through myth and astrology. The third transformation, the conversion of the hard-hearted Anaxarete into a marble statue at the sight of her dead suitor, is achieved through a series of parallels with the first part of the poem. As in his other long poems, Garcilaso uses the repetition of vocabulary to unify the various parts of the poem. Since transformations provide one of the major themes in the poem, the words for transformation abound, especially in the section on Anaxarete: "Sentió allí *convertirse* / en piedad amorosa el aspereza" (81–82), "los huessos *se tornaron* / más duros" (87–88), "y en sí toda la carne *convertieron*" (90), "las entrañas eladas / *tornaron* poco a poco en piedra dura" (91–92), and "en duro mármol *buelta* y *transformada*" (97). The word *convertido* occurs previously in the description of Mars: "el fiero Marte ayrado / a muerte *convertido*" (13–14), and in the description of the pallid lover: "*convertido* en vïola" (28). Along with the changes in nature produced by Orpheus's music and the changed nature of the lover described in lines 36–60, the repetition of the key word "convertido" and its synonyms provides a sense of unity to the diverse myths and sections of the poem.

In addition, other words link the fable of Anaxarete to the other sections of the poem. The word "fiera" occurs in the descriptions of Orpheus: "las fieras alimañas" (8), of Mars: "el fiero Marte" (13) and "el fiero cuello" (19), and of the lover: "ponçoñosa fiera" (58). The concept of death refers to Mars: "a muerte convertido" (14), the lover: "que 'stá muriendo vivo" (33), and Iphis: "el cuerpo muerto" (74). "Sangre" appears in the description of Mars: "de polvo y sangre y de sudor teñido" (15) and Anaxarete: "la sangre su figura / iva desconociendo" (94–95). "Figura" refers first to Venus: "tu figura" (30) and later to Anaxarete: "su figura" (94). "Amante" refers to the suffering Galeota: "el miserable amante" (30 and 50) and Iphis: "del miserable amante" (75). "Aspero" and "aspereza" refer to the locale of Orpheus' song: "en ásperas montañas" (6), the armor of Venus: "el aspereza de que estás armada" (25), the horse that the lover no longer controls "del áspero cavallo no corrige" (37), and the character of Anaxarete: "Sentió allí convertirse / en piedad amorosa el aspereza" (81–82). Finally there is great similarity in the phrases used to describe those conquered in war and Iphis, who commits suicide. The Germans and French are tied and led in defeat by the neck and Iphis hangs himself:

> el fiero cuello atados (19)
>
> y al cuello el lazo atado (76).

In addition, a number of words and phrases are repeated in the moral judgment that concludes the poem. "Ayrado" refers to Mars: "el fiero Marte ayrado" (13) and Nemesis: "de Némesis ayrada las saetas" (102). The concept of beauty refers throughout to the "hermosa flor de Gnido" (12): "la fuerça de tu beldad" (22), "por tu gran valor y hermosura" (27), and "tus perfettas / obras y hermosura" (104–5). "Miserable" and "miseria" refer to the weakened lovers (30 and 75) and the scandal that would occur if she persists in her cruelty:

> celebren la miseria
> d'algún caso notable
> que por ti passe, triste, miserable.
> (108–10)

The word "triste," which had previously referred to the lover: "tristes querellas" (48) also reappears in the last line with "miserable" in reference to the beloved. The word "notado" refers to the poetic process itself, describing the contents of the poem: "también seria notada / el aspereza de que estás armada" (24–25), the admonishment to the beloved to avoid the fate of Anaxarete: "no deve ser notada" (63), and resurfaces in the penultimate line as "d'algún caso notable" (109). The constant repetitions of vocabulary are quite numerous and remarkable for their density. The even flow and the elegant phrasing along with the shifts of focus tend to gloss over the numerous repetitions, which must be some of the most dense in any of Garcilaso's poems. The more heterogenous the material treated in the poem, the more intense are the repetitions to create on a subtextual level a sense of unity.

Another of the methods that Garcilaso uses to give unity to the ode is a constant distinction between wild, destructive, and uncivilized forces in contrast to the taming, soft, and cultured effects of civilization, a distinction represented mythically by Mars and Venus. From the description of the song of Orpheus to the moral conclusion of the story of Anaxarete, the distinction between the hard and the soft, the wild and the civilized is evident. In the description of Orpheus's song, the untamed elements, "la ira de animoso viento" (3–4), "la furia del mar" (5), "ásperas montañas" (6), and "las fieras alimañas" (8), are counterbalanced by the soft elements, "aplacase" (3), "el süave canto" (7), and "enterneciesse" (7). In the martial song he will not sing, the hostile elements, "fiero Marte ayrado" (13) and "fiero cuello" (19), are checked by the participles "atados" (19) and "domesticados" (20). In the description of the transformed lover, "el áspero cavallo" (37), "la furia y gallardía" (38), "importuno, grave y enojoso" (52), and "ponçoñosa fiera" (58) are balanced by "corrige" (37), "con freno la rige" (39), and "su puerto y su reposo" (55). In the story of Anaxarete, the words indicating hardness and harshness of the beloved, "dura tierra" (62), "el pecho empedernido" (72), "dureza" (85), "huessos" (88), "piedra dura" (92), and "duro mármol" (97), are contrasted by soft elements: "en piedad amorosa" (82), "terneza" (84), and "carne" (90); the fire and harshness, "arde" (70) and "el aspereza" (82), are opposed by the cowardly and suicidal, "temerosa" (66), "covarde" (67), and "el lazo atado" (76). In the moral conclusion, the "saetas" (102) of vengeance are to be combatted by the beauty and civilized deeds of the lady.

In the constant opposition between the untamed and the tamed, the hard and the soft, Mars and Venus, and their counterparts the real lovers, partake of both worlds; in fact, the argument of the poem rests on these changes. The central stanzas (lines 41–60) describing the transformed lover emphasize his transformation from his natural spirited self to a helpless, simpering lover. Conversely, Venus has become hard and harsh, and the story of Anaxarete warns her that her continued hardness will result in an unnatural state, not only for her lover, but also for herself. The stanza describing Venus (lines 21–25), the subject of the poem, rest on a duality. He will sing of the force of her beauty, "la fuerça de tu beldad (22), and also her harshness "el aspereza de que estás armada" (25). This, too, for Venus is an unnatural state, and the poet argues that she should avoid this hard exterior armor, inappropriate to her, in order to restore the lover to his natural state. The constant division of elements into the wild and domesticated provides an underlying unity to the poem and makes clear the central argument by tying together the various elements of the poem and showing how the central figures participate in both.

Another unusual element in this poem, and it is one of the few times Garcilaso employs it, is the use of puns, which are of sufficient number and thematic importance that they must form part of the plan of the poem:

1. **Gnido.** Dunn has pointed out that the reference to Gnidi, with the addition of the curious G, serves as a double reference to the beautiful inhabitant of the Seggio de Nido in Naples and to Venus who had an important temple at Cnidus, which was written "Gnidus" in Renaissance Latin and "Gnido" in Italian texts. This along with the reference to the shell in stanza 7 in which Venus was born firmly establish the presence of Venus in the poem.
2. **Marte / muerte.** In the phrase "el fiero Marte / a muerte convertido" (13–14), the closeness of the sounds of the two words and the verb "convertido" pun on the disastrous planetary sign of Mars. Since Saturn was known as the greater misfortune and Mars the lesser misfortune, it is easy to imagine Mars converted into a sign of death.
3. **Vïola.** As Sotelo Salas suggested (Garcilaso: *Obra* 151), and Whitby (136–40) later argued in a note, the "vïola" (27) is not only a flower, but also a viol which weeps the lover's misfortunes: "convertido en vïola, / llora su desventura / el miserable amante" (27–30).
4. **Figura.** A clearer reference to astrology occurs in stanza 6 with the

word "figura," which usually means "face" in Golden Age poetry, as it probably does in line 94. It is a horoscope, or plotting of the positions of the stars, as in Boscán's Sonnet VI. Here it refers to the face of the beloved and the planet Venus moving into the lover's horoscope.

5. **Galeote.** The pun on the lover's name, Galeota, and his servitude as an oarsman, "galeote," in Venus's shell, has already been explained.

6. **Concha de Venus.** Herrera first pointed out the erotic double-entendre of this expression: "Fingen que Venus va en concha por el mar, dejando la causa principal, que no es tan honesta que la permita nuestra lengua; porque el mantenimiento de este género conmueve el incentivo de la lujuria" (H-259).

7. **Cíthera.** There is another subtle reference to Venus in stanza 10, and like the previous references it involves a pun (Cruz, *Imitación* 68–69). The original edition spells the second syllable of "cítara" with "t, h, e," instead of "t, a." The spelling "cithera" recalls the island, Cythera, where Venus came ashore on her shell. Thus, the phrase "en lugar de" means both "in the place or site of" and "instead of." Likewise, the word "cíthera" serves double duty: (1) It is a sonorous musical instrument that has been replaced by the lover's laments and (2) it is the place from which his muse sings, inhabiting the very island of Venus's birth set in the resounding sea.

8. **Anaxarete.** As Don Cameron Allen has shown in case after case, Renaissance mythographers often looked to the etymology (or invented etymology) of the name as a clue to the hidden meaning of the myth. The extended argument of Garcilaso's lines "no fuiste tú engendrada / ni produzida de la dura tierra" (61–62), suggests that he too found a hidden meaning in Anaxarete's name. The *Dictionnaire Grec-Français* of J. Planché (1838) gives a verb and a noun similar to Anaxarete's name: *Anaxeraino* means to "faire secher; dessécher," and *Anaxeranois* is "desséchement, dessication." The fact that Anaxarete's name could be construed to mean to dry out suggests her earthlike nature, and makes logical, in a mythological manner, her conversion to stone. The idea that people are generated by the land in which they grew up was widely diffused. Horace may be the source of the idea in poetry, in his Ode I, xxii, as shown in Fray Luis's translation: "la tierra donde mora / el moro, de fiereza engendradora" (II, 924). Gracián quotes a stanza from Góngora that plays on the same idea:

> Estremo de la hermosas
> y estremo de las crueles:

hija al fin de sus arenas
engendradoras de sierpes.
(249a)

Garcilaso repeats the same idea in Elegy II: "en la arenosa Libya, engendradora / de toda cosa ponçoñosa y fiera" (176–77).

Considering the various puns and wordplays as a whole, such as "vïola," "galeote," and "cíthera," it is obvious that they represent the Neoplatonic desire for synthesis. Not only are the Neoplatonic texts filled with the words "harmony" and "concord"; they also try to synthesize unharmonious elements, such as pagan myth and Christianity, and pagan philosophy and Christian theology. While this juxtaposition and synthesis of diversity and opposites is not as marked as in seventeenth-century poetic conceits, which purposely juxtapose opposites, it still indeed occurs in sixteenth-century poetry.

One striking element in the ode is the many references to music. Ode in Greek comes from the verb signifying to sing, and it probably was originally a musical composition. Even though Garcilaso's ode is a written text, the imagery of song abounds throughout the poem. In line 1 he refers to "mi baxa lira." In line 2 he refers to the magical powers of the sound of his song. Line 7 mentions "el süave canto," and line 10 repeats the word "son." In addressing the flower of Gnido, he refers to his poem as singing " no pienses que cantado / sería de mí" (11–12). In naming the true subject of the poem, he repeats the verb "cantada" (22). As mentioned above, "vïola" (28) refers to a viol as well as a flower. In enumerating the changes wrought in the personality of the miserable lover, he mentions the "cíthera sonante" that the lover has abandoned because of his weeping. The continual reiteration of musical metaphors seems to be another element in Garcilaso's ode that takes its lead from Neoplatonic philosophy. The emphasis on world harmony and the music of the spheres is one of the more popular themes of Platonic philosophy.

Garcilaso's use of Neoplatonic imagery in the ode is quite different from the use in the sonnets, where he uses the ideas of Neoplatonic philosophy of love to describe his own emotions. In the ode his Neoplatonism is implicit rather than explicitly stated in the message. Unlike a Neoplatonic love sonnet, which teaches Neoplatonic philosophy by comparing the lover's experience to some aspect of that theory, Garcilaso does not didactically teach some aspect of Neoplatonic philosophy in this poem. In the sonnets of both Garcilaso and Boscán, Neoplatonism is a program or system of belief that the poems simultaneously explicate and use to describe the inner emotions of the poet-lover. In the ode the Neoplatonic imagery serves to unify the poem and to help make the argument that harmony in world affairs comes from requited love. Garcilaso is not proposing and explaining a program of action to reach mystical heights. To the contrary, he is referring to the ideas of Neoplatonic harmony as a system of received ideas that make his arguments more logical. The references to music and the use of puns remind one more of the Platonic dialogues themselves than the philosophical systems that had been extracted from them by Renaissance philosophers.

Garcilaso's major influences in his one ode derive from Bernardo Tasso's mandate to imitate the classical poets of antiquity. Garcilaso undertook this challenge and endeavored through his own studies to achieve in the vernacular the type of ode written by Horace and Pindar. In this chapter I have shown how he assumed the voice of the public good, in place of the plaintive voice of the courtly lover, and expressed the new morality of public good through striking imagery, typical of Horace and Pindar. Since Garcilaso was uncomfortable with a scintillating surface that failed to achieve a unified vision, he employed numerous repetitions of words and ideas to unify the disparate parts of the poem. He also employed several devices, such as puns, to draw upon the imagery associated with the Neoplatonic movement to achieve an overall effect of unity.

15

The Ode ad florem Gnidi as Iconological Mystery

As detailed in the last chapter Garcilaso's Ode ad florem Gnidi represented a major innovation in Spanish literature. The importance of this innovation is seen throughout the Spanish Renaissance. In spite of taking his inspiration in Tasso's metric formulation of the ode, Garcilaso treated the genre differently, creating various devices to give unity to a poem whose surface texture should surprise the reader with its discontinuous imagery. In this chapter I shall argue that Garcilaso brings to literature in his ode an imitation of the iconological mystery invented by Renaissance artists. In the Ode ad florem Gnidi, Garcilaso's employment of mythology—the *fabula* advocated by Bernardo Tasso—partakes of other Renaissance traditions, far exceeding the dissimulated use of myth in the Petrarchan manner and the use of mythology in the sonnets to break with the poetic posture of a compromised suffering lover. In his ode Garcilaso also takes a different direction from Tasso who re-creates the pagan spirit in his odes through descriptions of altars, incense, burning sacrifices, and other pagan rites. In Garcilaso's one ode myths are, as in Renaissance paintings and philosophy, presented as iconological mysteries—images whose symbolic allusions produce a complex structure of parallel meanings.

Mythology is essential to Garcilaso's ode. Mythological allusions become an integral part of the poetic exposition, and nearly every phase of the argument is expounded through myth. In the first ten lines the poet compares himself to Orpheus, wishing he had the powers of Orpheus to tame storms and wild beasts and move inanimate trees. Lines 11 through 20 discuss Mars and the martial style in poetry, those elements he would not treat had he Orpheus's powers. Lines 11 and 12 introduce the addressee, who is a Venus figure. Lines 26 through 35 deal with the force of Venus to subdue the warrior Mars. With line 35, the myth comparisons end as Garcilaso describes the changes brought about in his suffering friend. The fable in this poem is, however, mythic, relating the magical transformation of Anaxarete into stone. Even as he draws the moral lesson from the fable, Garcilaso mythifies the conclusion with the reference to Nemesis, the goddess of vengeance. The strategy of mythifying each section of the action provides further points of unity in the composition.

Garcilaso employs two aspects of the occult in his Ode ad florem Gnidi. The first is a reference to the astrological position of the planets Mars and Venus. This provides an added dimension to the metaphorical argument of the poem and recalls the newly forged Neoplatonic doctrines of astrological forces. In addition, the poem involves a second type of occult literature, for it is conceived in the tradition of the iconological mystery so popular among Florentine Renaissance writers and painters. Garcilaso's use of mythology in the ode far exceeds the casual sort of ornamental allusions common in other poems. Previous critics have argued that Garcilaso employed mythology essentially as an adornment to his poetry (Cammarata), or that the myths were personal, paralleling and revealing the poet's inner psychological state (Poullain, "Le Thème" 358–63, and Correa). Guillou-Varga maintains that all the myths in Garcilaso's poetry relate to the elements of water and fire, which she sees as a key to the poetic universe of Garcilaso (394): "C'est l'élémentisation' du mythe qui lui donne une vie poétique nouvelle, autentiquement personelle" (395). Dunn argues specifically that Garcilaso did not conceive of myth in his ode in the Neoplatonic manner of concealing deeper theological truths. Against these interpretations I shall argue that Garcilaso constructs his ode as an iconological mystery, a genre popular among Renaissance artists.

The iconological mystery, a type of Renaissance painting, grows out of the combination of two different Renaissance concepts concerning mythology and painting. In the first concept, pagan myths were believed to embody deep theological mysteries (Walker, "Orpheus" 105–6). The belief that the pagan myths hid mysterious meanings began with the Church fathers, who asserted that the great pagan philosophers had studied in Egypt with Moses and, even though the philosophers were aware of the Judeo-Christian revelation, they had to cloak these truths in fables in order to present them to a nonbelieving public, either to avoid debasing the truth or to cover it with a fable acceptable to pagans. Boccaccio in the fourteenth and fifteenth books of his *De geneologia deorum* argued that myths were fables invented to conceal theological truths that ancient sages feared to reveal to an unprepared and uniniti-ated public. These arguments were reinforced by the Renaissance Neo-platonists, who reiterated the arguments that the ancient poets had taken their learning from Moses in Egypt and thus had access to the true reve-lations of God, which they then masked in their fables in order to make the sacred truths available and acceptable to a large audience, at the same time blunting the full force of the revelation by enclosing it in pleasing disguises. The sixteenth-century Spanish writer Juan de Pineda in his *Diálogos familiares de agricultura cristiana* concluded that these veiled revelations to the pagans were part of God's plan and perhaps were even superior to Holy Scripture (1:72). He affirms they were quite effective since the Jews, who had a direct revelation, had not converted to Chris-tianity, but the pagans, receivers of the disguised revelation in mythology, had accepted Christianity (1:76). In his study *Mysteriously Meant*, Don Cameron Allen painstakingly documented the Renaissance reading hab-its that looked to pagan fable and myth for kernels of hidden truths, often Christian truths. The idea that all fiction, as well as nature itself, is a mask for hidden (occult) inner truths was a common Renaissance conception concerning mythology. Allen's study contradicts the earlier views of the Renaissance as a period that tired of medieval allegoriza-tions and reproduced much shortened allegories only as a moral pretext for enjoying the stories and myths of the pagans. To the contrary, Allen shows an increased interest in allegory beginning early in the Renais-sance and continuing, at times, well into the eighteenth century.

The second idea essential to the iconological mystery was the creation of a type of painting that would fulfill Horace's observation that poetry was like painting ("ut pictura poesis"). Renaissance painters and theore-ticians actually reversed the concept to read that painting was like poetry, and more important, read it prescriptively: that painting must be like poetry. There are two significant ways in which poetry and painting are not at all alike. Painting consists of a flat image which contains meaning only in the context of the written word or some mutually understood cultural context. Icons from prehistoric cultures have no intrinsic meanings to us, and the meanings established for them are conjectures by modern scholars—writing that supplies meaning to the image. Gombrich states succinctly the problem of ascribing meaning to icons: "Images apparently occupy a curious position somewhere between the statements of language, which are intended to convey a meaning, and the things of nature, which we only can give a meaning" (2). Painting also differs from poetry in that it does not manifest a temporal sequence. The painting can be viewed from left to right, top to bottom, or vice versa, but very few paintings can be said to contain a narrative sequence in which the various elements should be viewed. In fulfilling the prescription to make painting like poetry, Renaissance artists employed a variety of means. One was to use figures that could be identified, such as allegorical figures or mythological figures that could be juxtaposed in a variety of meaningful combinations or postures. These figures already contained deeper meanings, and their new context provided further reflections on possible meanings for the painting. They also solved the lack of sequential development by choosing a moment that carried greater import, either by representing a key moment in a narrative sequence, or an emblematic situation with meaning on several exegetical levels.

Renaissance mythology is much more complex than previously thought. As Seznec, Wind, Gombrich, and Panofsky have made clear, Renaissance myths are like classical pagan myths in that they use the same figures and utilize some of the same sources, but their unique elaborations in the Renaissance incorporate diverse later material, such as medieval moralizations, Platonic allegorizations, and scientific associations from both natural and occult sciences. The syncretic methodology that grew out of medieval thought, but was given a great boost by the Neoplatonic writers in Florence, attempts to synthesize not only pagan mythology and Christianity, but also science and mysticism with myth and Christian teachings. This syncretism, which becomes something of a mental habit among Renaissance writers, has its basis in occult beliefs in a hidden (occult) key to all of existence. Underlying the numerous associations of different beliefs and systems of knowledge is a belief that nature and the supernatural can be fathomed and its forces harnessed and utilized for the common benefit of human civilization. For these writers, pagan mythology, magical superstitions, and simple natural forces could all be clues leading to the comprehension of ultimate knowledge.

Several of the myths referred to in the Ode ad florem Gnidi share the composite nature of the Renaissance myth. In line 25, Garcilaso makes reference to the Armed Venus: "el aspereza de que estás armada." The mythological figure of the Armed Venus was important both in literature and to a lesser degree in art. Since no full treatment exists of this theme in Renaissance literature and art, I shall document part of its extension. Gyraldo in his *De Deis gentium* reported that the Armed Venus had a cult among the Lacedemonians where the women armed themselves and defended their country while their husbands were engaged in war. He quotes sources in Lactantius, Pausanias, and Quintillian (141), and he also quotes one of the major sources of the myth, a witty epigram from the *Greek Anthology:*

> Pallas, seeing Cytherea in arms, said: "Cypris, wouldst thou that we went to the judgment so?" But she, with a gentle smile, answered: "Why should I lift up a shield in combat? If I conquer when naked, how will it be when I arm myself?" (16:174)

This epigram, along with several others that mention Venus in arms, was very popular among the Neo-Latin poets, and there exist fifty-six Renaissance epigrams treating the Armed Venus (Hutton, *Greek Anthology* 78). First translated into Latin by Ausonius (c. 310–c. 395), a second Latin translation was added to the 1496 edition of Ausonius's works. This has been assigned to Giorgio Merula (c. 1424–94), a Milanese teacher and historian (Hutton, *Greek Anthology* 24–25; 102–5). Both versions (reproduced in Hutton, *Greek Anthology* 105) are close translations of the original Greek, as is the version by Minturno (Hutton, *Greek Anthology* 233). Such close reproductions of the original Greek epigram represent a desire to popularize Greek literature among a Latin reading public. This type of imitation is reproductive rather than eristic. Ariosto, however, gives the idea an original twist, stating that Venus has no need of armor to conquer:

> Arma, Venus, Martis sunt haec. Quid inutile pondus,
> Mortali bellum si meditare subis?

Nil opus est ferro, ferri cum nuda potentem
   Exueris spoliis omnibus ipsa deum.
                    (Hutton, *Greek Anthology* 162)

(These, Venus, are Mars's arms. What a useless weight,
   to put on if you are thinking of a war against mortals.
You do not need this iron, you will pluck all the spoils
   of iron from this powerful god with your nakedness.)

The two versions by Sannazaro (published in 1526) attempt to gloss the original, eliciting further points from its wit. In the first, he reworks the theme of the Armed Venus by placing Mars and Venus face to face (in opposition, as they appear in sixteenth-century iconology) and recalling Venus's role in the siege of Troy:

DE VENERE, ET MARTE
Dum Venus armatum complectitur obvia Martem,
   Distrinxit teneram fibula adunca manum.
Sensit, & ante Jovem ridens ait aemula Pallas;
   Bella iterum gessit cum Diomede soror.
                    (*Poemata* 127)

ON VENUS AND MARS
While Venus embraced face to face Mars armed
   she opened with tender hand the curved clasp of his armor.
Her rival Pallas noted it, and before Jove laughing she said:
   "His sister will wage war again with Diomedes."

In the second, the sun (Apollo) refers to Vulcan's entrapment of Mars and Venus in a strong invisible net that held them captives in the coital position and to the ridicule of the other gods:

DE VENERE ET SOLE
Induerat thoraca humeris, geleamque decoro
   Aptarat capiti Marte iubente Venus.
'Nil opus his,' Sol, 'Diva,' inquit; 'sumenda fuerunt,
   Cum vos ferratae circuiere plagae.'
                    (*Poemata* 154)

ON VENUS AND THE SUN

Venus had placed the breast-plate on her shoulders, and
  adjusted
the helmet beautifully on her head with Mars' help.
"None of this is necessary, goddess," said the Sun,
"you need only put an iron net around you."

The version by Navagero, the Italian poet who introduced Boscán to
the Italian style, enjoyed great popularity and was often reprinted. Following the precepts of competitive imitation, he found a contemporary
significance in the figure of the Armed Venus. The moralizing tone of the
closing phrases recalls the epigrams or commentary that explained the
hidden meaning of Renaissance emblems:

De imagine sui armata

Quid magis adversum bello est? bellique tumultu
  Quam Venus? ad teneros aptior illa iocos.
Et tamen armatam hanc magni pinxere Lacones,
  Imbellique data est bellica parma deae.
Quippe erat id signum forti Lacedaemone natum:
  Saepe et femineum bella decere genus.
Sic quoque non quod sim pugna versatus in ulla,
  Haec humeris pictor induit arma meis.
Verum hoc quod bello, hoc patriae quod tempore iniquo,
  Ferre vel imbellem quem libet arma decet.

(74)

(What is more averse to war and the tumult of war
than Venus? She is more suited to tender sport.
And yet, the great Spartans have depicted her armed,
and a warlike shield has been given the unwarlike goddess.
Indeed, it was a token natural to fierce Sparta,
and often adorned her females in war.
So also, the painter has depicted this armor on my shoulders,
not because I have taken part in any battle,
but because in this war, in this terrible time for our country,
it becomes everyone, however unwarlike, to bear arms.)

(75)

The theme was also very popular in Spanish in the Golden Age. The seventeenth-century Portuguese poet Antonio Barbosa Bacelar (1610–63) treated it in a sonnet in Spanish:

> Vestio-se Venus el arnes de Marte,
>   y le adornò de mucha pluma y galas:
>   Llegò en esto la Diosa Palas,
>   y sonriendo le dixo d'esta arte:
> Coraçon has tenido para armarte,
>   [¿]de adonde tanto brio, y tantas alas?
>   Venus, que via sus entrañas malas,
>   metiendo mano puso-se de parte.
> Con este braço, dize, y esta espada,
>   quando del Cielo todo el resto acuda,
>   le mostrarè que tu potencia es nada,
> Bien saben tu blason, pero quien duda
>   que oy te puedo rendir estando armada,
>   si cuando te vencì estaba desnuda.
>   (Pereira da Sylva 2:99)

As noted previously in treating Garcilaso's epigrammatic sonnets, the form of the sonnet produces a poem that is more wordy and padded than the original epigram. In sonnet form, as these examples make clear, the epigram loses its tautness and point.

A much earlier version by Diego Hurtado de Mendoza (1503–75) is a *copla*, the stanza he used to render successfully in Spanish several classical epigrams. His version, like Ariosto's, states that Venus need only use her nakedness to conquer:

> A Venus
> Vénus se vistió una vez
> En hábito de soldado;
> Páris, ya parte y juez,
> Dijo, de vella espantado:
>   «Hermosura confirmada
> Con ningun traje se muda:
> ¿Véisla cómo vence armada?
> Mejor vencerá desnuda».
>   (430)

This is certainly one of the more successful of the renditions in Spanish. The *copla*, with its tradition of wit and concision, is the perfect vehicle for rendering in the vernacular the effect of the Greek epigram. In the hands of the classical scholar and collector of antiquities, it is more successful than the sonnet.

Two anonymous sonnets, among those published by Foulché-Delbosc, also re-create the theme of Venus in armor. One of the sonnets refers to the Armed Venus as the conqueror who saps Mars's strength and fury, an important aspect of the myth of Mars and Venus in Garcilaso's ode. In this sonnet, Venus speaks more like a scholastic philosopher than the playful goddess of love:

> Dexó las armas Marte enamorado,
> tomólas Venus dulce y amorosa,
> y Palas, viendo tan disforme cosa,
> burlando de los dos ansi a hablado:
>   «Baxeza es el feroz ser delicado,
> soberuia es ser guerrera la medrosa,
> y aun poco es para mi ser vitoriosa
> de Venus fiera, y Marte afeminado».
>   Respondio Venus con desden y brio:
> «Si en los azeros Marte es siempre Marte,
> mudanza de accidente el ser no muda;
>   y a mi que prouarme es desuario,
> que pues vencer te pude ya desnuda,
> armada que hare sino matarte?»
>   (Foulché-Delbosc 512–13)

Lope de Vega also treated the theme in his *Rimas* (1602), using the longer sonnet form to develop sexually provocative love play between Venus and Mars:

> La clara luz, en las estrellas puesta,
> del fogoso León, por alta parte
> bañaba el sol, cuando Acidalia y Marte
> en Chipre estaban una ardiente siesta.
>   La Diosa, por hacerle gusto y fiesta,
> la túnica y el velo deja aparte,

sus armas y de la selva parte,
del yelmo y plumas y el arnés compuesta.
   Pasó por Grecia, y Palas vióla en Tebas,
y díjole: «Esta vez tendrá mi espada
mejores filos en tu blanco acero».
   Venus respondió: «Cuando te atrevas,
verás cuánto mejor te vence armada
la que desnuda te venció primero».

(Obras poéticas 106)

The other anonymous sonnet published by Foulché-Delbosc carries the wit a step further by playing on the fact that Venus not only outdoes Minerva (the goddess of wisdom) in beauty, but also in intelligence:

De relucientes armas la hermosa
Venus acaso armada estuuo vn dia,
a la qual viendo Palas le dezia
con vna risa falsa y desdeñosa:
   «Armada como estás, haze vna cosa,
y es que ambas conbatamos a porfia,
con tal que no aquel Paris que solia
iuzgue nuestra batalla peligrosa».
   Dixo Venus: «De ti estoy espantada,
pues siempre te e tenido hasta agora,
como todos te tienen, por sesuda.
   En que juyzio cabe, di, señora,
ansi menospreciarme estando armada,
si quando te venci estaua desnuda?»

(Foulché-Delbosc 512)

The theme also had some popularity among classical and Renaissance artists. The Armed Venus was one of the figures inscribed on Jason's cloak in the *Argonautica* (Shapiro 281–82). Wind found abundant evidence of the Armed Venus in antiquity: "But side by side with the jocose tradition, which was inherited from the Greek epigrammatists, the Romans retained toward the Armed Venus an attitude of religious respect. . . . she appears on gems and coins of Caesar and Augustus, as a martial figure of Roman peace, of victorious generosity relying on her

strength" (93). Whittkower also traces the Renaissance artistic representations to antiquity: "The gesture of holding a helmet in the outstretched
hand occurs in antiquity not only with 'Minerva Pacifica' but also with
'Venus Victrix', whose cult was set up under Pompey and who was ven-
erated together with 'Victoria' as Goddess of Victory" ("Transformations" 139). A plaquette in the National Gallery in Washington, D.C.
(Fig. 6) portrays the Armed Venus with the inscription "Veneram temeo
armatam" (I fear the Armed Venus) (Pope-Hennessey 108). In her left
hand, she holds Venus's mirror and in her left she holds an arrow. Whittkower studied the fusion of Venus and Minerva in two sixteenth-century
representations of Venus Victrix, an engraving by Agostino Veneziano
(Fig. 7) and a drawing by Marco Zoppo (Whittkower 139). In the engraving, the shield of Minerva lies on the ground to the left of Venus.
"In such a case one is tempted to argue that the artist was simply mistaken. But this is extremely unlikely" (139). Cartari's representations of
the images of the pagan gods, drawn from antique models, include the
Armed Venus and the Venus Victrix (Fig. 8). The Armed Venus (first
figure on the left) holds a shield and the Venus Victrix is seen seated,
holding a mirror and in a small cameo from behind in a pose similar to
that in the engraving of Veneziano. The third in full armor represents the
Venus worshiped by the Lacedemonians in honor of the valor of their
women. A common element in some of these representations is that
Venus is not fully armed, or even fully dressed. She is often nude with a

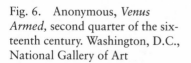

Fig. 6.   Anonymous, *Venus
Armed,* second quarter of the six-
teenth century. Washington, D.C.,
National Gallery of Art

Fig. 7.   Agostino Veneziano, *Venus Victrix*, early sixteenth century

Fig. 8.   Vincenzo Cartari, "Imagine di Venere armata, di Venere vittrice & di Venere in ceppi dinotante la fermezza . . ."

few pieces of armor, such as a headpiece or shield, but not sufficient to cover her nakedness. As stated by Ariosto and Hurtado de Mendoza, the real armor of Venus is her nudity.

Lope de Vega returned to the theme of the Armed Venus in 1624 in his poem *La Circe*. He carries the myth to its final limits, detailing the transformation of Mars into Venus (represented in Garcilaso's ode) and Venus into Minerva (as studied by Whittkower).

> Andaba entonces Marte riguroso,
> depuestas ya las aceradas mallas,
> en la conquista de su rostro hermoso,
> sin ordenar asaltos a murallas; . . .
>   Ya no sabes qué es guerra, ya no formas,
> Marte cruel, en plano o sobre montes;
> así en la hermosa Venus te transformas, . . .
>   Ya son galas de paz, ya son diamantes
> lo que era hebillas y dorados pernos;
> suspiros son los rayos fulminantes,
> que imitan los de Júpiter eternos;
> Venus, que vio sus armas arrogantes,
> sus banderas, sus tropas y gobiernos
> rendidas a sus pies, quiso piadosa
> ser Palas, a su lado, belicosa.
>   (*Obras poéticas* 1066–67)

The numerous representations of Venus in armor, show how a myth, taken from classical historical sources was elaborated and reworked by Renaissance artists and writers. Venus could no longer be just the goddess of love; with armor she becomes her opposite, the cruel unmoved lady, subject of courtly love poetry. Renaissance mythology incorporates numerous references, icons, and ideas to produce a complexity of imagery in which the myths are metamorphosed into new entities that correspond more closely to the reality of contemporary culture.

Returning to Garcilaso's poem, we note an essential difference between the Armed Venus in his ode and the numerous quotations in literature and representations in art. Garcilaso's Venus is armed, not with armor or nudity, but with "el aspereza," the quality in Garcilaso associated with barbarity. In Sonnet XXVIII "aspereza" is contrasted with tender love feelings and associated with the uncivilized "selvatiquez" and "torpeza." It is a major theme in Canción IV where love is an element that brings out the uncivilized and barbaric in the lover. Venus has a dual role as the goddess of love. She exists as a civilizing element that brings civility and culture to the rough and barbaric in society. As the goddess who subdues the savagery of Mars, she is a civilizing force and possesses sufficient power to overcome the fury of aggression. Garcilaso argues that when she rejects love and dons Mars's armor, she becomes an uncivilizing force. Since the Venus flower of Gnido has already conquered her Mars, the armor of her haughty and cruel rejection of him will make her as uncivilized as the forces she has domesticated. In the midst of a Renaissance commonplace, Garcilaso has produced a significant variant that speaks to the general conflict between Mars and Venus and between savagery and civilization in general.

Another mythic association in the Ode ad florem Gnidi is between Venus and violets, the flower into which the lover is converted into line 27. The sixteenth-century commentators clashed stridently over the identification of the beloved and her relationship to the flower. El Brocense claimed it was doña Violante Sanseverino, and she was referred to in the reference to the violet. Herrera was indignant at such an identification: "porque pensar que fue escrita a doña Violante, porque dice: 'Convertido en viola' es conjetura muy flaca, y de poco fundamento" (H-246). He seems offended at the idea of a pun in this passage, falling short of claiming that Garcilaso would never lower himself to such an association. It was Herrera, of course, who eliminated the pun in Gnido. There also exists the possibility that Herrera was aware of the association of the violet with Venus, and found other associations in this passage to be oversubtle. Lázaro Carreter has pointed out the association of violets and Venus in Renaissance literature: "esa flor aparece constantemente asociada a Venus" (120), citing poems by Poliziano and Giovanni Pontano. One could add to his list poems by Sannazaro, Crottus, Navagero, and Brixianus.[1]

The major Renaissance myth in the Ode ad florem Gnidi is the encounter of Mars and Venus. Like the other myths, it takes its lead from the

---

1. Sannazaro's poem De Violante Grappina, Femina Praeclarissima, in which Venus asks her son: "Unde mihi has violas affers, puer?" (Whence do you come bearing me violets?) (164); Julius Aelius Crottus's epigram Ad Veneram: "En violas, en & verno de cespite flores, / En breuia immistis lilia cum violis" (See the violets and see the flowers in the summer grass, see the small lilies mixed with violets) (Gherus 855); Navagero: "has violas dare tibi sancta Venus" (to give you these violets, holy Venus) (Gherus 2:106); and Faustus Sabaeus Brixianus: "Nudus Acidaliis Amor excerpebet in hortis / Pallentes violas, purpureasque rosas" (Naked Cupid cut in Venus's gardens pale violets and red roses) (Gherus 1:556).

pagan myths of antiquity, but by the time it has reached the Renaissance, it has gathered so many accretions from astrologers, mythographers, Platonists, and painters that its original story line has been reversed. The original myth, told by Homer, narrated an adulterous love affair between the god of war and the goddess of love, who was married to Vulcan. The references occurring in stanzas 6 through 12 serve to recall the myth of Mars and Venus. This myth is not, however, the love affair told by the mythographers and alluded to in Garcilaso's Canción IV. To the contrary, it represents the conjunction of two cosmic forces, one of which is capable of dominating the other. Doña Violante is obviously not the adulterous mistress of Mars, but is a force that has sapped his strength and converted him into a weeping lover. Dunn rejected the occult significance of this encounter, asserting that Garcilaso "was no neo-pagan mystagogue, and much of Ficino and Pico would have been a closed book to him" (304). In order to explain Venus's power over Fabio or Mario he must argue that "Donna Violante both 'is' and 'is not' Venus. She 'is' Venus (with Nido as her temple) by reason of her beauty, her irresistible attraction. She 'is not' Venus because she does not love" (305). A better explanation would be that she is not the Venus of antiquity, goddess of love, but she is the Renaissance Venus, an armed planetary force who at various conjunctions subdues her fierce warrior-lover in their continual wanderings through the heavens. Garcilaso's indoctrination into Renaissance philosophy was much more complete than has been thought previously, and in his ode he demonstrates his knowledge and use of this philosophy.

In these stanzas Garcilaso clearly evokes the famous astrological confrontation of Mars and Venus. Fritz Saxl has documented that the revival of the philosophy and sciences of antiquity consisted not only of the learning of the classical periods of Greece and Rome, but also included the writings of the more mystical philosophers of late antiquity. In the Hellenistic period, the occult science in question here, astrology, had become conflated with the popular stories of the pagan gods and goddesses (Saxl, "The Revival"). In this way, the love affair of Mars and Venus, as recounted in Homer, was not simply treated as a myth; it also became a part of the supposed effects of the astral planets of the same name. Astrologers posited a unique affinity between these two planets, and attributed special characteristics to their conjunctions and oppositions based on their mythical love affair. Leone Hebreo's *Diálogos de amor*, which describes at great length the positions of the stars and constellations, almost always devotes a special paragraph to the case of Venus and Mars because of their mythic love affair. He describes the importance of planetary conjunctions with great clarity:

> La conjunción de dos planetas es amorosa y odiosa según la naturaleza de los dos conjuntos; que si están conjuntos los dos planetas benignos, llamados Fortunas, esto es Júpiter y Venus, se tienen amor y benevolencia el uno al otro. (137)

> Pero la conjunción de cada uno de los dos planetas infortunios, Saturno y Marte, es odiosa con todos, excepto la de Marte con Venus, que hace lascivia amorosa y excesiva. (138)

He devotes a special passage to the relationship of Mars and Venus:

> Así que la concupiscente Venus suele enamorarse del ardientísimo Marte; por lo cual los astrólogos ponen grandísima amistad entre estos dos planetas, y dicen que Venus corrige con su benigno aspecto toda la malicia de Marte. (127)

He again states that Venus overcomes the evil of Mars: "También Júpiter fortunado corrige la dureza de Saturno, y Venus bien colocada corrige la crueldad y maldad de Marte" (138). These ideas come from Marsilio Ficino who had ascribed special characteristics to these two planets. In a letter (Book III, 10) titled "Venus subdues Mars, and Jupiter Saturn," he made clear the powers of the planets:

> . . . then I recalled what the ancient sages say, not without very good reason, in their fables about Saturn and Jupiter, Mars and Venus; they say that Mars is bound by Venus, and Saturn by Jupiter. This simply means that the benignity of Jupiter and Venus holds in check the malignity of Saturn and Mars. (15–16)

In his commentary on Plato's *Symposium*, he made more specific the effects of these conjunctions and oppositions:

> . . . Mars surpasses the other planets in courage, because he makes men braver. *Venus dominates him.* For when Mars is located at the corners of the heaven, in either the second or eighth

house of a nativity, he threatens evils to the person being born, but Venus often shackles, so to speak, the malignancy of Mars, by coming into conjunction or opposition with him, or by receiving him or by watching him from the trine or sextile aspect. . . . she seems to make Mars more gentle and to *dominate* him. *But Mars never dominates Venus.* (97)

Leone Hebreo explains clearly the nature of the conjunctions and oppositions of the planets:

Los planetas se aman el uno al otro cuando se miran de aspecto benigno, que es trino de distancia de ciento y veinte grados, el cual es aspecto de perfecto amor, o de aspecto sextil de la mitad de aquella distancia, que es de sesenta grados del uno al otro, el cual es aspecto de lento amor de media amistad. Empero, hácense enemigos y se aborrecen el uno al otro cuando se miran de aspecto opósito, de la mayor distancia que puede ser en el Cielo, que es de ciento y ochenta grados, el cual es aspecto de entero odio y enemistad y de total oposición; y también cuando se miran de aspecto cuadrado de la mitad de aquella distancia, que es de noventa grados del uno al otro, es aspecto de media enemistad y de odio lento. (137)

As one can see by these descriptions, Mars and Venus do not always love each other, but in their planetary wanderings they pass from positions of greater or lesser love and hatred. The positions in which Venus dominates Mars completely would be when Mars is in one of her zodiacal signs, either Taurus or Libra, and she faced him across the heavens from the signs of Scorpio or Aries. These would be the moments of her greatest power over the aggressive nature of Mars, when the "Venus fiera y Marte afeminado" would become manifest (Foulché-Delbosc 512). Francisco de Aldana encapsulates in a sonnet one of these moments of Mars's submission to Venus:

> Marte en aspecto de Cáncer[2]
> Junto a su Venus tierna y bella estaba
> todo orgulloso Marte horrible y fiero,
> cubierto de un templado y fino acero

---

2. This title is somewhat enigmatic, since it does not reveal which aspect. *Autoridades* lists five different "aspectos": "conjunción, sextil, cuadrado, trino y oposición." The houses of Mars and Venus are side by side, Aries (I) and Taurus (II), and Libra (VII) and Scorpio (VIII). They

que un claro espejo al sol de sí formaba;
   y mientras ella atenta en él notaba
sangre y furor, con rostro lastimero
un beso encarecido al gran guerrero
fijó en la frente y dél todo colgaba.
   Del precioso coral tan blando efeto
salió que al fiero dios del duro asunto
hizo olvidar con nuevo ardiente celo.
   ¡Oh fuerza estraña, oh gran poder secreto:
que pueda un solo beso en sólo un punto
los dioses aplacar, dar ley al cielo!

(233–34)

In the artistic circles of Renaissance Italy, the revival of mythology and antiquity came about not only because of an interest in the classics, but also because of an obsession with mystical thought. The use of the myths as conflated by late Hellenistic philosophers provided the material needed for this type of speculation.

The encounter of Mars and Venus was a favorite subject of Renaissance painters. One of the first representations would be that of Francesco del Cossa (1436–78) who in 1469–70 painted frescoes of the months in the Palazzo Schifanoia in Ferrara (Fig. 9). The part above the sign of Taurus shows the celebration of Venus. Taurus is a sign of one of the houses of Venus, and the sun is shown as in her sign, giving her extraordinary powers. The goddess is seated on a cart drawn by swans; kneeling before her is the figure of the warrior Mars, who is chained to her throne. The central scene is surrounded by groups of lovers and symbols, such as the rabbits, of Venus. This fresco is obviously astrological because it is painted above the figure of Taurus, one of the signs of Venus. It represents the power of Venus over the warrior, as occurs when their planets are in opposite positions, with Mars in one of the constellations (houses) of Venus. In this configuration, the heavens come to represent the domination of Venus over Mars as occurred during their love affair.

Even though Francesco del Cossa's painting is clearly astrological, the more famous representation of Venus and Mars by Botticelli (Fig. 10)

---

are also opposite each other in the heavens: Aries facing Libra and Taurus facing Scorpio. The poem seems to suggest a conjunction, perhaps with Mars moving into Libra with Venus in the same house, and Cancer at right angles ("quadrado").

Fig. 9. Francesco del Cossa, *Month of April*, c. 1470. Ferrara, Palazzo Schifanoia

Fig. 10.   Sandro Botticelli, *Mars and Venus*, c. 1483. London, National Gallery

has not been so easily understood; in fact many critics, including even recent ones (Lightbown 70), reject hidden meanings, claiming it is a work that exists for its aesthetic beauty alone, and its purpose is the re-creation of antique motifs, such as a Roman sarcophagus (Gombrich, *Symbolic*, plate 48). German art critics, however, such as Gombrich, Panofsky, and Wind, have debated the subtleties of the iconology of this painting. Even though Wind specifically denies the astrological interpretation advanced by Gombrich, it seems that the figures in the painting must take their disposition from the astrological motif of the dominating power of Venus over Mars. The painting shows Venus and Mars stretched out on the ground in a myrtle grove (the plant sacred to Venus). Venus stares fixedly and enigmatically into space and Mars sleeps deeply while baby satyrs play with his armor and one blows a shell into his ear without awakening him. Those critics who deny the Neoplatonic reading have no satisfactory explanation of why Mars is sleeping or the curious position of the lovers facing each other. The painting seems to represent Mars positioned in one of the zodiacal signs of Venus (either Taurus or Libra) at a time when the two planets are opposite each other in the heavens. According to astrologers, this is the position when two astral forces are in complete opposition, as previously stated by León Hebreo. The lines of the painting beginning with the nonperspective crosspiece of Mars's sword and following Mars's legs and Venus's arms lead the eye to Venus's jewel, which is a ruby surrounded by pearls. The ruby, because of its redness, is associated with the planet Mars; in this case it is sur-rounded by the pearls, associated with Venus because of her birth from the sea, a moment made immortal in Botticelli's *Birth of Venus,* and re-called in Garcilaso's stanza 7. In the painting of Venus and Mars, her stones completely surround and check his power. The fact that she is wearing his stone suggests the tradition of the Armed Venus. If the Mars and Venus of the painting did in fact celebrate the marriage of two his-torical figures by representing them as Mars and Venus, then the painting has many parallels with Garcilaso's ode, which also functions on a literal historical level, a mythological level, and an allegorical cosmic level.

The iconology of Botticelli's scene became something of a common-place in Renaissance art. Among others, Piero di Cosimo (1462–1521) copied the scene with Mars and Venus in the same positions (Fig. 11). His version is more obviously erotic, with its nude Venus and erotic sym-bols, not limited to the myrtle grove sacred to Venus, but it also includes

Fig. 11. Piero di Cosimo, *Mars and Venus*, c. 1498. Berlin, State Museum

Fig. 12. Piero di Cosimo, *Mythological Scene (Death of Pocris)*. London, National Gallery

Fig. 13.   Lucas van Leyden, *Mars and Venus,* 1530

the butterfly on her knee, the huge rabbit, the kissing doves, and the red lance placed above Mars's thigh. This picture was in the possession of Vasari (1512–74) who described it in this way:

> This master painted a picture of Mars and Venus, both nude, with troops of Loves hovering around them and carrying off the helmet and armor of Mars. A grove of myrtle forms part of the landscape, and here is a cupid alarmed at the sight of a rabbit. Venus' doves are also depicted, with other emblems of love. (208–9)

Porqueras Mayo has argued that Garcilaso portrayed another mythological painting by Piero di Cosimo (Fig. 12), the so-called *Death of Pocris,* in Eclogue III as the "ninfa degollada." Because of the similarity of style, subject, and even size of these two paintings, it is perhaps possible that

Fig. 14.   Paolo Veronese, *Venus and Mars*, 1550–60. Turin, Galleria Sabauda

they were painted for the same room or chest and Garcilaso saw them together.[3] That would imply that he recalled in this poem the painting by Piero instead of the one by Botticelli.

Later examples of this Renaissance tradition are an engraving (Fig. 13) by Lucas van Leiden (dated 1530) in which even though Mars and Venus face each other, Mars tries to avert his eyes from Venus's stare, and seems

3. The *Death of Pocris* is 65 cm by 183 cm, and the *Venus and Mars* is 72 cm by 182 cm (Bacci, *L'Opera* 90). Bacci comments on the similarity of the treatment of background landscape in both paintings (91).

to lack strength to rise. Two paintings by Paolo Veronese (1528–1588) present Mars and Venus facing each other. The first (Fig. 14), painted between 1550 and 1560, shows Cupid holding the reins of desire while Mars and Venice seem poised between resisting each other and making love. The second (Fig. 15), painted around 1580, shows Mars and Venus tied together by a Cupid while another holds the powerful horse in check. Finally in the seventeenth century, Velázquez rather humorously portrays the subdued Mars obviously in Venus's house as shown by the bed. His postcoital dejection and the absence of Venus are clues leading to the mystery of this allegorical scene, which recalls earlier versions of the subdued and dejected Mars under Venus's power.[4]

Garcilaso's poem not only lies squarely within this tradition; it also builds on the mythological-astrological motif established in Renaissance art. The Mars and Venus of his poem are not merely the adulterous lovers of mythology; they have become the Renaissance mythic figures represented by astrological planets, whose forces, when in opposition, check the rage of Mars (stanzas 3 and 4) and create the simpering lover portrayed in stanzas 8 through 12. Beginning with a simple stylistic rebellion against the close imitation of Petrarch, Garcilaso has created a poem that incorporates the best and the most subtle of Renaissance thought and art. The subtle puns that unite such disparate elements as a proud lady and a lovely Venus and a musical lyre and an island temple, as well as the lovers into mythological figures suggest the methods of the Renaissance Neoplatonists in their reconciliation of opposites. Like Botticelli's Venus and Mars (which may represent on a literal level the marriage of two patrons), Garcilaso's poem invokes its mystery through the subtle juxtaposition of seemingly inconsequential ornamental details, that convert the historical figures into allegorically cosmic forces. The simple admonition to return the love of a friend becomes a mandate placed on the level of universally controlled forces. Just as a metaphor conflates our understanding of an object with our knowledge of another, so too does the association of an earthly event with a mythic one serve to place the timebound succession of earthly events in an eternal prototypical world. The events are no longer understood as a single historical event, but are

4. My interpretation differs from traditional and even recent interpretations of this painting. Marsha Welles and Jonathan Brown portray the figure in more human and psychological terms. I would argue that the sleeping and lifeless Mars subdued by Venus found in the writing of the Neoplatonists and in earlier paintings is the proper background for Velázquez's conception of Mars.

Fig. 15. Paolo Veronese, *Mars and Venus United by Love,* c. 1580. New York,
The Metropolitan Museum of Art

projected into a realm of archetypes in which they assume greater significance. The fact that these mythological figures also represented cosmic forces further inflates the imagery into the realm of physical and cosmic powers in the universe.

Thus, Garcilaso's ode is not at all a precious plaything. In its depth, it evokes a series of correspondences and ideas that relate it to the essence of Platonic philosophy. The modern reader, suffering the collective historical experiences of rationalism, Romanticism, aestheticism, and scientific realism, can never participate in the Renaissance enthusiasm for a philosophy that taught that God is essentially truth, goodness, and beauty, and viewed all of creation as participating in and serving as examples of those essential aspects of the divinity. We may re-create these ideas in our understanding, but we can never experience them as truth or feel the thrill of their re-creation in art. If the ode seems trivial to us, its ideas antiquated, and uninteresting because it lacks sincerity, then we have missed the import of a work that was obviously at the pinnacle of Renaissance art. For the Renaissance, it incarnated, it re-created in its essence, the latest innovations in poetical form (the Horatian and Pindaric odes) and the latest advances in painting. Its beauty was not precious and trivial; rather, it was significant, profound, and vital.

Conclusion

These studies have identified three distinct stages in Garcilaso's Spanish poetry: the Hispanic *cancionero* style, the Petrarchan style (with the influence of Ausiàs March), and the Neoclassical style. The Neo-Latin odes constitute a fourth style with norms closely related to his Neoclassical style in Spanish. In addition to the stylistic characteristics that distinguish these poems, it is important to study in detail the postures of the speakers and the roles of the readers. The early style is characterized by the strong presence of the fictive beloved and one or more rivals in love. The fictive beloved tends to disappear in the Petrarchan period, while the presence and psychology of the suffering and anguished beloved dominates the poems. In the later period, the love message is distanced from the narrator. The addressee, if mentioned at all, becomes a "tú" instead of a "vos," and is often a male friend of the poet. If it is the beloved, she plays a far different role from the cruel mistress in the Petrarchan poems. These shifts of narrative and addressed reader constitute major changes in the aesthetics and artistry of the poems.

Garcilaso's attitudes toward imitation become important in distinguishing these periods. Garcilaso undoubtedly found Tasso's ideas on imitating the classics to suit his temperament better than the stifling imitation of Petrarch mandated by Bembo. In his early poetry, the themes of rivalry and personal superiority dominate. His orthodox Petrarchism is interrupted by a desire to rival and outdo the master and to affirm the strength of his will over the masochistic suffering prescribed by the Petrarchan tradition. The humanist Neo-Latin poets provided the key to enhance his poetic individuality. Not willing to be subsumed in the straitjacket of strict Petrarchism, he moved to the more personal and biographical style of the Italian humanists. These aspects are clearly evidenced in the encomiastic sonnets, Elegy II and the Ode.

In these studies I have focused on several themes that are not usually associated with Garcilaso, such as allegory, jealousy, allegorical mythology, and competitive imitation. All these themes place Garcilaso within the Neapolitan intellectual traditions of the 1520s and 1530s, and the Spanish poet emerges from these studies as a strong intellectual figure. The historical figure of Garcilaso has largely been lost. The documents tell us little of his character. The one personal letter and the beginning of Elegy II reveal a courtier and politician concerned with his worldly reputation. His audacity in battle at La Goleta (Tunisia) and at Le Muy in Provence reveal the fearless soldier who would become a legend in Luis Zapata's *Carlo magno*. The witty courtier portrayed in Zapata's *Miscelánea* can also be seen in the humorous *coplas* on dancing, but barely appears otherwise. The frustrated lover who emerges from the poetry corresponds more to poetic tradition and convention than to any evidence we have of his passionate involvement in unrequited love affairs. The evidence of the intellectual figure is more fully documented. The allegorical myths of several sonnets, the Ode and Elegy II, the allegorical treatment of the rudimentary concepts of primitivism and evolution in Canción IV, and the obvious delight in reversing the commonplace of the ideal of moderation in Elegy II clearly portray for us a thinker more inclined to humanistic speculation than to emotive outpourings. The role of Neoplatonism cannot be discounted from this revaluation. Although Garcilaso seems to employ Neoplatonism in the sonnets as a point of departure to express his own emotions, one cannot discount its importance in the worldview presented in Elegy II nor his masterly utilization of Neoplatonic ideas of philosophical and mythological syncreticism in the Ode. Even though he did not produce a Neoplatonic sonnet cycle, as did Boscán, his absorption of Neoplatonism seems to have been less doctrinal and much more profound and intellectual. In addition, the intense study of Horace with the idea that his own poetry would rejuvenate and make contemporary Castilian literature (for which he expressed contempt) reveal a writer consciously involved in a literary movement—not a frustrated lover pouring out his soul and committing his tears to paper. The stylistic study of the sonnets makes it at least as likely that they are more informed by aesthetic norms than by personal experiences. The degree to which one accepts this argument determines the extent to which the revaluation of Garcilaso's poetry has been completed.

As these studies show, the appreciation of the complexities of Garcilaso's aesthetic and cultural milieu provides new insights and new readings of individual texts. The poet who emerges from these new readings is not as superficially appealing as the older concept of a sincere grieving lover. The intellectual appreciation of his poetry requires a familiarity with several poetic and artistic traditions as well as a detailed understanding of their reception in the Renaissance. The conflict of emotions in Garcilaso's poetry is easily grasped, but the appreciation of the depth of poetic expression involves the study of sources, the analysis of sound structuring, the subtle interplay of multiple references, the incorporation of Renaissance literature and art, and the rhetorical and aesthetic norms that inform individual poems. Garcilaso seems to have been on the cutting edge of the artistic innovations of his contemporaries. In most cases, one needs to study the literature and art of the 1520s and 1530s, while the art and literature of the previous century seems to have held little interest for him. His interest in the Greek and Latin classics lay mainly in their reception and refashioning among the Italian humanists. The facile poet expressing his sorrowful love has disappeared in the complexities of Renaissance art, and has been replaced by a strong intellectual figure capable of understanding and utilizing the many aspects of Renaissance artistic traditions.

Works Consulted

Abad Nebot, Francisco. "Anotaciones formales al soneto XXIII de Garcilaso." *Archivium* 27–28 (1977–78): 17–20.

Abrams, M. H. *The Mirror and the Lamp: Romantic Theory and the Critical Tradition*. New York: Norton, 1958.

Academia Literaria Renacentista. *IV. Garcilaso*. Ed. Victor García de la Concha. Salamanca: Universidad de Salamanca, 1986.

Acuña, Hernando de. *Varias poesías*. Ed. Luis F. Díaz Larios. Madrid: Cátedra, 1982.

Alatorre, Antonio. "Garcilaso, Herrera, Prete Jacopín y Don Tomás Tamayo de Vargas." *Modern Language Notes* 78 (1963): 126–51.

———. "Sobre la 'gran fortuna' de un soneto de Garcilaso." *Nueva Revista de Filología Hispánica* 24 (1975): 142–77.

Albistur, Jorge. "La poesía en el siglo XVI: Garcilaso de la Vega." *Literatura española*. Montevideo: Ediciones de la Banda Oriental, 1975. 86–126.

Alcalá, Manuel. "Del virgilianismo de Garcilaso de la Vega." *Filosofía y Letras* 11, nos. 21–22 (1946): 59–78, 227–45.

———. "Virgilio en las odas latinas de Garcilaso." *Filosofía y Letras* 19, no. 37 (1950): 157–64.

———. "Virgilio y Garcilaso: Cinco escolios." *Tierra nueva* 1 (1940): 334–44.

Alcántara, Manuel. "La incorporación de la frase hecha en la poesía española." *Revista de Archivos, Bibliotecas y Museos* 63 (1957): 223–50.

Alciati, Andrea. *Emblematum liber*. Augsburg, 1531; repr. New York: Georg Olms, 1977.

Alciatus, Andreas. *Emblematum Fontes Quatuor*. Ed. Henry Green. London: Holbein Society, 1870.

Alda Tesán, J. M. "Fortuna de un verso garcilasiano." *Revista de Filología Española* 27 (1943): 77–82.

Aldana, Francisco de. *Poesías castellanas completas*. Ed. José Lara Garrido. Madrid: Cátedra, 1985.

Allen, Don Cameron. *Mysteriously Meant: The Rediscovery of Pagan Symbolism and Allegorical Interpretation in the Renaissance*. Baltimore: Johns Hopkins University Press, 1970.

Allen, John J. "Lope de Vega y la imaginería petrarquista de belleza feminina." *Estudios literarios de hispanistas norteamericanos dedicados a Helmut Hatzfeld con motivo de su 80 aniversario*. Ed. J. M. Solá-Solé, Alessandro Crisafulli, and Bruno Damiani. Barcelona: Ediciones Hispam, 1974. 5–23.

Almeida, José. "El concepto aristotélico de la imitación en el Renacimiento de las letras españolas de los siglos XVI y XVII." *Actas del Sexto Congreso Interna-cional de Hispanistas celebrado en Toronto del 22 al 26 agosto de 1977.* Ed. Alan M. Gordon and Evelyn Rugg. Toronto: University of Toronto Press, 1980. 41–43.

———. "Garcilaso a través de los nuevos aspectos del 'New Criticism.'" *Crítica Hispánica* 191 (1965): 325–56.

Alonso, Dámaso."El destino de Garcilaso." *Cuatro poetas españoles.* Madrid: Gredos, 1962. 17–46.

———. "Elogio del endecasílabo." *De los siglos oscuros al de oro.* Madrid: Gredos, 1958. 178–82.

———. "Garcilaso, Ronsard, Góngora (apuntes de una clase)." *De los siglos oscuros al de oro.* Madrid: Gredos, 1958. 183–91.

———. *La poesía de San Juan de la Cruz.* Madrid: Aguilar, 1966.

———. *Poesía española: Ensayo de métodos y límites estilísticos.* Madrid: Gredos, 1971.

———. "Raíz española: La tradición culta." *La poesía de San Juan de la Cruz.* Ma-drid: Consejo Superior de Investigaciones Científicas, 1942.

Alonso, José A. "Elementos mitológicos en la poesía de Garcilaso." *Proceedings of the Northwest Conference on Foreign Languages* 26, no. 1 (1977): 192–95.

Altolaguirre, Manuel. *Garcilaso de la Vega.* Madrid: Espasa-Calpe, 1933.

Alvarez Barrientos, Joaquín. "Dafne y Apolo en un comentario de Garcilaso y Que-vedo." *Revista de Literatura* 46 (1984): 57–72.

Anelli, Luigi. *Historium ed il Vasto attraverso i secoli.* Vasto: Guglielmo Guzzetti, 1929.

Araya, Guillermo. "La fuente y los ríos en Garcilaso." *Estudios Filológicos* 6 (1970): 113–34.

Arce Blanco de Vázquez, Margot. "Cerca el Danubio una isla . . ." *Studia Philoló-gica: Homenaje ofrecido a Dámaso Alonso.* Vol. 1. Madrid: Gredos, 1960; *La poesía de Garcilaso: Ensayos críticos.* Ed. Elias L. Rivers. Barcelona: Ariel, 1974. 103–17.

———. "La égloga primera de Garcilaso." *La Torre* 50 (1953): 31–68.

———. "La égloga segunda de Garcilaso." *Asomante* 5 (1949): no. 1, 57–73; no. 2, 60–78.

———. *Garcilaso de la Vega: Contribución al estudio de la lírica española del siglo XVI.* Río Piedras: Universidad de Puerto Rico, 1969.

Aristotle. *Ethics.* Trans. J. A. K. Thompson. Baltimore: Penguin, 1966.

Artigas, M. "Boscán y Garcilaso." *Las obras.* By Juan Boscán. Barcelona, 1543; fac-simile edition, Madrid: Biblioteca Nueva, 1936.

Ashcom, B. B. "A Note on Garcilaso and Cervantes." *Hispanic Review* 19 (1951): 61–63.

Atkinson, William C. "On Aristotle and the Concept of Lyric Poetry in Early Spanish Criticism." *Estudios dedicados a Menéndez Pidal.* Vol. 6. Madrid: Consejo Superior de Investigaciones Científicas, 1956. 189–213.

Aubrun, Charles. "Salid, lágrimas." *Bulletin Hispanique* 60 (1958): 505–7.

Augustine, Saint. *On Free Choice of the Will.* Trans. Anna S. Benjamin and L. H. Hackstaff. Indianapolis: Bobbs-Merrill, 1964.

Avalle-Arce, Joaquín Bautista. "Tres notas al Quijote." *Nueva Revista de Filología Hispánica* 1 (1947): 86–89.

Azar, Inés. *Discurso retórico y mundo pastoral en la* Egloga segunda *de Garcilaso.* Amsterdam: Benjamins, 1981.

————. "Metáfora, literalidad, transgresión: Amor-muerte en la *Celestina* y en la *Egloga II* de Garcilaso." *Lexis* 3 (1979): 57–65.

————. "La textualidad de la *Egloga II* de Garcilaso." *Modern Language Notes* 93 (1978): 176–208.

————. "Tradition, Voice and Self in the Love Poetry of Garcilaso." *Studies in Honor of Elias Rivers*. Ed. Bruno M. Damiani and Ruth El Saffar, 24–35. Potomac, Md.: Studia Humanistica, 1989.

Babb, Lawrence. *Elizabethan Malady: A Study of Melancholia in English Literature from 1580 to 1642*. East Lansing: Michigan State University Press, 1965.

Babín, M. T. "Garcilaso de la Vega y Sir Philip Sydney." *La Nueva Democracia* 33, no. 4 (1953): 64–74.

Bacci, Mina. *L'opera completa di Piero di Cosimo*. Milan: Rizzoli, 1976.

————. *Piero di Cosimo*. Milan: Bramante, 1966.

Baldacci, Luigi. *Il petrarchismo italiano nel cinquecento*. Milan: Riccardo Ricciardi, 1957.

Ball, Patricia M. "Sincerity: The Rise and Fall of a Critical Term." *Modern Language Review* 59 (1964): 1–11.

Barnard, Mary E. "The Grotesque and the Courtly in Garcilaso's Apollo and Daphne." *Romanic Review* 72 (1981): 253–73.

————. *The Myth of Apollo and Daphne from Ovid to Quevedo: Love, Agon, and the Grotesque*. Durham: Duke University Press, 1987.

Bataillon, Marcel. "Glosa americana al Soneto II de Garcilaso." *Varia lección de clásicos españoles*. Madrid: Gredos, 1964. 24–36.

Bayo, M. J. *Virgilio y la pastoral española del renacimiento, 1480–1530*. Madrid: Gredos, 1959.

Bembo, Pietro. *Prose della volgar lingua*. Ed. Carlo Dionisotti-Casalone. Turin: Unione Typographica, 1931.

————. *Prose della volgar lingua*. Ed. Mario Marti. Padua: Liviana Editrice, 1967.

————. *Prose della volgar lingua*. Ed. Mario Pozzi. *Trattatisti*.

————. *Prose e rime*. Ed. Carlo Dionisotti. Torina: Unione Tipografico–Editrice Torinese, 1960.

Benivieni, Girolamo. *Opere*. Florence: Philippo di Giunta, 1519.

Berenguer Carisomo, Arturo. "Una posibilidad dramática en la Egloga IIª de Garcilaso." *Homenaje: Estudios de filología e historia literaria lusohispanas e iberoamericanas publicados para celebrar el tercer lustro del Instituto de Estudios Hispánicos, Portugueses e Iberamericanos de la Universidad Estatal de Utrecht*. The Hague: Van Goor Zonen, 1966. 89–105.

Bertini, G. M. "Originalitá del Rinascimento spagnuolo." *Studi di Letteratura Ispano-Americana* 2 (1969): 9–35.

Blecua, Alberto. *En el texto de Garcilaso*. Madrid: Insula, 1970.

Blecua, José Manuel. "Corrientes poéticas en el siglo XVI." *Sobre poesía de la Edad de Oro*. Madrid: Gredos, 1970. 11–24.

————. "Garcilaso y Cervantes." *Homenaje a Cervantes*. Madrid, 1948; *La poesía de Garcilaso: Ensayos críticos*. Ed. Elias L. Rivers. Barcelona: Ariel, 1974. 367–80.

————. "Garcilaso y Cervantes." *Sobre poesía de la Edad de Oro*. Madrid: Gredos, 1970. 151–60.

————. "Las obras de Garcilaso con anotaciones de Fernando de Herrera." *Sobre poesía de la Edad de Oro*. Madrid: Gredos, 1970. 100–104.

Bloom, Harold. *The Anxiety of Influence*. Oxford: Oxford University Press, 1973.

Boccaccio, Giovanni. See Osgood, Charles.

Boccheta, Vittore. *Sannazaro en Garcilaso.* Madrid: Gredos, 1976.

Bohigas, Pere. "Más sobre la Canción IV de Garcilaso." *Ibérida* 5 (1961): 79–90.

Bongrani, Paolo. "Appunti sulle Prose della volgar lingua: In margine a una recente edizione." *Giornale Storico della Letteratura Italiana* 159 (1982): 271–90.

Bonora, Ettore. *Critica e letteratura nel cinquecento.* Torino: G. Giappichelli, 1964.

Bouterwek, Frederick. *History of Spanish and Portuguese Literature.* London: Boosey and Sons, 1823.

Boscán, Juan. *El cortesano.* See Castiglione, Baltasar.

———. *Las obras.* Ed. William I. Knapp. Madrid: Librería de M. Murillo, 1875.

———. *Obras poéticas.* Ed. Martín de Riquer, Antonio Comas and Joaquín Molas. Barcelona: Universidad de Barcelona, 1957.

Bourland, C. B. "Garcilaso de la Vega, Soneto XXV." *Homenaje a A. M. Huntington.* Wellesley, Mass.: Wellesley College, 1952.

Brancaforte, Benito. "Valor y límites de las *Anotaciones* de Fernando de Herrera." *Revista de Archivos, Bibliotecas ÿMDIÏ Museos* 79 (1976): 113–29.

Brand, C. P. *Ariosto.* Edinburgh: Edinburgh University Press, 1974.

Braschi, Giannina. "La metamorfosis del ingenio en la Egloga III de Garcilaso." *Revista Canadiense de Estudios Hispánicos* 4 (1979): 19–36.

Brown, Gary J. "Fernando de Herrera and Lorenzo de' Medici: The Sonnet as Epigram." *Romanische Forschungen.* 87 (1975): 226–38.

———. "Lope de Vega's Epigrammatic Poetic for the Sonnet." *Modern Language Notes* 93 (1978): 218–32.

———. "The *Peregrino Amoroso:* Four Movements of Poetic Configuration in the Spanish Love Sonnet." *Neophilologus* 60 (1976): 376–88.

———. "Rhetoric in the Sonnet of Praise." *Journal of Hispanic Philology* 1 (1976): 31–50.

Brown, Jonathan. *The Golden Age of Painting in Spain.* New Haven: Yale University Press, 1991.

Bustos, Eugenio de. "Cultismos en el léxico de Garcilaso de la Vega." Academia Literaria Renacentista. Vol. 4. *Garcilaso.* Ed. Victor García de la Concha. Salamanca: Universidad de Salamanca, 1986. 127–63.

Cabañas, P. "Garcilaso de la Vega y Antonio de Lofrasso (un soneto conocido y una glosa olvidada)." *Revista de Literatura* 1 (1952): 57–65.

———. "Garcilaso, Góngora y Arguijo (Tres sonetos sobre el mismo tema)." *Bulletin of Hispanic Studies* 47 (1970): 210–22.

———. *El mito de Orfeo en la literatura española.* Madrid: CSIC, 1948.

Calcagnini, Celio. "Super imitatione commentatio." *Trattatisti di poetica e retorica del cinquecento.* Ed. Bernard Weinberg. Bari: Laterza, 1970. 1:197–220.

Caldera, E. *Garcilaso e la lirica del Rinascimento.* Genova: Bozzi, 1966.

Cammarata, Joan. *Mythological Themes in the Works of Garcilaso de la Vega.* Madrid: José Porrúa Turanzas, 1983.

Capece, Scipione. *Il poema di principius rerum.* Trans. Francesco Maria Ricci. Venice: Stampe Remondiniane, 1754.

Carayon, M. "Le monde affectif de Garcilaso." *Bulletin Hispanique* 32 (1930): 246–53.

Carducci, Giosuè. "Dello svolgimento dell'ode in Italia." *Opere.* N.p.: Nicola Zanichelli, 1942. 15:1–81.

Cartari, Vincenzo. *Vere e Nove Imagini degli Dei delli Antichi.* Padova, 1615; facsimile reprint, New York: Garland, 1979.

Casanova O., Wilfredo. "Una coordenada poética en la obra de Garcilaso." *Boletín del Instituto de Filología de la Universidad de Chile* 23–24 (1972–73): 7–27.

Cascales, Francisco. *Tablas poéticas.* Ed. Benito Brancaforte. Madrid: Espasa-Calpe, 1975.

Cascardi, Anthony J. "The Exit from Arcadia: Reevaluation of the Pastoral in Virgil, Garcilaso and Góngora." *Journal of Hispanic Philology* 4 (1980): 119–41.

Castiglione, Baldesar. *El cortegiano. See* Castiglione, Baltasar.

Castiglione, Baltasar. *El cortesano.* Trans. Juan Boscán. Ed. Marcelino Menéndez y Pelayo. Revista de Filología Española. Anejo XXV. Madrid: Consejo Superior de Investigaciones Científicas, 1942.

Castillejo, Cristóbal de. *Obras.* Vol. 2. Ed. J. Domínquez Bordona. Madrid: Espasa-Calpe, 1957.

Cerboni Baiardi, Giorgio. *La lirica di Bernardo Tasso.* Urbino: Argalia, 1966.

Cernuda, Luis. "Tres poetas clásicos." *Poesía y literatura.* Barcelona: Seix Barral, 1960.

Cervantes Saavedra, Miguel de. *Don Quijote de la Mancha.* Ed. John Jay Allen. 2 vols. Madrid: Cátedra, 1977.

Chamberlin, Henry Harmon. *Last Flowers.* Cambridge: Harvard University Press, 1937.

Chevalier, Maxime. *L'Arioste en Espagne.* Bordeaux: University of Bordeaux, 1966.

———. "Fama Póstuma de Garcilaso." Academia Literaria Renacentista. 165–84.

Cienfuegos, Alvaro. *La heroyca vida, virtudes y milagros del grande S. Francisco de Borja antes duque de Gandia, y despues Tercero General de la Compañia de Jesus.* Madrid: Viuda de Juan Garcia Infanzon, 1717.

Ciocchini, Héctor. "Garcilaso, poeta europeo." *Cuadernos del Sur* 11 (1972): 117–26.

———. "Una hipótesis de simbología figurada en dos obras de Garcilaso." *Revista de Filología Española* 49 (1966): 329–34.

Cirot, Georges. "A propos des dernières publications sur Garcilaso de la Vega." *Bulletin Hispanique* 22 (1920): 234–55.

Cirot, Georges, and Paul Laumonier. "Ronsard et les Espagnols." *Bulletin Hispanique* 44 (1942): 168–71.

Cisneros, L. J. "Diego Mexía y Garcilaso." *Quaderni Ibero-Americani* 19–20 (1956): 182–84.

Clarke, Dorothy Clotelle. *Garcilaso's First Eclogue: Perspective, Geometric Figure, Epic Structure.* El Cerrito, Calif.: Shadi, 1977.

Codoñer, C. "Comentaristas de Garcilaso." Academia Literaria Renacentista. 185–200.

Consiglio, Carlo. "I sonnetti di Garcilaso de la Vega: Problemi critici." *Annali del Corso di Lingue e Letterature Straniere, Universitá di Bari* 2 (1954): 215–74.

Correa, Gustavo. "Garcilaso y la mitología." *Hispanic Review* 45 (1977): 269–81.

Cossío, José María. *Fábulas mitológicas en España.* Madrid: Espasa-Calpe, 1952.

Coudert, Allison. *Alchemy: The Philosopher's Stone.* Boulder, Colo.: Shambhala, 1980.

Covarrubias, Sebastián de. *Tesoro de la lengua castellana o española.* Ed. Martín de Riquer. Barcelona: S. A. Horta, 1943.

Cravens, Sydney P., and Edward V. George. "Garcilaso's Salicio and Vergil's Eighth *Eclogue.*" *Hispania* 64 (1981): 209–14.

Crawford, J. P. W. "Notes on the Chronology of Boscán's Verses." *Modern Philology* 25 (1927): 29–36.

Croce, Benedetto. "Intorno al soggiorno de Garcilaso de la Vega in Italia." *Rassegna Storica Napoletana di Lettere ed Arti* 1 (1894): 3–16.

Cruz, Anne J. *Imitación y transformación. El petrarquismo en la poesía de Boscán y Garcilaso de la Vega.* Amsterdam: John Benjamins, 1988.

———. "La mitología como retórica poética: El mito implícito como metáfora en Garcilaso." *Romance Review* 77 (1986): 404–14.

Culler, Jonathan. "Changes in the Study of the Lyric." *Lyric Poetry. Beyond New Criticism.* Ed. Chaviva Hosek and Patricia Parker. Ithaca: Cornell University Press, 1985. 38–54.

Darbor, Michel. "Le Mepris de la richesse dans la poésie espagnole de la Renaissance." *L'Or au temps de la Renaissance: Du mythe à l'économie.* Ed. Marie Thérèse Jones-Davies. Paris: Université de Paris–Sorbonne, 1978. 63–66.

Darst, David H. "Garcilaso's Love for Isabel Freire: The Creation of a Myth." *Journal of Hispanic Philology* 3 (1979): 261–68.

———. *Juan Boscán.* Boston: Twayne, 1978.

Davies, G. A. "Notes on Some Classical Sources for Garcilaso and Luis de León." *Hispanic Review* 32 (1964): 202–16.

De Armas, Frederick A. "Los excesos de Venus y Marte en *El gallardo español.*" In *Cervantes. Su obra y su mundo.* Ed. Manuel Criado de Val. Madrid: Edi-6, 1981. 249–59.

———. *The Return of Astraea. An Astral Imperial Myth in Calderón.* Lexington: University of Kentucky Press, 1986.

De Man, Paul. "Lyrical Voice in Contemporary Theory: Riffaterre and Jauss." *Lyric Poetry. Beyond New Criticism.* Ed. Chaviva Hosek and Patricia Parker. Ithaca: Cornell University Press, 1985. 55–72.

Diccionario de Autoridades. 3 vols. Madrid: Gredos, 1963.

Dionisotti, Carlo. Bembo. *Prose.* 1960.

Dionisotti-Casalone. Bembo. *Prose.* 1931.

Dionysius of Halicarnassus. *The Critical Essays.* Trans. Stephen Usher. Vol. 2. Cambridge: Harvard University Press, 1985.

———. *On Literary Composition.* Ed. and trans. W. Rhys Roberts. London: MacMillan, 1910.

———. *The Three Literary Letters.* Ed. and trans. W. Rhys Roberts. Cambridge: Cambridge University Press, 1901.

Dizionario biografico degli italiani. 30 vols. Roma: Istituto della Enciclopedia Italiana, 1960–84.

Duff, J. Wight, and Arnold M. Duff, eds. *Minor Latin Poets.* 2 vols. Loeb Classical Library. Cambridge: Harvard University Press, 1982.

Dunn, Peter N. "Garcilaso's Ode A la Flor de Gnido: A Commentary on Some Renaissance Themes and Ideas." *Zeitschrift für romanische Philologie* 81 (1965): 288–309.

Dutton, Brian. "Garcilaso's *sin duelo.*" *Modern Language Notes* 80 (1965): 251–58.

Echenique Elizondo, María Teresa. "¿Italianismo o cultismo semántico en Garcilaso?" *Neuphilologische Mitteilungen* 85 (1984): 367–68.

Entenza de Solare, B. E. "Fernando de Herrera ante el texto de Garcilaso." *Filología* 11 (1965): 65–98.

Entwistle, W. J. "La date de l'*Egloga primera* de Garcilaso de la Vega." *Bulletin Hispanique* 32 (1930): 254–56.

———. "The First Eclogue of Garcilaso." *Bulletin of Spanish Studies* 2 (1925): 87–90.

————. "Garcilaso's Fourth Canzon and Other Matters." *Modern Language Review* 45 (1950): 225–28.

————. "The Loves of Garci-laso." *Hispania* 13 (1930): 377–88.

Equicola, Mario. *Libro de natura de amore*. Venice: Lorenzo Lorio da Portes, 1525.

Espantoso Foley, Augusta. "Petrarchan Patterns in the Sonnets of Garcilaso de la Vega." *Allegorica* 3 (1978): 190–213.

————. "Synonymic Variations in Certain Sonnets of Petrarch and Garcilaso de la Vega." *Estudios sobre el Siglo de Oro en homenaje a Raymond R. McCurdy*. Ed. Angel González, Tamara Holzapfel and Alfred Rodríguez. Madrid: Cátedra, 1983.

Etcheverry, J. E. "Un soneto clásico: el X de Garcilaso." *Número* 3 (1951): 344–47.

Faria e Sousa, Manuel de. *Fuente de Aganipe o Rimas varias*. Parte tercera. Madrid: Carlos Sánchez Bravo, 1646.

————. *Rimas varias de Luis de Camoes . . . comentadas*. Part 2. Lisboa, 1689; facsimile reprint: Lisboa: Impresa Nacional-Casa da Moeda, 1972.

Ferguson, William. *La versificación imitativa en Fernando de Herrera*. London: Tamesis, 1981.

Fernández de Navarrete, Eustaquio. *Vida del célebre poeta Garcilaso de la Vega*. Collección de Documentos Inéditos para la Historia de España, vol. 16. Madrid: Viuda de Calero, 1850.

Fernández de Oviedo y Valdés, Gonzalo. *Las quinquagenas de la nobleza de España*. Ed. Vicent de la Fuente. Vol. 1. Madrid: Manuel Tello, 1880.

Fernández Morera, Darío. "The Dedication in Garcilaso's Third Eclogue." *Revista Canadiense de Estudios Hispánicos* 4 (1980): 123–32.

————. "Garcilaso's Second Eclogue and the Literary Tradition." *Hispanic Review* 47 (1979): 37–53.

————. *The Lyre and the Oaten Flute: Garcilaso and the Pastoral*. London: Tamesis, 1982.

————. "On Garcilaso's *Egloga I* and Virgil's *Bucolic VIII*." *Modern Language Notes* 89 (1974): 273–80.

Ferreiro Alemparte, Jaime. "Garcilaso de la Vega en Colonia y el culto de las once mil vírgenes en España." *Homenaje universitario a Dámaso Alonso*. Madrid: Gredos, 1970. 119–26.

Ficino, Marsilio. *Commentary on Plato's Symposium on Love*. Trans. Sears Jayne. Dallas: Spring Publications, 1985.

————. *Letters*. Vol. 2. London: Shepherd-Walwyn, 1978.

Flamini, F. "Imitazioni italiane in Garcilaso de la Vega." *Biblioteca delle Scuole Italiane*, 2d series, 8 (Milan, 1899): 200–203.

Fletcher, Angus. *Allegory. The Theory of a Symbolic Mode*. Ithaca: Cornell University Press, 1964.

Font, María Teresa. "Análisis estructural del soneto XII de Garcilaso." *Explicación de Textos Literarios* 7, no. 1 (1978): 63–68.

Forster, Leonard. *The Icy Fire*. Cambridge: Cambridge University Press, 1969.

Foster, David William. "Formulaic Structure in Garcilaso's Ode 'A la flor de Gnido.'" *Language and Style* 4 (1971): 144–52.

Foster, Kenelm. *Petrarch. Poet and Humanist*. Edinburgh: Edinburgh University Press, 1984.

Foulché-Delbosc, Ramon. "237 Sonnets." *Revue Hispanique* 18 (1908): 488–618.

Franco, Nicolò. *Rime . . . contro Pietro Aretino*. Lanciano: Carabba, 1916.

Franquini, Francesco. *Poemata*. Venice: Haeredum Natalis, 1554.

Frattone, J. G. "Influssi prepetrarcheschi nei sonetti di Garcilaso." *Italica* 25 (1948): 300–305.

Frye, Northrop. *Anatomy of Criticism*. Princeton: Princeton University Press. 1957.

———. "Approaching the Lyric." *Lyric Poetry. Beyond New Criticism*. Ed. Chaviva Hosek and Patricia Parker. Ithaca: Cornell University Press, 1985. 31–37.

Fucilla, J. G. *Estudios sobre el petrarquismo en España*. Madrid: Consejo Superior de Investigaciones Científicas, 1960.

———. "Un Italien, imitateur des poètes espagnols." *Bulletin Hispanique* 36 (1934): 195–97.

———. "Notes on Spanish Renaissance Poetry." *Philological Quarterly* 11 (1932): 225–62.

———. "The Present Status of Renaissance and 'Siglo de Oro' Poetry." *Hispania* 30 (1947): 182–93.

———. "Sobre dos sonetos [XI and XXV] de Garcilaso." *Revista de Filología Española* 36 (1952): 113–17.

———. *Superbi colli e altri saggi*. Roma: B. Carucci, 1963.

———. "Two Generations of Petrarchism and Petrarchists in Spain." *Modern Philology* 27 (1930): 277–95.

———. "Una versione sconosciuta dell'Egloga Primera di Garcilaso." *Quaderni Ibero-Americani* 24 (1959): 595–600.

Fulgentius. *Fulgentius the Mythographer*. Trans. Leslie George Whitbread. Columbus: Ohio State University Press, 1971.

Gale, G. R. "Garcilaso's *Sonnet XIII* Metamorphosed." *Romanische Forschungen* 80 (1968): 504–9.

Gallagher, Patrick. "Garcilaso's First Eclogue and the Lamentations of Love." *Forum for Modern Language Studies* 9 (1973): 192–99.

———. "Hacia una poética de Garcilaso: La subversión de la armonía en su arte; apuntes sobre la *Egloga primera*." *Cuadernos Hispanoamericanos* 319 (1977): 113–24.

———. "Liturgical Profanation and its Implications in Garcilaso's *Second Eclogue*." *Beiträge zur Romanischen Philologie* 7 (1968): 223–28.

———. "*Locus Amoenus*: The Aesthetic Centre of Garcilaso's Third Eclogue." *Hispanic Studies in Honour of Frank Pierce Presented by Former and Present Members of the Department of Hispanic Studies in the University of Sheffield*. Ed. John England. Sheffield: University of Sheffield Press, 1980. 59–75.

Gallardo, B. J. *Ensayo de una biblioteca española de libros raros y curiosos*. Vol. 4. Madrid: 1889. Cols. 1271–1325; vol. 3, cols. 317–330.

Gallego Morell, Antonio. *Antología poética en honor de Garcilaso de la Vega*. Madrid: Ediciones Guadarrama, 1958.

———. *En torno a Garcilaso y otros ensayos*. Madrid: Ediciones Guadarrama, 1970.

———. "La escuela de Garcilaso." *Estudios sobre poesía española del primer siglo de oro*. Madrid: Insula, 1970.

———. *Garcilaso: Documentos completos*. Barcelona: Planeta, 1976.

———. *Garcilaso de la Vega y sus comentaristas*. Madrid: Gredos, 1972.

———. *El mito de Faetón en la literatura española*. Madrid: Consejo Superior de Investigaciones Científicas, 1961.

———. *El poeta Garcilaso de la Vega en el teatro español*. Granada: Consejo Superior de Investigaciones Científicas, 1963.

———. "Sá de Miranda y Garcilaso de la Vega." Academia Literaria Renacentista. Vol. 4. *Garcilaso*. Ed. Victor García de la Concha. Salamanca: Universidad de Salamanca, 1986. 235–46.

García-Berrio, Antonio. "Estatuto del personaje en el soneto amoroso del Siglo de Oro." *Le personnage dans la littérature de siècle d'or: Statur et fonction.* Casa de Velázquez, Table Ronde, November 1979. Paris: Edition Recherche sur les Civilisations, 1984. 11–20.

———. "A Text-Typology of the Classical Sonnets." *Poetics* 8 (1979): 435–58.

García de la Concha, Victor. "La officina poética de Garcilaso." Academia Literaria Renacentista. 83–108.

García Gómez, J. J. "Algunas notas sobre el masoquismo y la estructuración de la Egloga I de Garcilaso de la Vega." *Humanitas* 10 (Mexico, 1969): 327–42.

García Lorca, Francisco. "Análisis de dos versos de Garcilaso." *Hispanic Review* 24 (1956): 87–100.

Garcilaso de la Vega. *Obra completa*. Ed. Alfonso I. Sotelo Salas. Madrid: Editora Nacional, 1976.

———. *Obras*. Ed. Tomás Navarro Tomás. Madrid: Clásicos Castellanos, 1911.

———. *Obras*. Ed. Tomás Navarro Tomás. Madrid: Clásicos Castellanos, 1924.

———. *Obras*. Ed. Tomás Navarro Tomás. Madrid: Clásicos Castellanos, 1963.

———. *Obras completas*. Ed. Amancio Labandeira. Madrid: Fundación Universitaria Española, 1981.

———. *Obras completas*. Ed. Elias L. Rivers. Madrid: Castalia, 1968.

———. *Obras completas con comentarios*. Ed. Elias L. Rivers. Madrid: Castalia, 1981.

———. *Works. A Critical Text with Bibliography.* Ed. Hayward Keniston. New York: Hispanic Society of America, 1925.

Gauthier, M. "A propos de l'harmonie des vers: Essai sur le consonantisme chez Garcilaso de la Vega." *Les Langues Néo-latines* 54, no. 152 (1960): 44–52.

Gendreau-Massaloux, Michèle. "La Folie d'amour de Garcilaso à Góngora: Epanouissement et métamorphoses d'un thème mythique." *Visages de la folie (1500–1650): Domaine hispano-italien.* Ed. Agustín Redondo and André Rochon. Paris: Publications de la Sorbonne, 1981. 101–16.

Gerhardt, M. I. "La pastorale de la Renaissance en Espagne: Garcilaso de la Vega." *La poesía de Garcilaso: Ensayos críticos.* Ed. Elias L. Rivers. Barcelona: Ariel, 1974. 177–96.

Ghertman, Sharon. *Petrarch and Garcilaso: A Linguistic Approach to Style.* London: Tamesis, 1975.

———. "Semiotics and the Self-Consuming Artifact: Garcilaso's 'Ode ad Florem Gnidi'." *Pacific Coast Philology* 14 (1979): 34–41.

Gherus, Ranuntius. *Delitiae CC. italorum poetarum huius superiorisque aevi illustrium.* 2 vols. N.p., Jonas Rosa, 1608.

Gicovate, Bernardo. *Garcilaso de la Vega.* Twayne World Authors Series 349. Boston: Twayne, 1975.

Gilman, Anita. "El viento como destino en la obra de Garcilaso de la Vega." *Sin Nombre* 14 (1984): 132–43.

Giovio [Jovio], Paolo. *Dialogo de las empresas militares y amorosas.* Trans. Alonso de Ulloa. Venice: Gabriel Giulito de Ferraris, 1558.

Girard, René. *Deceit, Desire, and the Novel: Self and Other in Literary Structure.* Trans. Yvonne Freccero. Baltimore: Johns Hopkins University Press, 1965.

————. *Violence and the Sacred.* Trans. Patrick Gregory. Baltimore: Johns Hopkins University Press, 1977.

Glaser, Edward. "El cobre convertido en oro: Christian *rifacimentos* of Garcilaso's Poetry in the Sixteenth and Seventeenth Centuries." *Hispanic Review* 37 (1968): 61–76; *La poesía de Garcilaso: ensayos críticos.* Ed. Elias L. Rivers. Barcelona: Ariel, 1974. 381–403.

————. "La crítica de las églogas de Garcilaso hecha por Manuel Faria y Sousa." *Estudios hispano-portugueses.* Valencia: Castalia, 1957.

————. "*Cuando me paro a contemplar mi estado:* Trayectoria de un *Rechenschafts-sonett.*" *Estudios hispano-portugueses.* Valencia: Castalia, 1957.

————. "Garcilaso's Minnesklave." *Modern Language Notes* 70 (1955): 198–203.

————. "On Plagiarism and Parody." *Studia Iberica: Festschrift für Hans Flasche.* Ed. Karl-Hermann Korner and Rühl Klaus. Bern: Francke, 1973. 175–87.

Godman, Peter. "Literary Classicism and Latin Erotic Poetry of the Twelfth Century and the Renaissance." Godman and Murray. 149–82.

————, and Oswyn Murray, eds. *Latin Poetry and the Classical Tradition.* Oxford: Clarendon Press, 1990.

Gombrich, E. H. *Symbolic Images. Studies in the Art of the Renaissance II.* Oxford: Phaidon, 1978.

Gómez Bedate, Pilar. "El castigo de la amada ingrata en Ovidio, Boccaccio y Garcilaso ('Oda a la flor de Gnido')." *Torre* 89–90 (1975): 11–30.

Gómez-Menor, José. "Tres escrituras suscritas por Garcilaso." *Boletín de la Real Academia Española* 51 (1971): 475–80.

González de Escandón, B. *Los temas del «carpe diem» y la brevedad de la rosa en la poesía española.* Barcelona: Universidad de Barcelona, 1938.

González Miguel, J.-Graciliano. *Presencia napolitana en el Siglo de Oro español: Luigi Tansillo (1510–1568).* Salamanca: Ediciones Universidad de Salamanca, 1979.

Goodwyn, Frank. "Garcilaso de la Vega, Representative in the Spanish Cortes." *Modern Language Notes* 82 (1967): 225–29.

————. "New Light on the Historical Setting of Garcilaso's Poetry." *Hispanic Review* 46 (1978): 1–22.

————. "Una teoría para la interpretación de la poesía, aplicada al primer soneto de Garcilaso de la Vega." *Hispanófila* 9, no. 26 (1966): 225–29.

————. "Tipos de verso y ritmo en la segunda égloga de Garcilaso." *Hispanófila* 10, no. 34 (1968): 1–25.

Gracián, Baltasar. *Obras completas.* Ed. Arturo del Hoyo. Madrid: Aguilar, 1967.

Greek Anthology. Trans. W. R. Paton. 5 vols. Cambridge: Harvard University Press, 1968–80.

Green, Otis H. "The Abode of the Blest in Garcilaso's Egloga Primera." *Romance Philology* 6 (1952–53): 272–78.

————. *Spain and the Western Tradition.* 4 vols. Madison: University of Wisconsin Press, 1963.

Greene, Thomas M. *The Light in Troy. Imitation and Discovery in Renaissance Poetry.* New Haven: Yale University Press, 1982.

Greimas, A.-J. *Structural Semantics: An Attempt at a Method.* Trans. Daniele Mc-Dowell, Ronald Schleifer, and Alan Velie. Lincoln: University of Nebraska Press, 1983.

Groult, P. "Sur deux vers de Garcilaso." *Lettres Romanes* 12 (1958): 189–92.

Guillén, Claudio. *Literature as System.* Princeton: Princeton University Press, 1971, 182–88.

———. "Sátira y poética en Garcilaso." *Homenaje a Casalduero*. Ed. Rizel Pincus Sigele and Gonzalo Sobejano. Madrid: Gredos, 1972. 209–33.

Guillou-Varga, Suzanne. *Mythes, mythographies et poésie lyrique au Siècle d'or espagnol*. Paris: Didier, 1986.

Gutiérrez Volta, J. "Las odas latinas de Garcilaso de la Vega." *Revista de Literatura* 2 (1952): 281–308.

Gyraldo, Lilio Gregorio. *De Deis gentium varia & multiplex historia*. Basil: 1548; facsimile reprint, New York: Garland, 1976.

Hauvette, Henri. *Un exile florentin à la cour de France au XVIe Siècle. Luigi Alamanni (1495–1556). Sa vie et son oeuvre*. Paris: Libraire Hachette, 1903.

Hebreo, León. *Diálogos de amor*. Trans. El Inca Garcilaso de la Vega. Buenos Aires: Austral, 1947.

Heiple, Daniel L. "The 'Accidens Amoris' in Lyric Poetry." *Neophilologus* 67 (1983): 55–64.

———. "[Al]chemical Imagery in the Poetry of Garcilaso de la Vega." *The Hermetic Journal* (1991): 121–32.

———. "Lope's *Arte poetica*." *Renaissance and Golden Age Essays in Honor of D. W. McPheeters*. Ed. Bruno Damiani. Potomac, Md.: Scripta Humanistica, 1986. 106–19.

———. "Renaissance Medical Psychology in *Don Quijote*." *Ideologies and Literature* 2 no. 5 (1979): 65–72.

Henríquez Ureña, P. "El endecasílabo castellano." *Revista de Filología Española* 6 (1919): 132–57.

Hermogenes. *On Types of Style*. Trans. Cecil W. Wooten. Chapel Hill: University of North Carolina Press, 1987.

Herrera, Fernando de. *Controversia sobre sus Anotaciones a las obras de Garcilaso de la Vega*. Ed. J. M. Asensio. Seville: Imprenta que fue de J. M. Geofrín, 1870.

Herrero García, Miguel. *Estimaciones literarias del Siglo XVII*. Madrid: Voluntad, 1930.

Hirst, Michael. *Sebastiano del Piombo*. Oxford: Oxford University Press, 1981.

Holzinger, Walter. "Garcilaso's Sonnet XVI in Poems by Gutierre de Cetina, Miguel de Barrios and Ben Jonson." *Hispano* 72 (1981), 13–18.

Hosek, Chaviva, and Patricia Parker, eds. *Lyric Poetry. Beyond New Criticism*. Ithaca: Cornell University Press, 1985.

Hurtado de Mendoza, Diego. *Obras poéticas*. Ed. William I. Knapp. Madrid: Libros Raros o Curiosos, 1877.

Hutton, James. "The First Idyl of Moschus in Imitations to the Year 1800." *American Journal of Philology* 49 (1928): 105–36.

———. *The Greek Anthology in Italy to the Year 1800*. Cornell Studies in English 23. Ithaca: Cornell University Press, 1935.

Iglesias Feijoo, Luis. "Lectura de la Egloga I." *Academia Literaria Renacentista*. 61–82.

Iventosch, Herman. "Garcilaso's Sonnet 'Oh ducles prendas': A Composite of Classical and Medieval Models." *Annali dell' Istituto Universitario Orientale di Napoli, Sezione Romanza* 7 (1965): 203–27.

Jakobson, Roman. *On Language*. Ed. Linda R. Waugh and Monique Monville-Burston. Cambridge: Harvard University Press, 1990.

Jedin, Hubert. *Girolamo Seripando. Sein Leben und Denken im Geisteskampf des 16. Jahrhunderts*. Wurzburg: Augustinus-Verlag, 1984.

Jones, Royston O. "Ariosto and Garcilaso." *Bulletin of Hispanic Studies* 39 (1962): 153–64.

———. "Bembo, Gil Polo, Garcilaso." *Revue de Littérature Comparée* 40 (1966): 526–40.

———. "Garcilaso, poeta del humanismo." *La poesía de Garcilaso: ensayos críticos.* Ed. Elias L. Rivers. Barcelona: Ariel, 1974. 51–70.

———. "The Idea of Love in Garcilaso's Second Eclogue." *Modern Language Review* 46 (1951): 388–95.

Keniston, Hayward. *Garcilaso de la Vega: A Critical Study of his Life and Works.* New York: Hispanic Society, 1922.

———. *The Syntax of Castillian Prose. The Sixteenth Century.* Chicago: University of Chicago Press, 1937.

Kennedy, William J. *Rhetorical Norms in Renaissance Literature.* New Haven: Yale University Press, 1978.

Kim, Judith G. "Garcilaso's Sonnet: 'O dulces prendas' reexamined." *Romance Quarterly* 21 (1974): 229–38.

Klibansky, Raymond, Erwin Panofsky, and Fritz Saxl. *Saturn and Melancholy: Studies in the History of Natural Philosophy, Religion, and Art.* New York: Basic Books, 1964.

Komanecky, P. M. "Epic and Pastoral in Garcilaso's Eclogues." *Modern Language Notes* 86 (1971): 154–66.

Lapadat, B. "Diferencias técnicas entre Boscán y Garcilaso." *Acta Philológica Aenipontana* 3 (1964): 203–20.

Lapesa, Rafael. "El cultismo semántico en la poesía de Garcilaso." *Revista de Estudios Hispánicos* (Puerto Rico) 1–4 (1972): 33–45; *Poetas y prosistas de ayer y de hoy.* Madrid: Gredos, 1977, 92–109; *Garcilaso: Estudios completos.* Madrid: Istmo, 1985. 239–54.

———. *Garcilaso: Estudios completos.* Madrid: Istmo, 1985.

———. "Poesía de cancionero y poesía italianizante." *De la Edad Media y nuestros días.* Madrid: Gredos, 1971. 145–71; *Garcilaso: Estudios completos.* Madrid: Istmo, 1985. 213–38.

———. *La trayectoria poética de Garcilaso.* Madrid: Revista de Occidente, 1968; *Garcilaso: Estudios completos.* Madrid: Istmo, 1985. 5–176.

Lasso de la Vega, J. S. "Un motivo literario." *Estudios Clásicos* 5 (1959–60): 311–22.

Lázaro Carreter, Fernando. "La 'Ode ad Florem Gnidi' de Garcilaso de la Vega." *Academia Literaria Renacentista.* 109–26.

León, Luis de. *Obras castellanas completas.* 2 vols. Ed. Felix García. Madrid: Biblioteca de Autores Cristianos, 1957.

León, Pedro R. "El soneto XIII de Garcilaso: Ensayo de explicación textual." *Explicación de Textos Literarios* 7, no. 2 (1978–79): 129–35.

Levenson, Jay A., Konrad Oberhuber, and Jacquelyn L. Sheehan. *Early Italian Engravings from the National Gallery of Art.* Washington, D.C.: National Gallery of Art, 1973.

Levisi, Margarita. "Elementos visuales en la *Egloga II* de Garcilaso." *Boletín de la Biblioteca de Menéndez Pelayo* 53 (1977): 39–59.

———. "La interioridad visualizable en Garcilaso." *Hispanófila* 73 (1981): 11–20.

Lewis, C. S. *The Allegory of Love.* New York: Oxford University Press, 1958.

Lida de Malkiel, María Rosa. "La abeja: Historia de un motivo poético." *Romance Philology* 17 (1963–64): 75–86.

———. "El amanecer mitológico en la poesía narrativa española." *Revista de Filología Hispánica* 8 (1946): 77–110.

──────. "Dido y su defensa en la literatura española." *Revista de Filología Hispánica* 4 (1942): 209–52, 313–82; 5 (1943): 45–50.

──────. "Perduración de la literatura antigua en Occidente." *Romance Philology* 17 (1963–64): 75–86.

──────. "La tradición clásica en España." *Nueva Revista de Filología Hispánica* 5 (1951): 183–223; *La tradición clásica en España.* Barcelona: Ariel, 1975. 339–97.

──────. "Transmisión y recreación de temas grecolatinos en la poesía lírica española." *Revista de Filología Hispánica* 1 (1939): 20–63; *La tradición clásica en España.* Barcelona: Ariel, 1975. 35–117.

Lightbown, Ronald W. *Sandro Botticelli.* Vol. 1. Berkeley and Los Angeles: University of California Press, 1978.

Lipmann, Stephen. "Garcilaso's Second Elegy." *Modern Language Notes* 86 (1971): 167–81.

──────. "On the Significance of the 'Trance de Lucina' in Garcilaso's First Eclogue." *Neophilologus* 67 (1983): 65–70.

López de Sedano, Juan José. *Parnaso español.* Vol. 2. Madrid: Joachin de Ibarra, 1770.

López Grigera, Luisa. "Notas sobre las amistades italianas de Garcilaso: Un nuevo manuscrito de Pietro Bembo." *Homenaje a Eugenio Asensio.* Madrid: Gredos, 1988.

Lovejoy, Arthur O., and George Boas. *Primitivism and Related Ideas in Antiquity.* Baltimore: Johns Hopkins University Press, 1935.

Loveluck, Juan. "Una nota para la *Egloga I* de Garcilaso." *Atenea* 30, no. 113 (1953): 69–75.

Lowes, John Livingston. "The Loveres Maladye of Hereos." *Modern Philology* 11 (1914): 491–546.

Lumsden, Audrey. "Garcilaso de la Vega as a Latin Poet." *Modern Language Review* 42 (1947): 337–41.

──────. "New Interpretations of Spanish Poetry: X. Sonnets [X and XXV] by Garcilaso de la Vega." *Bulletin of Hispanic Studies* 21 (1944): 114–16.

──────. "New Interpretations of Spanish Poetry: XII. Garcilaso de la Vega: Sonnet XXXII." *Bulletin of Hispanic Studies* 21 (1944): 168–70.

──────. "Problems Connected with the Second Eclogue of Garcilaso de la Vega." *Hispanic Review* 15 (1947): 251–71.

──────. "A Spanish Viceroy of Naples in the Sixteenth Century." *Bulletin of Hispanic Studies* 23 (1946): 30–37.

──────. "Two Echoes of the Bible and the Christian Liturgy in Garcilaso de la Vega." *Bulletin of Hispanic Studies* 29 (1952): 147–52.

Lumsden-Kouvel, Audrey. "Garcilaso and the Chatelainship of Reggio." *Modern Language Review* 47 (1952): 559–60.

──────. "Nature and Time in Garcilaso." *Romance Quarterly* 19 (1972): 199–209.

Ly, Nadine. "Garcilaso: Une Autre Trajectoire poétique." *Bulletin Hispanique* 83 (1981): 263–329.

Macdonald, Inez. "La segunda égloga de Garcilaso." *La poesía de Garcilaso: Ensayos críticos.* Ed. Elias L. Rivers. Barcelona: Ariel, 1974. 209–35.

Macrí, Oreste. "Recesión textual de la obra de Garcilaso." *Homenaje: Estudios de filogía e historia literaria lusohispanas e iberoamericanas publicados para celebrar el tercer lustro del Instituto de Estudios Hispánicos, Portugueses e Iberamericanos de la Universidad Estatal de Utrecht.* The Hague: Van Goor Zonen, 1966. 305–30.

————. "Revisión crítica de la controversia herreriana." *Revista de Filología Española* 42 (1958–59): 211–27.

————. "Un testo inedito del Soneto XXXIII di Garcilaso." *Quaderni Ibero-Americani* 31 (1965): 247–52.

Maddison, Carol. *Apollo and the Nine: A History of the Ode.* Baltimore: Johns Hopkins University Press, 1960.

————. *Marcantonio Flaminio. Poet, Humanist & Reformer.* Chapel Hill: University of North Carolina Press, 1965.

Maravall, José Antonio. "Garcilaso: Entre la sociedad caballeresca y la utopía renacentista." *Academia Literaria Renacentista.* 7–47.

Marichalar, A. "El uso de *Don* en Garcilaso." *Revista de Filología Española* 35 (1951): 128–32.

Marín, Nicolás. "La blanca filomela: Un lugar de Garcilaso comentado por el Abad de Rute." *Explicación de Textos Literarios* 2 (1974): 278–82.

Marti. Bembo. *Prose.* 1967.

Martínez Fernando, J. Ernesto. *Privilegios otorgados por el Emperador Carlos V en el Reino de Nápoles.* Barcelona: Consejo Superior de Investigaciones Científicas, 1943.

Martínez Lopez, Enrique. "El rival de Garcilaso: 'esse que de mi s'está reyendo' (Egl. I. 180)." *Boletín de la Real Academia Española* 61 (1981): 191–281.

————. "Sobre 'aquella bestialidad' de Garcilaso (égl. III.230)." *PMLA* 87 (1972): 12–25.

Mas, A. "Le mouvement ternaire dans les hendecasyllabes de la troisième eglogue de Garcilaso." *La poesía de Garcilaso: Ensayos críticos.* Ed. Elias L. Rivers. Barcelona: Ariel, 1974. 243–66.

Maylender, Michele. *Storia della Accademie d'Italia.* 5 vols. Bologna: L. Capelli, 1926–30.

McCormick, Beverly A. "Garcilaso de la Vega y la poesía española contemporánea." *Hispania* 48 (1965): 837–40.

McFarlane, I. D. *Renaissance Latin Poetry.* New York: Barnes and Noble, 1980.

McNerney, Kathleen. *The Influence of Ausiàs March on Early Golden Age Castilian Poetry.* Amsterdam: Rodolpi, 1982.

Mele, Emilio. "In margine alle poesie de Garcilaso." *Bulletin Hispanique* 32 (1930): 218–45.

————. "Lettre autographe de Garcilaso au cardinal Seripando." *Bulletin Hispanique* 25 (1923): 134–35, 192.

————. "Las poesías latinas de Garcilaso de la Vega y su permanencia en Italia." *Bulletin Hispanique* 25 (1923): 108–48, 361–70; 26 (1924): 35–51.

————. "Sonetti spagnoli tradotti in italiano." *Bulletin Hispanique* 16 (1914): 448–57.

Menéndez Pidal, Ramón. "Cartapacios literarios salmantinos del siglo XVI." *Boletín de la Real Academia Española* 1 (1914): 43–55, 151–70 and 298–320.

Menéndez y Pelayo, Marcelino. *Antología de poetas líricos castellanos. Boscán.* Vol. 10. *Obras completas.* Vol. 26. Madrid: Consejo Superior de Investigaciones Científicas, 1945.

————. *Horacio en España.* Vol. 2. (La Poesía Horaciana.) Madrid: A. Pérez Durull, 1885.

Michaelis de Vasconcellos, Carolina. *Poesias de Francisco de Sa de Miranda.* Halle: Max Neimeyer, 1885. 831–38.

Mill, John Stuart. "Thoughts on Poetry and its Varieties." *Collected Works.* Vol. 1. *Autobiography and Literary Essays.* Ed. John M. Robson and Jack Stillinger. Toronto: University of Toronto Press, 1981. 343–65.

Minian de Alfie, Raquel. "La *Elegía I* de Garcilaso." *Filología* 16 (1973): 167–74.

Minturno, Antonio Sebastiano. *L'Amore innamorato.* Venice: Francesco Rampazetto, 1559.

——. *L'Arte poetica.* Venice, 1564; facsimile reprint, Munich: Wilhelm Fink Verlag, 1971.

——. *Poemata.* Venice: Io. Andream Valussorem, 1564.

Moir, Duncan. "Bances Candamo's Garcilaso: An Introduction to *El César africano.*" *Bulletin of Hispanic Studies* 49 (1972): 7–29.

Montero, Juan. "Algo más sobre las peripecias editoriales de las *Obras de Garcilaso de la Vega con anotaciones de Fernando de Herrera.*" *Archivo Hispalense* 66, no. 201 (January–April 1983): 157–72.

Montesinos, J. F. "Centón de Garcilaso." *La poesía de Garcilaso: Ensayos críticos.* Ed. Elias L. Rivers. Barcelona: Ariel, 1974. 41–50.

Montgomery, Thomas. "Sound-Symbolism of Close Vowels in the Sonnets of Garcilaso." *Modern Language Notes* 93 (1978): 209–17.

Montoliu, M. de. "La lengua española en el siglo XVI: Notas sobre algunos de sus cambios fonéticos." *Revista de Filología Española* 29 (1945): 151–60.

Moya del Baño, Francisca. "Los comentarios de J. de Fonseca a Garcilaso." Academia Literaria Renacentista. 201–34.

Mustard, Wilfred P. "Later Echoes of the Greek Bucolic Poets." *American Journal of Philology* 30 (1909): 245–83.

Muzio, Girolamo. "Dell'Arte poetica." *Trattati di poetica e retorica del cinquecento.* Vol. 2. Ed. Bernard Weinberg. Bari: Gius. Laterza & Figli, 1970.

——. [Mutio Iustinopolitano]. *Rime diverse.* Venice: Gabriel Giolito de Ferrari, 1551.

Navagero, Andrea. *Lusus.* Trans. Alice E. Wilson. Niewkoop: B. de Graaf, 1973.

Navarro Durán, Rosa. " 'Entretano / que el sol al mundo alumbre . . .': Una hipérbole fosilizada." *Bulletin Hispanique* 85 (1983): 5–19.

Navarro Gónzalez, Alberto. "Garcilaso y Gracián." Academia Literaria Renacentista. 247–69.

Navarro Tomás, Tomás. "El endecasílabo en la tercera égloga de Garcilaso." *Romance Philology* 5 (1951–52): 205–11.

——. "La musicalidad de Garcilaso." *Boletín de la Real Academia Española* 49 (1969): 417–30.

Nelson, John Charles. "Platonism in the Renaissance." *Dictionary of the History of Ideas.* Vol. 3. Ed. Philip P. Wiener. New York: Charles Scribner's Sons, 1973. 508–14.

Nessi, A. O. "La plástica del mito en Garcilaso." *Humanidades* 31 (1948): 515–26.

Nichols, Fred J., ed. *An Anthology of Neo-Latin Poetry.* New Haven: Yale University Press, 1979.

Norris, Margarit Van Antwerp. "The Rejection of *Desengaño:* A Counter Tradition in Golden Age Poetry." *Revista Hispánica Moderna* 36 (1971): 9–20.

Norton, Richard. "La relación entre la voz 'sauz' y la identidad de Flérida en el Canto amebeo de la Egloga III de Garcilaso." *Explicación de Textos Literarios* 5 (1976): 191–95.

Osgood, Charles, trans. *Boccaccio on Poetry.* New York: Bobbs-Merrill, 1956.

Panofsky, Erwin. "The Early History of Man in Two Cycles of Paintings by Piero di Cosimo." *Studies in Iconology.* New York: Harper and Row, 1967.
———. *Problems in Titian, Mostly Iconographic.* New York: New York University Press, 1969.
Parker, Alexander A. "Theme and Imagery in Garcilaso's First Eclogue." *Bulletin of Hispanic Studies* 25 (1948): 222–27; *La poesía de Garcilaso: Ensayos críticos.* Ed. Elias L. Rivers. Barcelona: Ariel, 1974. 197–208.
Paterson, Alan K. G. "Ecphrasis in Garcilaso's *Egloga tercera.*" *Modern Language Review* 72 (1977): 73–92.
Patterson, Annabel M. *Hermogenes and the Renaissance: Seven Ideas of Style.* Princeton: Princeton University Press, 1970.
Peers, E. A. "The Alleged Debts of San Juan de la Cruz to Boscán and Garcilaso." *Hispanic Review* 21 (1953): 1–19; 93–106.
Pereira da Sylva, Mathias, ed. *A fenix renasida, ou obras poeticas dos melhores engenhos portugueses.* 5 vols. Lisbon: Antonio Pedrozo Galvam, 1746.
Perosa, Alessandro, and John Sparrow. *Renaissance Latin Verse.* Chapel Hill: University of North Carolina Press, 1979.
Petrarca, Francesco. *Il canzoniere.* Ed. Giuseppe Rigutini and Michele Scherillo. Milan: Ulrico Hoepli, 1925.
Pettenati, Gastone. "Il Bembo sul valore delle 'lettere' e Dionisio D'Alicarnasso." *Studi di Filologia Italiana* 18 (1960): 69–77.
Pico de la Mirandola, Giovanni. *Commentary on a Canzone of Benivieni.* Trans. Sears Jayne. New York: Peter Lang, 1984.
———. *Heptaplus or Discourse on the Seven Days of Creation.* Trans. Jessie Brewer McGaw. New York: Philosophical Library, 1977.
Pigman, G. W., III. "Neo-Latin Imitation of the Latin Classics." Godman and Murray. 199–210.
———. "Versions of Imitation in the Renaissance." *Renaissance Quarterly* 33 (1980): 1–32.
Pineda, Juan de. *Diálogos familiares de agricultura cristiana.* 5 vols. Biblioteca de Autores Españoles 161, 162, 163, 169, 170. Madrid: Ediciones Atlas, 1963–64.
Pintor, Fortunato. *Delle liriche di Bernardo Tasso.* Pisa: Fratelli Nistri, 1902.
Piras, Pina Rosa. "'Yo' tra metafora e letteralità: Lettura del sonetto 'Quando me paro a contemplar mi 'stado' di Garcilaso de la Vega." *Annali Istituto Universitario Orientale, Napoli, Sezione Romanza* 24 (1982): 427–32.
Plato. *Phaedrus and Letters VII and VIII.* Trans. Walter Hamilton. Harmondsworth, Middlesex, England: Penguin Books, 1983.
Pol, Ferran de. "El paisaje en Garcilaso de la Vega: de la naturaleza muerta al *Cántico espiritual.*" *Filosofía y Letras* 9 (1945): 79–90.
Poliziano, Angelo. *Opera omnia.* Turin: Bottega d'Erasmo, 1970.
Polo de Bernabé, José Manuel. "Tensión metafórica y transmisión del lenguaje poético: De Garcilaso a San Juan." *Revista de Estudios Hispánicos* 16 (1982): 275–85.
Pons, J. S. "Note sur la Canción IV de Garcilaso de la Vega." *Bulletin Hispanique* 35 (1933): 168–71.
Pope-Hennessy, John. *Renaissance Bronzes from the Samuel H. Kress Collection.* London: Phaidon, 1965.
Porqueras-Mayo, A. "La ninfa degollada de Garcilaso (Egloga III, versos 224–232)." *Actas del Tercer Congreso Internacional de Hispanistas.* Ed. Carlos H. Magis. Mexico City: El Colegio de México, 1970.

Poullain, C. "Garcilaso de la Vega." *Revue des Langues Romanes* 76 (1965): 79–90.
———. "Le mouvement strophique dans les églogues de Garcilaso." *Revue des Langues Romanes* 77 (1966): 61–90.
———. "Le Thème central de Garcilaso." *Revue des Langues Romanes* 83 (1978): 357–78.
Pozzi, Mario, ed. *Trattatisti del cinquecento*. Vol. 1. Milan: Riccardo Ricciardi, 1977.
Prete Jacopín. Herrera, Fernando de.
Prieto, Antonio. *Garcilaso de la Vega*. Madrid: Sociedad General Española de Librería, 1975.
———. *La poesía española del siglo XVI*. Vol. 1. Madrid: Cátedra, 1984.
Quinn, David. "Garcilaso's *Egloga primera*: Autobiography or Art?" *Symposium* 37 (1983): 147–64.
Quintana, Manuel José. *Tesoro del Parnaso español*. Paris: Baudry, Librería Europea, n.d.
Regan, Mariann Sanders. *Love Words: The Self and the Text in Medieval and Renaissance Poetry*. Ithaca: Cornell University Press, 1982.
Reichenberger, Kurt. "Garcilasos 'Ode ad florem Gnidi': Spanische Renaissancelyrik oder Prototyp des literarischen Manierismus." *Studia Iberica: Festschrift für Hans Flasche*. Ed. Karl-Hermann Körner and Rühl Klaus. Bern: Francke, 1973. 511–27.
Rendall, Stephen F., and Miriam D. Sugarmon. "Imitation, Theme and Structure in Garcilaso's First Elegy." *Modern Language Notes* 82 (1967): 230–37.
Richards, I. A. *Practical Criticism*. London: Routledge and Kegan Paul, 1966.
Rico, Francisco. "De Garcilaso y otros petrarquismos." *Revue de Littérature Comparée* 52 (1978): 325–38.
———. "Reseña del *Cancionero de Gallardo*." *Romanistisches Jahrbuch* 15 (1964): 375–76.
Riffaterre, Michael. *Semiotics of Poetry*. Bloomington: Indiana University Press, 1978.
Rime di diverse signori napolitani, ed d'altri. Libro settimo. Venice: Giolito di Ferrari, 1556.
Rime diverse di molti eccellentissimi auttori nuovamente raccolte. Libro primo. Venice: Giolito di Ferrarii, 1549.
Riquer, Martín de. *Juan Boscán y su cancionero barcelonés*. Barcelona: Archivo Histórico, 1945.
Rist, Anna, trans. and comm. *The Poems of Theocritus*. Chapel Hill: University of North Carolina Press, 1978.
Rivers, Elias L. "Albanio as Narcissus in Garcilaso's Second Eclogue." *Hispanic Review* 41 (1973): 297–304.
———. "Las églogas de Garcilaso: Ensayos de un trayectoria espiritual." *Atenea* 401 (1963): 54–64; *Actas del Primer Congreso Internacional de Hispanistas*. Ed. Frank Pierce and Cyril A. Jones. Oxford: Dolphin Book, 1964.
———. *Garcilaso de la Vega. Poems. A Critical Guide*. Critical Guides to Spanish Texts 27. London: Grant and Cutler, 1980.
———. "Garcilaso divorciado de Boscán." *Homenaje a Rodríguez-Moñino*. Vol. 2. Madrid: Castalia, 1966. 121–29.
———. "Garcilaso y los géneros poéticos." *Studia Hispanica in Honorem R. Lapesa*. Ed. Eugenio Bustos et al. Vol. 2. Madrid: Gredos, 1972. 495–99.
———. "The Horatian Epistle and its Introduction into Spanish Literature." *Hispanic Review* 22 (1954): 175–94.

————. "L'Humanisme lingüistique et póetique dans les lettre espagnoles du XVIe siècle." *L'Humanisme dans les lettres espagnoles.* Ed. Augustin Redondo. Paris: J. Vrin, 1979.

————. "Nymphs, Shepherds, and Heroes: Garcilaso's Second Eclogue." *Philological Quarterly* 51 (1972): 123–34.

————. "On the Text of Garcilaso: A Review Article." *Hispanic Review* 42 (1974): 43–49.

————. "The Pastoral Paradox of Natural Art." *Modern Language Notes* 77 (1962): 130–44.

————, ed. *La poesía de Garcilaso: Ensayos críticos.* Barcelona: Ariel, 1974.

————. "El problema de los géneros neoclásicos y la poesía de Garcilaso." Academia Literaria Renacentista. 49–60.

————. "Some Ideas about Language and Poetry in Sixteenth-Century Spain." *Bulletin of Hispanic Studies* 66 (1983): 379–83.

————. "The Sources of Garcilaso's Sonnet VIII." *Romance Notes* 2 (1960–61): 96–100.

————. "The Spoken and the Written Word." *The Dialectic of Discovery: Essays on the Teaching and Interpretation of Literature Presented to Lawrence E. Harvey.* Ed. John D. Lyons and Nancy J. Vickers. Lexington, Ky.: French Forum, 1984. 62–71.

Roberts. Dionysius of Halicarnassus. *On Literary Composition.*

Rodríguez-Luis, J. "Algunos aspectos de la evolución de lo pastoril de Garcilaso a Góngora." *Hispanófila* 8, no. 22 (1964): 1–14.

Rodríguez Marín, Francisco. *Luis Barahona de Soto.* Madrid: Sucesores de Ribadeneyra, 1903.

Roig, Adrien. "*¿Quienes fueron Salicio y Nemoroso?*" *Actas del Sexto Congreso Internacional de Hispanistas celebrado en Toronto del 22 al 26 agosto de 1977.* Ed. Alan M. Gordon and Evelyn Rugg. Toronto: University of Toronto Press, 1980. 637–40.

Rosales, Luis. *Lírica española.* Madrid: Editora Nacional, 1972.

Rota, Bernardino. *Sonetti et Canzone . . . con l'egloghe pescatorie.* Naples: Giovanni Maria Scotto, 1560.

Rothberg, Irving Paul. "The Greek Anthology in Spanish Poetry: 1500–1700." Ph.D. dissertation. Pennsylvania State University, 1954.

Saavedra Fajardo, Diego de. *República literaria.* Ed. Vicente García de Diego. Madrid: Espasa-Calpe, 1973.

Sabor de Cortázar, Celina. *La poesía de Garcilaso de la Vega.* Buenos Aires: Centro Editorial de América Latina, 1967.

Salinas, Pedro. "The Idealization of Reality: Garcilaso de la Vega." *Reality and the Poet in Spanish Poetry.* Baltimore, Md.: Johns Hopkins University Press, 1940.

Salvá, Vicente. *Nuevo diccionario de la lengua castellana.* Paris: Librería de Don Vicente Salvá, 1846.

Sánchez Romeralo, Antonio. *El villancico.* Madrid: Gredos, 1969.

Sannazaro, Jacobo. *Poemata.* Bassano: Typographia Remondiniana, 1805.

Santangelo, Giorgio. *Il Bembo critico e il principe d'imitazione.* Florence: Sansoni, 1950.

Sarmiento, E. *Concordancias de las obras poéticas en castellano de Garcilaso de la Vega.* Madrid: Castalia, 1970.

Saxl, Fritz. *A Heritage of Images.* Harmondsworth, Middlesex, England: Penguin, 1970.

Seaver, Henry Latimer. *The Great Revolt in Castile: A Study of the Comunero Movement of 1520–1521*. Boston: Houghton Mifflin, 1928.

Selig, Karl-Ludwig. "Further Observations on Garcilaso, Egl. II, Son. 29." *Revista Hispánica Moderna* 37 (1972–73): 210–13.

———. "Garcilaso and the Visual Arts: Remarks on Some Aspects of Visualization." *Interpretation und Vergleich: Festschrift für Walter Pabst*. Ed. Edo Eberhard Leube and Ludwig Scharder. Berlin: Erich Schmidt Verlag, 1972. 302–9.

———. "Garcilaso in Seventeenth-Century Germany: Two Citations and an Excursus Bibliographicus." *Revista Hispánica Moderna* 40 (1978–79): 72–75.

———. "Garcilaso in Sixteenth-Century England." *Romanische Forschungen* 84 (1972): 368–71.

Serra, L. "Sannazaro e Garcilaso." *Convivium* 17 (1948): 173–81.

Il sesto libro delle rime de diversi eccellenti autori nuovamente raccolte, et mandate in luce. Venice: Al segno del pozzo, 1553.

Seznec, Jean. *The Survival of the Pagan Gods*. Trans. Barbara F. Sessions. New York: Harper and Row, 1961.

Shapiro, Alan H. "Jason's Cloak." *Transactions of the American Philological Association* 110 (1980): 263–86.

Shumaker, Wayne. *The Occult Sciences in the Renaissance: A Study in Intellectual Patterns*. Berkeley and Los Angeles: University of California Press, 1979.

Sito Alba, Manuel. "¿Un tiento de Garcilaso en poetas portugueses? (notas a la lectura de la *Egloga III*)." *Boletín de la Real Academia Española* 56 (1976): 439–508.

Snell, Ana María. "Tres ejemplos del arte del soneto en Garcilaso." *Modern Language Notes* 88 (1973): 175–89.

Sobejano, G. *El epíteto en la lírica española*. Madrid: Gredos, 1970.

Soterinus, Io[hannes] Baptistae. "Prima Paneg[yrica] ad Illustris[simum] et excellentis[simum] Principem Alphonsum Davalum." ms. Newberry Library, Chicago, Ill. Case ms Y 682 .S717.

Spaulding, R. K. "And who is Flérida?" *Hispanic Review* 6 (1938): 76–77.

Speroni, Sperone. *Dialogo della rettorica. Opere*. Vol. 1. Venice: Domenicho Occhi, 1740.

———. *Dialogo della rettorica*. Ed. Mario Pozzi. *Trattatisti*.

Spitzer, Leo. "Garcilaso, Third Eclogue, Lines 265–271." *Hispanic Review* 20 (1952): 243–48.

Stanton, Edward F. "Garcilaso's Sonnet XXIII." *Hispanic Review* 40 (1972): 198–205.

Symonds, John Addington. *The Greek Poets*. 2 vols. New York: Harper and Brothers, 1880.

———. *Renaissance in Italy*. 3 vols. New York: Henry Holt, n.d.

Tansillo, Luigi. *Poesie liriche edite ed inedite*. Ed. F. Fiorentino. Naples: Domenico Morano Libraio, 1882.

Tasso, Bernardo. *Delle lettere*. 2 vols. Ed. Anton-Federigo Seghezzi. Padova: Giuseppe Comino, 1733.

———. *Libro primo degli amori*. Venice: Giovan. Antonio & Fratelli da Sabbio, 1531.

———. *Libro primo e secondo degli amori*. Venice: Joan. Ant. da Sabbio, 1534.

———. *Libro terzo de gli amori*. Venice: Bernadino Stagnino, 1537.

————. *I tre libri de gli amori, ai quali nuovamente dal proprio autore s'à aggiunto il quarto libro.* Venice: Gabriel Giolito de' Ferrari, 1555.

————. *Rime.* Venice: Gabriel Giolito de' Ferrari, 1560.

————. *Rime.* 2 vols. Ed. Pierantonio Serassi. Bergamo: Pietro Lancellotti, 1749.

ter Horst, Robert. "Time and Tactics of Suspense in Garcilaso's *Egloga Primera.*" *Modern Language Notes* 83 (1968): 145–63.

Terpening, Ronnie H. "The Representation of Charon in the *Siglo de Oro:* Innovation in the Myth of Orpheus." *Romance Quarterly* 22 (1975): 345–64.

Toffanin, Giuseppe. *Il cinquecento.* Milan: Dottor Francesco Vallardi, 1945.

Topsfield, L. T. *Troubadours and Love.* Cambridge: Cambridge University Press, 1975.

Torraca, F. "Gl' imitatori stranieri di J. Sannazaro." *Scritti varii.* Milan: Società Editrice Dante Alighieri, 1928. 109–210.

Torres Bodet, Jaime, A. Quintero, and R. Solana. *Tres ensayos de amistad lírica para Garcilaso.* Mexico City: Taller Lírico, 1936.

Toscano, Giovanni Matteo. *Carmina illustrium poetarum italorum.* Paris: Aegidius Grobinus, 1576.

Trend, J. B. "Musical Settings of Famous Poets." *Revue Hispanique* 71 (1927): 547–54.

Trissino, Giovan Giorgio. *Rime. 1529.* Ed. Amedeo Quondam. Vicenza: Neri Pozza Editore, 1981.

Triwedi, Michael D. "Garcilaso as an Authority in Covarrubias' *Tesoro de la lengua castellana o española.*" *Romance Notes* 15 (1973): 155–58.

Turner, John H. *The Myth of Icarus in Spanish Renaissance Poetry.* London: Tamesis, 1976.

Usher. Dionysius of Halicarnassus. *The Critical Essays.*

Utley, Francis L. "Must we Abandon the Concept of Courtly Love?" *Medievalia et Humanistica* 3 (1972): 199–324.

Valbuena Prat, Angel. "Isabel Freyre en las 'Eglogas' de Garcilaso." *Homenaje al Excmo. Sr. Dr. D. Emilio Alarcos García.* Vol. 2. Valladolid: University of Valladolid, 1965–67. 483–93.

Valdés, Juan de. *Diálogo de la lengua.* Ed. Juan M. Lope Blanch. Madrid: Clásicos Castalia, 1969.

Valency, Maurice. *In Praise of Love: An Introduction to the Love-Poetry of the Renaissance.* New York: Schocken Books, 1982.

Vance, Eugene. "Greimas, Freud, and the Story of Trouvère Lyric." *Lyric Poetry. Beyond New Criticism.* Ed. Chaviva Hosek and Patricia Parker. Ithaca: Cornell University Press, 1985. 93–105.

————. *Mervelous Signals: Poetics and Sign Theory in the Middle Ages.* Lincoln: University of Nebraska Press, 1986.

Vasari, Giorgio. *The Lives of the Painters, Sculptors and Architects.* Trans. A. B. Hinds. 4 vols. London: Dent, 1965.

Vega, Lope de. *Obras poéticas.* Vol. 1. Ed. José Manuel Blecua. Barcelona: Editorial Planeta, 1969.

Vitaliani, D. *Antonio Brocardo. Una vittima del bembismo.* Longino: Papolo & Granconato, 1902.

Vosters, Simon A. "Dos sonetos de Garcilaso. Análisis estilístico." *Hispanófila* 13, no. 37 (1969): 1–37.

Walker, D. P. "Orpheus the Theologian and Renaissance Platonists." *Journal of the Warburg and Courtauld Institutes* 16 (1953): 100–120.

————. "The Prisca Theologia in France." *Journal of the Warburg and Courtauld Institutes* 17 (1954): 204–59.

Waley, Pamela. "Garcilaso, Isbael and Elena: The Growth of a Legend." *Bulletin of Hispanic Studies* 56 (1979): 11–15.

————. "Garcilaso's Second Eclogue Is a Play." *Modern Language Review* 72 (1977): 585–96.

Weinberg, Bernard. *A History of Literary Criticism in the Italian Renaissance.* 2 vols. Chicago: University of Chicago Press, 1961.

————, ed. *Trattati di poetica e retorica del cinquecento.* 4 vols. Bari: Laterza, 1970–74.

Weiss, Roberto. *The Spread of Italian Humanism.* London: Hutchinson University Library, 1964.

Wellek, René. *Discriminations: Further Concepts of Criticism.* New Haven: Yale University Press, 1971.

————, and Warren, Austin. *Theory of Literature.* New York: Harcourt, Brace & World, 1956.

Welles, Marsha. *Arachne's Tapestry: The Transformations of Myth in Seventeenth-Century Spain.* San Antonio: Trinity University Press, 1986.

Whitby, William M. "Transformed into *What?*: Garcilaso's 'Ode ad Florem Gnidi.'" *Revista Canadiense de Estudios Hispánicos* 9 (1986): 131–43.

Whitfield, J. H. *A Short History of Italian Literature.* Westport, Conn.: Greenwood, 1976.

Whittkower, Rudolf. "Transformations of Minerva in Renaissance Imagery." *Allegory and the Migration of Symbols.* Boulder, Colo.: Westview, 1977. 129–42.

Wilkins, Ernest Hatch. "A General Survey of Renaissance Petrarchism." *Studies in the Life and Works of Petrarch.* Cambridge: Mediæval Academy of America, 1955. 280–99.

Williamson, Edward. *Bernardo Tasso.* Rome: Edizioni di Storia e Letteratura, 1951.

————. "Form and Content in the Development of the Italian Renaissance Ode." *PMLA* 65 (1950): 550–67.

Wilson, Carolyn C. *Renaissance Small Bronze Sculpture and Associated Decorative Arts at the National Gallery of Art.* Washington, D.C.: National Gallery of Art, 1983.

Wilson, Edward J. "La estrofa sexta de la canción a la Flor de Gnido." *Revista de Filología Española* 36 (1952): 118–22.

Wilson, Edward M. "La estética de don García de Salcedo Coronel y la poesía española del siglo XVII." In his *Entre las jarchas y Cernuda: Constantes y variables en la poesía española.* Barcelona: Ariel, 1977.

————. "La estrofa sexta de la canción a la Flor de Gnido." *Revista de Filología Española* 36 (1952): 118–22.

Wind, Edgar. *Pagan Mysteries in the Renaissance.* New York: Norton, 1968.

Woods, M. J. "Rhetoric in Garcilaso's First Eclogue." *Modern Language Notes* 84 (1969): 143–56.

Yates, Frances A. *The Art of Memory.* Chicago: University of Chicago Press, 1966.

Zapata, Luis. *Miscelánea. Colección de documentos, opúsculos y antigüedades.* Vol. 11. Madrid: Imprenta Nacional, 1859.

Zardoya, Concha. "Valores cromáticos de la poesía de Garcilaso." *Cuadernos Americanos* 19, no. 90 (1960): 221–37.

Index

PQ 6392 .H45 1994   95 2017

Heiple, Daniel L.

Garcilaso de la Vega and the
  Italian Renaissance

CABRINI COLLEGE LIBRARY
610 KING OF PRUSSIA RD.
RADNOR, PA 19087-3699

DEMCO